OBSESSIONS
AND
COMPULSIONS

The Century Psychology Series

James J. Jenkins
Walter Mischel
Willard W. Hartup

Editors

OBSESSIONS AND COMPULSIONS

Stanley J. Rachman
Institute of Psychiatry

Ray J. Hodgson
Institute of Psychiatry

PRENTICE-HALL, INC., Englewood Cliffs, New Jersey 07632

Library of Congress Cataloging in Publication Data

Rachman, Stanley.
    Obsessions and compulsions.

    (Century psychology series)
    Bibliography: p.
    Includes index.
    Obsessive-compulsive neurosis.   I. Hodgson,
R. J., joint author.   II. Title.
RC533.R3   616.8'522   79-18440
ISBN   0-13-629139-2

Editorial/production supervision and interior design by Alison D. Gnerre
Manufacturing buyer: Harry P. Baisley

Printed in the United States of America

10   9   8   7   6   5   4   3   2   1

Prentice-Hall International, Inc., *London*
Prentice-Hall of Austrialia Pty. Limited, *Sydney*
Prentice-Hall of Canada, Ltd., *Toronto*
Prentice-Hall of India Private Limited, *New Delhi*
Prentice-Hall of Japan, Inc., *Tokyo*
Prentice-Hall of Southeast Asia Pte. Ltd., *Singapore*
Whitehall Books Limited, *Wellington, New Zealand*

Contents

Acknowledgments

We are grateful to the many colleagues who assisted and encouraged us in the work described in this book. Some of the research was carried out in collaboration with past and present colleagues and we are indebted to them for their contributions and for agreeing to our publication of these joint efforts. Mr. P. de Silva, Dr. I. Marks and Dr. G. Röper all made substantial contributions and these are indicated at the appropriate points in the text. The section on preparedness is based mainly on two papers written in collaboration with Professor M. E. P. Seligman, who introduced the concept and who kindly agreed to our use of much of this jointly produced material. We owe thanks to Edna Foa, Peter Lang, Lesley Parkinson, Clare Philips, Ted Rosenthal, Harriet Shackelton, and Terence Wilson. We have also benefited from the help and advice of many other people and wish to thank them collectively. Even though many of our conclusions differ from theirs, the stimulation provided by the work of Dr. R. Beech and his colleagues (V. Walker, A. Liddell, and J. Perigault) has been most helpful. We are of course most strongly indebted to the patients who participated in the various studies.

The Medical Research Council provided essential support for different parts of the research. Much of Stanley Rachman's contribution was written at the Center for Advanced Study in the Behavioral Sciences, at Stanford. The generosity of the Center and the valuable assistance provided by its excellent staff are acknowledged with gratitude.

Chapter 1

Introduction

This book describes and analyzes the nature of obsessions and compulsions, their common and distinguishing features, the conditions that are thought to maintain obsessions and compulsive behavior, and our ability to modify these disorders for therapeutic purposes. Although there is little reliable information relative to the genesis of these disorders, we have attempted to assemble such information as there is and have placed our own interpretation on its significance.

In a justifiably famous lecture delivered to members of the Royal Society of Medicine in December 1935, Professor Aubrey Lewis asserted rather grandly that "it may well be that obsessional illness cannot be understood altogether without understanding the nature of man" (Lewis, 1936, p. 325). Certainly, obsessions and compulsions present intellectual problems of some magnitude, and Prof. Lewis continued to think and write about them for the remainder of his life.

The main puzzle is why people who in all other respects are rational, and indeed often possess superior intelligence, persistently engage in unwanted, self-defeating behavior—at least partly against their will. In the most straightforward cases, obsessions and compulsions provide the clearest examples of essentially irrational behavior carried out by rational people. In this sense of the term, obsessions and compulsions are prototypes of *abnormal behavior*.

In the course of the book we will examine the adequacy of the customary definitions of obsessions and compulsions, but, in the interest of simplicity, the weaknesses of the traditional approach will be set aside for the moment. For introductory purposes the conventional definition of obsessions as repetitive, intrusive, and unwanted thoughts or impulses is sufficient. Their recurrence is generally resisted, and they are difficult to remove. The ideas and impulses are usually abhorrent, and frequently involve the possibility of harm coming to innocent people. Compulsions are stereotyped, repetitive patterns of behavior, and, like obsessions, usually are resisted by the person executing them. People complaining of these problems generally recognize that they have an irrational basis, and indeed, for many of them, the persistence of the compulsive acts or intrusive thoughts is distressing precisely because it is felt to be irrational. Although obsessions and compulsions can occur independently, most often the two types of problems arise in association. In a majority of instances, the affected person is or has been subject to episodes of depression. For a considerable time obsessions and compulsions were regarded as illnesses, neurotic illnesses. In keeping with the move away from a purely medical approach to problems of this kind, many psychologists, ourselves among them, are now of the opinion that obsessions and compulsions are better construed as emotional and behavioral problems than as illnesses.[1] Nevertheless, there are exceptional cases that undoubtedly qualify for the diagnosis of illness (e.g., obsessional-compulsive problems that are secondary to an infectious illness, brain damage, etc.).

However, the undiscriminating extension of the medical model to all obsessional-compulsive problems is felt to be unhelpful. Although reconstruing them as emotional or behavioral problems is a constructive change, the satisfactory development of the consequences of adopting this new perspective is hampered by our failure to produce a new and more appropriate vocabulary to match the new perspective. For want of a better term, and because most of the people who participated in the research and controlled trials that we will be describing were in fact registered patients at National Health hospitals, the older terminology is used throughout the book, despite our reservations about the conceptual justification for such use.

When the manifestations of obsessional and compulsive problems are described in print, it frequently is difficult for the reader to appreciate the seriousness of these problems. Without experience of people who have suffered from these difficulties, it is hard to imagine how a persistent compulsive urge to check the security of one's home before leaving for work each morning can grow into a problem of such magnitude as to distort and diminish the person's entire life. In the case of someone who is constantly troubled by intrusive, unacceptable thoughts, it is hard to imagine the amount of suffering involved, and how it can reach such proportions as to imprison the person and prevent

---

[1] The weaknesses of a medical approach to abnormal behavior are discussed by Rachman and Philips (1978). These weaknesses include an unjustified extension of the disease model to emotional and behavioral difficulties, a misleading vocabulary (*illness, patients, symptoms*), the use of inappropriate diagnostic procedures, the groundless presumption of a fundamental underlying causation, a bias against direct modification of the person's difficulties, the encouragement in the patient and his or her relatives of misconceptions and passivity, and so on.

him or her from carrying out any constructive work. Even more extreme, it is hard to imagine how a grossly exaggerated fear of dirt and disease can lead an entire family to move to a new house every six months and to avoid entire regions of the country. Of course, most people who suffer from obsessional-compulsive problems do not have them in this degree of severity, but it would be a mistake to underestimate the intensity and extent of the suffering involved. In an attempt to convey the psychological effects of these disorders, we have included a fair amount of case material—both because of its intrinsic interest and in order to convey to nonclinicians the seriousness of the problem.

Like the word *neurotic*, the term *obsessional* has crept into everyday language: It is used to denote a propensity to carry out some activity with particular care, or to be excessively concerned with some idea or activity. Like most terms of this kind, it is used loosely in everyday language. Nonetheless, it retains its utility. There is in fact an interesting although not invariant relationship between obsessional personality characteristics and the disorder described as obsessional-compulsive neurosis. As we hope to show, the earlier view that there is an identity between obsessional personality characteristics and obsessional neuroses is mistaken.

It is impossible to work with obsessional-compulsive patients for any length of time without becoming intrigued by the nature of the disorder itself. In particular, the extraordinary persistence of unwanted, aversive, and self-defeating obsessions and compulsions is a major puzzle. The irrationality of the disorder, generally recognized by the person affected, is another source of intellectual interest. The irrational, abnormal quality of obsessional-compulsive disorders is emphasized by the fact that the people affected are in almost all other respects rational, intelligent, stable people.

While pursuing some of these problems, it became necessary to collect additional information about the phenomenology of the disorder and the extent to which the different manifestations of the various forms of obsessional-compulsive problems are related both to themselves and to other types of neurosis. It turns out that although obsessional-compulsive problems have a good deal in common, there are certain respects in which compulsive cleaning rituals are closer to circumscribed phobias than to other obsessional problems, such as checking rituals. In the course of these studies, we also came across a definable, discrete manifestation that had not been previously described. For reasons to be given later, we chose to call it primary obsessional slowness.

Although our interest in the nature of obsessions and compulsions grew as a result of our increasing acquaintance with the patients and their problems, our original purpose was to develop an effective treatment. In the attempt to help these people, we encountered some of the intriguing puzzles just alluded to. Not for the first time, however, our ability to modify a psychological disorder has outstripped our understanding of the therapeutic processes involved and, indeed, of the nature of the disorder itself.

It is generally agreed that the first important successes achieved by behavior therapists were in the modification of phobias. Wolpe's (1958) invaluable pioneering work in the 1950s and 1960s was later consolidated by the addition of new information and new techniques. Among these, flooding and participant modeling appear to be the most promising. Unfortunately, the early successes in the treatment of phobias were not accompanied by similar progress in dealing with obsessional disorders, and until recently therapists approached the treatment of obsessional patients with realistic caution.

Our greatly improved capacity for modifying these powerful and resistant problems can be attributed mainly to two developments. In the first place, there has been a transition from imaginal to *in vivo* procedures as an inevitable part of the development of participant-modeling and flooding techniques. These *in vivo* procedures appear to make a powerful contribution to the treatment of obsessional difficulties. The second contributor to therapeutic progress was the introduction of response prevention methods in the late 1960s. Prompted by the encouraging developments in research on therapeutic modeling and flooding, and by the success reported by Meyer (1966) in treating two severely disabled obsessional-compulsive patients, a number of psychologists began experimenting with *in vivo* modification procedures. These developments, including our own research on the subject, are described in Chapters 11 to 13. Although some valuable progress has been made, there is a long way to go in refining these methods and improving our understanding of how they operate. Nevertheless, we now have a behavioral treatment, combining *in vivo* exposure, modeling, and response prevention, that is at least moderately effective in reducing obsessional-compulsive problems. The improvements are reassuringly stable and are seldom followed by the emergence of new problems. Although we are getting closer to providing an adequate descriptive account of the conditions that are necessary and sufficient for inducing therapeutic change, a comprehensive explanation of the processes involved remains elusive.

Before starting the exposition, a few words about our sources are required. We have used five sources of information in preparing this book. In the first place, there is a large volume of information contained in the psychiatric literature. Almost all of it is descriptive and epidemiological, and for the most part it is lucid and instructive (e.g., Black, 1974; Jaspers, 1963; Kringlen, 1965, 1970; Pollitt, 1959; etc.). The concise, unambiguous and thoughtful writings of Lewis (1934, 1936, 1957, 1966) are especially helpful. Unlike many parts of the psychiatric literature, the accounts of obsessions and compulsions are comparatively free of interminable disputations about problems concerning diagnostic purity. The limitations of this literature are that the information is based solely on clinical assessments, rarely goes beyond the descriptive level, assumes the validity of the medical conception of the disorder, and contains virtually no experimental evidence. The most striking feature of the psychiatric approach to the problem is that it has been nonexperimental.

Our second source of information, the psychological literature, is surprisingly meager and consists mainly of psychometric studies of nonrandom samples of psychiatric patients and attempts to find animal analogs for the disorder. This literature shares some of the limitations of the psychiatric brand, including the widespread adoption of the medical model of the disorder.

Our third source of information is the slowly growing literature describing the results of experimental analyses of different aspects of the disorder. Thus far the information is of assistance mainly in attempting to understand the maintenance of compulsive behavior. It is also useful for delineating the similarities and differences among different manifestations of obsessions and compulsions, and their relation to phobias. So far it has been of little value in clarifying the genesis of the disorder.

A fourth source of information is the new literature on the modification of obsessions and compulsions by behavioral methods. In addition to telling us how to assist people suffering from the disorder, this research is beginning to yield information about the conditions that maintain and modify compulsions and, to a lesser extent, obsessions. These findings are limited by the weakness of current assessment techniques.

Our fifth source of information is the experience that we have accumulated over the past years in assessing, studying, and treating a considerable number of people with moderate to severe obsessional-compulsive disorders. At many points we have been obliged to draw water from our own well.

SECTION A

Chapter 2

Obsessions and Compulsions: The Concepts

From the introduction of the concept well over 100 years ago until the present, the definition of an obsessional-compulsive disorder has produced little controversy. As a result of recent research and clinical findings, it now seems desirable to clarify and review this and related concepts. Jaspers's (1963) definition is representative and comprehensive.

> In the strict sense of the term, compulsive thoughts, impulses etc., should be confined to anxieties or impulses which can be experienced by the individual as an incessant preoccupation, though he is convinced of the *groundlessness* of the anxiety, the *senselessness* of the impulse and the *impossibility* of the notion. Thus, compulsive events, strictly speaking, are all such events the *existence* of which is strongly resisted by the individual in the first place, and the *content* of which appears to him as groundless, meaningless or relatively incomprehensivel. [p. 134, original emphasis]

The concise definition offered by Lewis (1966) is in the same tradition: "In this condition the characteristic feature is that, along with some mental happening, there is an experience of subjective compulsion and of resistance to it. Commonly the mental happening (which may be a fear, an impulse, or a preoccupation) is recognized on quiet reflection, as senseless; nevertheless it persists" (p. 1199).

An obsession is an intrusive, repetitive thought, image, or impulse that is unacceptable and/or unwanted and gives rise to subjective resistance. It generally produces distress. Obsessions are difficult to remove and/or control. It is said that during calm periods the person acknowledges the senselessness of the thought or impulse. The content of an obsession is repugnant, worrying, blasphemous, obscene, nonsensical—or all of these—and frequently takes the *form* of doubting (see Akhtar et al., 1975).

The following are clinical examples of obsessional *thoughts*: "Am I a lesbian?" "Did I kill the old lady?" "Christ was a bastard." Examples of obsessional *impulses* are the following: "I might expose my genitals in public"; "I am about to shout obscenities in public"; "I feel I might strangle a child." Examples of obsessional *images* include mutilated corpses, decomposing fetuses, my husband involved in a serious motor accident, my parents being violently assaulted. Obsessional impulses often are accompanied or preceded by a fear of losing control—in fact, the impulses are rarely acted upon.

In a recent phenomenological analysis of eighty-two obsessional neurotics, Akhtar and his associates (1975) classified the content of the obsessional material into five broad categories. In order of frequency of occurrence, the categories were dirt and contamination, aggression, orderliness of inanimate objects, sex, and religion. Although this is interesting information, it should be remembered that most of the examples given by these investigators are obsessional ideas—presumably, they did not seek information about obsessional impulses and images, and hence their data are incomplete. In support of Lewis's (1966) claim that "the content of the obsession is of little use prognostically" (p. 1201), they found no relation between content and outcome. (The introduction of more effective methods of treatment may, however, produce disconfirmatory evidence; e.g., it may well be the case that compulsions arising from fears of dirt and disease will respond particularly well to behavior therapy—see Chapters 11 to 13.) As Akhtar and his colleagues observed, approximately half of their patients were troubled by a single obsession. Or, to look at it another way, half of their patients had multiple obsessions.

It is not their intrusiveness per se that makes obsessions disturbing—they are *unwanted* intrusions. The significance of the unwanted quality of intrusive obsessional thoughts can be illustrated by contrast with the extremely welcome intrusive thoughts described by Mozart. Bartlett (1958) quotes this description from one of Mozart's letters:

> Thoughts crowd into my mind as easily as you could wish. Whence and how do they come? I do not know, and I have nothing to do with it. Those which please me, I keep in my head and hum them; at least others have told me that I do so. Once I have my theme, another melody comes,

linking itself to the first one, in accordance with the needs of the composition as a whole; the counterpoint, the part of each instrument, and all
the melodic fragments at last produce the entire work. [p. 195]

In characteristic style, Beethoven gave a vivid and powerful account of his
experiences:

> You will ask me where I get my ideas. That I cannot say with certainty.
> They come unbidden, indirectly, directly. I could grasp them with my
> hands; in the midst of nature, in the woods, on walks, in the silence of the
> night, in the early morning, inspired by moods that translate themselves
> into words for the poet and into tones for me, that sound, surge, roar,
> until at last they stand before me as notes. [quoted by Landon, 1970,
> p. 163]

Incidentally, this description of Beethoven's musical inspiration gives us one of
the clearest examples of intrusive ideas that owe very little to external stimulation, in this case auditory stimulation.

COMPULSIONS

Compulsions are repetitive, stereotyped acts. They may be wholly unacceptable
or, more often, partly acceptable, but are regarded by the person as being excessive and/or exaggerated. They are preceded or accompanied by a subjective
sense of compulsion, and provoke subjective resistance. They generally produce
distress. In his or her calmer moments, the person usually acknowledges the
senselessness of these activities. A compulsive ritual is a prescribed style of
performing some activity. Although the activities are within the person's voluntary control, often the urge to carry out the acts is exceedingly strong, and
hence the person experiences a sense of diminished volition. The two major
types of compulsive activity (often referred to as compulsive rituals) are cleaning
and checking. The classic example of the former type is the compulsive hand
washer, and a common example of the second type is the person who
compulsively checks the security of appliances and of entrances to his or her
home.

There is a close and probably causal relationship between compulsive urges
and compulsive acts, with the former producing the latter. Obsessions and
compulsions are closely related, and in the opinion of some authorities the
occurrence of a compulsive activity implies the earlier (causal) occurrence of
an obsession. There are exceptions, especially in cases of primary obsessional
slowness. It is agreed, however, that obsessions are not necessarily translated
into observable acts, compulsive or otherwise. For example, obsessional doubts
may fill the person's conscious activities without provoking any overt behavior.

In the study by Akhtar and his colleagues, it was found that 25 percent of the reported obsessions were not associated with overt acts. As we will see, however, they may well have been associated with *covert* attempts to neutralize the obsession. In their study of 150 obsessional in-patients, Welner and his associates (1976) found that 103 (69%) patients had both obsessions and compulsions, 38 (25%) had only obsessions, and 9 (6%) had only compulsions.

The relations between obsessions and compulsions can be summarized in a series of short statements. Although they are often found together, patients can have one or the other of these difficulties. The most characteristic sequence is of an obsession leading to a compulsion (e.g., an obsessional doubt about whether one has caused an accident might result in compulsive checking of police records and/or compulsive seeking of reassurance from relatives). In one of our patients, described on page 255, the obsessional thought involved the danger of violence being done to his parents. This provoked a powerful urge to remove the idea, and the mode of escape (the compulsive act) was a stereotyped pattern of washing his hands. Obsessions and compulsions can run independent courses, even when the same patient suffers from both of these phenomena. Compulsions can occur in the apparent absence of an obsession, especially in patients whose main problem is primary obsessional slowness, but are also seen in some compulsive hand washers. Compulsive acts can be followed by an obsession, especially by doubting after the completion of a checking ritual. Obsessions can persist without translation into any overt activity, compulsive or otherwise.

OBSESSIONAL-COMPULSIVE DISORDERS

One can describe someone as having an obsessional-compulsive disorder if his or her major complaint is the repeated occurrence of an obsession and/or a compulsion, if there are accompanying behavioral signs of such experiences, and if the complaint and signs are associated with at least a moderate degree of distress and at least a moderate degree of impairment of psychological functioning (e.g., socially, occupationally, sexually, etc.). The experience of subjective compulsion, the report of internal resistance, and the presence of insight are three key indicators of an obsessional-compulsive disorder. Outside of his or her obsessional and compulsive problems, the person generally has an "intact personality."

PROBLEMS

Although this conception is sufficient for most purposes, the matter of definitions and concepts is more complex than might at first appear to be the case. First, there are semantic difficulties. For example, what precisely is meant by the term *insight* when it is used as a diagnostic criterion for this disorder? The term can be interpreted in more than one way. To take other examples, what does the term *intrusive* imply? And is it logically related to *subjective resistance?* When does a pattern of behavior qualify for the adjective *stereotyped?*

The second major problem is that no one has offered a systematic statement of the necessary and sufficient conditions for deciding when and whether a reported experience is an obsession and when and whether a behavioral pattern should be described as compulsive. It is true that we have some excellent clinical descriptions and persuasive commentaries, but few writers (Lewis, Jaspers, and Janet are notable exceptions) have taken the risks involved in attaching differential weights to the various features of obsessions and compulsions, and none appear to have asserted which of these features are necessary and sufficient for defining the disorder. Despite these limitations, there have been few disputes about the meaning of the key terms, and as we have already remarked, the present definition is serviceable. It is likely that a comparison among the definitional and diagnostic practices of a collection of psychiatrists and psychologists would reveal a considerable amount of agreement—unlike, say, the serious disagreements about the meaning and diagnosis of schizophrenia (see, e.g., Kendell, 1971).

The third problem arises from the fact that most of the important phenomena of obsessions and compulsions are subjective and, hence, more difficult to grasp and define. It is no easy matter to define *feelings of compulsion* or *subjective resistance* or *the intrusion of an idea.* Proof of this claim, if it is needed, will be found in the discussion that follows.

The concept of compulsion is of central importance in any consideration of the phenomena. In everyday language, *compulsion* refers to a sense of feeling pressed or driven to act, and its use in the scientific literature is not dissimilar. It is a subjective experience inferred from a verbal report given by the person affected; such inferences are sometimes supported by observations of the person's overt behavior, but an inference drawn solely from behavioral observations is less satisfactory. The essence of a compulsion is the person's sense of being influenced by a pressure that is, at least in part, unwelcome. In the most blatant examples, people describe the experience as one in which they feel that they are being driven to do or think something against their will. Some authorities, such as Lewis, distinguished in their phenomenological analyses between unwelcome forces that appear to originate within the person and those that appear to originate from without. In the latter case, one might infer that the person is experiencing a psychotic phenomenon rather than a compulsion. The statement "I feel that I *must* wash all the germs off my body," implying an internal prompt, is a compulsion. The statements "I feel that someone is making me wash myself" and "The secret radio messages are making me wash myself," implying external pressures, are delusional. To quote Lewis (1966, p. 1201): The obsessional "feels that it comes from within his own mind, whereas in the schizophrenic phenomena he feels that it comes from without, it is imposed upon him."

The three key characteristics of a sense of compulsion are experienced pressure to think or act in a particular manner, an unwillingness to comply with this pressure, and an internal source of the pressure.

Assessing the validity of the verbal information provided by the affected person is as difficult here as it is with all subjective phenomena. As the inference is based largely or wholly on this subjective information, it is impossible to avoid problems of validity. Although external referents such as behavioral observations are helpful, they do not in themselves provide an adequate basis for identifying a sense of compulsion. It is comparatively simple to assess unwillingness in behavior (but not in thoughts), but behavioral observations may give little clue as to the source or quality of the sense of coercion.

Another difficulty is that in practical situations one sometimes encounters compulsive behavior that, paradoxically, occurs in the absence of an accompanying sense of internal compulsion. So, for example, it is not uncommon to find compulsive hand washers who yield to or accept the pressures to wash repetitively and excessively. While acknowledging a sense of some pressure to carry out their washing rituals, they express a willingness or even a desire to do so: "I have an overwhelming need to wash my hands. I want to do so." They may well regret the need to wash excessively, but their compliance is not unwilling. They prefer washing over not washing.

In light of this paradox, it is interesting to notice that Lewis (1957) and Akhtar and his associates (1975), among others, distinguish between the *yielding* and *controlling* compulsions. In most cases it is comparatively easy to determine the origin of the pressure; direct attributions to external forces are recognizable, especially if they have a bizarre quality (e.g., radio waves, ghosts, historical figures, etc.). In some instances the distinction between external and internal origin is blurred, however, and the description of the behavior must rest on other criteria.

To what extent are obsessions and compulsions involuntary? If human motives were unmixed and if they operated sequentially rather than simultaneously, the task of distinguishing between voluntary and involuntary behavior would be greatly simplified. As motives display neither of these properties, it is inevitable that in many circumstances a conflict of motives will arise. A compulsive checker may wish to avoid the social disapproval provoked by his irritatingly repetitive and slow behavior while at the same time striving to ensure his child's safety by engaging in the rituals. In clear-cut cases these finer points of distinction do not arise. Patients who complain that they find themselves carrying out compulsive rituals, or having thoughts against their wishes, present little problem: "I can't help myself—I keep saying the numbers over and over again"; "I can't stop the thoughts—they keep coming back no matter how hard I try to prevent them."

Perhaps it was clear-cup examples of this type that led Carr (1974) to state that "in both states, obsessional and compulsive, the patient is disturbed by a loss of volition, a loss of control over his own behavior" (p. 311). But it is difficult or even impossible to tease out the motives that prevail at any particular time. There is another sense in which Carr's view is open to misinterpretation. Even the most powerful, demanding compulsive activities are under a considerable degree of voluntary control. Without any great effort a compulsive cleaner or checker can abbreviate, extend, curtail, or postpone a compulsive act. Experimental illustrations of this degree of voluntary control are provided in Chapters 11, 14, and 15. Obsessional thoughts, images, and impulses are also open to voluntary control, but probably to a lesser extent. Furthermore, patients can initiate their compulsive behavior or obsessions without difficulty. This can be achieved directly or indirectly (e.g., by arranging to touch a provoking stimulus or by entering a provoking situation). Although the whole process can be initiated by the person acting on his or her own initiative, it is most readily instigated by simple instructions from someone else (see Rachman and de Silva, 1978).

Of course, this is not the whole story. If obsessions and compulsions were under voluntary control in all circumstances and under all conditions, there would be no obsessional-compulsive disorders—and no books about them. There is in almost all obsessions and compulsions a crucial element of diminished control. When an appropriate degree of self-regulation is restored, by formal treatment or otherwise, the disorder is overcome. In all, it is more profitable, and indeed more accurate, to speak of the *extent* of voluntary control rather than to categorize the behavior in question as voluntary *or* involuntary. The parameters involved in voluntary control include the frequency of the behavior, its intensity, its duration, its situation-specificity, and so on.

The qualify of *intrusiveness* is most prominent in obsessions but can also be seen in some compulsive activities. The person typically complains that the thoughts or images are unwelcome and interfere with ongoing activities: "The thoughts keep returning and prevent me from concentrating on my work." The essential characteristics of intrusive thoughts are that they make an unwanted and usually unwelcome entry into consciousness. Obsessional thoughts, impulses, or images generally fit this definition of intrusiveness—they make an unwelcome entry. Their arrival and persistence usually cause distress, and they are regarded as being alien and interfering. Moreover they often cause or are accompanied by a sense of pressure—almost like a head pain.

Most patients complain that once the obsession has made its unwelcome entry it is exceedingly difficult to remove. As we have seen, an obsession often promotes a compulsive urge, and this generally is translated into ritualistic behavior. Other techniques for dealing with intrusive thoughts include *distraction, neutralizing* activities and seeking *reassurance* (see Chapter 19 and Rachman and de Silva, 1978).

Intrusive thoughts are by definition unwanted, and most of them are also morally and personally unacceptable. Our clinical impression is that patients whose main complaint consists of intrusive, unacceptable thoughts are correct, upright, moral citizens who aspire to high standards of personal conduct. In our research into the obsessions of a nonclinical sample of people, we found that their thresholds for personal acceptability were significantly lower and wider than those of the patients. The intrusive thoughts of the people in the nonclinical group were unwanted, but infrequently unacceptable (Rachman and de Silva, 1978).

Most patients report that they try to prevent the thoughts from intruding. They resist. To quote Jaspers again (1963, p. 113), "The self finds itself in conflict faced with a content which it wants to suppress but cannot. This content then acquires the character of a psychic compulsion." Patients also resist the *continuation or repetition* of the thoughts, and it would appear that this form of psychological resistance is similar to resisting the execution of compulsive rituals. The concept of resistance, defined here as an attempt to prevent or curtail an obsession or compulsion, was regarded by Jaspers, Lewis, and others as the hallmark of obsessional-compulsive disorders. It is evident, of course, that resistance implies a sense of compulsion; there is some pressure that has to be opposed. If the essential features (i.e., a feeling of subjective compulsion and immediate resistance to this) are kept in view, "it is seldom difficult to distinguish between obsessions on the one hand, and delusions, hallucinations, ideas of reference or self-reproach . . . etc., on the other" (Lewis, 1966, p. 1200).

There is no denying the prominent and striking quality of such resistance in many patients. However, we have encountered numerous patients who display undeniably compulsive behavior and/or experience undeniably clear obsessions, but show little sign of resistance. Even patients in whom resistance is evident often accept or yield to some of their compulsive urges. Resistance is not necessarily uniform, nor is it consistent.

In our psychometric research, described in Chapter 10, 23 out of a group of 34 obsessional-compulsive patients indicated that they did *not* always resist their obsessions or compulsions. We also found signs of a connection between resistance and type of compulsion—checkers showing a greater tendency to resist than cleaners. Examples of obsessions without resistance are reported by Rachman and de Silva (1978).

In sum, resistance is an important feature of obsessions and compulsions. However, some patients show little or no sign of internal resistance; it is neither a necessary nor a sufficient condition for an obsessional-compulsive disorder. Resistance is not uniformly provoked. Some compulsive urges do not produce resistance, and others do so only inconsistently (e.g., "Sometimes I resist it, but at other times I simply yield to it"). Lastly, resistance may not be randomly distributed across the different varieties of obsessions and compulsions. In support of this possibility, it is worth mentioning that obsessional impulses, which usually are aggressive or obscene in content, are always (?) resisted successfully. Apart from the exceptions of kleptomania and some instances of child abuse, obsessional-compulsive patients seldom act on their obsessional impulses. Apart from these exceptions, we have no knowledge of an obsessional-compulsive patient translating his or her obsession concerning a serious aggressive impulse into an act of violence. This is in some respects remarkable, because the impulses often are extremely violent (actual examples include "I may blind my infant daughter"; "I may strangle a child"; and "I may push an old lady onto the railway line"), and because of the patient's strong and genuine fears of losing control. To quote Lewis, "Few obsessionals give way to anti-social impulses, e.g., to suicide, homicide, delinquency . . . Obsessionals rarely yield directly to an impulse they have resisted or need to have 'irresistible impulse' urged in extenuation of a crime. Sexual offences and perversions are rarely obsessional" (1966, p. 1201). Fear of losing control is often associated with fear of impending insanity.

Clinicians are of course familiar with the relief experienced by many patients when they receive the reassuring information that they are most unlikely to act on their impulses. However, the relief generally dissipates, and the patient then needs to be reminded of the fact and to receive a repeat dose of reassurance.

At what stage does repetition of an action become excessive, even to the point of abnormality? In cases of compulsive cleaning, there is seldom any doubt. Washing one's hands 100 times a day is excessive to the point of abnormality. There are many intermediate examples about which there is less certainty. There is no saying exactly how many repetitions of checking the safety of the gas taps is within normal limits, or when the tidiness of one's room is excessive, or how long it should take to prepare oneself in the morning. Even when the overall pattern of a person's behavior is seriously distorted by obsessions and compulsions, one encounters many individual pieces of behavior that hover on the borderline of acceptability. These borderline examples provide grist for the obsessional patient's mill, and the unwary clinician may be sucked into protracted discussions of how many pieces of toilet paper one should use, how long it should take to have a bath or tidy one's papers, and so on. In part compensation, therapists are often rewarded by the excellent records maintained by many of these patients. Provided that there are few uncertainties about the format of the data collection, obsessional patients collect impeccable baseline data.

Attempts to establish "norms" for the everyday activities that so often present problems for these patients are hardly justified. Rather, it is preferable to decide in each case what is excessive and exaggerated behavior for the person in question. In our clinical work we found it best to estimate the extent to which the behavior produces stress or social disapproval and the extent to which it prevents or interferes with other, more productive and desirable behavior. Repetitive washing that occupies an entire hour, prevents other people from using the bathroom, and makes the hand washer late for work is excessive on all counts. Observation of the entire ritual quickly reveals the redundancies, and in practice we find that a few sessions of therapeutic modeling (see Chapter 21) are generally sufficient to establish acceptable guidelines.

Some compulsive activities are extraordinarily stereotyped. It would appear that with increasing practice the ritualistic behavior becomes increasingly mechanical, precise, and unchanging.Although there are exceptions in which new compulsions show this kind of rigidity, there appears to be a correlation between chronicity and stereotypy. For our purposes stereotypy can be defined as repetitive, unchanging, mechanical behavior. So, for example, one of our patients spent more than 30 minutes each morning, and again each evening, brushing his teeth. He cleaned each tooth separately, rinsing his brush before moving on to the next tooth. He cleaned the front, rear and top aspects of each tooth in sequence—counting 10 strokes of the brush for each part of the tooth. He always started with his rear-most upper left tooth, and always cleaned the others in an unchanging sequence, moving from left to right and from top to bottom. Another patient carried out multiple checks of the windows, doors, taps, and so forth before he could leave his home. The entire sequence, moving from item to item, from room to room, took up to two hours to complete and was rigidly repeated day by day. Observers watching this performance on video-tape were struck by the mechanical quality of his action; his hands and arms seemed to be powered and controlled by some independent force. Once the sequence was switched on, his hands began tapping away at the window panes in a rhythmic, unchanging pace and style.

In our view this type of repetitive, stereotyped behavior is reminiscent of the precise, smooth avoidance jumping described by Solomon, Kamin and Wynne (1953). After exposure to a punishing stimulus, the experimental animals learned to avoid further punishment by jumping over a barrier and out of the aversive compartment of the apparatus. Despite repeated extinction trials the avoidance behavior persisted, and the experimenters were "impressed with certain behavioral changes . . . Latencies of response to the CS gradually decreased and the behavior of the animals became more stereotyped" (Solomon, Kamin, and Wynne, 1953, p. 293). Between trials the animals sat quietly and showed few signs of disturbance. Then, on "the next trial, the behavior was precisely the same." Moreover, "the frequency and intensity of overt emotional reactions, both to the CS and in the inter-trial interval, decreased markedly" (p. 293). With practice the avoidance behavior became more precise, more stereotyped, and calmer.

When used in discussions of the nature of obsessions and compulsions, the term *insight* refers to the affected person's ability and willingness to recognize the essential irrationality of his or her obsessions and/or compulsions—hence the common statement that "in his/her calmer moments" he/she can acknowledge the senselessness of his/her worry or action. For most writers the presence of insight, so defined, appears to be a necessary feature of an obsessional disorder. It is particularly important for distinguishing between obsessions and psychotic delusions—in the latter case, the person is persuaded of the truth or the validity of his or her irrational belief. The test of insight is also applied when there is a doubt about whether one is dealing with an obsessional personality trait or an obsessional disorder. An extremely meticulous person may be well content with his own behavior. It is an accepted and coherent part of his personality. Or, to use the technical term, it is *ego-syntonic*. If, on the other hand, a person complains that she feels compelled to carry out excessively meticulous acts, resists the urges, and finds them ego-alien, then this *insight* may well be an indicator of disorder.

As is so often the case, the use of the term *insight* is perfectly adequate for deciding relatively clear instances, one way or the other. In practice, however, one encounters cases in which the term lacks a cutting edge. Some patients who display all of the major signs of an obsessional-compulsive disorder (e.g., distress, compulsive and stereotyped hand-washing rituals, intact personality, etc.) cling to the view that their obsessions and compulsions do have a rational basis. To quote an example, one of our compulsive hand-washing patients repeatedly argued that unless she cleaned well and used disinfectants, she might contract an illness. If pressed, she would agree that her cleaning precautions were excessive, but customarily added that it was "better to be safe than sorry" and always insisted that her behavior was rational, even if exaggerated. Another patient carried out multiple counting rituals to protect her parents from injury or illness. She agreed that her rituals did not afford them direct protection but felt that the rituals were helpful in the same way that prayers are. She concluded that her rituals were irrational only to the extent that prayers are irrational. A third patient argued that the meticulous record keeping she had developed in early childhood was excessive but fundamentally sound and rational, and she supported her view with instances in which her records had proved to be useful. A particularly striking example of the bluntness of the insight criterion may be seen in a case described by Dr. Meyer (1973). The patient, a religious middle-aged Jewish woman who spent long periods carrying out multiple eating and checking compulsions, argued that her behavior had a rational foundation. After many inconclusive discussions Meyer finally secured his point by arranging for a distinguished rabbi to visit the patient and confirm that she had taken her ritualistic activities to irrational extremes.

Although it usually can be seen that the psychological cost of the behavior greatly exceeds the risks involved, there are a significant number of cases in which one cannot easily conclude that the behavior is fundamentally irrational. We found ourselves labeling the behavior as irrational more easily and more rapidly than later appeared to be justified. Not uncommonly *rationality* is, for these purposes, a sensible balance between the risks and the costs involved. Hence, the test of insight is less sharp than one might wish. In working with these patients, we found that some of them (perhaps the submissive types postulated by Lewis—see page 54) too readily complied with our views, or their estimation of what our views might be. With increasing experience we learned that early and easy compliance can be skin deep. Another complication is that some patients agree that one (or more) aspect of their obsessional-compulsive behavior is irrational, but warmly dispute that all of it is senseless. They may even justify one type of checking ritual while disowning another as senseless. Moreover, their confidence in the rationality of their compulsions fluctuates (see Shackleton, 1977).

A further complication is that patients often have different levels of explanation for their behavior. A superficial question elicits a superficial answer. For example, if one asks simply, "Why are you washing your hands?" the superficial answer may well come back, "In order to remove the dirt." If the question is pressed, however, the next answer may well be, "As a protection against disease." If the patient is pressed still further, the answer may express a belief that washing affords protection against unrelated threats, such as the possible death of a relative. Puzzled pragmatists sometimes say that they wash in order to obtain subjective relief, and this reply is almost bound to be correct. It is neither senseless nor irrational and, strictly speaking, cannot be classified as lacking insight. For other reasons, such as the occurrence of feelings of compulsion and/or stereotyped behavior, one might nevertheless feel assured that the behavior in question is undoubtedly obsessional-compulsive.

From these conceptual problems we turn to some psychometric data collected from firmly diagnosed obsessional-compulsive neurotics (see Chapter 10 for a full account). One of the statements contained in our questionnaire was "My washing/checking is sensible/senseless." Even allowing for the fact that the question, constructed in the earliest stages of our research, was unacceptably superficial, it is nevertheless interesting that only 18 of the 34 patients chose the adjective *senseless*. Contrary to the widespread view that insight is an essential feature of obsessional-compulsive disorders, a significant minority of the patients replied to our simple question in an unpredicted manner. Our clinical experience, however, is entirely consistent with this psychometric information, and we no longer share the opinion that *insight*, as defined here, is an essential feature of obsessional-compulsive disorders. We also found a correlation between *senselessness* and duration of the disorder. That is, patients with a long history of obsessional problems were more likely to describe their rituals as senseless. (The rituals also seem to become more mechanical over time.) Although we do not have sufficient evidence to prove the point, it seems possible that resistance declines during a chronic disorder (see Rachman and de Silva, 1978, for examples).

To sum up, the only necessary condition for deciding whether behavior is compulsive is an experienced sense of pressure. By itself this criterion is not sufficient to reach a decision. The criterion of *internal origin*, if the source of the pressure can be determined, is a strong supporting sign; the combination of a sense of pressure and an internal source provides the necessary and sufficient conditions for defining a compulsion.

Unwillingness to comply, while neither necessary nor sufficient, is nevertheless an important confirmatory feature. The combination of unwillingness and a sense of pressure is not sufficient—the source may be external, and if so, the decision is likely to be in favor of a delusion rather than a compulsion. It can be argued, correctly in our view, that unwillingness implies the presence of pressure, but there are practical reasons for looking beyond the expression of unwillingness. There are cases meriting the term *compulsive* in which the person experiences an (internal) sense of pressure but is *willing* to comply (e.g., "I feel a strong urge to wash and I wish to do so").

The necessary and sufficient conditions for defining an idea, impulse, or image as *obsessional* are intrusiveness, internal attribution, unwantedness, and difficulty of control. The criterion of internal attribution is necessary in order to exclude delusions, ideas of reference, ideas of influence, and so on. Intrusiveness describes the essential experience of an obsession; one becomes aware of the entry into consciousness of an unwanted thought, image, or impulse. An obsession is insinuating. If it is not unwanted, or indeed if it is welcomed, it cannot be described as an obsession. Enjoyable ideas, images, or impulses do not qualify for the term. It is possible for an idea or impulse to be intrusive, internal in origin, and unwanted, and yet fall short of the term *obsessional* if the person finds it easy to control or banish it. Such power reduces the idea, impulse, or image to a mere flash or a stray thought, lacking the adhesiveness of an obsession.

The most important confirmatory indicators are internal resistance and the rejection of the idea or impulse as alien and/or unrealistic. Obsessions generally produce distress (unlike, say, a mere preoccupation).

An obsessional-compulsive disorder is one in which the person's major complaint is of distress caused by obsessions or compulsions (as defined here) or both. The overt indications are repetitive, stereotyped behavior and at least some degree of psychological, occupational, and social impairment that appears to bear a direct relationship to the person's complaints.

Chapter 3
History and Natural History

The concept of obsessions has survived three historical stages—religious, medical, and psychological. Prior to the emergence of medical theories, obsessions were considered to be distorted *religious* experiences ("It is a religious melancholy") and often were regarded as the work of the Devil. For example, John Bunyan construed his blasphemous obsessions as a trial instigated by the Devil. Or, in the words of Baxter (1696), quoted by Hunter and Macalpine (1963), "Those that were never guilty of fornication, are oft cast into long and lamentable trouble by letting Satan once into their Phantasies" (p. 240). The early *medical* view emphasized the role of fevers and disordered imaginations, and the first comprehensive psychopathological theory, *psychoanalysis*, postulated that obsessions are defensive reactions to psychosexual anxiety. This theory was succeeded by the incomplete account proposed by psychologists engaged in testing the applications of learning theory to abnormal psychology. In the course of these changes, from religious to medical to psychological, the emphasis and interest shifted from obsessions to compulsions.

Bearing in mind the blasphemous content of many obsessions, it must be said at the outset that attributing the cause of obsessions to the intrusions of the Devil is more immediately understandable than ascribing them to the vagaries of infant bowel training. The religious attribution was certainly more firmly grounded in contemporary thought than psychoanalysis. Although the form of psychoanalytic theory was continuous with medical theories of the time (i.e., it was a pathological theory, seeking an inner etiology and describing symptoms), the content of psychoanalysis ran counter to prevailing social thought.

Extracts printed in Hunter and Macalpine's (1963) treasure house of British psychiatric history confirm that religious obsessions were among the first to attract the attention of philosophers and physicians. The case of William of Oseney, described by Jeremy Taylor in 1660, is an example of what contemporary writers regarded as a religious melancholy. William was an exceedingly devout man and spent a great deal of his time studying religious texts. However, his devotion eventually got out of control, He decided to devote 3 hours each day to study and to read each of the books 3 times. This was later extended to 6 hours each day reading the same books, and each of them had to be read 6 times over. This chore was then doubled until William had little time left for anything but religious ruminations. His religious concerns had become "vexatious and intolerable," but he was unable to set them aside because of pervasive uncertainties and fears. In Taylor's description people afflicted with these difficulties think too much, "but think of nothing"; the scruple (obsession) is, in his striking phrase, "a doubt when doubts are resolved." In his account of religious melancholy, John Moore (1692), quoted by Hunter and Macalpine (1963), described well the intense preoccupation with religious duties and the associated feelings of guilt. The people affected are troubled by "naughty and sometimes Blasphemous Thoughts" which start in their minds despite "all their endeavours to stifle and suppress them" (p. 252).

The *indecisiveness* of obsessional ruminators had already been identified in 1638 by Richard Younge (quoted by Hunter and Macalpine, 1963). Younge describes how these irresolute people hover in their choices: "Like an empty Balance with no waight of Judgement to incline him to either scale . . . he does nothing readily . . . when he begins to deliberate, never makes an end . . ." (p. 116). An interesting description of the onset of an obsessional delusion was given by John Woodard in 1757 (also quoted by Hunter and Macalpine, 1963). After three miscarriages and the loss of two other children, a woman in her sixth pregnancy observed a large porpoise in the Thames and "was much delighted with the viewing of it" (p. 338). However, two weeks later she experienced considerable abdominal pain and then for no apparent reason recalled the image of the porpoise. She began to fear that the porpoise might "mark her child" and was unable to reason the thought away. It began to absorb more and more of her attention—"It molested, teized, and put her into a disorder so great as almost to distract her" (p. 339). Thereafter the thought fluctuated, seemingly in correspondence with the return of the pain. At times it "became as vexatious as ever, upon the increase of the pain," but at other times she was free of it. Later she developed some additional obsessional ideas and, finally, some obsessional impulses as well. Among other obsessions, she "had thoughts of the Devil, as tempting and vehemently urging of her to ill; particularly to flinging her child into the fire, beat its brains out and the like; to which she had the utmost horror and aversion; being naturally mild, good-natured, and very virtuous" (p. 340).

These antique obsessional fears appear to have been based on fears of contemporary diseases, especially the plague. In later centuries, the fear of syphilis featured prominently; more recently, cancer has taken its place as a common obsessional fear. One of our patients embodied this historical change: She had an extremely serious obsessional disorder, having devoted virtually her entire adult life to escaping from contamination by carrying out intensive, prolonged cleaning rituals. In the early stages of her thirty-five-year-long disorder, she had an intense fear of syphilis; the expressed intention of scrubbing and disinfecting herself in this repeated fashion was to protect herself from contacting syphilis. She avoided entire sections of the city that she felt carried an elevated risk of contamination and took particular care when walking in public places to avoid trampling on discarded condoms. After some ten years the content of the fear changed. She was considerably less worried by the threat of syphilis but became preoccupied with the danger of contracting cancer. The cleaning rituals showed very little alteration either in form or in content—she continued carrying out extensive multiple washes, with water and disinfectant, many times each day.

For a considerable period obsessions were regarded as a manifestation of depression or, as it was then called, melancholia. At most, they were construed as a subclass of depressive phenomena. The 1895 edition of Henry Maudsley's influential textbook *The Pathology of Mind* contains, in the chapter on melancholia, an excellent and colorful account of obsessional ideas and impulses but a single, dismissive mention of compulsions (acceptance of the view that obsessions were better regarded as a separate, although related, disorder came some fifty years later):

> In another group of cases of simple melancholy the cause of affliction is a morbid impulse to utter a bad word or to do an ill deed. The impulse is bad enough, but the essence of the misery is not always so much the fear of actually yielding to it as the haunting fear of the fear. It is that which is the perpetual torture, an acute agony when active, a quivering apprehension of recurrence when quiescent. Sometimes the impulse is of a dangerous character, as when it prompts a father to kill himself or urges a mother to kill her children; not unfrequently it is an impulse to utter aloud a profane or obscene word or to do an indecent act; now and then it is the impulse to do some meaningless and absurd act which has taken hold of the fancy and will not let it go, and to repeat the act over and over again, since thus only can peace of mind be obtained.
>
> Bad as the impulses are, worse still perhaps is the persistent intrusion of evil thoughts, horrible and detestable, into the mind, despite the most earnest wish to turn and keep them out. They come and stay there against the will, a haunting horror, a maddening torture; agonies of praying are as futile to exorcise them as agonies of will to expel them. [Maudsley, 1895, pp. 170-71]

Thus he is in despair because he has the urgent impulse to do some ridiculous thing which it has come into his mind to do and has no peace until he does it; or cannot help repeating an act foolishly over and over again, only because he feels he must, when he would be only too glad to have done with it; or is constrained to think of doing an indecent act and is in a fright lest he should some day do it; or feels impelled to utter aloud a blasphemous or obscene word, and is obliged either to bite his tongue to prevent himself from speaking or to compromise matters by whispering the word to himself; or is urged by a morbid spirit of metaphysical curiosity continually to ask himself the reason of this and the reason again of that reason and so backwards the reasons and reasons without end. [p. 184]

Before leaving the early psychiatric literature on the subject, it is worth mentioning in passing some famous obsessionals of the past. Samuel Johnson, John Bunyan, and Charles Darwin all had obsessional traits and at one time or another suffered from an obsessional disorder. It is interesting too that in each case their work bears the marks of their obsessional tendencies—collecting, systematically ordering and organizing, making increasingly fine distinctions, struggling with unacceptable thoughts, and so on. As Dr. R. Levy has observed (personal communication), Marthe de Meligny, the wife of the French painter Bonnard, was a compulsive washer. Bonnard left an artistic record of her activities, with many beautiful paintings on the themes of "nude in bath," "woman at toilet," and so on.

It would appear that in his declining years Howard Hughes suffered from a severe obsessional disorder, among many other problems. Although the information is scanty and of unknown reliability, it seems extremely probable that he had a strong obsessional fear of contamination. In order to avoid infection, he constructed for himself a sterile, isolated environment in which his contact with potentially contaminating people was kept to a minimum. For the most part he successfully avoided touching any person or object directly—instead, he covered himself with paper tissues and other protective materials. His barber was required to repeatedly sterilize all of his instruments by immersing them in alcohol. There was a complicated ritual for handling objects. Before handing Hughes a spoon, his attendants had to wrap the handle in tissue paper and seal it with cellophane tape. A second piece of tissue was wrapped around the first protective wrapping to ensure that it would be protected from contamination. On receiving the protected spoon, Hughes would use it only with the handle covered. When he finished with it, the tissue was discarded into a specially provided receptacle. The spoon itself had to be carefully cleaned.

Hughes also developed a complicated series of requirements surrounding eating, even though in the course of the disorder his appetite diminished and the range of foods acceptable to him became extraordinarily narrow. In addition to the many bizarre cleaning rituals that he adopted, a striking feature of his obsessional life style was the manner in which he withdrew from the world into a small, sealed, germ-free environment serviced by a small group of carefully selected attendants. His wealth enabled him to pay these people to carry out compulsive rituals on his behalf. On one occasion, for instance, he observed that a bottle had been broken on the steps of his ranch. He wrote out a series of instructions that involved marking out a grid of one-inch squares on each step and then meticulously cleaning one square at a time to ensure that every splinter of glass had been removed. This set of rituals was delegated to a hired cleaner whom Hughes observed from a window.

Skoog (1959) reviewed most of the early psychiatric literature on the subject of obsessions and compulsions, starting with the 1838 treatise by Pinel's protégé Esquirol. This historical material combines clinical description and philosophical analysis. The major themes are the basis for diagnosis, the relation of obsessions to personality and to psychiatric disorders (especially schizophrenia and depression), and the causal role of hereditary and organic factors. The absence of suitable investigative procedures hampered progress, and none of the major questions was resolved. It was, for example, impossible to determine the relation between obsessional disorders and intelligence as long as the investigators were obliged to rely on their personal impressions of the patient's intelligence. Similarly, the relation between the patient's illness and personality, and the personality of the patient's close relatives, could not be determined with any degree of satisfaction in the absence of reliable methods of assessing personality. Moreover, as this type of information also provided the basis for assessing the hereditary contribution to the illness, it is no surprise that estimates ranged from as low as 5 percent to as high as 90 percent. Speculations about the role of organic factors were poorly grounded because of the absence of reliable means of assessing organic impairment.

Notwithstanding these difficulties, the historical material has many interesting features. Early on, a measure of agreement was reached on the matter of definitions. So in 1925 Schneider was able to propose three defining qualities of obsessions: the experience of subjective compulsion, their immovable quality, and the retention of insight (under calm conditions). (The term *anancastic* personality, drawn from the Greek word for fate, was apparently introduced in 1896, but as it serves no useful purpose it can be dispensed with). Janet (1903) was one of the earliest writers to emphasize the importance of personality factors; he concluded that all obsessional patients have a clearly abnormal personality (he used the term *psychasthenia*) that antedates the onset of the illness. The main characteristics of psychasthenia are lack of energy, anxiety, doubting, indecisiveness, pedantry, excessive worrying, and feelings of weakness. Many of these adjectives can be found in the pre-medical literature, and the concept also bears some relationship to the modern concept of dysthymia (Eysenck, 1957). Janet was a supporter of the genetic view and reported that a mere 8 percent of the 170 parents of obsessional patients investigated were normal. However, even if the data were precise and reliable (they are not), they would not enable one to reach definite conclusions. The same findings about the personality of the patient and his or her relatives can as easily be recruited in support of an environmental theory of causation.

The dispute about the relationship between obsessional-compulsive illness and schizophrenia was considered to be of central importance, and it continued for decades. Numerous authorities claimed that there is a continuous relationship between obsessional-compulsive disorders and schizophrenia—indeed, it was argued that obsessions are a premonitory sign of schizophrenia. Other writers denied any relationship between the two illnesses, and yet others claimed that an obsessional illness protects one from schizophrenia. On the question of obsessions and depression, there was, and still is, greater agreement. The two are closely related and often occur together. Although the early writers exaggerated the etiological importance of organic impairments, they did succeed in making a useful distinction between "normal" obsessions and those in which organic impairment plays a part. The latter were said to be more primitive, stereotyped, and free of intellectual content.

The style and content of this early work can be illustrated by Skoog's own research, which is embedded in the classical psychiatric tradition. He selected for special study the 285 "anancastic syndromes" extracted from 5732 patients attending the Gothenburg University Clinic between 1947 and 1953. The incidence figure of 5 percent of the total psychiatric population is higher than usual and suggests that perhaps not all of the cases were typical of those reported elsewhere. It is worth mentioning, however, that 80 percent of these "anancastic" patients gave a history of depression, a large majority reported fears of various types, 40 percent reported sexual difficulties, 47 percent reported acute onset of their illness, and 67 percent claimed that they had been under emotional stress at the time of onset. However, in a comparison with nonanancastic patients similarly high figures were reported for the occurrence of depression and emotional stress. One of the major differences between the anancastics and the control patients was seen in the mode of onset—47 percent of the former group reported acute onset of their disorder, while a mere 4 percent (a curiously low number) of the controls reported acute onset of their disorder.

Despite the serious limitations of these writings, a broad but blurred picture did emerge. There is a disorder, or a collection of related disorders, characterized by the experience of compulsion, incomplete subjective resistance, repetitive and stereotyped behavior, unwanted intrusive thoughts, and the rest. It is relatively uncommon, occurs equally in both sexes, is associated with depression, is unrelated to schizophrenia or to intellectual capacity, and so on. Many of these observations have been confirmed to some degree by contemporary workers.

In retrospect it may well seem that the most important conceptual fault transmitted by the early writers was to regard obsessions and compulsions as illnesses. Even though many writers distinguished between the concepts of obsessional personality and obsessional illness, it was universally assumed, but never argued, that the abnormal form of this type of behavior was indeed an *illness*, as opposed to an abnormality of behavior and experience that is not an illness and certainly is nonpathological in the narrow sense of that term. From the first systematic descriptions provided in the middle of the nineteenth century until a few years ago, obsessions and compulsions were regarded as signs and symptoms of a (neurotic) illness and, hence, best dealt with practically and theoretically within the medical framework. One might ask why they ever came to be so regarded, and the answer must surely be found in the historical development of psychiatry and the later growth of the separate subject of abnormal psychology. No doubt many people troubled by obsessions and compulsions, then as now, did not seek medical assistance but, rather, sought help from relatives, friends, healers, and priests. When medical assistance for psychiatric and psychological problems became available, large numbers of people with obsessional problems sought this professional help. Clinical psychology developed some time after clinical psychiatry, and in its early stages most psychologists were employed by, and hence subordinate to, psychiatrists. As clinical psychology approached maturity, alternate conceptions of abnormal behavior emerged, and for the first time a nonpathological, nonreligious view of obsessions and compulsions was offered.

THE NATURAL HISTORY
OF OBSESSIONAL-COMPULSIVE DISORDERS

Studies of the natural history of a disorder are of course compilations of the major features of the disorder, the prominent characteristics of the affected population, and the course of the disorder. They are based on group data and are descriptive and atheoretical.

Before entering a discussion of the merits and limitations of studies of the natural history of disorders such as obsessions and compulsions, it is as well to draw attention to their most obvious and significant value—they enliven the definitions of the disorder and delineate the scope, nature, and path of the problem. Undue reliance on the findings of these studies can, however, lead to serious errors. With few exceptions, and the available studies of obsessional-compulsive disorders are not exceptions, the data are retrospective, imprecise, incomplete, nonrandom, and of unknown reliability. Comparisons between studies are awkward because of variations in diagnostic concepts and practices, base rates, health service facilities, and so forth. In all, the difficulties are so numerous that only lightheaded optimists expect to derive anything of value from them. On the subject of obsessions and compulsions, however, their optimism is justified.

As will be seen from the following quotations, there is a surprising amount of agreement about the general characteristics and course of obsessional disorders. The only serious disagreement concerns the prognosis of the disorder, with estimates of improvement ranging from 25 percent (Kringlen, 1965) to 71 percent (Lo, 1967). The disparity is traceable, in part, to different improvement rates for in-patients and out-patients.

In summary, the evidence suggests that of patients who are developing an obsessional illness, about a third will give a history of neurotic symptoms in puberty or early adolescence but this incidence may be no higher than in patients who develop other neurotic illnesses. Persistent phobic, ritual or perseverative features are perhaps the only precursory ones more specific to obsessional disorder. The illness most often begins between the ages of 10 and 15 years and by the age of 25 it has started in over half of the cases; only one person in 20 becomes ill for the first time after the age of 40. Significant changes in life events are associated with the onset of illness in one-third to two-thirds of the cases, but again these frequencies may be no different from those found in other neurotic conditions. The type of precipitating factors most commonly described are sexual and marital difficulties, pregnancy and delivery, and illness or death of a near relative, but there is little agreement on the absolute or relative importance of these. In most patients the initial illness follows a slowly progressive course, sometimes punctuated by exacerbations; in others, the onset is acute and continuous, or presents with discrete phasic attacks. The main illness—persisting symptoms, eventually leading the patient to seek psychiatric help—usually develops in the mid-20s, with a mean age of 28 years. About half the patients will not come to psychiatric attention for two years or more, and in an appreciable minority of cases, this delay may be more than 10 years. If admission to hospital becomes necessary, this tends to occur in the mid-30s. [Black, 1974, p. 41]

A review of 13 follow-up studies on obsessional neurosis reveals that the disease has an onset in childhood or early adult life, a course that is chronic but variable, and a prognosis that is more favorable than is often believed. The data suggest that obsessional neurosis does not involve an increased risk of suicide, homicide, alcoholism, drug addiction, anti-social behavior, chronic hospitalization, or the development of another mental disorder, such as schizophrenia. [Goodwin, Guze, and Robins, 1969, p. 186]

Patients with a typical obsessional neurosis usually suffer from a variety of neurotic symptoms as children and most of them have obsessional traits prior to their main illnesses. These patients have a relatively early onset of symptoms, more than half of them developing symptoms before the age of 20. During the first years of illness, the course is usually episodic. In some cases there is a complete disappearance of symptoms, but later the course is characterized by fewer remissions and fewer improvements. Most of the patients have both obsessive thoughts, obsessive acts and phobic anxiety. In addition, many are suffering from tenseness, headache, sleeping difficulties and depressive thoughts. The typical obsessional is usually a hard worker and only in periods of decompensation with depression is his working ability impaired. Most of them have a miserable life; they are frequently socially isolated and if married, unhappy with their spouses. Obsessive pre-morbid personality and severe clinical picture on first admission seems to be associated with a significantly less favorable prognosis. In samples of in-patients one can expect that roughly three-fourths will be unchanged 20-30 years after onset (10-20 years after admission) and one-fourth will be much improved. In samples of out-patients with a less severe clinical picture, one can expect that half the patients are much improved after some years. Misuse of alcohol and drugs frequently occurs, but typical chronic alcoholism and drug addiction are rare. Development into psychosis is also rare in typical cases and the suicidal risk is small. [Kringlen, 1970, p. 418]

The obsessive-compulsive neurosis is a rather uncommon psychiatric disorder. The onset is usually in childhood, adolescent, or early adult life; and it may or may not have environmental precipitants. First born and only children are especially prone to this disorder. There appears to be no appreciable sex predilection. The most common complication is depression. Yet the suicide rate of depressed obsessive-compulsives is less than in other depressed patients. Obsessive-compulsive neurotics tend to be of above average intelligence. Although relatives have a high incidence of a variety of psychopathological entities, the role of heredity is unclear. Although obsessive-compulsive symptomatology is often noted in both schizophrenics and organics, it would probably be unwarranted to say that either schizophrenia or brain pathology is present in the majority of typical obsessive-compulsives. The prognosis is generally regarded as not good. [Templer, 1972, p. 382]

Similar descriptions can be found in most psychiatric textbooks or in specialized papers on the subject (e.g., Lewis, 1936, 1966; Pollitt, 1957; Lo, 1967). In passing, it is of interest to note the growing evidence of cross-cultural similarities in the natural history of the disorder. Descriptions of patients in Egypt (Okasha et al., 1968), Hong Kong (Lo, 1967), China (Dai, 1957), India (Akhtar et al., 1975), Lebanon (Katchadourian & Racy, 1969), Norway (Kringlen, 1965), the United States (Welner et al., 1976), Sudan (Elsarrag, 1968), and England (Lewis, 1936, 1966) are broadly similar. These reports also contain some amusing sidelights. Commenting on their Egyptian findings, Okasha and his associates say, "This illness was relatively common . . . and may be attributed to the fact that cleaning plays an important role in Moslem religious rituals" (p. 952). In another article in the same issue of the *British Journal of Psychiatry*, Elsarrag interpreted the lower than usual incidence among Sudanese patients—an adjacent territory, sharing a common religion—as reflecting "a culture pattern [that] is not conducive to obsessionality" (p. 946). Cultural evidence can be recruited to show that the glass is half full of water—or half empty.

Some of the more important aspects of the natural history of the disorder are discussed in detail later, but first it is worth elaborating on the value of this type of study. As mentioned earlier, such studies provide us with a useful outline of the disorder, and this in turn enables one to give informed advice to people who have these problems and to their relatives. They also provide a backdrop against which one can evaluate the significance of new findings, and a basis for making prognostic estimates.

An important virtue of these studies is that they provide a starting point for the introduction of risk research strategies. By combining the available evidence, suitably weighted, it should be possible to calculate the risk that a particular person or group of people will develop an obsessional-compulsive disorder during a prescribed period.

The theoretical value of these data is that they allow one to develop alternative, multideterminant conceptions of "etiology." Acceptance of the traditional medical model leads to a search for one (or sometimes more than one) etiological cause of the putative illness. On the analogy of organic illness, there should be a specific time at which the cause begins to exert a pathological influence. Once started, the pathological process gives rise to symptoms and signs.

An alternate, psychological model emphasizes the *continuity* of behavior; obsessions and compulsions are regarded as abnormalities of behavior. They need not have a cause or causes in the restricted medical sense. It is instead more profitable to ask what *generates* the behavior and what *maintains* it. One attempts to delineate the multiple determinants of the (abnormal) behavior. Instead of seeking the cause of the illness, one should ask *which conditions and factors promote the development of obsessions and compulsions.*

From our point of view, it is no more sensible to ask "What is the cause of tardiness?" than it is to ask "What is the cause of excessive checking?" In both examples the questions can be more fruitfully posed as follows: "What conditions and factors promote tardiness/checking?" The alternate question emphasizes the continuity of behavior, normal or abnormal, and thereby helps distinguish this conception from the illness model.

An alternate psychological approach might deal with the *general* question of genesis (as opposed to an analysis of the specific psychological mechanisms— see Chapters 11, 12, and 19) by constructing a table of risk factors. As an illustration of the form this approach might take, we compiled the following list of high- and low-risk factors, without regard to their differential weighting. The high-risk factors include the following: one (or more) obsessional parent, overcontrolling parental behavior, firstborn or only child (Kayton and Borge, 1967; Tseng, 1973), ritualistic behavior during childhood, unfavorable significant life event within the past 12 months, episodes of depression, obsessional traits, and an age of 15-25 years. The low-risk factors would include absence of a family history of obsessional-compulsive disorders, minimal obsessional traits, a stable extroverted personality, no history of depression, no significant unfavorable life events in the recent past and an age over 40.

It must be emphasized that the introduction of risk research strategy in dealing with the problem of the genesis of obsessional-compulsive disorders, while more congruent with a psychological than with a medical model, is not the major distinction between medical and psychological theorizing on the subject. Also, the present list of risk factors was compiled to illustrate the point rather than to provide a basis for counseling or specific predictions.

We are fortunate in having a number of excellent reviews of the natural history of obsessions and compulsions, and it would serve no useful purpose to repeat the exercise. Instead, we have chosen to give a short account of the most salient points and to provide references for readers who wish to obtain more detailed information on a particular aspect of the subject. Where available, new material has been added to the general picture. These data are drawn from a sample of 83 patients, most of whom were studied in the early years of our research program. They constitute a nonrepresentative, incomplete sample, having been chosen primarily for participation in therapeutic trials, and hence the information can be regarded as no more than a supplement. However, on the most important features of the disorder it would appear that the overwhelming majority of our patients were characteristic of a severe, chronic, in-patient population.

DEMOGRAPHY

The best recent estimates of the demographic attributes of obsessional patients are provided by Hare, Price, and Slater (1972), and their information serves as a point of reference for the other reports. In considering this information, and indeed other features of the natural history of the disorder, it is helpful to distinguish between the statistics for in-patients and out-patients. Incidentally, a disproportionately large proportion of obsessional patients are admitted to psychiatric hospitals.

Hare and his colleagues compared the characteristics of 446 obsessional patients who attended the Bethlem-Maudsley Hospital in London between the years 1952 and 1966 with those of 831 obsessional patients admitted to other English psychiatric hospitals for the first time during the period 1965-1966. After drawing attention to some of the limitations of their data (e.g., a slight overlap between the two samples, disparity between the in-patient status of the two groups, etc.), the authors drew some important conclusions. They calculated that obsessional neurosis accounts for 3 percent of all neuroses and 0.5 percent of all first-admission psychiatric cases. In the national series (comprising in-patient admissions only), 40 percent of the obsessional cases were male, whereas the percentage rose to 49 percent in the Bethlem-Maudsley series (in which out-patients as well as in-patients were included). They argue that the excess of female patients in the national series results from the policy of "more readily admitting" females as in-patients. Overall, males and females were equally represented. Hare and his associates provide a detailed comparison of the age distributions in obsessional neuroses, all neuroses, schizophrenia, and affective psychoses; the peak distribution of obsessional neuroses lies between that of schizophrenia and all other neuroses combined, but is different from that of affective psychosis. The celibacy rate was high, particularly for males; both male and female obsessional patients tended to marry at an older age than other types of patient. Fertility in marriage was low, falling even below the rate for schizophrenic patients. "The proportion of childless marriages in obsessional neurosis is greater than in all neuroses or in affective psychoses, and for females the proportion exceeds that in schizophrenia" (p. 202. These data, and our clinical experience, suggest that this results from a combination of severe social problems and specific sexual difficulties. It is perhaps of interest to mention that in one of our studies we observed a correlation between our concept of "impaired reproductive capacity" and severity of the disorder, as well as a relationship between impaired reproductive capacity and poor therapeutic outcome (de Silva, Rachman, and Seligman, 1977). Using the information provided by Hare, Price, and Slater (1972) as a basis for comparison, we can now examine the other studies.

INCIDENCE

Black (1974, p. 21) provided an excellent tabular summary of 11 studies reported up to 1964. The percentage of psychiatric out-patients who were diagnosed as having an obsessional-compulsive disorder lies between 0.3 and 0.6 percent. (The larger figure of 2.9% reported by Blacker and Gore in 1955 is, judging from the comparative data compiled by Hare et al., a reflection of the fact that the hospital concerned, the Bethlem-Maudsley, deals with a disproportionately large percentage of neurotic patients.) As mentioned earlier, obsessionals constitute a slightly larger percentage of the in-patient population, probably of the order of 2 percent. Between 3.5 and 4.5 percent of all neurotic in-patients and roughly 3 percent of all neurotics are classified as obsessional. The incidence among children was estimated by Berman (1942) to lie between 0.1 and 0.8 percent of the psychiatric population.

Sex Ratio

With the exception of the Hong Kong Chinese sample described by Lo (1967)—which he explains in terms of cultural bias—the sex distribution of the disorder is apparently random. As Hare and his associates point out, however, more female psychiatric patients are admitted to hospitals. Hence, the figure for in-patient obsessionals shows a slight excess of females. In our own nonrepresentative sample of 83 patients, there were more women (65%) than men, perhaps because we were actively seeking patients with disorders sufficiently severe to merit admission to a hospital. On available evidence there is no reason to suppose that women are more or less likely to develop the disorder (Black, 1974; Ingram, 1961). However, a reexamination of our own data revealed an interesting and previously unremarked association between cleaning compulsions and gender. No less than 86 percent of our compulsive cleaners were female; the ratio of females to males was 6:1. Male and female patients were nearly equally represented among the compulsive checkers (males = 55%). Bearing in mind the greater incidence of fears and phobias among women (Marks, 1969), this new finding is consistent with our argument that there is a close association between phobias and cleaning compulsions (see Chapter 25). Moreover, if our interpretation of cleaning rituals in terms of escape and passive avoidance behavior is correct, the present finding suggests that women are more likely than men to engage in this type of behavior.

The celibacy rate is high in obsessional neurosis; as we have seen, Hare and his colleagues estimate that the rate is higher for these patients than for any group other than schizophrenics. Our own data, showing an overall celibacy rate of 37 percent, are consistent with their estimates and with Kringlen's (1965).

Of the 51 patients in our group who were married, slightly less than half (47%) were judged to have a satisfactory marital relationship. In Kringlen's group, 30 out of 55 (i.e., 54%) were thought to have a satisfactory marital relationship. As mentioned earlier, Hare and his associates reported a low fertility rate and an excessive number of childless marriages (28.5%)—the national average is given as 19 percent. In our group 23 percent of the married patients were childless, and many of the parents experienced considerable difficulty in rearing their children. The fertility rate was low.

Intelligence

In the early literature it was widely supposed that obsessional patients are, on average, of superior intelligence. This assumption was based on flimsy impressionistic evidence. When standardized psychometric tests were introduced and a small amount of appropriate evidence collected, the impressions of the clinicians were confirmed—an uncomfortable lesson, perhaps. The work of Slater (1945), Ingram (1961), Payne (1960), and Eysenck (1947) provides the necessary support, but is based on small samples. Slater compared the scores of 25 obsessional patients with those of a like number of hysterics, cases of anxiety neurosis, and miscellaneous neuroses, on the Progressive Matrices. The obsessional patients did significantly better than the other three groups, who did not differ among themselves. The investigation was repeated on a comparable sample, first using the Cattell tests of intelligence and then a vocabulary test.

The same result emerged—the obsessional patients were of superior intelligence and the remaining three groups did not differ among themselves. Substantially the same pattern of results was obtained by the other research workers mentioned. The matter was taken a little further by Eysenck (1967), who compared the scores obtained by dysthymics (i.e., neurotic introverts) with those obtained by hysterics (neurotic extraverts) and concluded that the former were more intelligent than the extraverts. As obsessional patients fall squarely in the dysthymic quadrant, this result is consistent with Slater's. Eysenck then went on to compare the patterning of intelligence in these two groups of neurotic patients and demonstrated that dysthymics show a low intelligence/vocabulary ratio—in other words, the introverts are found to have a good vocabulary relative to their intelligence.

Despite the small samples, these findings seem to settle the matter; except in the negative sense of excluding some possibilities, confirmation of the slightly superior intelligence of obsessional patients, as a group, appears to have no further theoretical or practical significance. This provides us with a rare opportunity to conclude that further research on this topic is *not* necessary.

Age

It is agreed that the age for obsessions is late adolescence and early adulthood. The mean age of onset is the early 20s (see Ingram, 1961; Pollitt, 1957). In Black's (1974) words, "By the age of 25, over half of the patients have symptoms and by 30, nearly three-quarters" (p. 38). Less than 5 percent of the patients report an onset after the age of 40. The available evidence is summarized in the useful figure compiled by Black, which is reproduced here. (See Figure 3.1) Our own data are consistent with his analysis. Sixty-five percent of our sample of 83 patients reported an onset age of less than 25 years, and his estimate, based on a review of other papers, is approximately 56 percent.

A considerable time may pass before the affected person comes to the attention of the health services. According to Pollitt's (1957) evidence, the mean waiting period is 7.5 years, but the improvement of services and education has probably reduced this gap. Even in Pollitt's now dated study, half of the patients sought help within two years of onset.

It is not clear why obsessional-compulsive disorders develop in early adulthood. None of the theories advanced so far has dealt with this aspect of the disorder. If, as we will argue presently, there often is a close relationship between depression and obsessions, we need to explain why obsessions appear to be ignited at a young age. There is no simple overlap between the age of onset of depressions and of obsessions; depressions have their onset in later life (Robins and Guze, 1972; Schuyler, 1974). "There is no quarrel from any quarter with the conclusion that depression, by comparison with all other functional mental illnesses, is an ailment of aging" (Levitt and Lubin, 1975, p. 85). It appears to

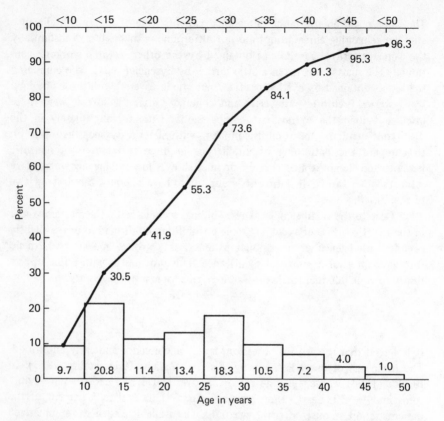

FIGURE 3.1.   Age of onset of first symptoms in obsessional illness expressed as percentage distribution and cumulative frequencies. (N=357-667) (from Black, A., 1974).

follow from this epidemiological mismatch (and others to be discussed later, see p. 81) that the link between depressions and obsessions must be a complex one.

One possibility is that depression may indeed facilitate obsessions but that there is a critical time (early adulthood) during which this process can take place. For example, some of the recognized precipitants of obsessional disorders, such as childbirth (e.g., Ingram, 1961), occur during the critical period for onset.

A related and strong possibility is that the association lies between obsessional-compulsive disorders and neurotic (reactive) depression. For example, Kiloh and Garside (1963) found significant correlations between obsessionality and neurotic depression, on the one hand, and endogenous depression and late age of onset, on the other. In line with this possible link, Schuyler (1974) reviews evidence indicating that endogenous depressions reach a peak incidence in women between 45 and 50 years of age, and in men at the age of approximately 60. Reactive depression, by contrast, reaches its peak incidence at a younger age; in females, it ranges between 26 and 40; in males, between 36 and

40. The argument that obsessional-compulsive disorders are associated with reactive depression rather than endogenous depression is taken up in detail later and rests on the assumption that the distinction between reactive and endogenous depressions can be justified.

In a study of prepared obsessions, de Silva, Rachman, and Seligman (1977) found a positive relationship between early age of onset and severity of the disorder, but the age of onset was not related to the preparedness of the obsession (see Chapter 25). Nor was the age of onset, early or late, related to therapeutic outcome. The important question of why obsessions and compulsions emerge at a comparatively early age remains unanswered.

Finally, Black (1974) has conveniently summarized the four major reports on the natural course of obsessional disorders, with the following results. In a comparatively small number of cases, between 11 percent and 14 percent, the disorder is phasic. In another 25-35 percent, the disorder shows a fluctuating course in which the major complaint never disappears. In just over half of the patients (between 54% and 61%), the problem remains relatively static. In the remaining one-third of the cases, a steady deterioration is observed. Similar percentages were reported by Lo (1967).

Chapter 4

Factors Promoting
and Precipitating the Disorders

THE GENETIC CONTRIBUTION

Proponents of the argument that there is a significant direct genetic contribution to the development of obsessional-compulsive disorders have not proven their case. There is, however, plausible support for the argument that there is an important genetic contribution to general emotional oversensitivity or neuroticism (see Eysenck, 1967; Shields, 1973; Slater and Cowie, 1971; Rosenthal, 1970). In addition to their relevance for analyses of the causation of the disorder, genetic studies can make an indirect contribution to nosology.

As the genetic evidence and arguments are admirably presented in excellent texts (Shields, 1973; Slater & Cowie, 1971, Rosenthal, 1970), our discussion will be confined to points of greatest theoretical interest. The genetic evidence is of three main kinds: studies of familial incidence, comparisons between monozygotic and dizygotic twins, and studies of adoptive parents and children. Although these methods have produced valuable clarification of the genetic contribution to psychiatric disorders, especially schizophrenia, relatively little research has been undertaken on the genetics of obsessions and compulsions. This comparative neglect is a result, in part at least, of the infrequency with which the disorder is encountered. In addition, the confusing problem of distinguishing between obsessional disorders and obsessional personality traits presents a serious obstacle to genetic research.

As far as research into familial incidence is concerned, the information is of interest, but there are problems of interpretation. The presence of obsessions and compulsions in close relatives of diagnosed obsessional patients does not prove a genetic contribution; on the other hand, the absence of obsessional problems in close relatives may weaken those theories of the genesis of obsessional-compulsive disorders that are based on observational learning. The observation of an elevated rate of obsessional disorders in close relatives, taken in isolation, can as easily be interpreted as evidence for a genetic or an environmental contribution.

Although the twin method, particularly when separated pairs have been traced, has produced valuable results in other spheres, the few twin studies on obsessional-compulsive disorders are disappointing. In accounts in which a high concordance rate between monozygotic twins has been claimed, there are doubts about the quality of the diagnostic conclusions. To take an example, Inouye (1965) claimed an 80-percent concordance rate for ten monozygotic obsessional patients, but the supporting case material is unsatisfactory. Both the index cases and their co-twins seemingly suffered from a range of mild psychological difficulties and a few serious ones. In all of the cases quoted, there is doubt about whether a firm diagnosis of obsessional-compulsive neurosis was justified. As an extreme example of the dubious quality of the diagnostic procedures, Inouye's fourth index case was aggressive, hysterical, and engaged in compulsive coprolalia, with earlier signs of a possibly neurological disorder in which tics and yelling were prominent. The putative obsessional symptoms in the retarded, brain-injured co-twin, who was a deaf mute, were "milder and more primitive than those of the index twin and the formation of obsession-compulsion was less marked" (p. 1174). In his commentary on this material, Black (1974) is critical of Inouye's study and that of Tienari (1963), who also claimed a high concordance rate—91 percent. We accept Black's reservations, and he is probably correct in concluding that in Tienari's published material "there is no support for the diagnosis of obsessional neurosis in a single case" (Black, 1974, p. 23).

The third tactic, assessment of the behavior and disorders of adoptive children and their biological and adoptive parents, which has been so valuable in research into schizophrenia, has not yet made a mark on research into obsessions. The results of such research are awaited with interest.

According to the thorough reviews carried out by Slater and Cowie (1971) and by Rosenthal (1970), there are no grounds for assuming any degree of genetic identity between obsessional-compulsive disorders and either schizophrenia or depressive illnesses. Although there is sound evidence indicating an increased frequency of psychiatric disorder among the close relatives of obsessional patients, no specific associations have emerged. As Rosenthal points out, the "degree of association between schizophrenia and neurosis" is in any event low; and the schizophrenic morbidity rate for siblings of obsessional patients is correspondingly low (p. 117). Our argument is that, insofar as obsessions are related to depression, it is likely to be the reactive type of depression rather than the endogenous type. According to Slater and Cowie (p. 108) and Shields (1973, p. 575), the genetic contribution to reactive depression is nonspecific and the family risk for reactive depression is low.

Although the research of Tienari (1963), Inouye (1965), and Marks and his associates (1969), among a few others, has yielded high concordance rates for monozygotic twins, there are reasonable doubts about the quality of the evidence and/or ambiguities of interpretation. We have already noted some evidential weaknesses; the fascinating pair of monozygotic twins reported by Marks, Crowe, Drewe, Young, and Dewhurst (1969) is an illustration of the dangers of using raw figures of twin concordance as a basis for concluding that obsessional-compulsive disorders are determined largely by genetic factors. Their detailed account of the personality of the index and co-twin, and of their relationship, makes it plain that there was a degree, perhaps a very large degree, of direct and vicarious transmission of obsessional ideas and compulsive habits from the co-twin to the index twin. Apparently, the co-twin was the dominating partner in the twinship, and at least one instance is quoted in which he transmitted his "profound distaste for dog's feces (even seen at a distance) and the patient quickly followed suit . . . From that time the patient and his brother developed a complicated ritual of avoidance of dogs which involved many aspects of their lives" (p. 991). At the age of 10, the twins agreed that butter and milk bottles were dirty and "if contaminated [the co-twin] would wash scrupulously and make the patient do the same before he would accept him" (p. 991). As the authors point out, "The similarity of *content* of the disorder in both twins is probably the result of mutual social interaction between them with the patient's brother deciding the rules to be followed with the disorder, just as he did in normal activities before the disorder developed. The brother withdrew from the patient if he did not comply. The patient accepted this dominance even later after many arguments had occurred between them and they no longer saw one another" (p. 993, original emphasis).

Although this example is correctly coded as an instance of concordance between monozygotic twins, the importance of environmental transmission from the co-twin to the patient is beyond dispute; the genetic contribution to the patient's obsessional disorder cannot be demonstrated.

Before turning to evidence that runs contrary to claims of a major genetic component in the genesis of obsessional disorders, it should be noted that in the Medical Research Council's meticulously collected data (gathered by Slater, Shields, and their co-workers over a period of many years) there is a concordance rate of three out of six for obsessional neurosis (quoted by Shields, 1973). The significance of this finding and the others on twin concordance (e.g., Woodruff and Pitts, 1963, persuasive cases), bearing in mind the doubts expressed about the significance of this evidence, has to be read against the following astonishing statistic. Basing their calculations on the prevalence of obsessional neurosis in the general population and the occurrence of identical twins (one in 200 adults),

Marks and his colleagues (1969) concluded that "by chance alone . . . about one in 400,000 . . . of the general adult population could be expected to be a monozygotic twin with obsessive-compulsive neurosis, and one in 800 million . . . would be expected to be one of a pair of identical twins with the same illness if concordance was only random" (p. 992). As we have tried to argue, however, concordance is not "only random." Bias is almost bound to enter into the selection, assessment, and diagnosis of co-twins of monozygotic obsessional patients. Moreover, the opportunities for direct social transmission of obsessional and compulsive ideas and behavior are considerable. The case for an important genetic contribution, based on twin concordance, can be resolved only by comparisons between separated monozygotic twins in which the most careful blind and independent assessments are carried out. Bearing in mind the very low incidence of obsessional neuroses, the likelihood of these requirements being met is rather small. The alternate strategy of using adoption studies is more likely to provide some early answers.

The case for a specific genetic contribution to the development of obsessional-compulsive disorders is inconclusive, but the possibility of a *general* genetic contribution, through the vehicle of an increased predisposition to anxiety, or to neuroses generally, cannot be excluded. So, for example, Brown (1942) found little evidence (7.5%) of obsessional-compulsive disorders among the parents of his obsessional patients, but a significantly elevated percentage of what he called "anxious personalities" (32%). Similar evidence bearing on obsessional-compulsive disorders is provided by Kringlen (1965) and by Rosenberg (1967), while the case for a general predisposition is argued by numerous writers, including Eysenck (1979) and the psychogeneticists referred to earlier.

Rosenberg's (1967) study of the familial aspects of obsessional neurosis produced an important result. In his study of 547 first-degree relatives of 144 patients with obsessional neurosis, "classical obsessional neurosis" was "found in only two cases. However, several were diagnosed as suffering from a phobic anxiety state, which some authors classify as an obsessional neurosis" (p. 412). He correctly concluded that although his findings indicate that "psychiatric illness occurs frequently among relatives of obsessional neurotics," they do not support "the view that the obsessional personality or classical obsessional neuroses (obsessions accompanied by compulsions) are genetically determined" (p. 412).

Using the information provided by Slater and Cowie (p. 105) as a basis, we have constructed a small table that incorporates the findings on familial incidence of obsessional traits and obsessional symptoms—indicated separately. We have added to the information provided by Slater and Cowie the figures provided by Gittelson (1966d), Kringlen (1965), Lo (1967), and Rosenberg (1967). It can be seen that, with the exception of one study (Lewis, 1936) that provided inordinately high estimates of familial incidence, the siblings of obsessional patients seldom display obsessional traits. Even smaller percentages

TABLE 4.1:   PERCENTAGE OF PARENTS AND
              OF SIBLINGS (OF OBSESSIONAL PATIENTS)
              SHOWING OBSESSIONAL TRAITS
              OR OBSESSIONAL SYMPTOMS, VARIOUS

	TRAITS	SYMPTOMS
Parents	5, 9, 10, 10, 23, 37	0, 0.1, 5, 8
Siblings	3, 5, 9, 14, 21	0.1, 2, 7, 36

of the siblings of obsessional patients (from 0.1% to 7%) have comparable symptoms. The evidence on obsessional traits in the parents of obsessional patients shows a wide range, from 5 percent to 37 percent (Lewis's high figure). On the score of obsessional symptoms, however, the parents of these patients show, perhaps surprisingly, a low incidence of obsessional symptoms—from 0.1 percent to 8 percent (see Table 4.1).

SOCIAL TRANSMISSION

Even allowing for the poor quality of much of this evidence, the figures neither confirm nor disconfirm the hypothesis that there is a significant genetic contribution to obsessional disorders. However, they do bear on the hypothesis that obsessional symptoms are transmitted by observational learning. If direct social transmission, by observational learning and indeed by instruction, were a major factor in the development of obsessional-compulsive disorders, then the figures on familial incidence—especially those of the parents—should be considerably higher than those recorded. If direct social transmission were the main vehicle for obsessional-compulsive disorders, we might also have expected the siblings of obsessional patients to show a far higher incidence of obsessional symptoms than they do. On the available evidence the hypothesis of a *direct social transmission* of obsessional-compulsive disorders receives little support.

The possibility remains, however, that there may be some less direct form of social transmission. References to the parental incidence of obsessional traits is not incompatible with this possibility, nor indeed are the figures for obsessional traits in the siblings of obsessional patients. If, instead of looking for evidence of direct transmission of obsessional-compulsive *disorders*, it is argued that obsessional traits are socially transmitted and, given additional contributing factors, may develop into a disorder, then the debate is left open. This second possibility is of course a modern version of the older view that when people with premorbid obsessional personality traits become disturbed, frustrated, or depressed they develop obsessional-compulsive disorders. In light of the evidence on the emergence of obsessions without prior obsessional traits, even at its most successful, this hypothesis would not achieve comprehensiveness.

Before considering the effect that obsessional-compulsive patients may have on their children (another important source of information pertinent to the hypothesis of social transmission of this kind of behavior), some brief comment on psychogenetic research needs are in order. In the first place, there is a need for improved methods of assessment; virtually all of the available information is marred by the reliance on unconfirmed, potentially unreliable ratings. Some of these problems can be overcome by the increased use of standardized psychometric, interview, and behavioral tests. It is also important to abandon the practice of confusing obsessional-compulsive disorders and obsessional personality. In most of the studies relevant to the question of inheritance of obsessional-compulsive problems, the co-twins and relatives are almost always classified as having *obsessionality*, without further specification. It is of course essential to distinguish between the disorder and the personality traits that are assumed to be related to them. Furthermore, the search for relationships should extend beyond the postulated connection between obsessional-compulsive problems in the index case and in the relatives, to include a search for potential connections between obsessional-compulsive disorders and other neurotic problems, especially phobias. There are reasons for supposing that compulsive cleaning and compulsive checking are disorders that, whatever their similarities, have some important differences (see Chapter 9). Consequently, the investigation of genetic determinants may be more productive if this distinction is taken into account.

There is a need for more evidence on the occurrence of the two main types of obsessional-compulsive disorder, and other neurotic disorders, in monozygotic and dizygotic twins—and of course, if any separated monozygotic twins turn up, they should be studied with particular care. From a practical point of view, however, bearing in mind the low incidence of the disorder, it is preferable to think in terms of adoptive studies. At present, there is little information on the incidence of obsessional personality traits, obsessional-compulsive disorders, and related neurotic disorders in the children of identified compulsive neurotics. It would also be extremely interesting to study the development of children who are adopted by people with marked obsessional traits and/or identified obsessional-compulsive disorders.

CHILDREN OF OBSESSIONAL PATIENTS

Although the evidence on familial incidence does not encourage the view that the disorder is transmitted socially, it is not conclusive because the information is indirect, approximate, and largely unconfirmed. Investigation of the accounts of obsessional-compulsive problems in the children of identified obsessional patients provides a more direct test of the hypothesis. If direct and vicarious social transmission contributes in any significant degree to the genesis of obsessions and compulsions, then the children of obsessional-compulsive patients should display a significantly elevated incidence of these problems.

We began by carrying out a retrospective analysis of the data obtained from our first series of 83 patients, with the following results. The number of children over the age of 4 years known to us to be showing signs of psychological difficulty was a mere 4 (out of 39). Of these, 3 displayed excessive fears and one (a 14-year-old girl) had experienced a moderately severe depressive episode. None of the offspring was showing signs of significant obsessional-compulsive behavior (this is consistent with Rosenberg's observation on first-degree relatives). Although many of the offspring were reported to be compliant with the abnormal demands of the affected parent, none of them developed obsessions or compulsions that had a life independent of parental pressure. The graft failed to take, and in the absence of the affected parent (e.g., when admitted to a hospital), their behavior quickly returned to normal. We found no evidence to support the hypothesis that obsessional disorders are transmitted directly. Even when allowance is made for the fact that obsessions and compulsions generally develop in late childhood or early adulthood, our information must be seen as damaging to the notion of direct transmission of specific obsessional-compulsive behavior. Some signs of the emergence of this kind of behavior should have been evident, particularly as some of the offspring had already reached early adulthood, but we could find none. The occurrence of significant fears in 3 of the 39 children may be an underestimate, but, if taken at face value, it is no higher than the incidence of fear in children of non-obsessional parents.

More weight should be attached to the methodical study of the offspring of psychiatrically disturbed mothers carried out by Cowie in 1961. Cowie obtained information about 330 offspring of the 152 (psychiatrically ill) index cases and compared them with 342 offspring of nonpsychiatric control subjects. Twenty of the 152 psychiatric patients had a diagnosis of obsessional-compulsive disorder, and between them they had 30 offspring. Cowie assembled evidence to show that there is a "higher incidence of neurosis amongst the offspring of obsessional than amongst the offspring of patients of the other diagnostic categories investigated (schizophenia and affective psychosis), which is in keeping with the common observation by child psychiatrists of psychiatric disturbance in the children of rigid and obsessional parents" (p. 49). The incidence of neurotic disturbances in the children was particularly marked when the mother, rather than the father, had an obsessional disorder. Seven of the 38 children of the obsessional patients had required psychiatric treatment at some time, and 6 of these were the offspring of female obsessional patients. Of special interest is the fact that 2 of the 7 children were said to suffer from "obsessional illnesses." However, the most important outcome of this study was the demonstration that the children of obsessional patients have widespread psychological difficulties. As Cowie observes, "All of the offspring . . . showed a common tendency to be overdependent on the mother," regardless of whether it was the mother or the father who was the obsessional parent. In addition, the children of obsessional parents showed common signs, apart from "an overt tendency to cling to the mother, including faddiness with food, excitability, stubbornness, temper tantrums, timidity, an inclination to cry easily, attention-seeking behavior, specific fears, and gratification habits such as thumb-sucking" (Cowie, 1961, p. 56). In light of the importance attached to anal functions by psychoanalytic writers, it is interesting that "none of the children in this group suffered from encopresis," and only two of the children were reported as having had enuresis.

With minor exceptions, the comparable study carried out by Rutter (1966) on the children of sick parents is consistent with Cowie's findings. The nine children of obsessional parents were, by comparison with the offspring of most other types of psychiatric patient, found to be suffering from widespread psychological dysfunctions. Eight of the nine were showing signs of excessive anxiety and disturbed maternal relationships. Sleeping and eating disorders were also conspicuous; in addition, six of the children were overly aggressive and disobedient. Four of them had obsessional symptoms, and another four had signs of depression.

In contradiction to deductions from psychoanalytic theory, only one of the nine children had problems associated with defecation. Three of the children had micturition difficulties. There were few indications of antisocial conduct. In contrast to Cowie's findings, Rutter observed that seven of the nine children suffered from "tension habits." It is also of some interest that obsessional symptoms were observed in 10 percent of the offspring of patients with anxiety neuroses, and 7 percent of patients suffering from depression (Rutter, 1966, pp. 137-38).

In their study of "house-proud" housewives (the women on whom the Leyton Obsessional Inventory was standardized), Cooper and McNeil (1968) found some support for the widely held belief that obsessional parents tend to be overly conscientious (e.g., Lewis, 1966). In a detailed study of 19 pairs of matched families, they detected that "the children of the house-proud mothers" had "more intense interaction with adults, more time alone and more time on physical restriction than those of the controls, who appear to experience rather more easy-going, less structured and more peer-oriented days" (pp. 187-88).

This report, taken in conjunction with the evidence reviewed by Rutter (1966), supports the view that obsessional parents may well engage in distinctive parental behavior. In fact, Cooper and McNeil's observations are notably similar to the description given by Tseng (1973) of the mother-son relationship noted in ten young men with obsessional-compulsive neuroses. Like Cooper, he drew attention to the "excessive intimacy," the restriction of physical activity, and so on. Also consistent with this description is Lo's (1967) report that the parental attitudes of obsessional neurotics were marked by overprotection and perfectionism. Although the clinical reports on the childhood training of obsessional patients are compatible with Cooper's observations on the maternal behavior of house-proud housewives, the other evidence (except for Rutter's report) fails to show an increased incidence of obsessional-compulsive problems in the children of obsessional parents. In the absence of direct observations, the best reconciliation we can offer is the following. Bearing in mind Cowie's (1961) findings and Rutter's (1966) review, it seems likely that a high percentage of obsessional parents transmit behavior that emerges as a *general* maladjustment rather than as a specific problem with an obsessional character. The attributes most likely to be influenced by these parents are timidity, overdependence, and anxiety—rather than specific obsessional preoccupations. This hypothesis—that general neurotic predispositions are transmitted socially—is worth pursuing for plausible theoretical reasons (e.g., Bandura, 1969, 1977). A detailed prospective study, including behavioral observations, of the children of identified obsessional-compulsive patients, is much needed. Supplementary evidence on the development of adopted children of obsessional patients would be invaluable.

To sum up, it is improbable that *specific* patterns of obsessional-compulsive thought and/or behavior are transmitted by observational learning or by direct instruction. There remains, however, a strong possibility that these social-learning processes play an important part in generating and maintaining general behavior tendencies such as timidity, overdependence, and the like, and that these dispositions provide fertile soil for the growth of obsessions and compulsions. There appear to be four major determinants of obsessions and compulsions: social learning, a genetic component, specific learning exposures, and mood disturbances.

OBSESSIONS AND COMPULSIONS IN CHILDHOOD

Although obsessions and compulsions do arise in children, our own experience of this phenomenon is limited to a small number of unquestionably valid cases, and we can add little new information. According to Berman's (1942) survey, it is an uncommon disorder in childhood.

The rarity of the disorder was confirmed by the results of the Isle of Wight survey (Rutter, Tizard, and Whitmore, 1970). "Of the total population of 2,199 ten- and eleven-year-old children screened, 118 (5.4 percent) were found to have a clinically significant psychiatric disorder" (p. 200). Seven of these children had disorders with prominent obsessive features, but no fully developed obsessional disorders were diagnosed. Although Adams's (1972) report is too short on descriptive information to be helpful, Judd's (1965) detailed account of five confirmed cases is of interest.

All five children showed the following characteristics. The onset of the illness was sudden and often dramatic, and the obsessional and compulsive symptoms were always encountered in combination. The children possessed a "rigid, absolute" moral code and frequently expressed guilt. None of the five children was ever considered to be psychotic. Four of the five children showed the following characteristics: There were no premorbid signs of disturbance, but there was a significant psychiatric history in parents or near relatives, "very often with prominent obsessive-compulsive traits or symptoms" (p. 139). Some "transient phobic phenomena" were frequently observed in these children, and they showed aggressive feelings toward one or both parents. In light of the psychoanalytic theory of the genesis of this disorder, it is significant that in four of the five children "the bowel training was nonpunitive, uneventful, and accomplished in the normal time range without any regressions" (p. 139). Similarly, neither the ten young obsessional-compulsive patients described by Tseng (1973) nor the three described by the psychoanalyst Dai (1957) had undergone strict toilet training.

An examination of the childhood problems reported by the 83 patients in our first series, taking care to exclude any information of dubious reliability, revealed a comparatively low incidence of obsessional-compulsive difficulties. It should be remembered, however, that the data are incomplete and mostly unconfirmed. Fifty-five of the 77 patients on whom we had useful data reported having neither obsessional nor compulsive traits or problems during childhood. Fourteen of them (i.e., 18%) reported having had clearly obsessional traits, and 8 (10%) had recognizable obsessional-compulsive difficulties during childhood. Similarly low incidence figures were reported by Ingram (1961) in his study of 89 obsessional patients. Only 16 percent of them had displayed rituals or phobias associated with rituals during childhood. An additional 9 percent of the sample reported having had phobias during childhood—a larger percentage than the control groups of hysterical and anxiety-neurotic patients. By contrast, Kringlen (1965), in his comparison of 91 obsessional and 91 nonobsessional neurotics, reported that 38 percent of the index cases had experienced phobias in childhood and an additional 25 percent had obsessional-compulsive difficulties; these figures are significantly greater than those for the control patients. Remarkably similar findings were reported by Lo (1967). Twenty-one of his 59 obsessional patients (i.e., 35%) reported having had significant phobias during childhood, and an additional 20 percent had carried out compulsive rituals. The combined percentage of phobias and compulsions of 62 percent is almost identical to the 64 percent reported by Kringlen. In the smaller sample of ten obsessionals described by Tseng (1973), 50 percent had had obsessional symptoms early in childhood. Eight out of 24 obsessional patients in the group studied by Bridges and his colleagues (1973) reported childhood phobias, and 22 percent of Tan, Marks, and Marset's (1971) sample of 37 obsessional patients did so. Only 3 of the 37 patients reported having had "childhood obsessions."

Fifty percent of Videbech and his associates' (1975) 104 obsessionals had phobias in childhood.

There is no basis for deciding whether these reports are overestimates or whether the findings from our own series and that of Ingrams are underestimates. The range of incidence is from 22 percent to 64 percent. Pending new information, it is more profitable to draw attention to the apparent association between childhood phobias and obsessional-compulsive problems in adulthood. This association is of course compatible with the view put forward earlier that general behavior tendencies such as timidity and overdependence are generated by social-learning processes and provide fertile soil for the growth of obsessions and compulsions.

MODE OF ONSET

All theories that address the genesis of obsessions and compulsions need to explain the mode of onset of the disorder and the events that precipitate that onset. Information about these two aspects of the disorder is of practical value and in time may contribute to counseling techniques and preventive programs. The information is also useful for making prognostic estimates. Unfortunately, the only practical methods for obtaining the information are retrospective and unreliable. It is difficult to secure the information and even more difficult to gauge its validity. Bearing these weaknesses in mind, it has been estimated that in many cases no specific point of onset can be determined (see Black, 1974). Similarly, no specific precipitating events can be discerned in 30 to 50 percent of all cases (Goodwin et al., 1969; Black, 1974). Even in cases with apparently acute onset, the earlier occurrence of other and possibly related psychological difficulties cannot be excluded. In our own series 51 percent of the 83 patients reported an apparently acute onset. There was, however, no significant relationship between mode of onset and therapeutic outcome. Nor was there a significant relationship between mode of onset and degree of preparedness (de Silva et al., 1977). On the other hand, mode of onset was related to the severity of the disorder. A patient whose obsessional disorder was rated "less severe" was more likely to have experienced a gradual onset.

PRECIPITATING EVENTS

Until the recent development of "life events research," our knowledge about the nature and role of precipitating events in psychological disorders was based mainly on guesswork. The application of these methical procedures to the analysis of obsessional-compulsive disorders is awaited with impatience, as the available evidence cannot be relied upon to provide more than a rough guide.

Lo (1967) reports that 56 percent of his 88 patients were able to recall a precipitating event. Ingram (1961) reports that 70 percent of his 89 patients were able to do so; Rudin (1953), 58 percent of 130 patients; Pollitt (1957), 62 percent of 150 cases; and Bridges and his associates (1973), 90 percent of 24 patients.

Kringlen (1970) offered a clear summary of the position:

> In many cases however the obsessional symptoms started acutely and were precipitated by emotional stress in family or in work. This is particularly so for women, 65 percent of whom had a more or less acute onset; this was true for only 40 percent of the men. The stresses frequently were anxiety-provoking . . . For women rather typical stresses were pregnancy, abortion and birth of the first child. Family conflicts and somatic disease were also common . . . In men the precipitating factors were usually less clear, but included some family conflicts and stress in connection with hard work . . . In some cases obsessional symptoms started in mild degree around puberty and later developed into more serious symptoms. Initially, the course of the illness was often episodic; symptoms would disappear or improve only to recur after a few years. [p. 407]

As to the nature of the precipitating events, the absence of an agreed system for defining and assessing these events precludes sound comparisons or conclusions. So, for example, when we attempted to classify the precipitating events reported by our own patients we encountered serious obstacles. Using Black's (1974) review as a basis, we compiled four categories of precipitating event—sexual and marital difficulties, pregnancy and birth, illness or death of a relative, and frustration and overwork—but soon found it necessary to add sub-classifications and additional classes. We inserted Lo's category of pubertal problems and then had to include "fear" and "increased responsibility," as well as some subclasses of the original four groups. Having unwisely failed to make a systematic collection of this information from the start of our research, we were unable to convert the available fragments into usable data.

Pollitt (1957) concluded that sexual and marital precipitants were common, but Lo (1967) emphasized the importance of frustration and overwork among his sample. Kringlen's analysis confirms the occurrence of both these examples of precipitation and adds that, in general, precipitants tend to be anxiety evoking. We have of course encountered both the specific and general precipitants mentioned so far, and can add to this some personal impressions. In some of our patients the disorder appeared to have emerged after an increase in responsibility—occupational, marital, or social (a point raised in his later work by Pollitt, 1969). In a small but significant number of (mainly immature) patients, their obsessional-compulsive difficulties seemed to surface in the midst of a cauldron of adolescent problems. We have also seen some dramatic examples of obsessional-compulsive disorders emerging during the course of a depressive episode and then remaining to torment the patient long after the depression has waned.

Perhaps the clarification of these diverse findings depends on a set of sub-analyses. Instead of searching for a simple mode of onset for all obsessional disorders, we can begin by subdividing them into cleaners and checkers, for example. Also, the association with depression may play a critical role in onset.

One pointer in this direction is the study reported by Kiloh and Garside (1963), who were able to distinguish between neurotic depression and endogenous depression in 143 depressed patients. The factor of obsessionality was significantly correlated with a diagnosis of neurotic depression as opposed to endogenous depression. Moreover, patients who fell into the neurotic-depression category were more likely to have reported a precipitating event and to have experienced a sudden onset of the disorder. Retardation, common in endogenous depression but rarely present in reactive depression (Woodruff et al., 1967), is seldom associated with obsessions (see p. 82).

CHECKERS AND CLEANERS

Prompted by our review of the epidemiological findings on mode of onset, we carried out a retrospective analysis of the data gathered from our own sample of 83. To our surprise they contained a clear distinction between the mode of onset (sudden vs. gradual) in compulsive checkers and compulsive cleaners. Bearing in mind that many patients have some elements of both problems, it was nevertheless possible to divide our patients into those whose problems were mainly checking or mainly cleaning, or both, or mainly ruminative, or mainly slowness. Two patients were unclassifiable.

The results, shown in Table 4.2, indicate that most cleaners reported a sudden onset of the disorder. Most checkers, on the other hand, reported a

TABLE 4.2:   MODE OF ONSET AND TYPE OF DISORDER

TYPE OF DISORDER	GRADUAL	SUDDEN ONSET	$n =$
Compulsive checking	21	8	29
Compulsive cleaning	8	24	32
Cleaning and checking	5	2	7
Ruminations	2	4	6
Obsessional impulses	0	2	2
Primary slowness	4	1	5
Unclassifiable	1	1	2

gradual onset. The numbers in the other categories are too small for us to draw any conclusions but are given for the sake of completeness.

The interpretation and possible significance of the main findings are discussed in Chapters 9 and 10, on checkers and cleaners. For present purposes we need merely add that the exceptions gave rise to fresh hypotheses.

First, 6 of the 8 checkers who reported a sudden onset (as opposed to the general pattern of *gradual* onset in this subgroup) developed their compulsive problems during or shortly after a clear depressive episode—in each of the 6 cases, antidepressant treatment had been provided independently. As against this figure of 6/8, only 6 out of 21 of the checkers with *gradual* onset developed their problem in close association with depression. Broadly speaking, compulsive checking develops gradually except when a depressive episode occurs, in which case the onset is more likely to be sudden.

Second, 6 of the 8 compulsive cleaners who reported a gradual onset rather than the usual sudden onset had fears and problems of an atypical, unprepared nature (see Seligman, 1971; and Rachman and Seligman, 1976). Only 3 of the remaining 24 cleaners with sudden onset had unprepared fears or problems. The 6 exceptions expressed obsessional fears of chocolate, fiery colors, warts, car oil, any word or photograph or object associated with the city of Birmingham, and religious books or paraphernalia. The 3 patients with unprepared obsessional fears who nevertheless reported a sudden onset complained of unattached electric shavers, animal fats, and invisible chemicals. To conclude, compulsive cleaning develops suddenly except in cases in which the content of the fear or problem is atypical, unprepared.

In summary, then, the factors that promote obsessional disorders appear to include a nonspecific genetic component, observational learning experiences that promote them indirectly (by fostering dependent, noncoping, fearful behavior), reactive depression, and, in compulsive cleaning disorders, a precipitating event.

Chapter 5

Personal and Social Aspects

PERSONALITY

Present knowledge about the childhood precursors of obsessional-compulsive disorders is unsatisfactorily vague. Roughly one-quarter to one-half of obsessional patients report having had obsessions and/or phobic difficulties during childhood, and according to Ingram's (1961) comparison these figures are significantly larger than those obtained from cases of anxiety neuroses or hysteria. Are the *adult* precursors even more closely related to the development of obsessions and compulsions than those of childhood?

There are three major approaches to this question: the conventional (psychiatric) analysis, the psychoanalytic view, and, in a general sense, Eysenck's personality theory. For present purposes we will set aside our doubts about the value of the concept of the *obsessional personality*. As Mischel (1968, 1972) has argued, global concepts of this order can be globally misleading.

The term *obsessional personality* was "originally a description of premorbid personality characteristics in obsessional patients. The description was widely accepted and came to be applied to a wide range of people; it is now used to describe a type of personality whose possessors are said to be subject not only to obsessional illness but to depressive and anxiety states" (Ingram, 1961, p. 1016). One of the earliest writers on the subject, Janet, held the view that all obsessional patients have a premorbid personality that is causally connected to the genesis of the disorder. On these lines Skoog (1959) produced evidence of many abnormalities of personality in the group of patients he described as anankastic. However, as early as 1936 Lewis was cautioning against acceptance of the view that there is a necessary connection between the predisposing personality and the emergence of an obsessional illness:

> Of course many obsessionals have shown excessive cleanliness, orderliness, pedantry, conscientiousness, uncertainty, inconclusive ways of thinking and acting. These are sometimes obsessional symptoms themselves, sometimes character traits devoid of any immediate experience of subjective compulsion. They are, however, especially in the latter case, just as commonly found among patients who never have an obsessional neurosis, but who get an agitated melancholia . . . I have verified this on a large number of patients at the Maudsley Hospital. The traits are also, of course, common among healthy people. They are, conversely, sometimes undiscoverable in the previous personality of patients who now have a severe obsessional neurosis. [p. 328]

This important point was reiterated thirty years later: "Obsessional traits occur, however, in many people who never become mentally ill, and in many who become mentally ill otherwise than with an obsessional disorder. Consequently these traits cannot be rigidly held to be the forerunners or nonmorbid counterparts of obsessional illness" (Lewis, 1966, p. 1199).

Current knowledge, concisely reviewed by Black (1974), can be summarized as follows. In the seven studies he examined, marked obsessional traits were found in 31 percent of 254 obsessional patients, moderate traits in 54 percent of 166, and no obsessional traits in 29 percent of 451 obsessional patients. As Black points out, direct comparisons among these seven studies are inadvisable because of variations in methodology and sample selection. Nevertheless, the general picture is one of a close but not invariant relationship between premorbid personality and obsessional illness, with roughly 16 to 36 percent of cases showing no premorbid traits. It is an imperfect fit.

Some of Lewis's other observations have received recent confirmation. For example, Pollitt (1959) has shown that obsessional traits are also associated with a range of nonobsessional psychiatric problems such as depression, anorexia, and so forth. In Kringlen's (1965) important series, 72 percent of his obsessional patients showed at least moderate obsessional traits—but so did 53 percent of his nonobsessional control patients. Rosenberg (1967) found that roughly half of his sample of 47 obsessional patients were judged to have "predominantly obsessional premorbid personalities," but, he goes on to add, "the immature and schizoid personalities accounted for a further 30 percent of cases" (p. 473).

The results of recent research into the traditional view of the relation between obsessional personality and illness, while confirming Lewis's analysis, also raise some important theoretical problems. For example, one might ask why it is that such a significant minority of obsessional patients give a history that does not include a premorbid "obsessional personality." In these patients, what is the predisposing soil? And from there, of course, one goes on to ask whether it is possible to distinguish between the obsessional disorders of patients with or without a premorbid obsessional personality. In our view little progress can be expected as long as the research remains confined to a search for connections between the so-called obsessional personality and obsessional disorders. As it is clear that there are other routes to the emergence of the disorder, the search for precursors should be widened to include other aspects of personality, and the most promising of these would appear to be general timidity, overdependence, and more generally, dysthymia. Another obstacle to progress in untying the complicated connections between predisposing factors and the onset of the disorder is the adherence to an oversimplified view of the concept of the obsessional personality. Furthermore, continued adherence to the view of obsessional disorders as a unitary state or illness will hamper progress. At least two major variants of obsessional disorder, compulsive checking and compulsive cleaning, can be distinguished—and others such as obsessional doubting and primary obsessional slowness may have to be added to the list.

An early attempt to distinguish between different types of obsessional personality is worth mentioning. In his 1936 lecture Lewis postulated that there are two types of obsessional personality—"the one obstinate, morose, irritable, the other vacillating, uncertain of himself, submissive" (p. 328). When, some twenty-five years later, Ingram (1961, pp. 1017-18) attempted to recruit support for this idea, he was only partly successful. Only 30 of the 77 obsessional patients he examined could be described as falling into one or the other of the two categories proposed by Lewis—"The majority cannot be described in this way." For what it is worth, he found twice as many of the submissive type as the obstinate, morose type.

Although it is obvious that the matter cannot be brought to a conclusion unless and until systematic and reliable assessments are carried out, our curiosity was sufficiently provoked to carry out a retrospective examination of the data collected on our 83 early patients. The outcome was surprisingly fruitful and justifies a more thorough investigation of Lewis's classification.

Allowing ourselves what must have been a more flexible system of classification than that adopted by Ingram, we successfully sorted all 83 patients. Unlike him, we found the two types to be represented almost equally—44 were classified as "submissive, vacillating, uncertain" and the remaining 39 fitted into the "morose, obstinate, irritable" category. Furthermore, we found that the compulsive cleaners were overrepresented in the morose/irritable category in a ratio of two to one. Among the compulsive checkers, however, the ratio was two to one in favor of the submissive/vacillating category. Significantly more of the morose/irritable patients had a sudden rather than a gradual onset, but we detected no association between the two personality categories and prognosis (i.e., the morose/irritable patients fared as well, or as badly, as the submissive/ vacillating patients).

According to Freud (1908) the premorbid personality of obsessional patients is what he called "anal-erotic." He described this personality as a "triad of characteristics which are almost always to be found together—orderliness, parsimoniousness and obstinacy" (1908), and wove an elaborate theory to account for the dynamic relationship between the anal character and obsessional illness. A full discussion of the theory is given elsewhere; here we need merely note that the theory rests on two important assumptions (among others) that are relevant to the present account of ideas relating personality and obsessional illness (Hodgson and Rachman, 1979). In the first place, the theory assumes a necessary and indeed sufficient causal connection between the "anal" personality and obsessional illness. Although the theory incorporates a *constitutional* predisposing factor, which allows one to account for instances in which the personality and illness failed to develop despite the occurrence of the required childhood experiences, the occurrence of an obsessional illness in the absence of an anal obsessional personality is automatically excluded. There is no route to the obsessional illness other than through the development of an anal obsessional personality.

The theory also makes the important assumption of *continuity* of development from the anal personality into the illness. This assumption is, of course, related to the one just mentioned: There is only one route to the illness (via the anal personality), and it is a continuous one. Both of these assumptions were shared by Janet, who also believed that a predisposing obsessional personality was a requisite for the development of the illness—although he did not, of course, subscribe to the concept of an anal personality. Nowadays few non-analytic writers would agree that a premorbid obsessional personality is a necessary condition for the development of an obsessional illness, but there is widespread recognition of a close relationship between premorbid obsessional characteristics and the disorder.

The third approach to the relation between personality and illness is to be found in the general personality theory advanced by Eysenck (1947, 1952, 1957, 1965, 1967). The development of this elaborate theory of personality is described in detail in Eysenck's voluminous writings. For present purposes we draw attention to the place of obsessional neurosis in his wider conception.

There are three major dimensions of personality—neuroticism, psychoticism, and introversion—and people who are highly endowed with neuroticism and introversion are called dysthymic. This concept incorporates most of the neurotic disorders and certainly those in which anxiety plays a prominent role; phobics, anxious personalities, and obsessional-compulsive people all fall within this group. People who score highly on neuroticism and extraversion fall into the category of hysteria-psychopathy. In Eysenck's (1957) words, "additional to the dimension of neuroticism, and orthogonal to it, we have another dimension, that of extraversion-introversion, which finds its prototype in the neurotic population in the hysteric-psychopathic (extraverted) and the anxious-obsessional (introverted) type of personality" (p. 88). In *The Dynamics of Anxiety and Hysteria*, Eysenck (1957) assembled the evidence that supported this conception. In most studies patients who suffered from anxiety, obsessional disorders, phobias, and so on obtained high scores on neuroticism and introversion, whereas psychopaths and criminals tended to obtain high scores on neuroticism and average or above-average scores on extraversion. Eysenck carried the theory forward from a dimensional analysis toward a psychogenetic theory in which great emphasis was placed on differences in conditioning. "We may say that in our general system introverts are postulated to condition more easily and, therefore, to acquire the conditioned anxieties and fears of the dysthymic more easily than other people, whereas psychopaths and prisoners generally are people who condition poorly and who, therefore, fail to acquire the conditioned responses characterizing the socialization process" (Eysenck and Rachman, 1965, pp. 24-25). In a later development of the theory, described in *The Biological Basis of Personality*, an attempt was made to connect the dimensional and psychological differences to variations in biological function (Eysenck, 1967).

To sum up, three main approaches to the subject of personality and obsessional illness can be distinguished: the conventional psychiatric model, psychoanalytic theory, and Eysenckian personality theory. There appears to be a close but not unvarying relationship between premorbid obsessional traits and the occurrence of obsessional-compulsive disorders; a significant minority of the people who develop obsessional-compulsive disorders do so without having shown evidence of premorbid obsessional traits. It was noted that the psychoanalytic theory, while sharing the form of the conventional psychiatric approach, is markedly different in content. The Eysenckian dimensional analysis, according to which obsessional disorders fall into the dysthymic sector, has attracted psychometric support.

RIGIDITY

When affected people discuss their obsessional problems, they may appear to be rigid and inflexible, unresponsive to rational debate, and excessively eager to remove uncertainty. As a result psychologists have been tempted to ask whether rigidity and intolerance of uncertainty are general obsessional traits or whether they are specifically related to particular fears and compulsions. A number of investigations of obsessionals' decisions, concepts, and personal constructs are consistent with the view that some obsessional people cannot tolerate uncertainty or ambiguity (Hamilton, 1960; Rosenberg, 1953; Milner, Beech, and Walker, 1971), tend to form underinclusive concepts (Reed, 1969b), and use personal constructs that cluster into isolated groups with no linking construct (Makhlouf-

Norris, Jones, and Norris, 1970). Although these studies suggest avenues of research to be pursued, the claim that there is a specifically obsessional-compulsive cognitive style cannot be justified at present. The failure of other attempts to identify stable, general cognitive styles of any kind is, however, a discouraging cloud.

Before leaving the subject of the conventional approach to the relation between the obsessional personality and obsessional disorders, we should draw attention to the traditional distinctions between these two concepts. Unlike an obsessional disorder, the person with a so-called obsessional personality does not regard his compulsive thoughts and ruminations as being alien or, to use the technical term, ego-dystonic. Nor does he find his obsessional and compulsive thoughts and acts distressing.

OBSESSIONAL LIFE STYLES

Part-timers and Full-timers

Obsessional-compulsive disorders can be "malignant" or "benign." In some instances the disorder distorts the person's life almost to the point of destruction (although, curiously, the suicide rate for obsessional-compulsive patients is lower than that observed in other psychiatric disorders). Virtually all of the person's waking time is devoted to avoiding provocation and to planning and carrying out compulsive rituals. Such people may be called "full-time obsessionals." In some cases the disorder leads to almost total immobilization. At its most malignant, the damage and suffering caused by the disorder are equal to or exceed that produced by any other psychological disorder.

At the other extreme, numbers of people, the "part-timers," succeed in making a productive and satisfying life for themselves, in spite of their obsessional disorders. The number of people who have relatively benign obsessional-compulsive disorders is bound to be underestimated because the majority of them do not seek professional help and, hence, go unrecorded. Lewis (1965) has pointed out that "the social efficiency of an obsessional may have little discernible relation to the characteristic symptoms of his neurosis" (p. 300). He quotes the obsessional problems of Bunyan and Luther as illustrations of "how energy and achievement can be compatible with persistent severe obsessions" (p. 302). His argument and illustrations leave no doubt that "mental vigor and practical activity coexist with obsessional illness in people of diverse social and intellectual quality. Conversely there are many people who have gradually reduced their field of activity because (they believe) of their obsessional symptoms, in whom these obsessional symptoms seem, to the dispassionate observer, trivial" (p. 303). As mentioned earlier, Lewis expressed the view that there are at least two discernible types of obsessional personality: the "obstinate, morose, irritable" personality and the "vacillating, insecure, submissive" personality. He argued that the patient's personality is reflected in the adequacy of his or her adjustment. "Whether they become social invalids, surrendering to their complaint, or pursue active lives in spite of their symptoms, depends much less on the form and severity of their obsession than on their personality structure, and probably on their genetic affinities" (p. 305). Although there is a risk of circularity in this argument, it nevertheless provides a basis for constructing hypotheses about the relation between personality and disorder, and between disorder and life style.

When people with creative energy succeed in putting their obsessional personality traits to constructive use, everyone benefits. Orderliness and meticulousness are essential attributes of the successful classifier and lexicographer. The best fruits of the combination of creativity and obsessionality can be seen in the works of Samuel Johnson and Charles Darwin.

Among those with less creative talents, controlled orderliness and meticulousness are useful qualities for accountants, information scientists, timetablers, catalogers, and the like. Uncontrolled or controlled obsessionality in bureaucrats can be a source of unending frustration and irritation. When it is combined with gross inefficiency, the results greatly exceed the common, everyday irritations, and quiet desperation sets in.

A detailed description of obsessional life styles is interesting from a theoretical point of view because of the relation between personality and disorder, and from a practical point of view because it provides a basis for constructing a prognostic measure. In a retrospective study of eighty-two of our own cases (de Silva, Rachman, and Seligman, 1977), we unearthed only one significant correlation between the characteristics of the obsessional disorder and therapeutic outcome: The patients who followed an obsessional life style had a poorer outcome than those with a confined form of the disorder. Furthermore, although the data do not permit a systematic analysis of this point, in our own series a disproportionately large number of compulsive cleaners displayed an obsessional life style. By contrast, a smaller percentage of compulsive checkers showed this malignant form of the disorder; or, to put it another way, more of the compulsive checkers were able to continue living something approaching a normal life.

At its worst, an obsessional disorder causes considerable misery and distress, and interferes with the person's capacity for social, occupational, and sexual adjustment (e.g., Kringlen, 1965). One of our patients, who participated in the second clinical trial described in Chapter 22, feared contamination by germs. As a result she engaged in prolonged and intensive washing and cleaning rituals. Her young child was restrained in one room of the four-bedroom house, as it was the only one that she could keep satisfactorily free from germs. Three of the rooms were kept permanently locked because she was incapable of ensuring that they were sufficiently sterile. She used an extraordinarily large amount of disinfectants to clean her house and to wash herself and her child. As is common with many of these patients, she was particularly agitated by contact with doors and doorknobs, and therefore learned how to open a door with her feet in order to avoid contaminating her hands. The large and complicated series of rituals that had to be carried out in preparing food meant that the family was kept on a restricted diet. Meals were seldom complete and rarely ready on time. The patient's fear of contamination made her virtually housebound, and her child was not permitted to leave the house except on a very few essential occasions. On returning from work each day, her husband was obliged to go through a series of decontaminating-cleaning rituals. Their sexual relationship, never satisfactory, had been abandoned because of her fears of contamination. Their social life was damaged beyond repair, and they had lost all but one of their friends; even the members of their families could neither visit them nor be visited by them. Although the patient had been a competent, trained secretary, returning to work was out of the question.

Another patient, a severely disturbed woman, was similarly dominated by her obsessional fears and washing compulsions. Practically every action of every day was planned and assessed in terms of the probability of contracting cancerous contamination. It determined where she lived, and when she moved (frequently), it determined what clothing she was free to wear (very few items indeed). It determined whom she could speak to and whom she could touch (practically no one). It determined the homes and public places that she could visit (very few). It determined the type of work she could undertake (very limited and always unsatisfactory). The risk of contamination precluded any form of sexual activity. She was unable to pick up any reading material except and unless she wore protective clothing. Her conversation was confined mainly to a discussion of her fears and the actions she was obliged to take in order to avoid or escape from them. Ultimately, after thirty years of this form of existence, the obsessions and compulsions had become the core and substance of her entire life.

A competent, articulate engineer was able to rearrange his working day in such a manner as to avoid entire sections of the city in which he lived. His central fear was of sexual contamination, and in order to continue his sexual activities he developed an elaborate technique for ensuring his safety. He could engage in sexual activity only in a specially designated sterile room in his house. This room, which contained only one item of furniture, a bed, was reserved for sexual activities and kept locked at all other times. He and his sexual partner had to carry out elaborate cleaning rituals before entering the room, both naked, and the cleansing rituals were then repeated immediately upon leaving the room. Any item of clothing or object that was inadvertently contaminated was either cleaned and disinfected or, if that failed to suffice, discarded. As can be imagined, the strain on his partner was considerable, and it was at her request that he repeatedly sought treatment.

The disorder called primary obsessional slowness insidiously invades all aspects of the victim's life. The middle-aged accountant whose story is described in Chapter 15 is a clear example of the obsessional life style of someone affected by this brand of the disorder. As his need to engage in increasingly prolonged and meticulous self-care activities increased, he was obliged to rise earlier and earlier in order to get to work on time. He would start his preparations at 3 or 4 o'clock in the morning and, with a great deal of effort and concentration, be ready to leave for work by about 10 o'clock in the morning. Even when he began his preparations at such an ungodly early hour, he was unable to arrive at work on time and as a result was discharged from successive jobs. When he came to the hospital for his initial assessment, it was taking him up to ten hours to wash, shave, and dress himself. This meant that he awoke at 6 in the morning and finally was able to leave his apartment by 4 o'clock in the afternoon. As the preparation of a meal was such an arduous business, he left his apartment each day in midafternoon in order to eat at a restaurant. Upon completion of his meal, he would either return home or pay a short visit to his parents before going home. His preparations for retiring took approximately three hours, and he would start the process by about 9 o'clock in the evening. In an unsuccessful attempt to come to his assessment appointment at the hospital, scheduled for 2 P.M., he spent the entire night preparing himself. He spent virtually all of his waking time planning and carrying out his self-care rituals. Most of his life was devoted to the execution of these rituals, and as is true of most of the patients who sink into an obsessional life style, it was impossible for anyone to live with him. Most of these patients live in isolation.

A minority of compulsive checkers had adopted an obsessional life style, but the people suffering from primary obsessional slowness, although few in number, were with only one exception wholly immersed in their obsessional style of living.

Miss T, a successful teacher in her mid-20s, managed to contain her compulsive checking activities and continue living a normal life. She had recurrent worries about securing her flat at night and, in particular, ensuring that there was no possibility of gas leaks or accidental fires. Each night she carried out a long and complicated series of checking rituals, but during her working hours and while in the company of other people she was able successfully to inhibit her impulses to check. Another young woman, who carried out compulsive hand-washing rituals because of her fear of dirt, succeeded through careful planning and considerable effort in disguising her problem while at work. She continued to work successfully and without apparent problems for a number of years, but upon returning home each evening she carried out a full cleansing ritual. Unless and until she had completed these cleaning rituals, she was unable to undertake any other activities. Another patient, a successful professor of food sciences, arranged his life in such a way as to avoid eating in public, as he had powerful obsessional fears about the potentially harmful effects of eating an extremely wide range of foods, even though his work took him to many conferences and other public occasions.

As we have already mentioned, patients who adopt an obsessional life style has a poorer prognosis (with behavioral treatment), and it is likely that their prognosis is less hopeful under all conditions and all forms of therapy. In the series of 83 patients on whom we have detailed information, 37 exhibited an obsessional life style. Only 6 of the 83 had successfully managed to contain their problems, and the remaining 40 patients displayed moderately distorted life styles. It should be remembered, of course, that the patients who make up this series were by no means representative. All of them had had previous psychological and psychiatric assistance at other institutions, and the majority fell into the severe and chronic category. As a group they were significantly less successful in establishing or maintaining satisfactory personal relationships; a disproportionately high number were single, separated, or divorced (see Chapter 15). Although many of them were highly intelligent and even gifted people, their productivity was low because of the damaging effects of their disorder. Most of them had required extensive professional help, and many were entirely unable to support themselves financially. In a significant majority of cases, their freedom to travel was impaired, and some of them were almost immobilized. A significant minority were obliged to avoid entire sections of the city in which they lived, or entire regions of the country. In the most extreme cases, the immobilization was so severe that they were obliged to spend a large part of each day sitting in one comparatively safe spot. Thus, Mrs. A, who had intense fears of contamination from other people, was able to sit in only one chair in her own home. Moreover, she repeatedly had to disinfect the chair each morning and evening. Naturally, no one else was ever allowed to touch it, let alone sit on it. Mrs. D, an affectionate mother of three lively children, was eventually reduced to spending most of her day sitting in the only safe chair in her home. Her fears of contamination were so intense that she was unable to touch her children; in the closing stages, shortly before her admission to the hospital, she had reached the point of insisting that they keep two or three feet away from her, lest their breathing contaminate her. Similarly, as described earlier, it would appear that Howard Hughes in his declining years constructed for himself a psychologically sterile, safe environment in order to protect himself from contamination. As far as he was able to do so, he constructed a hermetically sealed environment and restricted his movements to the point at which the greater part of each day was spent reclining on a disinfected couch.

The devastating effects of an obsessional-compulsive disorder on the affected person are almost matched by the consequences for that person's relatives and friends.

Just as an obsessional-compulsive disorder can come to dominate the pattern of a person's life, the presence in a family of a severely obsessional person can distort the lives of all of its members. As the incapacitation of the affected member spreads, the demands made on spouse, parents, and children increase. Not only are they required to take over many of the patient's functions— domestic, personal, financial, and social—they also have to devote increasing time and effort to the protection and comforting of the affected person. In cases of severe and chronic disorders, the social, personal, and financial damage to the entire family can be extensive and irreversible.

The effects on the children of obsessional patients are twofold (see Chapter 4). Firstly, there is a danger that abnormal behavior (especially dependence and timidity) will be transmitted directly to the children, and here our clinical observations are in accord with what is now known about the pervasiveness and power of observational learning (Bandura, 1969, 1977; Rachman, 1976c). Secondly, the development and emotional sustenance of the children are at risk (e.g., Rutter, 1966).

One of our patients, a 32-year-old woman, was prompted to seek professional help when she observed that her 5-year-old daughter had acquired a strong fear of dogs and was beginning to demonstrate extensive avoidance behavior and the beginnings of cleaning rituals. The patient herself was a compulsive handwasher whose core fear was of contamination from the excrement or urine of dogs and other small animals. She was successfully treated and, with some guidance, was able to help her daughter overcome the growing fears and compulsions. The severely incapacitated mother of three children referred to earlier was so terrified by the possibility of contracting cancer that she had become virtually immobilized. She forbade the children to touch her or any of her intimate belongings. They were also prohibited from walking near pharmacies or hospitals, or playing with children from "suspect" households. Upon returning from school each day, they had to discard their outdoor clothing and carry out decontaminating cleaning rituals. As her disorder had grown, her husband had been obliged to assume more and more of the household duties—with consequent financial loss.

A young married woman with two young children was troubled by religious and other obsessions and attempted to deal with them by engaging in extensive and intensive checking and cleaning rituals. These rituals had gradually absorbed most of the domestic activities of her children and husband. So, for example, the children were obliged to undress at specific times in specific places and only when the patient herself was seated in a particular chair downstairs. Their rooms were dirty and disorganized, as she was unable to touch most of the objects in them. They were not allowed to bring any visitors into the home, and certain objects had to be discarded before they reentered the house after

62

school. Another intensely frightened mother confined her only child and husband to one of the four rooms available in their house. The child was forbidden to play with other children, or indeed to leave the house, except in carefully circumscribed conditions in the company of one or both of her parents. In yet another case, the schooling and social development of a 6-year-old child were jeopardized by the frequent moves that were dictated by her mother's contamination fears. About every six months the contamination in their home grew to intolerable levels and the entire family was obliged to move to another house, sometimes to another suburb.

Broadly speaking, parents appear to react either by rejecting an obsessional child or by overindulging his or her fears and problems. In cases of rejection, the obsessional patient becomes isolated and, when it is practically possible, he or she departs from the home. Parents who increasingly indulge an obsessional child's fears and compulsions find that they get drawn into more and more complex rituals and avoidance behavior. This may involve helping the patients carry out their cleaning rituals directly—by helping to wash them, by disinfecting their clothes and belongings, and so forth. In these instances it is common to find that the parents have to provide special diets in order to cope with the increasingly restricted tolerance and appetite of the patient. Among patients with compulsive cleaning rituals, it is common to find that a great deal of friction is caused by excessively long use of the bathroom and toilet. In extreme cases the family bathroom might be out of bounds for up to three hours at a time while the patient completes his or her rituals.

A family that is occupied in maintaining a safe and/or sterile home learns to discourage visitors. The social isolation of the obsessional patient inexorably squeezes the family into an exclusive and isolated social unit. Quite apart from the unhappiness and inconvenience experienced by members of the family, they frequently are bewildered by the obsessional disorder and do not know how to help the affected person. It is common to find that they have received conflicting advice from professional advisers, friends, and relatives. Many of them vacillate between adopting a restrictive and nonaccepting way of responding to the requests made by the patient, or unquestioning compliance with his or her wishes and demands. In our view, the best advice to give to members of the family is one of firm but sympathetic noncompliance in ritualistic behavior. As adoption of this style of responding can produce some initial distress for all parties, it is strongly recommended that professional advisers arrange for members of the family to receive support when the family's pattern of responding is in the process of being changed. It is not uncommon to find that an obsessional child will, under pressure, display verbal and even physical aggression towards his or her parents.

Many spouses find living with an obsessional patient intolerable, and as we have already mentioned, the marital casualty rate in this group of patients is higher than average. The spouses who continue to live with a severely obsessional husband or wife are inevitably the more patient and devoted ones. However, many of them have told us that they have remained in the marriage simply for the sake of the children. There is a conflict, however, as they recognize that on the one hand the children face the hazards of a broken home, but if the marriage endures, the children are vulnerable to the psychological ill effects of close contact with a parent affected by a serious psychological disorder. As we have already mentioned, the unaffected spouse may gradually take over more and more of the domestic, personal, and social functions of the obsessional patient. Where the patient's obsessions have a sexual element, the sexual relationship between the partners is inevitably affected—in our series at least, the occurrence of sexual disorders was significantly elevated. It is not certain, however, whether the incidence of sexual disorders in an obsessional patient sample is greater than that encountered in nonobsessional groups of patients.

The sexual problems may result in total abstinence or a very low frequency of sexual relations. In some instances the frequency of sexual relations is seemingly unaffected, but pre- and postcoital rituals neutralize whatever pleasure might have been achieved. However, we have also observed numbers of obsessional patients, even some severely affected ones, whose sexual activities have been unimpaired. This aspect of their lives continues satisfactorily, protected from contamination or other obsessions by a form of psychological disengagement. So it is possible to find a patient who is obsessionally preoccupied with avoiding bodily products of all kinds, other than sexual fluids. The patient whose fear of contamination from the waste products of dogs and other animals obliged her and her family to make repeated changes of residence was fastidious and concerned about toilet hygiene and cleanliness but continued throughout to have a vigorous and highly satisfactory sexual relationship with her husband.

In some notable cases the affected person, or patient, exercises inordinate power over the lives of family members, even to the point of tyranny. Here are some examples. One compulsive hand washer, an immature man of 17, insisted that his parents remove their "outdoor" clothes and shoes before entering the house, on pain of provoking a tantrum accompanied by abuse. His mother was required to wait on him, having cleaned all his utensils and crockery several times, and as he was unwilling/unable to touch a sugar bowl or salt cellars, she had to flavor his food for him. Among other restrictions, another immature young patient forbade her parents to read newspapers for fear of their spreading the dirty newsprint and thus contaminating her. A third such patient forbade his mother to carry out any household cleaning when he was at home (which was most of the time) lest he become contaminated by the dust; hence, his mother had to clean intermittently and usually at inconvenient times. A middle-aged woman whose obsessions and compulsions arose from a strong fear of chocolate forbade her husband to eat chocolate anywhere at any time, regardless of whether she was present or not. Upon returning home each night, he was obliged to recount precisely what he had eaten that day. In some instances obsessional patients successfully demand that valuable but contaminated objects, including comparatively unused automobiles, be exchanged. At the most extreme, they insist on repeated changes of residence. One of our patients had forced six changes of home in three years, each move involving some financial loss and, of course, great disruption.

In the course of carrying out the research and treatment described in this book, we have visited the homes of a considerable number of obsessional patients. After the first dozen or so visits, our capacity for being surprised was greatly reduced. We learned to expect that the homes of compulsive cleaners would contain a bizarre mixture of excessively clean areas and indescribably dirty parts as well. In the same home, the lavatory might be brightly clean and strongly disinfected while parts of the kitchen were caked with month-old food remains. (Incidentally, this peculiar contrast is often encountered in the patients themselves—a compulsive cleaner who washes her hands 200 times per day may leave her legs and feet unwashed for months and wear the same dirty underwear for weeks on end.) In some cases the accumulation of debris and dirt was directly attributable to the patient's inability to come into contact with dirty or contaminated objects. In other cases the dirt and disarray reflected the patient's inability to cope with the daily requirements of living.

Visiting the home of a patient who engages in compulsive hoarding can also be a memorable experience. Entire rooms are set aside for the collection of old newspapers, used cans, bits of string, nails and screws, and the rest. The inability to start or complete a task, observed in many of these patients, is reflected in the partly completed tasks whose remains are sprinkled throughout the house. One sees cupboards without doors, curtains without seams, rooms that are half-painted, appliances left in their original wrappings, and so on. In one extreme case the patient had been trying to complete the cleaning of the motor of his second automobile for almost three years. He had succeeded in taking out some of the parts and cleaning them, but had gotten no further. This immobilized car was kept in the well-protected garage, while the more valuable vehicle that was in daily use was left unsheltered in the street outside.

Telltale signs of compulsive cleaners are easily spotted. One encounters endless boxes of tissue paper, rolls of paper toweling, bottles of disinfectant, hordes of soap bars, washing powders of all sizes, makes, and varieties, innumerable pairs of rubber gloves, and all the other signs of the dedicated cleaner. Quite commonly the lavatory is the most carefully tended room in the house and is overstocked with extra rolls of toilet tissue.

The homes of compulsive checkers are less obviously different. Here the distinguishing features are excessive tidiness and orderliness. Each piece of furniture has its designated place; the pictures hang straight; and attempts by others to rearrange things quickly produce alarm. Checklists are placed at strategic points, and the common habit of making lists is elevated to a fine art.

Sometimes members of the family are drawn into these checking rituals. Watching someone engage in this kind of repetitive, stereotyped activity is intrinsically irritating, and the amount of time wasted is an additional source of annoyance to other people. For these reasons relatives often attempt to truncate the process.

In the case of compulsive checkers and ruminators, and to a lesser extent compulsive cleaners, relatives and friends frequently are bombarded with requests for reassurance. "Will the children be safe?" "Did I cause an accident?" "Is the house safe?" "Are you sure the gas taps are securely closed?" As we will argue presently, these repeated requests for reassurance can be construed as functional equivalents of compulsive rituals. When the requests are successfully met by an authoritative person, they result in a temporary relief. Where requests of this kind play a prominent part in the disorder, it is essential to include them in the overall treatment program.

It should not be mistakenly thought that the effects on relatives and friends are always and necessarily deleterious. As mentioned earlier, the repetitive, compulsive cleaning carried out by Monet's wife inspired a series of exquisite paintings.

A CASE ILLUSTRATION

This description of his 19-year-old son's fears and rituals, and their awful ramifications was given by his elderly father:

When George wakes in the morning, usually at 11 A.M., he feels that his hands are contaminated and so he cannot touch his clothing. He won't wash in the bathroom because he feels that the carpet is contaminated and he won't go downstairs until he is dressed. Consequently, I have to dress him, having first cleaned his shoes and got out a clean shirt, underclothes, socks and trousers. He holds his hands above his head while I pull on his underpants and trousers and we both make sure, by proceeding very cautiously, that he doesn't contaminate the outside of his clothing. Any error or mishap and he will have to have clean clothes because he must avoid at all costs passing on the contamination to others. George then goes downstairs, washes his hands in the kitchen and thereafter spends about twenty minutes in the toilet. This is quite a palaver. He has to roll up his shirt and vest to make sure they do not touch the toilet seat and I have to check that he does it properly. I then have to stand in the doorway and supervise him, my main function being to give reassurance that he has not done anything silly to contaminate his clothing. Thankfully he is now managing on some occasions to cope in the toilet without my close supervision but I still have to be on call so that I can help him if he starts to panic for any reason. Incidentally, I have to put newspapers down on the floor of the toilet and change them daily to make sure that his trousers never come into contact with any contaminating substances. If he only wants to urinate then my task is made easier. I simply have to check his trousers and boots for splashes, sometimes getting down on my hands and knees with a torch. I am forever telling him how ridiculous I think these rituals are especially because I never ever find anything wrong. George never flushes the toilet because he fears that his clothing could be splashed, so one of my duties is to pull the chain and to cope with the frequent blockages which occur because of George's excessive use of toilet paper. Recently he has been checking that there are no pubic hairs on the floor and he asks me to get down on my hands and knees to check the floor meticulously. Basically he has to be completely sure that there is no contamination around because if he is not sure then he will start to worry and ruminate about it later on. He has to be completely sure and therefore needs a second opinion. As soon as he has zipped up his trousers I have to march in with a pad soaked in antiseptic and give the zip a quick onceover. When he washes his hands after toileting, he meticulously scrubs each finger and methodically works his way up as far as his elbow. I used to have to watch him at every step of the way but now he only calls me in occasionally. Sometimes he will have washed and dried his hands and then decide that he is not sure whether he washed properly. At this stage I usually have to supervise him so that when he is finished he is absolutely certain that the job has been done perfectly without missing a square inch of contamination.

By the way, I forgot to say that the first thing I do is always give him breakfast in bed. He doesn't mind eating with contaminated hands because his worry is not his own health but passing on contamination to others and being personally responsible for a plague or an epidemic.

The afternoon is the easiest part of the day but at no time can I get away from George's problems. For example, if he is driving I have to keep looking around to check that he hasn't injured a cyclist or a pedestrian. I have to reassure him that there is not some poor fellow bleeding in the gutter. He keeps questioning me incessantly; for example, he'll ask:

"Is there a cyclist there?"

"Is the cyclist all right?"

"Did I give that car enough room?"

"What was that bang?"

His whole life seems to be spent making sure that he is not responsible for causing harm to others.

"If he sees a brown speck in the car I have to check closely and reassure him that it is not a dog dirt. I have to reiterate it a few times before he is convinced and sometimes he remains unconvinced so that I have to clean out the car before he will sit in it. Occasionally I will have to wait for him to re-wash before going out. On one occasion he suddenly decided to have a bath and this delayed our departure for three hours.

There are many contaminating events which will make him change his clothing in the afternoon; for example, if he drops food on himself he will imagine the flies that will be attracted and the dog dirt and dustbins that the flies have been buzzing around. This means that I have to do a lot of clothes washing during the average week. Actually I find it very difficult to get on with my own work because I am frequently called upon to cope with some disaster. Of course, the disasters are not only time-consuming but also expensive. I spend three pounds per week on paper tissues, two pounds on toilet rolls, I don't know how much on antiseptics and soap, and of course we must use gallons of hot water. If George gets angry and frustrated because of my inefficiency in coping with contamination he gets rather violent and recently he has broken dishes, glasses and cups, the headboard of his bed, windows and doors. Only the other day I was helping him to wash and I didn't do something properly so he just threw the soap through the window. He then started to worry about bits of broken glass.

Dogs and cats are a very big problem. This particular worry started or was exacerbated after George had seen a program about the damage dogs can do to little children. It seems that there is a bug which can get into the eye or brain. We therefore have to avoid dog dirt especially in the garden and sometimes I've had to go out at night with a torch and check meticulously because he imagined that he had heard a noise which could have been a dog. If we are walking in the street and he spots dog dirt I have to walk behind him to check that he does not step into it.

When George arrives home the first thing that he does it take off his boots and place them on a piece of newspaper ready for me to wash. He then walks up the stairs to change his trousers and I have to check that his trousers do not touch the stairs because he must avoid contaminating the house. The other night I remember he came home feeling very contaminated and it took about four hours to clean him up and prepare a meal. I even had to wash his legs whilst he sat in his bedroom with his feet in a basin of water. You would not imagine that it would take so long but it is a constant struggle to do the right thing all the time; for example, sometimes I have to clean his boots two or three times before he is satisfied. In George's eyes the bathroom carpet is contaminated and this adds to the ritual. You see, after helping him off with each garment, I have to wash my hands in the bathroom but this contaminates my feet and so George insists that I walk around my own bedroom to get rid of this contamination. My bedroom has become a sort of decontamination chamber.

If he comes home after a very contaminating day he will have a bath in the evening and this will last for hours. On one occasion I was helping him with his bathing rituals almost continuously from 10 P.M. until 3 A.M. Because he can't be certain that he has washed himself properly I had to do most of the hard work myself and also make sure that he didn't recontaminate himself. He kept asking me to watch him to make sure that he didn't touch the wall as he turned around. Three times the water had to be changed. I had to repeatedly check that all the soap had been rinsed out of his hair, check that he dried himself properly and watch him walk into his bedroom to make sure that he didn't touch anything on the way.

I have described all the main rituals that I have to go through for George's peace of mind but I can't start to describe everything. From the moment that I see him first thing in the morning to the time he goes to bed there are a thousand little things that I have to reassure him about. At least half of my life at the moment seems to be involved in George's rituals.

It is pleasing to report that George's fear and avoidance were substantially reduced and his rituals virtually eliminated as a result of domiciliary treatment of the type described in Chapters 21 and 22.

Chapter 6

Obsessions, Compulsions, and Depression

The relation between obsessions, compulsions, and depression is widely recognized to be of considerable importance (e.g., Lewis, 1966; Welner et al., 1976; Videbech, 1975; Noreik, 1970, etc.), but the nature of this association is unclear. As an illustration of this relationship, Rosenberg (1968) found that 34 percent of his sample of 144 obsessional patients had received treatment for moderate or severe depression within a few years of the onset of their obsessions.

Although obsessions and depressions are often associated, sometimes intimately so, the relations between them are complex. Obsessions and depressions can arise independently, and even in instances in which they are associated at the time of onset, they can then *develop* independently. As mentioned earlier, for a period many psychiatrists, such as Maudsley, made no distinction between obsessions and depression. Almost all of the (scattered) information on the relations between obsessional-compulsive phenomena and depression concerns obsessions rather than compulsions, with treatment research providing the main source of data on compulsions. For present purposes it will be assumed that obsessions and compulsions do not differ in their relations with depression. While it is currently convenient, this assumption will be found wanting when data on compulsions and depression are accumulated; there is already one hint of a divergence between obsessions and compulsions. Nevertheless, it would be prematurely overanalytic to separate the two phenomena at this stage. To prevent unnecessary repetition, in this chapter the term *obsessions* is taken to include compulsions as well.

There are many opinions on the subject of how depression and obsessions are related. Some writers have argued that depression "activates" dormant obsessions, while others contend that depression develops when the person's obsessional defences fail him. Still others regard obsessions as little more than one of the numerous manifestations of depression. It will be recalled that in the early days obsessional ideas were considered to be an accompaniment of melancholia, particularly religious melancholia.

The division of "obsessional depressions" into two types, primary and secondary, was advocated by Lewis (1966). "Obsessional patients are in most cases depressed; their illness is a depressing one. Besides the secondary depression, however, there is frequently an association of a more intimate kind in which depression—or mania—is the essential or main part of the illness, and the concurrent obsessions seem to be symptoms of this affective disorder" (p. 1200). Lewis's view that most obsessional patients are or have been depressed is widely shared (and is consistent with our own clinical experience), but it should not be forgotten that there are many cases in which the obsessional disorder is not accompanied by or preceded by any clear indications of depression (e.g., Welner et al., 1976). Kringlen (1970), in a careful study of 91 obsessional patients, found that roughly one-fifth of them displayed depressive symptoms (see also Welner et al., 1976). In our own series of 83 patients, 55 percent were seemingly free of depressive complaints at the onset of the disorder. However, in many instances the sequence was of the obsessions leading to depression. Welner and his associates (1976) found that the transition from obsessions to depression occurred three times as often (38 percent of the cases) as the reverse sequence (11%). It is of great interest that the latter group had a far better prognosis.

In addition to direct clinical observations of the relationship between obsessions and depressions, there is some indirect evidence of a correlative kind. In a statistical study Kiloh and Garside (1963) found a significant correlation between the presence of obsessional symptoms and reactive depression. Other indirect evidence is provided in the statistical study reported by Klerman (1972) and the questionnaire survey carried out by Young, Fenton, and Lader (1971) on a nonclinical sample—the depression and obsessional scales correlated 0.46.

Our own evidence is contained in the results of the treatment trials described in Chapters 22 and 23. In many of these clinical trials, our own and others, the patients were assessed before and after treatment on a range of behavioral and psychiatric scales, including ratings of depression. In all of the relevant studies, the obsessional patients were, as a group, rated by themselves or others as having elevated scores on the depression scales. Some indirect evidence of the relation between the two phenomena is also to be found in a number of studies on the structure and course of depressive illnesses, in which the presence of obsessions before, during, or after a depressive illness was recorded (e.g., Videbech, 1975). Before undertaking an examination of the evidence, one should be forewarned that the literature can be confusing, partly because of the complexity of the relationship and partly because of some conceptual difficulties.

To begin with, there are important disagreements about the nature of depression; for example, is it a unitary or binary disorder? In addition, there is considerable ambiguity about the relationship between obsessional-compulsive disorders and the so-called obsessional personality. In many parts of the literature, this essential distinction is lost. Taking care to distinguish between an obsessional disorder and an obsessional personality is more than a matter of personal fastidiousness, particularly as the concept of "the obsessional personality" is of questionable value. Because of these ambiguities it seems that at times psychologists and psychiatrists are seeking to relate two unknowns (obsessional personality and depression) or, more precisely, seeking to relate two compound concepts of uncertain validity and unknown boundaries. To make matters worse, much of the information on which one has to rely in interpreting the phenomena is of poor quality. This is partly a reflection of inadequate research methodology but is in large measure attributable to conceptual ambiguities.

In approaching the relationship between the two phenomena, one can start either from the depressive end or from the obsessional end. The latter tactic is less popular because of the shortage of suitable clinical material. So for people who are interested primarily in obsessions and compulsions the literature is meager. Studies in which the main focus of attention is on the nature and course of a depressive illness (and they are the majority) provide one with occasional glimpses of the fate of obsessions. Moreover, there is reason to doubt whether the obsessions that are observed to occur in depressive populations are identical to those that constitute the core of an obsessional-compulsive disorder. There are phenomenological differences that may prove to be critical. So, for example, Gittelson (1966c) found that in just over 50 percent of his 124 depressive patients who reported obsessional phenomena, the *content* of the obsession was aggressive—mainly homicidal or suicidal. Kendall and di Scipio (1970) and Videbech (1975) have reported a similar pattern. By contrast, the obsessions reported by obsessional-compulsive patients have a much lower frequency of aggressive themes. Instead, their obsessions are more widely distributed, with ideas of dirt and contamination, impersonal entities, and sexual and religious themes being prominent.

Nothwithstanding the sparse and often confusing information, we have constructed eight generalizations, more in the hope that they will help to organize and clarify the subject than with great conviction of their accracy or durability.

1. In most instances there is a close relationship between the occurrence of obsessions and/or compulsions and depression.

2. In some, perhaps many instances, the depression contributes to the genesis of the obsessions or compulsions; more frequently the emergence of obsessions and compulsions contributes to the genesis of a depressive period.
3. Obsessions and/or compulsions may covary with depression or vary independently of depression.
4. There is an epidemiological mismatch between depression in general and obsessions and compulsions.
5. Indecisiveness is a common (but not invariable) feature of both depressions and obsessional-compulsive disorders.
6. Obsessions and depressive retardation are negatively correlated.
7. The relation among obsessions, compulsions, and depressions is not an exclusive one; obsessions and compulsions are also encountered in other types of psychiatric disorders, such as schizophrenia (e.g., Black, 1974).
8. There is a positive correlation between severity of depression and the occurrence of obsessions/compulsions.

Although there is insufficient evidence on which to risk a generalization at this stage, there may be a close relationship between agitated depression and obsessions (Kiloh and Garside, 1963; Rachman, 1971; Vaughan, 1976). Similarly, it is possible that obsessions and mania are negatively correlated. No attempt has been made to formulate generalizations about the role of depression in *maintaining* obsessions and compulsions, or of the reverse relationship, as there is insufficient information. It is of course a subject of considerable importance, and will be discussed later.

Before entering upon a detailed consideration of these generalizations, it is necessary to digress in order to devote some time to an examination of two key concepts, depression and obsessional personality. Even if we assume that there is such an entity as "an obsessional personality"—and the justification for such an assumption is weak—there is no satisfactory instrument for assessing it. In addressing the relationship between depressions and obsessions, most workers have determined the categorical presence of an obsessional personality or of obsessional traits on the basis of secondhand or even thirdhand information. For example, in estimating the occurrence of obsessional personalities in the parents of his index case, Gittelson (1966a, b, c) was obliged to rely on the information recorded in hospital case notes. Hence, his decisions were based on the unsystematic and unvalidated inferences drawn by the original psychiatrist (who may never have seen the parents) as long as ten years prior to Gittelson's carrying out his examiniation of the data. Attempting to reach conclusions about the nature of obsessions and depression on the basis of such poor-grade information, and regrettably much of it is in this class, is a risky undertaking. Obviously, the conclusions have to be treated as tentative. A fuller analysis of the concept of the obsessional personality is undertaken in Chapter 10.

The long dispute about whether depression is unitary or binary dominated discussions of the subject throughout the period in which the research on the relation between obsessions and depression was carried out, but it may be approaching a partial resolution. If this optimism is justified, we can look forward to a welcome increase in the clarity of the research on the relation between depression and obsessions. The resolution, if it is achieved, may also contribute to reducing the serious differences in diagnostic practice that still persist and of course make it difficult to generalize from one study to the next. It has been demonstrated that there are important differences in international diagnostic practices with respect to both schizophrenia and depression. For example, Kendell and his colleagues (1971) showed that depression is diagnosed more frequently in the United Kingdom than in the United States, while schizophrenia is more commonly diagnosed in the United States than in the United Kingdom. These differences in diagnostic practice exceed the greater base rate for depression that exists in the United Kingdom. (According to Levitt and Lubin (1975), the incidence of depression in the United Kingdom is three to ten times as great as it is in the United States.)

The unitary theory of depression posited that the observed differences between depressed patients do not reflect differences in quality but, rather, are variations along a continuum of severity. The opposing theory, the binary conception, states that two major types of depression can be distinguished—neurotic depression and endogenous (psychotic) depression. According to a major version of this theory, the main features of neurotic depression are that it is reactive to external precipitants, is characterized by agitation, makes psychological sense, is accompanied by anxiety and tension, affects a younger age group, and is less severe than the endogenous variety. This latter type of depression is identified by marked biological dysfunctions (sleep, appetite, sexual, etc.), occurs in the absence of a clear precipitant, is characterized by retardation and apathy, affects an older age group with a family history of depression, and is more severe. According to Shields (1973, p. 575), the genetic evidence is consistent with a binary division of this kind.

An important test of the binary theory was carried out on 143 depressed patients by Kiloh and Garside (1963). The results of their detailed investigation supported the binary view, and what is of more immediate interest, they found that the presence of obsessional traits was positively correlated with reactive depression and negatively correlated with retardation. Obsessionality was one feature in a list of fourteen (which included irritability, sudden onset of depression, reactivity, etc.) that distinguished neurotic depression from endogenous depression. The main features of endogenous depression were early awakening, weight loss, retardation, an age over 40, and so forth. The results and interpretation of this and other studies were subjected to a spirited critical evaluation by Kendell (1968), who argued that much of the information could be accounted for by diagnostic bias in the original selection of the patients. His own results favored the unitary theory. Although the controversy has not ended, more recent work by Kiloh and his colleagues (1972) and the research of Everitt and his associates (1971) are indications of growing agreement between the opposing theorists. In their recent work the advocates of the binary system, Kiloh and others, continue to argue that depression is not unitary and that a category called endogenous depression can be isolated. However, they go on to add that the nature of the second type (or, more probably, *types*) of depression needs to be clarified. Further indications of increasing agreement can be found in the analysis carried out by Eysenck (1970). In his view the argument continues because of some misunderstanding between the opposing parties. He argues that the evidence indicates that depression is binary and adds that the entire problem has become muddled by the introduction of a second question, that of whether depressions are categorical or dimensional. He argues that reconstruing the problem in binary but dimensional terms facilitates a clarification of the persisting difficulty. The "existence of two independent and separate factors of depression does not preclude the existence of patients suffering from both endogenous and reactive depression, and showing symptoms of both" (Eysenck, 1970, p. 248).

Given the distinction between neurotic and psychotic depressions, obsessional-compulsive disorders (conventionally classified as neuroses) must surely be associated with the neurotic rather than the psychotic variety. Certainly, the list of attributes presumed to be indicative of neurotic depression comes much closer to the description of obsessional patients than the characteristics of psychotic depression do, and as we have already mentioned, there may well be a negative correlation between retardation (more characteristic of psychotic depression) and obsessions. Leaving aside the complications introduced by the probable existence of several forms of neurotic depression, the connection between obsessions and depression should be sought among neurotic depressed people. Indirect support for this contention can be found in the statistical study carried out by Klerman (1972). Granted the identification of psychotic depression, there are grounds for supposing that any connection between this kind of depression and obsessions is likely to be both uncommon and uncharacteristic. Two of the defining characteristics of psychotic depression (retardation and biological dysfunctions) are not commonly observed in obsessional patients. Furthermore, as mentioned earlier, there is an important difference between the two in age of onset. The confusion may have arisen because of the tendency for psychotic depressions to be more severe than neurotic depressions, coupled with a possible association between severity of depression and obsessions.

GENERALIZATIONS

The first of our eight generalizations states that there is a close relationship between the occurrence of depression and obsessions/compulsions.

Despite methodological weaknesses in the studies reported by Gittelson (poor-grade evidence, qualitative differences in phenomenology, etc.), they do provide some estimations of the frequency with which obsessions and depressions are associated, and equally interesting, they contain some evidence of the synchronous and desynchronous relations between the two phenomena. That is, although obsessions and depressions often are related, they are also seen to vary independently. Gittelson (1966a) studied the detailed case notes of all inpatients who were admitted (suffering from depressive psychoses) into the Professorial Unit of the Maudsley Hospital between January 1, 1956, and December 1959. (This unit followed the unitary theory.) "Of the 398 cases, 31 percent had obsessions, 64 percent did not, and 5 percent showed transition of obsessions into delusions . . . depressives with obsessions attempted suicide 6½ times less frequently than depressives without obsessions or the obsession-delusion transition group" (Gittelson, 1966a, p. 258). (Incidentally, all patients diagnosed as suffering from obsessional neurosis were excluded from the analysis.) Gittelson found surprisingly few differences between the patients whose depressive illness had been associated with obsessions and those who had not experienced this phenomenon. The claim that the patients who experienced obsessions had a high incidence "of obsessional personalities in the parents" is based on indirect inference, and in any event the differences were not large—16.5 percent versus 10.9 percent. Gittelson is perhaps on firmer ground in concluding that patients who experienced obsessions had "twice the incidence of obsessional premorbid personalities" than depressives who did not experience obsessions—69.4 percent versus 29.3 percent.

Gittelson concluded, without further explanation or justification, that the obsessions that occur during the course of a depressive psychosis "are based predominantly on the activation of premorbid personality traits and furthermore they appear to have a marked 'protective' effect against suicidal attempts" (p. 258). Whatever the theoretical explanation, the finding that the risk of a suicidal attempt being made by a patient who has obsessional experiences during a depression is greatly increased if the obsession begins to turn into a delusion is of considerable practical importance. It is of interest that the presence or absence of obsessions made no difference whatsoever to the manner in which the illness was treated (two-thirds of the patients were given ECT).

In a second report on the same group of patients, Gittelson (1966b) provided fascinating information about the synchronous and desynchronous changes in obsessions and depressions. He introduced three whimsical but appropriate and useful labels to describe the main patterns: *Keepers* are the patients who showed obsessional traits before the onset of depression and continued to experience them during the course of the illness; *losers* are those whose obsessional traits disappeared during the course of the depressive illness; and *gainers* are of course those who developed obsessional ideas for the first time during their depressive illness. He found that of the 52 cases "exhibiting pre-depressive obsessions, 25 percent lost their obsessions during the depression. Of the 346 without pre-depressive obsessions, 25 percent exhibited obsessions throughout the depression and 4 percent exhibited obsession-delusion transition during the depression" (1966, p. 707). The percentages of gainers and losers were approximately equal, and as Gittelson concluded, "During an attack of depressive psychosis, those with pre-morbid obsessions are just as likely to lose them as those without them are to gain them. For both, the chance is 1 in 4" (p. 707). Incidentally, it should not pass unnoticed that there were three times as many keepers as losers; patients who have predepressive obsessions are likely to maintain them during the depressive illness. Moreover, 62 percent of the depressive patients failed to experience obsessions either before or during their illness. A possible explanation of the "losers" phenomenon may lie in the inhibiting influence of depressive retardation.

It was also found that 13.5 percent of patients with predepressive obsessions experienced a "permanent worsening of their obsessions after the resolution of their depression" (p. 707). If we look at the total sample of 398 depressive patients, however, only 2.8 percent showed a permanent worsening of their obsessional problems after the resolution of the depression.

In a comparable study carried out on 104 depressed but "anancastic" Danish patients, Videbech (1975) obtained results similar to Gittelson's, despite the latter's exclusion of obsessional patients from his sample. There is a close association between obsessions and depression; the incidence of obsessions increased during depressive episodes; and so on. In the Videbech study the number of obsessions increased from 23 percent to 66 percent of all cases, but interestingly, the incidence of compulsions remained steady. He also found a high incidence of aggressive obsessions and (once again) a negative correlation between obsessions and retardation.

Consistent with Gittelson's observations concerning gainers, Kendell and di Scipio (1970) found that "patients with few obsessional traits are just as likely to develop obsessional symptoms when they become depressed as those with many, and perhaps even more so" (p. 68). In their study of 92 depressed patients, these authors assessed the development of obsessional symptoms by administering the Leyton Obsessional Inventory. The inventory was administered during the course of the illness and once more after recovery. The authors' general conclusions were that "obsessional symptoms are common in depression and tend to be aggressive in content. They are equally common in psychotic and neurotic depressions but are more extensive and more severe in deep depression than in mild depression" (Kendell and di Scipio, 1970, p. 72). Their findings tend to confirm Gittelson's and Videbech's with respect to the frequency of obsessional symptoms in depression, and are also consistent with their observation that the content of the obsessions is largely aggressive. As in his earlier work, Kendell found no evidence of an association between obsessions and neurotic depression, as opposed to psychotic depression (contrary to Kiloh and Garside, 1963). The possibility that the association between obsessions and depressions is in part a function of the severity of the depression received some support from their findings. (Incidentally, the authors' dismissal of an association between obsessions and *neurotic* depression is not entirely justified by their own data. In Table 4.2 the neurotic and endogenous depressives showed different changes on the Leyton Inventory, associated with recovery from the illness, but this difference is not evident in Table 7.1, where a slightly different sample is analyzed.)

Unfortunately, the value of this interesting study is lessened by its use of the Leyton Inventory, which is designed to assess obsessional symptoms, traits, resistance, and interference—as separate dimensions. As we will see, there is reason to doubt the independence of these scales, and indeed the study by Kendell and di Scipio adds to these doubts. So, for example, there is a significant reduction in the trait score after recovery from the illness—but presumably, being a trait score, a stable attribute of personality, it should have been resistant to transient change. Moreover, Kendell and di Scipio report a highly significant positive correlation of 0.78 between the trait scores and the symptom scores on the inventory; these are not independent scales. Lastly, the obsessional-trait score was found to correlate significantly with a score of general neuroticism derived from the Eysenck Personality Inventory (EPI)—0.48.

Kendell and di Scipio's conclusion that the tendency for obsessional symptoms "to develop or to get worse during a period of depression is widespread" (p. 70) is not quite borne out by their evidence. The conclusion appears to be based on the fact that the scores on some of the scales declined when the patients had recovered from their depressive illness—but in the absence of pre-illness scores the conclusion is not justified. At best, one might conclude that there is a tendency for (some) obsessional characteristics to decline with recovery from depression, but even this conclusion needs qualification. Although 58 percent of the patients had higher symptom scores "when they were depressed than they did after recovery," the reverse of this is of course that 42 percent of the patients did *not* have higher obsessional-symptom scores during the depression. For the moment this question must remain open.

Another interesting finding was that "a high proportion of those who develop new obsessional symptoms when they become depressed do not have prominent obsessional personality traits" (Kendell and di Scipio, 1970, p. 70). This information damages the hypothesis that depression merely activates pre-existing obsessional inclinations. Taken in conjunction with Gittelson's (1966b) results on gainers, Kendell and di Scipio's findings show that, at the least, the hypothesis needs first aid.

Even though we have followed Kendell and di Scipio in their use of the terms *obsessional symptoms, traits,* and so on, in order to avoid giving a misleading impression it should be noted that although the scores obtained by their depressive patients on the Leyton Inventory were higher than those obtained by normal adults, they were significantly lower than the scores obtained by obsessional neurotic patients. So interpretation of these findings needs to be qualified not only by the phenomenological differences mentioned earlier but also by the significant differences in intensity of the obsessional characteristics. In sum, the depressive patients reported obsessions that were somewhat different in content and significantly less intense than those of a group of obsessional patients.

The observation that obsessional characteristics decline after the patient's recovery from depression receives support from a small piece of indirect evidence contained in a report by Orme (1965). On the other hand, a systematic study recently reported by Paykel, Prussof, and Tanner (1976) clearly illustrates the independent development of obsessions and depressions. Thirty-three depressive patients were assessed first at the height of their illness and then some months later during a relapse following their initial recovery from the depressive episode. Although their depression was significantly less severe at relapse, the obsessional scores were almost identical at both assessments (i.e., they were unchanged even though the level of depression had dropped).

It will be evident that we have not come very far in tracking the changing relations between obsessions and depressions, and progress will depend on the adoption of improved tactics. So far we know little more than that there frequently is a close relationship between the two phenomena, that gainers slightly exceed losers, and that keepers exceed both. Most of the available evidence has been drawn from samples of depressive patients, and it remains to be seen whether or not their obsessions are comparable *in essential features* to those of obsessional patients. Also, the poor quality of the information demands a cautious acceptance. Despite this, however, at least one hypothesis—that depression merely activates premorbid obsessions—has been damaged.

For students of obsessions and compulsions, the evidence on the role of depression drawn from studies of obsessional patients (e.g., Welner et al., 1976) rather than from depressive patients is more satisfactory because it is more direct. Until the necessary experiments have been conducted, one is obliged to rely on incidental findings, especially those obtained in the course of clinical trials of behavior therapy. In our research we observed that depressive episodes were common before treatment and less common, but not rare, during and after treatment. In our first study on ten patients (Rachman, Hodgson, and Marks, 1971), we observed a small but significant decline in depression shortly after the patients were admitted to the hospital—but before behavioral treatment was commenced. Broadly speaking, this lowered level of depression remained constant throughout and after the completion of the behavioral-treatment program. Apart from this intial drop in depression consequent on admission to the hospital, there was no covariation between changes in obsessional-compulsive problems and feelings of depression. The point is made even more decisively by reference to Figure 6.1. This illustrates the unchanging level of moderate depression in a group of twenty patients who underwent behavioral treatment. From the beginning of treatment until the two-year follow-up, their depression

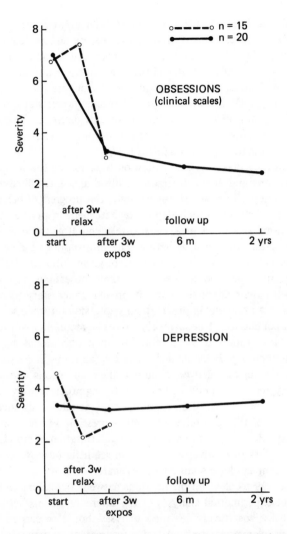

FIGURE 6.1. Changes in obsessional complaints and depression during treatment and follow up.

scores showed no significant change. In marked contrast, however, after behavioral treatment there was a steep decline in obsessional-compulsive problems. In brief, there was a marked desynchrony between depression and obsessions consequent upon the completion of behavioral treatment—the steep decline in obsessions was accompanied by an unchanging course in the low to moderate levels of depression that characterized these patients on admission to hospital.

The results obtained by Boersma, Den Hengst, Dekker, and Emmelkamp

(1976) reveal a different relation, however. "The improvement of the clients was shown by the measurement *in vivo*, the anxiety and avoidance scales, and by all the scales of the Leyton Obsessional Inventory. In addition it was shown that at the end of treatment the clients had become less depressed . . . The amelioration of depression as a consequence of response prevention is particularly noteworthy . . . On the whole these improvements persisted until follow-up" (p. 22). There is no obvious explanation for this discrepancy, particularly as both groups of patients appear to have been at approximately the same level of depression prior to entering the treatment trial.

Although they make little contribution to clarifying the complex relations between obsessions and depression, some clinical anecdotes illustrate the variations one encounters. In some of our patients, the progress of behavior therapy was brought to a halt when their depression returned. In most instances, when the full behavioral treatment program was resumed after the dissipation of the depression, progress continued as before. The interruptions seemed to have no long-term effects. In a few patients who were given antidepressant medication prior to beginning behavioral treatment, their obsessions and compulsions disappeared with their depression—and it proved unnecessary to carry out the planned treatment program. In others, their depression returned some time after the successful conclusion of behavior therapy. The recurrence of their depressed mood was seldom followed by a return of their obsessional and compulsive problems, except perhaps in a mild and easily treated form. There were, however, one or two patients whose lives, including their obsessions and compulsions, were shaped by recurrent mood swings. Painstaking progress in overcoming their obsessions and compulsions, often requiring courage and persistence, was wiped out within a day of the recurrence of black depression. From a clinician's point of view, perhaps the most obvious effect of a deterioration in mood is to be seen in the patients' loss of motivation. They can see little purpose in pursuing the treatment program and have scant energy to spare.

The best way to clear up the relations between obsessions and depressions is to carry out experimental analyses of the interconnections between the two phenomena. These specifically designed analyses should be carried out notwithstanding the problems of definition and measurement, and the difficulties that arise from the differing time spans of depressions and obsessions. Experimental analyses carried out in order to test specific hypotheses, preferably derived from substantial theories, are of course those that are most likely to lead to useful results.

In interpreting the covariation and independent variation of obsessions and depressions, it must be remembered that obsessions are also observed to occur in association with other disorders. The relation between obsessions and depression is close, but it is not an exclusive relationship. Also, a number of behavioral abnormalities other than obsessions (e.g., phobias—see Gurney et al., 1972; Marks, 1969) are associated with variations in depression, and Rosenberg

(1968) reports that while 34 percent of the obsessional patients in his sample had significant depression, so too did 25.7 percent of his cases of anxiety neurosis.

A MISMATCH

There is an epidemiological mismatch between depression and obsessional disorders. As none of the epidemiological studies on which this argument relies included a separation into endogenous and other kinds of depression, our conclusions might in the long run prove unduly negative. If and when epidemiological studies that distinguish between psychotic and neurotic depression are carried out, the conclusions might require qualification. Insofar as some of the epidemiological data are drawn from studies confined to in-patients, it is likely that a disproportionate emphasis is placed on the psychotic varieties of depression—they are more severe and therefore are more likely to lead to hospital admission.

Unlike depression, obsessional-compulsive disorders tend to take a chronic, constant course. "In 8 studies, a chronic depressive state was judged as having supervened in from 1 percent to 23 percent" (Robins and Guze, 1972, p. 287). On the other hand, obsessional problems more commonly follow a chronic (constant or slowly declining) course. Ingram (1961) reports a figure of 39 percent showing this pattern; Lo (1967) quotes a figure of 58 percent and Ray (1964) a figure of 61 percent. A second difference is that depression affects an older age group. According to Levitt and Lubin (1975), the modal first-admission rate for women occurs between 50 and 60 years of age, whereas the modal first-admission rate for obsessional women is approximately 30 years of age (Hare, Price, and Slater, 1972). Third, the peaks of the age-incidence curves vary for the two disorders: According to Hare and his associates, the age-incidence curve for obsessionals spikes in early adulthood, and this distinguishes them from the three major categories in psychiatric illness. In particular, the peak incidence for affective psychoses occurs just over ten years later.

Referring back to our argument about the greater likelihood of there being an association between *neurotic* depression and obsessions, it is worth noting in passing that Schuyler (1974) has adduced some evidence to indicate that endogenous depressions reach their peak incidence in women at between 45 and 50 years of age and in men at approximately 60 years of age. Reactive depressions, on the other hand, show a peak incidence that is much closer to that of the obsessional population (i.e., between 26 and 40 years of age for females and between 36 and 40 years for males). A fourth epidemiological difference between the two disorders is seen in the sex ratio. As mentioned earlier, men and women are equally represented in the obsessional population. However, the female:male ratio in depressive disorders is 2:1 (Levitt and Lubin, 1975; Schuyler, 1974). A fifth difference is seen in the marriage rate. Among depressives the rate is the same as for the rest of the population (Levitt and Lubin, 1975), but it is significantly lower for obsessional patients (Hare et al., 1972). Sixth, the fertility rate of female patients with affective disorders is comparable to that of women in the rest of the population (Stevens, 1969) and therefore is significantly higher than the abnormally low rate of obsessional patients (Hare et al., 1972). In considering all of this information, the relative incidence of depressions and obsessions should be borne in mind. In the national series reported by Hare and his colleagues, obsessional neurosis accounted for only 0.5 percent of all cases, whereas affective illnesses accounted for over 50 percent.

Before concluding this examination of the relation between the two phenomena, a number of smaller points, mostly little more than suggestions from the literature, are worth mentioning. In pursuing our clinical impression that there is a relationship between agitated depression and the onset of maintenance of obsessive-compulsive problems, we came across five independent mentions of a negative correlation between obsessions and depressive retardation. The relation was commented on by Stengel (1945), and negative correlations were reported by Kiloh and Garside (1963), by Videbech (1975), and by Gurney and his associates (1972). If this relationship is confirmed, it will become necessary to seek an explanation. At first sight it would appear that in a state of retardation the ability and desire to execute tiring, repetitive, compulsive acts is dissipated; even if this is correct, it remains to be explained why *obsessions* appear to decline or even disappear during retardation. As for the hypothesis of an association between agitated depression and obsessions (Rachman, 1971), some encouragement was provided in a study reported by Vaughan (1976). The case records of 168 cases of depression were rated for obsessional personality and the presence of obsessions and of depressive symptoms. Vaughan found that obsessional personality was significantly associated only with a decreased frequency of apathy. "Obsessions and depression were associated with rapid changes of mood, anxiety, agitation and over-activity and with a relative absence of retardation" (p. 36). Similar findings with respect to mood changes, agitation, and retardation were reported by Videbech (1975).

It has been suggested by Stengel (1945), among others, that there is a negative correlation between obsessions and mania. "Certainly it is difficult to visualize how the fruitless compulsion to resist that is the essence of an obsessional symptom could survive in the presence of the euphoria and disinhibition of mania. The authors have encountered one lifelong obsessional neurotic who developed recurrent manic illness in middle age and this man's normally incapacitating fears and compulsions faded away dramatically for the duration of each manic episode" (Kendell and di Scipio, 1970, p. 71). On the other hand, we were given the opportunity to administer our Obsessional Questionnaire (see Appendix A) to five consecutive manic patients. Although it proved difficult to get them to complete the forms adequately, to our considerable surprise all five of them turned in high obsessional scores. Whether this reflected a manic attitude toward test taking (unlikely in view of the composition of the scale) or whether these patients were in fact experiencing obsessions was unclear. With two exceptions, there was no evidence of anything resembling compulsive stereotyped activities. It is interesting that Lewis (1966) apparently accepted the existence of a *positive* relationship between obsessions and mania, if his opinion may be judged from one complex sentence. Earlier we quoted his view that sometimes the association between depression and obsessions is primary. That quotation also contained the following statement: "There is frequently an association of a more intimate kind, in which depression—*or mania*—is the essential or main part of the illness, and the concurrent obsessions seem to be symptoms of the affective disorder" (p. 1200, italics added). Videbech's (1975) research suggests that the occurrence of manic symptoms in association with obsessionality is uncommon, and he also found a negative relation between "flight of ideas" and obsessionality.

In the same article Lewis (1966) made another, rather more important suggestion. He postulated that in cases in which the obsessional illness is "a symptom of this affective disorder," then "the obsessional illness is very often cyclical in its course" (p. 1200). If confirmed—and Welner and his colleagues' (1976) research is a useful beginning—this relationship would be of theoretical and practical significance. A careful comparison of obsessional disorders that follow a constant course with those following a cyclical course would be welcome.

The possibility that obsessions are related to the severity of the depression arises from the statistical research of Raskin and his associates (1971) and of Kendell and di Scipio (1970). There is an obvious explanation for this relationship, but the evidence on which it is based has so far been confined to data gathered from patients suffering from depression. This putative relationship may not be confirmed when checked on a group of *obsessional* patients.

We have drawn attention to the finding of a considerable degree of indecisiveness among depressed patients, regardless of obsessions, because of the weight attached to this characteristic of obsessional patients in a number of theories. Indeed, as we will see presently, at least two prominent theoreticians (Beech, 1974; Carr, 1976) assign considerable importance to the role of indecisiveness in the maintenance and even in the genesis of obsessional-compulsive disorders. Levitt and Lubin (1975) report that 80 percent of 500 depressed patients complained of indecisiveness, and 22 percent of an unselected group of 153 patients at a general hospital also complained of this difficulty. Similarly, Woodruff and his associates (1967) reported that more than half of their 72 depressed patients complained of indecisiveness. Insofar as indecisiveness is a prominent feature of an obsessional disorder, it might be a secondary manifestation of depression in many instances.

Lewis (1966), among others, has commented on the fact that few obsessionals "give way to antisocial impulses, e.g., to suicide, homicide, delinquency" (p. 1201). Confirmation of the low suicide rate in obsessional patients is provided by Gittelson (1966a) and by Goodwin and his colleagues (1969). So far we have no explanation for this low rate of suicidal attempts. One possibility is that because of the strong moral and/or religious views that many obsessional patients hold, they are less likely to contravene the moral objections to suicide, and indeed to other antisocial acts. It should, however, be remembered that when depressed patients show signs of a transition from an obsession to a delusion, the suicidal risk increases to the high level prevailing among samples of depressive patients.

DISCUSSION

Genesis

Depression is not a necessary condition but may be a sufficient one for generating obsessions. In a moderately high percentage of cases, it may well be facilitative. It is not a necessary condition for the development of obsessions (at least in the immediate sense) because they can develop in the absence of discernible depression—as mentioned earlier, 55 percent of our patients reported no depression at the onset of the disorder. Delayed effects cannot be ruled out at this stage. However that is, 52 of Gittelson's (1966b) 398 patients had exhibited obsessions prior to the onset of depression, and more than half of Welner and his colleagues' (1976) 150 obsessionals had little or no prior depression.

In a certain number of cases, depression may be a sufficient condition; certainly, the incidence of obsessions (but not of compulsions?) increases during depressive episodes (Videbech, 1975). Also, there is some evidence that obsessions develop during depression even in a substantial percentage of people who have no predepressive experience of obsessions. Gittelson (1966b) reports that 85 of the 398 patients included in his study were gainers. There is, however, no certainty that the relation is causal. For example, the gainers may develop depressions and obsessions as parallel co-effects of some other process. However, it is safe to conclude that depression can promote obsessions.

Next we turn to the genesis of depression. The frequency of depression greatly exceeds that of obsessions; hence, obsessions cannot be a necessary condition. It is widely supposed, however, that persistent obsessional and compulsive problems can produce depression. "Obsessional patients are in most cases depressed; their illness is a depressing one" (Lewis, 1966, p. 1200), and our own experiences support this view. In a certain number of cases, the persistence of obsessional and compulsive problems is sufficient to produce depression. The most recent evidence (Welner et al., 1976) indicates that it might be a large percentage. At the very least, it is probable that persisting obsessional problems facilitate the onset of depression.

Maintenance

It is easier to make a case for the role of depression in generating obsessional-compulsive behavior than it is to argue for the role of depression in *maintaining* such behavior. A marked disturbance of mood is likely to result in behavioral changes, and given the presence of other contributing factors such as prior learning, "premorbid personality," and the like, the emergence of obsessional-compulsive behavior is not too surprising. At the other end of the chain, however, it is more difficult to see how a mood disturbance can help maintain obstssional-compulsive behavior. In keeping with traditional psychological analyses of behavior maintenance, one would be more inclined to look for the presence of reinforcing contingencies than for disturbances of mood. Insofar as depression does play a role in maintaining the behavior, it is likely to do so in an indirect manner. To take one possibility, discussed in detail in Chapters 11 and 12, the compulsive behavior may persist because it achieves temporary relief from an unpleasant affective state (e.g., anxiety or depression). By this reasoning the need for compulsive rituals, and the opportunities for their reinforcement, should decline when the depression dissipates. As we have seen, the evidence on this point is incomplete.

What, then, is the evidence for supposing that depression helps maintain obsessions? Clinically, the connection seems to be clear—in some instances the successful reduction of depression is accompanied or followed by a decline in obsessions and compulsions. In our own experience the successful treatment of depression sometimes removes the need to deal directly with the obsessional difficulties. The persuasive clinical reports of Capstick (1975) and others on the value of antidepressant medication in overcoming obsessional problems, if confirmed, would be useful evidence—provided, of course, that one could rule out the possibility that the drugs have a directly antiobsessional effect. On the other hand, Paykel and his associates (1976) have shown that in a group of 185 depressed patients, recovery from the depression left the average level of obsessional *traits* unaffected. This apparent conflict of evidence (it is not a true conflict, and in any event it needs confirmation) could be resolved by postulating that depressions may help maintain obsessional and compulsive disorders but have little or no influence on obsessionality when seen as a trait of personality. Gittelson's studies provide examples in which depression presumably helped maintain obsessions (39 of the 52 patients who exhibited obsessions before the onset of depression retained them—these were the keepers) and other examples in which the onset of depression failed to maintain existing obsessions. In his series there were 13 losers among the 52 patients who had obsessions prior to becoming depressed. As mentioned, many of our own patients had persisting obsessions in the absence of depression. Hence, depression cannot be regarded as a necessary condition for the maintenance of obsessions or compulsions; in some cases it may be a sufficient condition—or, more correctly, depression may promote the maintenance of obsessions and compulsions.

Obviously, obsessions are not necessary for the maintenance of depression, but as in the genesis of depression, the persistence of obsessional-compulsive problems may serve to maintain depression. The results of the treatment trial reported by Boersma and his colleagues (1976), and others discussed in Chapter 23, support this possibility in that the successful reduction of obsessional problems was followed by a significant reduction in depression. As mentioned earlier, our own experiments did not produce this result. The mild (average) level of depression present in our own patients before treatment showed little alteration despite the successful reduction of obsessional-compulsive problems. Other factors and influences were serving to maintain the (mild) depression. At present, these seemingly discrepant findings cannot be reconciled. Relying on Boersma's result and our clinical impressions, we come down on the side of postulating that obsessions can promote the maintenance of depression.

Naturally, many factors influence the onset and course of depression, and in confining our discussion to the role of obsessions we have taken for granted the contributory influences of premorbid personality, biological inheritance, precipitating events, and so on. A comprehensive theory of depression, such as Seligman's (1975), makes allowance for the operation of influences of this kind—and insofar as obsessional-compulsive problems play a part in determining the course of depression in a particular person, Seligman's theory can accommodate this information (see Chapter 25).

Chapter 7

The Relation Between Obsessional Disorders and Other Psychiatric Problems

For some time, particularly at the turn of the century, it was widely believed that there is a close association between obsessions and schizophrenia. Whether it was fed by the fact that some schizophrenic patients at one time or another display obsessional-compulsive features (Rosen, 1957) or whether it was based on a confusion between delusions and obsessions, the belief has taken a long time to wither. With the exception of two studies, contemporary evidence is consistent in showing that only a tiny percentage of obsessional patients subsequently develop schizophrenia. Moreover, this percentage is no higher than it is for other neurotic disorders. The data, neatly summarized by Black (1974, p. 51), show that the incidence of schizophrenia developing in patients with an obsessional neurosis varies between 0 percent (this figure is based on 3 studies involving over 300 patients) up to 3.3 percent. For example, Lo (1967) found that only 2 of his 88 obsessional neurotics developed schizophrenia (both with paranoid delusions). Ray (1964) found that only 1 out of 42 consecutive cases of obsessional neurosis developed schizophrenia. In his study of 82 obsessional patients followed up for a year or more, Pollitt (1957) observed that only 1 out of 82 developed schizophrenia. None of the 83 patients in our early series developed schizophrenia. The present view on the subject can be illustrated by quoting from some reviews of contemporary literature: "The great majority of gross obsessionals, however, do not become schizophrenic or anything else than obsessional" (Lewis, 1966, p. 1201); "It would be unwise to suggest that obsessional illness and schizophrenia are closely linked" (Ingram, 1961, p. 400); "Development into psychosis is also rare in typical cases" (Kringlen, 1970,

p. 418). [Incidentally, when a transition to schizophrenia does occur, paranoid delusions are claimed by both Rosen (1957) and Lo (1967) to form part of the clinical presentation]

Lewis (1966), among others, has, however, pointed out that there are many psychiatric and psychological disorders in which obsessional features may be observed, transiently or constantly. He comments on the association between obsessions and phobias, and points out that depersonalization, anorexia (e.g., Welner et al., 1976), and depression often are found in association with at least some obsessional features. Kringlen (1965) has also shown that many obsessional patients develop somatic symptoms, with head and chest pains being especially common. Somewhat surprisingly, the widely held belief that obsessional patients are particularly prone to mood swings, supported in part by Videbech's study (1975) has not been confirmed. For example, Kringlen (1965, p. 713) found that, among his patients, four times as many nonobsessional neurotic controls as obsessionals were subject to mood swings (20 controls to a mere 5 obsessionals).

The association between obsessions and the psychological dysfunctions that arise as a result of organic impairment is important not because of the frequency with which they are encountered but, rather, because of the bearing of this association on the argument in favor of retaining a medical conception of obsessional-compulsive disorders. It was argued earlier and elsewhere (Rachman and Philips, 1978) that psychological disorders such as obsessional-compulsive difficulties are best construed as psychological disorders rather than illnesses in the strict medical sense. Insofar as it can be demonstrated that at least some obsessional-compulsive disorders are a result of, or closely associated with, organic impairment, then the case for total rejection of the medical conception is untenable. Allowance has to be made for the small percentage of obsessional-compulsive disorders that are best construed as illnesses.

ORGANIC IMPAIRMENTS

Confirmation of a causal relationship between organic impairment and significant obsessions and/or compulsions would be of greater theoretical than practical importance. For the particular patients concerned, and for the people responsible for their care, detection of the organic impairment may well be critical, but the number of cases in which organic factors play a significant part is, by general agreement, likely to be very small (e.g., Lewis, 1966, p. 1199; Templer, 1972, p. 386). (Incidentally, the involvement of organic dysfunctions need not preclude the beneficial application of psychological treatment techniques.)

Cases in which the obsessional-compulsive disorder results from organic impairment are a challenge to the generalization that these disorders are best construed as psychological problems rather than as illnesses. On the other hand, obsessional disorders in which the organic impairment is incidental should continue to be regarded as psychological disorders.

In order for an obsessional disorder to qualify unreservedly for inclusion in the medical model, it should be shown that it resulted from (or was "produced by"—see Lewis, 1966, p. 1200) the organic impairment. The association between the impairment and the disorder must occur in a particular sequence and with a frequency that exceeds chance. Two such claims have been made: It is said that encephalitis and diabetes can lead to obsessional-compulsive disorders. It has also been claimed, tangentially, that obsessional patients have a disproportionately high incidence of abnormal (electrical) activity in the brain.

In his exhaustive study of the psychiatric symptoms of 144 patients with penetrating head injuries, Lishman (1968) found only two cases with obsessional-compulsive disorders. However, 28 percent of the sample had phobias or morbid anxiety; 50 percent were excessively irritable; and 40 percent suffered from episodic or continuous depression. Plainly, there is an association between head injuries and affective disorders but no sign of a link with obsessional-compulsive disorders. Establishing a connection between affective disorders and head injuries cannot, of course, be interpreted as showing that the psychiatric problems "derive in a more or less direct manner from organic lesions of the brain" (Lishman, 1968, p. 373). Lishman correctly points out that it is far easier to establish this kind of causal connection between lesions and cognitive impairments, while in cases of emotional and behavioral disorders "there can be no such ready answer."

Barton (1965) has urged the recognition of a new syndrome in which obsessional neurosis and diabetes are associated. "The syndrome consists of polydipsia, polyuria, and obsessional-compulsive rituals. Other features include depression and possibly bladder dysfunction . . . chilling, shivering, sweating . . . obesity, sleep disturbance, and mania" (1965, p. 133). It cannot be said that Barton's nine illustrative cases provide a satisfactory basis for establishing a new syndrome. With the exception of the first three cases, it is far from clear that the patients were suffering from obsessional-compulsive disorders. At most, a mild to moderate obsessional trait of one type or another is described. There is no suggestion that the incidence of these putative obsessional traits is more common among diabetic patients than among members of the general population. Even if the last six cases were to be taken as indicating a special connection between obsessions and diabetes (and this conclusion is not justified), the possibility that there might be a causal connection is not seriously argued. For example, case number 8 developed diabetes in her old age, having displayed meticulous behavior throughout her adult life. At most, this case illustrates the development of diabetes in an elderly person with a lifelong mild obsessional disorder. Barton's first three cases undoubtedly had obsessional-compulsive problems, notably counting rituals, but the case for a causal connection is not presented. It is of some interest that two of these three obsessional patients, unusually, had in addition at least one atypical and serious symptom suggestive of psychosis. One patient suffered from ideas of reference, and the other was deluded. The third patient appears to have had a sexual abnormality. Thus, the possibility of an association between diabetes and obsessional-compulsive disorders cannot be dismissed, but it has not been established.

The most thorough investigation of the relation between electrical activity of the brain (EEG) and obsessional illness was carried out by Ingram and McAdam (1960) on twenty-two confirmed cases of obsessional neurosis. Only one of the patients had an abnormal EEG—"a woman of 43 with a long-standing obsessional-compulsive neurosis which had its onset in adolescence and had run an unremitting course." The "only atypical feature was her considerable irritability which frequently led to outbursts of temper when her rituals were interfered with in any way. The EEG showed several bursts of synchronous, generalized delta waves. There was no clinical or family history of epilepsy. The history and EEG findings are reminiscent of the case described by Jarvie" (p. 689). In passing, it should be mentioned that Ingram found only 2 cases of epilepsy in a series of 105 obsessional patients (see Grimshaw, 1964, for a confirmatory view).

In sharp contrast, Pacella, Polatin, and Nagler (1944) found abnormal EEG signs ranging from "mild to severe" in 20 out of 31 reportedly obsessional patients. Neither the EEG findings nor the clinical data are convincing, and the sheer frequency of abnormal records is sufficient to raise doubts about the validity of their diagnoses. Few people would care to dispute that phobias are rarely functionally related to organic impairments, but 3 of the 4 phobic patients in this series surprisingly produced abnormal EEG records. The EEG diagnoses were based on loose criteria, were of unknown reliability, and apparently were interpreted by informed judges. The clinical data are also unsatisfactory; for example, patients with tics or phobias as their sole or main problem were classed as obsessional. On the ground that a hypothesis with such serious implications should not be proposed on the basis of poor evidence, Pacella and his colleagues' claim can be dismissed.

The Jarvie (1953) case referred to by Ingram and McAdam (1960) describes a young man who complained of longstanding irritability and episodic rages. This patient produced abnormal EEG records containing irregular delta wave activity of a type observed in Ingram and McAdam's patient, and eighteen months or so after the first recording was made he began to engage in mild checking rituals. According to Jarvie, there was no history of compulsions, but the patient reported some phobias and anxiety that antedated his first EEG examination. On the face of it, Jarvie attached undue significance to the mild compulsions, influenced no doubt by his belief that "anxiety-phobic symptoms are in a sense a stage towards more formalized compulsive phenomena" (p. 255). This case report contains no more than a slight hint of a link between an unspecified cerebral abnormality and compulsive behavior.

Rockwell and Simons (1947) recorded the EEGs of 24 patients with obsessional symptoms. Only 1 of the 11 patients with an uncomplicated obsessional neurosis produced an abnormal recording. The results obtained from one of the patients in the sample is instructive in demonstrating the difficulties involved in research of this kind. The first recording taken from this man, after a course of 55 subcoma insulin treatments, was abnormal. However, when the recording was repeated three months later it was found to be entirely normal. In the one patient from whom an abnormal record was obtained on more than one occasion, they adduced an interesting connection between the abnormal recording and the obsessional symptoms. The first recording was made when the patient's obsessional thinking was pronounced, and an excessive quantity of slow-wave activity was observed. The second recording, made when the patient was free of all symptoms but was experiencing "feelings of unreality," produced a different but still abnormal pattern. This suggests a possible association between the manifestation of his obsessional symptoms and organic disturbance.

Apart from these 11 clear-cut cases, Rockwell and Simons also took recordings from another 13 patients who were diagnosed as "psychopathic" but in addition had some obsessional symptoms. Interpretation of the finding that almost all of the second group produced abnormal EEG patterns is made difficult by the fact that they were psychopathic and were "characterized as follows: low ethical and moral standards, loose organization of personality and vague thinking and general inadequacy of personality" (Rockwell and Simons, 1947, p. 74). This description scarcely fits that of the typical obsessional patient, who, as we have seen, is rarely guilty of "stealing, lying, truancy and irresponsibility with regard to social and financial obligations" (p. 74). It would be inadvisable to treat these results as supporting the view that obsessional-compulsive disorders are associated with abnormal brain activity.

Placing greatest reliance on the report by Ingram and McAdam, we conclude that there is insufficient evidence to support the claim of a heightened incidence of EEG abnormalities in obsessional patients; there is no reason at all to assume a causal connection between some (unspecified) cerebral abnormality and obsessional disorders.

In his analysis of the neurological histories of 103 obsessional patients compared with those of 105 nonobsessional neurotic patients, Grimshaw (1964) found three cases of encephalitis among the obsessionals and none among the controls. There was also a significantly elevated incidence of convulsions in infancy, and of diphtheria and chorea. Overall, the incidence of neurological illnesses among the obsessional group was larger (19%) than in the control group (7.6%). The significance of this finding is not clear, and in the absence of supporting evidence it would be unwise to reach the premature conclusion that neurological impairment plays a major role in either the genesis or the maintenance of obsessional-compulsive problems. As Grimshaw points out, the earlier view proposed by Schilder (1938), that two-thirds of the patients with obsessional disorders have a neurological component of significance, is not supported.

Lewis (1966) stated that "encephalitis leghargica and a few other cerebral diseases may *produce* typical obsessional symptoms in persons previously free from demonstrable tendencies in this direction. Apart from the difficult instances in which lesions of the brain are accompanied by obsessions, the pathology is at present wholly a matter of psychopathology" (pp. 1199, 1200, emphasis added). After endorsing the idea that there is a causal connection between encephalitis and obsessional symptoms, he went on to express the view that neurological factors play a significant part in only a very small minority of obsessional disorders. Sternberg (1974) also supports the view that "brain damage may precede the onset of obsessional symptoms, as in encephalitis" (p. 294).

Their opinion is of course based on more evidence than the three cases contained in Grimshaw's retrospective survey. In the older literature there is a lengthy list of case descriptions purporting to demonstrate a relationship between postencephalitic conditions (and other neurological impairments) and obsessional neuroses. As the majority of these case reports rest on an unacceptably wide definition of obsessions and compulsions, there is no need to reexamine their details. Instead, we can accept that a connection (albeit rare) between the occurrence of unduly repetitive, stereotyped acts and neurological impairments has been demonstrated—but there is good reason for distinguishing between these repetitive activities and the obsessional-compulsive disorders that are the subject of this book. The distinction is well illustrated by reference to the work of Brickner, Rosner, and Munro (1940) and of Schilder (1938). Incidentally, in rejecting the undiscriminating extension of the term *obsessional neurosis* to the activities described in their writings, we are not also rejecting the possibility that there may be a functional relation of some sort between postencephalitic states and true obsessional disorders.

Brickner and his colleagues described seven cases in which there was an association between neurological impairment (postencephalitic states or epilepsy) and obsessional states, which they define widely to include "repetitive and fixed states" (p. 380), that range from automatisms, through echolalia and catatonia, to typical compulsive activities. "Such repetitive or fixed behavior . . . in the motor field is called compulsive, and in the strictly motor sphere it has a variety of names—perseveration, catatonia, propulsion, iteration, echolalia, pallilalia, stereotype of movement or thought" (p. 370). They go on to state that "the uniform thread of repetitiveness or fixedness which runs through all of these suggests that a common physiological mechanism may underlie them."

Case number 1 was a patient with a left temporal lobe abnormality whose epileptic seizures were "initiated by an auditory repetition . . . of whatever words or sounds reached her ears at the time" (p. 371)—clearly not the obsessional-compulsive phenomena with which we are concerned. The compulsion lacks intellectual content, purpose, or intentionality, and is mechanical. These authors' postencephalitic examples include mechanical and purposeless repetitions of puffing, blowing, scratching, rubbing one's eyes, rolling one's tongue, compulsive swallowing, grimacing, and so forth. In short, very few of their examples bear a close resemblance to obsessional-compulsive phenomena as currently defined. The exceptions are patients who felt compelled to repeat certain phrases and/or resist unwanted intrusive thoughts. The relationship between these obsessional phenomena and neurological impairment (notably postencephalitic states) is lost in the mass of descriptions of predominantly irrelevant clinical details. Clarification will not be achieved until more precise, contained, methodical studies are undertaken.

Given that a tiny percentage of obsessions and/or compulsions appear in close association with certain kinds of organic impairment, do they have any distinguishing features? Our view, based, it must be said, entirely on the evidence described in the literature, is that there are such features. They appear to include the following: (1) the patient has a history of injury, illness, or birth complication; (2) the obsession or compulsion lacks intellectual content; (3) the obsession or compulsion has no intentional component; (4) there are associated deficits (e.g., impairments of memory or learning, intelligence significantly below that of other members of the family, etc.); (5) the compulsions have a stereotyped, mechanical quality; (6) the compulsions have a primitive quality. If the regular occurrence of a combination of these features can be confirmed, and if it can be shown that they are critical, then the best course would be to regard these "organic obsessional-compulsive disorders" as being psychologically and phenomenologically distinct. Insofar as our analysis and argument is supported, the psychological—as opposed to medical—conception of obsessional-compulsive disorders is preferred. If, on the other hand, new evidence indicative of a causal and common link between organic impairments and obsessions is presented, the explanatory value of a purely psychological theory will be narrowed.

OBSESSIONS AND PHOBIAS

It has been argued that

> most forms of phobia are best construed as instances of passive avoidance; hence one would expect to find an affinity between phobias and compulsive cleaning. There should be less similarity between phobias and compulsive checking . . . compulsive cleaners are more likely to have concurrent phobias or a history of earlier phobias. They might also show evidence of a wider range of ordinary fears and perhaps at a more intense level than is encountered in the general population . . . It is predicted that

they are more fearful than compulsive checkers. [Rachman, 1976, pp. 271-72]

The distinctive nature of characteristic obsessional fears, focused most often on dirt/disease and contamination, leads naturally to the execution of extensive avoidance behavior. People who are excessively frightened of dirt/disease/contamination take particular care to avoid coming into contact with disease or dirt (this is mainly a passive form of avoidance). When these attempts at avoidance fail, then the person attempts to "escape."

Translated into concrete examples, the obsessional phobic passively avoids dustbins, public facilities such as lavatories and washrooms, doorhandles and telephones, sick people, hospitals, and so forth. Failure to avoid any one of these stimuli leads to escape behavior designed to remove or reduce the danger signals. The classical form of escape behavior is repetitive cleaning—hence, compulsive cleaning behavior can be construed as the natural consequence of a dirt/disease/contamination phobia. If this construction is correct, then obsessional-compulsive cleaning behavior is best seen as a subclass of the larger category of phobias. This argument is continued and expanded in Chapters 9 and 25.

Pieces of supporting evidence for the view that there is a close association between phobias and obsessional-compulsive disorders can be assembled from a number of investigations of the natural history of obsessional disorders. For example, Skoog (1959) found that his large sample of "anancastic" patients was excessively fearful. Kringlen (1965) reported that over 50 percent of the 91 obsessional patients included in his series complained of phobic symptoms. Kringlen subdivided the obsessional patients into four categories and concluded that one-third of the group had a mixture of obsessional thoughts, acts, and phobias while 19 percent had "predominantly or solely phobias" (p. 714). The stability of the phobic symptoms is attested to by the fact that when the follow-up investigation was carried out, an average of 16 years after admission to the hospital, no less than 69 percent of the remaining 84 patients complained of phobic symptoms. These symptoms were in fact the most common complaint at follow-up. Forty percent of Videbech's (1975) 104 depressed obsessionals reported phobias, but Welner and his colleagues (1976) found associated *phobias*, as opposed to phobic symptoms, in only 7 out of 150 severely obsessional patients. Orme (1965) administered two psychometric scales to a variety of psychiatric patients. As the 15 obsessional patients and the 15 phobic patients gave "almost identical mean scores on both scales" (measuring obsessionality and emotional stability), the results were combined. This combined phobic and obsessional group returned the highest scores on the emotional-instability scale and on the obsessional scale.

Additional supporting evidence is found in the significantly high incidence of reported phobias in the childhood of obsessional patients (see Chapter 5). For example, Lo (1967, p. 827) reports that 35 percent of his 59 obsessional patients had significant phobias during childhood, and Videbech (1975) reported the same for half of his 104 depressed obsessional patients. Similarly, Ingram (1961) reports that 25 percent of his 89 obsessional patients had significant phobias in childhood. In their follow-up of 100 adolescent school-phobics, Berg, Butler, and Hall (1976) found that within the brief space of three years, 4 patients had developed obsessional disorders and another 26 had "persistent neurotic symptoms including those of anxiety, depression and obsessions" (p. 82). Five of Warren's (1960) 15 adolescent obsessional patients had "phobic symptoms at some time" (p. 821).

It is also of some interest that, according to Rosenberg (1967, p. 410), a considerable number of the relatives of obsessional patients suffer from anxiety neurosis. In his sample of 47 patients, only 2 of the relatives had been treated for "a definite obsessional neurosis," whereas 14 of them had been treated for an anxiety neurosis. Overall, the clinical material drawn from different samples and for different purposes contains many hints of an affinity between phobias and obsessional disorders. If the present argument is sustained, the association between phobias and obsessional-compulsive problems will become more evident when the obsessional-compulsive population is subdivided into those who are concerned predominantly with compulsive cleaning rituals and those who are engaged mainly in compulsive checking.

Finally, it should be said that recognition of an affinity between obsessions and phobias is inherent in Eysenck's general theory of personality. It will be recalled that both of these neurotic disorders are classed as dysthymic and fall into that quadrant that contains people who return high scores on both neuroticism and introversion.

CLASSIFICATION

We are disinclined to devote much attention to the diagnostic problems that face psychiatrists in dealing with actual or potential cases of obsessional-compulsive neurosis because, as we have argued, the nonmedical construction of the disorder is preferable. At the same time, it is idle to ignore the fact that many psychiatrists and a minority of clinical psychologists will continue to use prevailing diagnostic habits. The need to decide between one or another type of difficulty will not disappear, even if the medical model is abandoned. Our preference is to carry out a behavioral and psychological analysis of the problems presented by the person, and for these purposes, as well as current diagnostic practice, it might prove useful to have a broad guide to the distinguishing characteristics of obsessional-compulsive problems and related difficulties (see Table 7.1). This guide is intended to be used not as a basis for conventional diagnosis or rigid classification but, rather, as an aid to decision making in the broad sense.

TABLE 7.1: DISTINCTIVE FEATURES OF OBSESSIONAL-COMPULSIVE
DISORDERS AND THEIR RELATION TO SCHIZOPHRENIA,
ORGANIC IMPAIRMENTS, MORBID PREOCCUPATIONS, AND
"OBSESSIONAL PERSONALITY"

Obsessions

- are unwanted
- have aggressive/sexual themes
- provoke internal resistance
- cause distress
- are recognized to be of internal origin
- are recognized to be senseless (insight)
- are ego-alien
- are associated with lack of confidence in memory or reality of memory
- are associated with depression

Compulsions are distinguished by repetitive, stereotyped behavior that

- is preceded or accompanied by a sense of compulsion that is recognized to be of internal origin
- provokes internal resistance
- is recognized to be senseless (insight)
- may cause embarrassment or distress
- is difficult to control over the long term

Schizophrenic Conditions differ in that the intrusive ideas, images, or impulses are

- attributed to external forces
- not necessarily ego-alien
- not regarded as senseless (lack of insight)
- unlikely to provoke internal resistance

Organic Impairments may involve repetitive ideas or acts that

- lack intellectual content
- lack intentionality
- have a mechanical and/or primitive quality

Morbid Preoccupations (see Rachman, 1973) involve intrusive, repetitive ideas that are

- ego-syntonic
- rational (but exaggerated)
- realistic, and current in content
- seldom resisted

"Obsessional Personality" Traits

- show greater stability than obsessional disorders
- are ego-syntonic
- seldom cause distress
- are seldom accompanied by a sense of compulsion
- seldom provoke resistance

Chapter 8

Conventional Treatment and Prognosis

The pessimism that permeates the psychiatric literature on obsessions and compulsions is most evident in discussions of the outcome of the disorder. Most writers discount the possibility that the outcome can be influenced by treatment.

The outcome statistics are usually presented without reference to treatment. Instead, the evidence is assembled and estimates of recovery are proposed without regard to the type or duration of treatment provided, despite the fact that few obsessional-compulsive patients fail to receive some treatment. There is so little confidence in conventional treatment that few writers take the trouble to distinguish between spontaneous remission rates and treatment remission rates. In addition to the more familiar expressions of therapeutic pessimism [e.g., "In others, whose affliction is chronic, recovery is out of the question" (Lewis, 1966, p. 1201)], one finds lengthy discussions of prognosis in which the influence of formal treatment is dismissed in a perfunctory paragraph (e.g., Kringlen, 1970; Lo, 1967). Although some writers cautiously allow that psychosurgery may influence the natural course of the disorder, there is little enthusiasm for this or any other form of treatment.

In his interesting retrospective study of the fate of 100 obsessional patients followed for a mean of 5 years, Grimshaw (1964) reported that "64 percent were improved as far as symptoms were concerned, with full social adaptation, 40 percent to the point of recovery or very considerable improvement . . . Improvement could not be attributed to any definite form of treatment" (p. 1055). He concluded the discussion by pointing out that his findings were "in agreement with Lewis and Pollard that improvement cannot be attributed to a definite form of treatment. In fact, the proportion of improved cases is not markedly different in any of the major treatment groups; the group receiving no specialist treatment fared the best of all, with about 70 percent having a satisfactory result" (p. 1055). In similar style, Goodwin, Guze, and Robins (1969) concluded from their review of thirteen follow-up studies that "obsessional neurosis is a chronic illness for which, at this time, there is no specific, definitive treatment. The road to recovery is seldom smooth, and some patients never get well." Black (1974) argues that "with the exception of leucotomy, no treatment has been shown to influence long-term outcome of obsessional illness, so fortunately, in this respect, the influence of different therapies can be discounted" (p. 43).

Although the therapeutic value of leucotomy will be considered presently, it should be said that Black's optimism is not widely shared. For example, in his analysis of the effects of treatment Cawley (1974) argues that the improved outcome observed in patients who have undergone the operation "is likely to be a comment on the selection procedures for leucotomy rather than on specific effects of the operation" (p. 281). Ingram (1961) and Sternberg (1974) express similar opinions (see p. 104). Goodwin and his associates (1969) argued that there is a limited place for the operation, but were careful to point out the dangers. "For a small minority of patients, therefore, lobotomy may warrant consideration. Before undertaking such a radical, irreversible treatment, evaluation by 2 or more psychiatrists is highly desirable . . . If used at all, [it] should be reserved for the severely disabled obsessional patient with classical symptoms (especially rituals) who fails to respond to other treatments and is totally disabled for a prolonged period" (p. 186).

ANTIDEPRESSANT MEDICATION

Given the close association between depression and obsessional disorders, it is reasonable to expect that *any* successful antidepressant treatment, using drugs or other means, should produce useful changes in many obsessional cases. As there are grounds for supposing that depression can act as a facilitator or as a maintaining factor in obsessions, successful antidepressant treatment may in some cases truncate an ongoing disorder and in others serve a preventive function. The antidepressant drug that has attracted most attention so far is clomipramine. If there is a particular reason for this preference, it is the hypothesis that clomipramine, in addition to its antidepressant properties, has a specific therapeutic effect on obsessions.

It has been claimed by Fernandez and Lopez-Ibor (1969) and Capstick (1973), among others, that clomipramine is effective in the treatment of obsessional-compulsive complaints, and an impressive number of clinical reports point to a similar conclusion (Walter, 1973; Rack, 1973; Waxman, 1975; Beaumont, 1973; Capstick, 1975; Yaryura-Tobias, 1975). On the other hand, Rigby and his colleagues (1973) had a poor result.

Insofar as clomipramine is an effective antidepressant and depression is a prominent feature of many obsessional disorders, it should be capable of reducing obsessional difficulties—at least as a secondary consequence. However, Capstick (1973, 1975) claims that the drug has, in addition, a specially antiobsessional action—surely a valuable advance. However, these claims were based on inadequate evidence. No randomized control trial employing blind assessments, placebo comparisons, and the rest had been reported before the conclusion of the MRC Project directed by Marks and Rachman (1979). The outcome of this trial is described in Chapter 22 and supports the claim that clomipramine has a primary effect on depression and a secondary effect on obsessional problems.

Sternberg (1974) offers a list of drugs that, on present evidence, should be avoided, as there is no evidence that they help and some indication that they may be harmful: lysergic acid, methyl amphetamine, intravenous acetylcholine, insulin, stilboestrol, reserpine, metrazole, and carbon dioxide abreactions.

There is little support for the use of ECT (e.g., Grimshaw, 1964), with the possible exception of its use with patients in whom depression is a prominent and complicating factor (Goodwin et al., 1969; Sternberg, 1974).

OUTCOME

Notwithstanding the inadequacies of the available evidence, it is necessary to sketch the broad course of obsessional disorders, regardless of treatment. It is difficult to improve on the succinct conclusion reached by Cawley (1974):

> If a series of patients with obsessional illnesses, severe enough to be treated at some time in hospital, is looked at after about 5 years have elapsed, it can be expected that one-fourth will have recovered; about one-half will have improved a good deal, though they will still experience symptoms, possibly incapacitating; and the remaining one-fourth will be unchanged or worse. Of the last sub-group, a few will have come to be recognized as schizophrenic. For a series not having needed hospitalization, about two-thirds will be much improved in terms of symptom relief and social adjustment, whilst the remainder will have improved to a lesser extent, or be unchanged or worse. These remarks apply to patients treated by the routine methods which have been available at various times over the last 30 years or so. [p. 280]

Overall, it would appear that the outlook for obsessional patients is slightly worse than that for people suffering from other types of neurotic disorder (see

Rachman, 1971). In the light of the current evidence, the advice offered by Goodwin and his associates (1969) is worth bearing in mind. "The data justify a certain measure of optimism about the 'natural' course of obsessional neurosis. It is evident that spontaneous improvement occurs rather often, and the patient can be apprised of this. He can be reassured that his impulses to commit injury or socially embarrassing acts almost certainly will not be carried out, given the nature of his illness. He can be reassured that he will not—as he often fears—lose his mind" (p. 186). Some interesting examples of patients who reported spontaneous improvements are given by Grimshaw (1964). Although one or two of the patients in his series, and indeed in our own, attributed part of their troubles to excessive pressure at work, it is interesting to notice that some of the patients described by Grimshaw attributed their *improvement*, in some measure, to persisting in employment. Lewis (1966) was persuaded of the therapeutic value of work and recommended that "patients should be encouraged to continue at their occupation" (p. 1201). This advice has an excellent pedigree. In 1692 John Moore recommended in his book *Religious Melancholy* that people so affected should avoid idleness. "I exhort you not to quit your Imployment . . . for no business at all is as bad for you as too much," and he went on to make the memorable remark that "there is always more Melancholy to be found in a Cloyster, than in the Market-place" (quoted by Hunter & McAlpine, 1963, p. 253).

The traditional recourse to recommending work as therapy can also be found in Maudsley's (1895) *Pathology of the Mind*. "How to do best in order to subdue the present temptation and to lay the good foundations of recovery? To inhibit and starve morbid function by discharging the energy of it into other channels of activity, either of thought or of movement: of thought, by a resolute and steady application of mind to wholesome intellectual work, so as to strengthen sound and weaken unsound function . . . of movement, by the temporary expedient of active and even violent exertion of some sort," on the indisputable ground that "no one who is racing for a wager or for his life would be sorely troubled with the impulse to utter obscene words or to do an indecent act" (pp. 185-86).

In the absence of any specific form of treatment, Lewis (1966) recommended that patients be given emotional support and practical advice "about the management of their lives," including encouragement to continue working. Grimshaw (1964) concluded his survey of the effects of different types of treatment with similar recommendations. Arguing that "no elaborate type of therapy seems indicated," he advised "a regime of emotional support, with or without simple sedation or stimulation, sufficient to fortify the patient's morale during a difficult time is probably the most practical of all" (p. 1055). Having concluded that "there is no evidence to support or refute the proposition that formal psychotherapy helps patients with obsessional disorders," Cawley (1974) recommended the use of informal therapy, supplemented by drugs or other procedures that seem likely to help in the particular case. His conclusion that obsessional disorders are "unlikely to be helped on any large scale by formal psychotherapy" appears to be shared by most writers other than those of the psychoanalytic persuasion. That Cawley and the other critics are well advised to refrain from recommending psychotherapy for obsessional disorders is consistent with present knowledge of the effects of psychotherapy (Rachman, 1971). On the question of psychoanalytic treatment, it is worth while quoting Lewis (1966). "Obsessional patients, so prone to rumination and endless questioning, often clamor to be psychoanalyzed. There is no evidence that psychoanalysis, however, prolonged, benefits them more than methods that are not so exigent of time and money" (p. 1201). Similarly, Grimshaw (1964) concluded that psychoanalysis yielded no better results than other forms of treatment, all of which were in any event ineffective (for an evaluation of psychoanalytic treatment in general, see Rachman and Wilson, 1979).

PROGNOSIS

In view of the incomplete, unconfirmed, and retrospective nature of the evidence, it is scarcely surprising that we have little reliable information about prognostic indicators. So, for example, on the question of premorbid obsessional personality some findings suggest that this is a favorable prognostic sign while others indicate that it is an unfavorable prognostic sign. A third study yielded no relation whatever between premorbid personality and outcome (see Black, 1974, p. 45). Similar conflicts of evidence are found on the question of the prognostic significance of episodic versus constant course, the presence or absence of precipitating factors, and the presence or absence of atypical symptoms. There is some agreement, however, that patients with a long history of obsessional difficulties do worse than those with a short history, and that patients with marked affective symptoms and/or stable personality do better (e.g., Sternberg, 1974). There is some slight evidence that obsessional problems in childhood, unmarried status, and nervousness in childhood are unfavorable prognostic signs (Black, p. 46). Lastly, there is reasonable agreement about the following factors, which are said to be unrelated to prognosis: age, sex, intelligence, family history, content of obsessions (Black, p. 46; Lewis, 1966). Reviews of this information are provided by Goodwin and his colleagues (1969); Kringlen (1965, 1970); Lo (1967); Black (1974), and Sternberg (1974).

In our own research (de Silva, Rachman, and Seligman, 1977), retrospective and incomplete though it is, we found that severity was correlated with an unfavorable outcome, as were an "abnormal personality" and the adoption of "an obsessional life style." Unlike some other workers, we found no correlation between age of onset and outcome. An account of the lack of success in identifying prognostic indicators in a series of connected *prospective* clinical trials is given in Chapter 22.

PSYCHOSURGERY

The claim that psychosurgery is an effective method of treating obsessional disorders incorporates three main elements. It is argued that the operation is (1) especially suitable for treating obsessional neuroses and (2) is most effective in treating chronic and (3) intractable cases. If sustained, these claims would be particularly convenient and welcome, offering as they do some hope for patients who (by definition) are beyond help by other methods. In the course of briefly reviewing the evidence on the effects of psychosurgery on obsessional neuroses, an attempt will be made to evaluate this triple claim (a detailed evaluation is provided by Rachman, 1979).

Although there was a short period during which it was believed, or hoped, that psychosurgery might provide an effective way of treating obsessional disorders, current enthusiasm for these procedures is confined to a small group of advocates. Contemporary advocates are careful to express the view that surgical intervention should be restricted to only the most intractable and chronic cases (e.g., Goktepe, Young, and Bridges, 1975, p. 279).

The view expressed by Kolb in 1973 is representative: "Probably the best results in lobotomy are secured in agitated depressions and in severe obsessive-compulsive reactions accompanied by so much tension that the patient is incapacitated" (p. 653). Unfortunately, there is no basis for this claim with respect to obsessional disorders. If anything, it is the mild cases that respond most, but even that possibility is a slender one.

Is the operation carried out solely on chronic cases? If "chronic" is taken to mean an illness duration of five years or more, then it is not confined to chronic cases. The operation is performed, not uncommonly, on patients with an illness duration of two years or less—and, of related importance, on people in their early 20s. Bearing in mind the occurrence of spontaneous remissions among obsessional patients (e.g., Pollitt, 1957), it seems preferable to adopt a strict definition of chronicity when considering psychosurgery. Even though we are handicapped by inadequate evidence, a conservative estimate of the spontaneous-remission rate for all neuroses, over a two-year period, is ± 60 percent (Rachman, 1971). The crude, estimated rate for obsessionals is lower, at 40 percent. In these circumstances, performing a serious operation on a patient who has not passed the two-year high-remission rate is difficult to justify. For purposes of psychosurgery, even the advocates of the operation would do well to adopt a strict definition of chronicity. The term should be restricted to disorders that have persisted for more than five years.

In order to appreciate the role of psychosurgery in the treatment of obsessional disorders, it is necessary to remember that these operations (Knight, 1964, listed seven variations) were introduced as a cure not for obsessions but for schizophrenia [e.g., 60% of an early sample of patients reported on by Kolb (1973) were schizophrenic and only 10% were neurotic (see also Sternberg, 1974; Willett, 1960)]. As might have been predicted, the use of psychosurgery was soon extended to include disorders ranging from depression to hypochondria (Bernstein, 1975), delinquency, alcoholism, anxiety states, and so on (see Sykes and Tredgold, 1964; Strom-Olsen and Carlisle, 1971). It was even claimed that psychosurgery is marginally helpful in alleviating tuberculosis (Cheng, Tait, and Freeman, 1956).

Imperceptibly, a shift in emphasis took place, and by 1960 a number of textbook writers gave the opinion that leucotomy was useful primarily in treating obsessions rather than schizophrenia. The skepticism about the value of psychosurgery for treating schizophrenia (e.g., Willett, 1960) has now spread to its use on obsessional patients (e.g., Cawley, 1974; Sternberg, 1974). It need hardly be argued that the use of such radical procedures can be justified only on the ground of demonstrable success, in the absence of satisfactory alternatives. It is argued that neither of these conditions is met and that therefore the psychosurgical treatment of obsessional paients cannot be justified at present.

What are the reasons for the present misgivings about operating on obsessional and, indeed, other psychiatric patients? It is an intervention that carries a slight risk of serious danger for the patient. There is an absence of persuasive evidence that the operation produces therapeutic benefits. Alternate and considerably less dangerous methods are available, including the newly developed behavioral treatments. No serious attempt has been made to explain why surgery should reduce obsessional disorders; even if there were acceptable empirical proof of its therapeutic value, we would remain in the dark about the process of change. The earlier, but now discredited, claim that psychosurgery is an effective treatment for schizophrenia is doubly worrying. In the first place, it provides another sharp warning about our credulity in therapeutic matters, and in the second place it reminds us that the recommendation of surgery for *obsessional disorders* is secondhand and atheoretical.

Are we in a position to dispel these misgivings? Unfortunately, we are not; hence, advocates who continue to recommend and use psychosurgery are obliged to provide suitably powerful reasons for so doing. Their arguments are empirical (see Rachman, 1979).

It is worth pointing out that the use of surgical interventions is based on and helps perpetuate the notion that obsessional disorders are illnesses. There can be little doubt that acceptance of the alternate view, that obsessional disorders are better construed as psychological problems, would reduce the likelihood of anyone's proposing a surgical solution. To place the matter in perspective, however, it is necessary to preface the discussion by noting that, to the best of our knowledge, no randomized, controlled clinical trial has ever been reported. The most satisfactory reports, all of them of recent origin, are those describing the results obtained in prospective series of patients. Although prospective studies are superior to those in which the material is collected retrospectively, this advantage should not obscure the fact that in none of the reported series was any attempt made to compare the effects of psychosurgery with those of conventional treatment, drug treatment, behavior therapy, and so forth. In addition, there is no series in which allocation to treatment was determined randomly (i.e., selection or rejection for treatment was itself a clinical decision). In none of the reports was the independent assessor, where one was employed, kept ignorant of the type of treatment provided. Of course, one must recognize the problems involved in providing an independent assessment of the effects of psychosurgery. In all therapeutic-outcome research, it is difficult to ensure that the independent assessors remain ignorant of the type of treatment the patient has received, and in assessing the effects of psychosurgery it may be impossible to achieve single-blind control. Despite its theoretical desirability, the use of a double-blind control procedure would rapidly lead to a depletion of the sample. The fact remains that the evidence of these clinical assessors is open to bias. Other defects of the series reported so far include the selection and use of inappropriate psychometric tests and the failure to obtain preoperative assessments of function and disorder.

A certain number of obsessional patients will experience improvements after undergoing psychosurgery, but it remains unclear whether these changes exceed in magnitude or duration those following other treatments or no treatment at all. The report by Mitchell-Heggs and her colleagues (1976) suggests that the changes occur far too rapidly to be regarded as spontaneous remissions, but the weaknesses of their study preclude a firm conclusion about the specific value of the operation. It seems most unlikely that the operation produces a specific improvement in the course of an obsessional disorder, and in any event there are preferable alternatives. Although the spontaneous-remission rate among obsessional patients is almost certainly lower than that observed among other forms of neurotic disorder, the rate is not insubstantial (see Chapter 8). Obsessional patients who receive conventional treatment or no specific treatment do not necessarily have a bleak outlook. Of 30 nonleucotomized patients followed up for 3 months to 15 years, "21 showed this [considerable] degree of improvement or recovery"; that is, 64 percent were "either free of symptoms or able to carry on a normal life" (Pollitt, 1957, p. 198). More recently, Lo (1967) reported an encouraging outcome of 71 percent improvement in a group of 87 obsessional patients, none of whom had undergone psychosurgery. Cawley (1974) has argued that even though leucotomized patients are sometimes observed to do well after the operation, this is likely to reflect the selection procedures for leucotomy rather than the specific effects of the operation. Sternberg (1974) reached a similar conclusion: "While half the patients with obsessional disorders who have some form of leucotomy may be expected to benefit greatly, there are also the patients who have a better prognosis without leucotomy. Those undergoing operation run a 1.5 to 4 percent risk of dying and 16 percent may be expected to have up to 12 epileptic fits" (p. 303). Ingram's (1961) summary is still applicable. "Many of the factors said to favor the outcome of operation are seen to be the same as those favoring spontaneous improvement. The prominence of affective symptoms, the absence of motor symptoms, and late onset are all held to favor a good leucotomy result; here they are associated with spontaneous improvement" (p. 399).

In view of the fact that psychosurgery was originally introduced as a method for the treatment of schizophrenia, it is scarcely surprising to find that there is no theoretical rationale for recommending surgery for obsessional patients; at best, it is sometimes argued that the operation will produce general changes (e.g., reduced tension) and that these may produce secondary benefits in the form of reduced compulsive behavior and the like. To the best of our knowledge, no one has made a serious attempt to trace a specific connection between psychosurgery and the reduction of obsessional-compulsive problems. It follows, of course, that if the rationale for using psychosurgery on these patients is to be an indirect one—that is to say, the benefits are secondary—then it is not unreasonable to look for a rationale of the primary effects *and* of the relation between these effects and the putative secondary benefits. So, for example, if it is argued that the operations reduce psychological tension, one needs to know why. Furthermore, the putative relation between reduced tension and an improvement in the obsessional disorder needs to be explained and defended. As mentioned earlier, if improvements in obsessional difficulties are secondary to some other change, then it is essential to show that the *primary* action (e.g., reduced tension) cannot be achieved by other, safer, simpler, nonintrusive methods.

Returning to the opening question of this assessment, it has to be said that on present evidence none of the three elements of the therapeutic claims made on behalf of psychosurgery is supportable. The operations are not especially suitable for treating obsessional disorders, and they are not most effective for treating either chronic or intractable cases. In one sense the use of psychosurgery for treating obsessional disorders is a scientific curiosity. Proponents of psychosurgery justify its use on empirical grounds, but on inspection it turns out that this empirically based treatment has an inadequate empirical basis.

In the present circumstances there is little reason to recommend psychosurgery for obsessional disorders. The alternatives include behavioral treatment, antidepressant medication, and supportive counseling. It is when all of these meethods have failed that the desperate but unwise resort to psychosurgery is raised [except in some of the series reviewed by Rachman (1979), in which there was a more hasty resort to the knife]. The belief that psychosurgery is of value in dealing with the most intractable cases is even less well founded than the hope that it is of value in improving the prospects of tractable cases.

SECTION B

Chapter 9

Cleaning
and Checking Compulsions

In this chapter an account is given of the central features of cleaning and checking compulsions—the two major forms of abnormal compulsions. Their similarities and differences are analyzed, and it is argued that there is an affinity between cleaning compulsions and phobias. This analysis, which moves from cleaning to checking compulsions, should not be misinterpreted to mean that the two types are mutually exclusive. Many people display features of both forms, usually with one predominating.

At many stages it has been helpful to construe abnormal compulsions as forms of avoidance behavior in which attempts are made to avoid aversive experiences. In both of the major forms of compulsion, there appears to be a large element of active avoidance; the person carries out certain acts in an attempt to avoid an aversive outcome. However, in cleaning compulsions there is, in addition, a significant element of *passive* avoidance, in which one avoids aversive stimulation by *refraining* from carrying out various actions. So while checking and cleaning compulsions appear actively to forestall anticipated aversive events, the cleaning compulsions are, in addition, associated with passive avoidance of contact with dirt, germs, or other contaminants. When attempts at passive avoidance fail, as in everyday life they frequently are bound to do, the compulsive cleaner *escapes* from the immediate aversiveness of the contaminant by removing it—in short, by cleaning. The term *compulsive cleaning* is preferred because it includes activities in which people compulsively clean objects in addition to, or instead of, cleaning or washing themselves and others. *Cleaning* includes the term *washing* and a variety of similar rituals that do not involve washing (e.g., dusting).

A compulsion is defined as a repetitive, partly stereotyped type of behavior that is preceded or accompanied by a sense of pressure, usually provokes internal resistance, is at least partly irrational, and often causes distress or embarrassment. Although cleaning compulsions can take several forms, the most common type is the classical hand-washing syndrome that for many people epitomizes obsessional-compulsive behavior.

COMPULSIVE CLEANING

Although compulsive cleaners are able in their quieter moments to recognize irrationality in their behavior, they passively avoid many places, people, and objects and feel compelled to carry out repetitive, excessive, stereotyped cleaning. The expressed intention of carrying out compulsive cleaning rituals is to remove dirty or contaminated material (to escape), with the longer-term aim of ensuring the health and comfort of the patient and of other people with whom he or she is likely to come into contact (active avoidance of future aversiveness). If someone whose expressed intention is to remove dirt is pressed for an explanation of that conduct, one almost always reaches a level of explanation that the patient recognizes as partly irrational. So, for example, a patient might say that he is washing his hands in order to remove the dirt contacted while cleaning the garbage container (a common source of trouble for many compulsive cleaners). If he is pressed to explain why this process requires so many repetitions, he might say that his aim is to achieve certainty about the removal of the dirt. If pressed further, he might explain that failure to remove every last speck of dirt might have untoward consequences. The next level of explanation almost always involves some fear of contamination leading to ill health or a disease process. When asked to specify the kind of disease and the likelihood of contracting it, the person's explanations become vague, and ultimately the irrational level is acknowledged. The irrationality need concern not the act of cleaning but, rather, the gross disproportion between the risks involved and the amount of repetitive and excessive cleaning that is undertaken. In many instances the concern about dirt or disease has all of the most important qualities of a phobia. It is an excessive, largely irrational fear.

It is not uncommon to find that there is a nonrational, even magical quality to the fear and the consequent cleaning rituals. So, for example, one of our patients carried out up to fifty compulsive washes each day in order to neutralize his unacceptable, violent thoughts about his parents. Another patient feared that she might contract a fatal disease from germs that were capable of jumping across large spaces and finding their way to her two hands. If for some practical reason she was unable to carry out her daily compulsive washing, she successfully resorted to a "magical" wash in which she removed all contaminating germs by wiping her hands with a linen handkerchief that she had imbued with supernatural cleaning powers. In other exceptional cases a sense of contamination can be contracted simply by reading some disturbing material, from a television program, or from a remark made by some other person. When the resulting emotional state is attributed to some contaminating process, the person is able to achieve immediate, if temporary, relief by carrying out a cleaning ritual. As can be imagined, people who have a propensity to develop these intensive cleaning rituals tend to have a hard time of it when caring for infants and young children. Not infrequently their fears of contamination are transferred, in part, to the child and help compound both the fears and the cleaning rituals.

Compulsive cleaners are mainly trying to avoid contact with danger, discomfort, or fear, whereas compulsive checkers often appear to be taking steps to avoid future criticism or guilt. Compulsive cleaning rituals are predominantly *restorative* whereas compulsive checking rituals are predominantly attempts at *prevention.* The person takes care to avoid coming into contact with any of the potentially upsetting stimulus situations; when attempts at passive avoidance fail, he or she engages in escape behavior.

Clinical examples of cleaning rituals include the following: A 24-year-old woman had a fear of passing on infectious diseases, particularly to children, old people, and close relatives. As a result she engaged in extensive avoidance behavior. Whenever she was unable to avoid contact with a possible source of disease, she carried out extensive washing rituals, disposed of contaminating clothing and other property, and avoided places where the imagined contamination had been experienced. The fear and associated rituals were of 6 years' duration. A 22-year-old married woman had an intense fear of contamination from dogs. Over 5 years the problem had generalized to include many areas of England; even reading or hearing about these places triggered prolonged washing rituals. Her fears led to repeated changes of residence. A 42-year-old woman practiced hand-washing and house-cleaning rituals over a 26-year period. The rituals were prolonged and seriously interfered with her social life and her relationship with her husband. She found it impossible to truncate her rituals in order to prepare dinner for the family or get to bed at a reasonable hour. Any contact with dirt, dust, dustbins, toilets, carpets, floors, and so forth triggered excessive hand washing. A 38-year-old mother of one child was obsessed by a fear of contamination for over 20 years. Her concern with the possibility of being infected by germs resulted in washing and cleaning rituals that invaded all aspects of her life. Her child was restrained in one room, which was kept entirely germ free. She opened and closed all doors with her feet in order to avoid contaminating her hands. A 37-year-old woman had for 8 years feared the possibility of being contaminated by the water supply, and as a result she avoided toilets and washed her hands and arms compulsively. A 45-year-old man was troubled for 28 years by his intense fear of semen and dirt. As a result he engaged in extensive washing rituals and avoided large areas of the London region. A 26-year-old married woman had an intense fear of sexual contamination and over a 5-year period engaged in prolonged and demanding hand-washing rituals.

※ Most of these patients engaged in extensive passive-avoidance behavior, taking care to keep away from entire suburbs, towns, and even regions. Many of them were careful not to touch a wide range of household objects or certain kinds of people, or to read certain kinds of material. Carried to its extreme, the adoption of passive-avoidance behavior leads to immobilization. The patient who was too frightened to touch her own children was reduced to sitting in a single safely disinfected chair for most of her waking hours. Many other patients became virtually housebound. It is not stretching the analogy too far if one calls to mind the descriptions of the immobilized behavior displayed by experimental animals in whom neuroses were artificially induced (e.g., Masserman, 1943; Wolpe, 1958; etc.). Many of these animals developed pathological passivity and avoidance.

When passive avoidance fails, the patients, like the experimental subjects, attempt to escape. In the case of fears based on the perceived dangers of contamination, the appropriate escape behavior is to engage in cleaning activities.

At what point do cleaning rituals qualify for the label "abnormal"? There is no clear dividing line, but a fully developed cleaning ritual is easy to recognize. As a general rule, one can say that when any cleaning activity becomes excessively repetitive and stereotyped, and is accompanied by a degree of internal resistance, the adjective *abnormal* may well be appropriate. In the case illustrations mentioned earlier, there was little doubt about the abnormality of the behavior.

Although this question will be gone into in some detail later, it is worth mentioning that the frequency with which comparable compulsive cleaning rituals develop in many different people runs contrary to the so-called "equipotentiality premise." It is straining credulity to suggest that the frequency with which compulsive hand washing is observed follows a random pattern of distribution. It cannot be a matter of mere coincidence that so many of the patients develop contamination fears, are concerned about dirt and disease, and engage in such similar forms of cleaning ritual.

Bearing in mind that our own clinical series cannot be regarded as representative, we found equal numbers of compulsive cleaners showing narrow or broad generalization of their fears and associated rituals. On the other hand, the proportion of patients who described a sudden onset to those who described a gradual onset was on the order of 3 to 1. Moreover, the association between a gradual onset of the disorder and a circumscribed focus was extremely uncommon. Sudden onset and circumscribed focus were (weakly) associated.

We found in our psychometric studies that compulsive cleaning rituals tend to be shorter, more often restorative than preventive, and less often associated with indecisiveness than was the case with checking rituals. They were far more often said to result in immediate, if temporary, relief than checking rituals. This self-report information is, as we will see, concordant with the results of our experiments on the effects of executing the appropriate ritualistic behavior (see Chapter 11).

Like checking rituals, compulsive cleaning can be triggered by an external or an internal precipitant. Our strong impression from clinical experience is that most cleaning rituals are triggered by contact with an external precipitant and that in this respect they are slightly different from checking rituals. An example of an internally provoked cleaning ritual is the intrusion of an unacceptable thought, which the person then attempts to subdue by carrying out some sort of cleaning action. The best-known dramatic example of this kind is Lady Macbeth's repeated attempts to wash away her guilt.

The disturbance experienced by obsessional-compulsive cleaners can be provoked with ease (see Chapter 11). Provocation by contact with a contaminated object results in a steep and immediate increase in subjective discomfort, psychological disturbance, and an urge to engage in escape behavior. Generally speaking, ordinary fear reactions are as easily provoked by contact with the relevant stimulus, and in most circumstances the three components of fear show the same course of change. In these respects (easy provocation and patterns of disturbance), the reactions to phobic stimuli and to stimuli that provoke compulsive cleaning are similar. The subjective reactions are comparable, the psychophysiological reactions appear to be closely similar, and the escape and avoidance responses are similar to some extent. Perhaps the greatest similarity exists between the reactions to circumscribed phobic stimuli and to circumscribed contaminating stimuli. There is one difference that may be of some significance. Whereas visual and auditory stimuli appear to play the major role in precipitating fear reactions, tactile stimuli play an especially important part in obsessional-compulsive cleaning reactions. This difference may be significant, not merely because of the variation in modality but, rather, because the escape (or avoidance) responses of obsessional-compulsive and ordinary fear reactions differ in some respects. There is a natural connection between the fear reaction induced by a tactile stimulus (such as dirt) and the consequent cleaning behavior. The natural reaction to visually or auditorily induced fear is to remove oneself from the situation in which the danger signal appears. In the first case, one removes the stimulus from one's body or possession; in the second case, one removes oneself from the situation. This distinction may prove to be functionally insignificant. However, if one construes obsessional-compulsive cleaning disorders as having their basis in a fear of contamination (liberally defined to include "mental contamination"), the removal of the offending fear stimulus by washing it away is the natural, fitting escape behavior.

As for the important question of how to modify these disorders, if we press our analysis of the relation between cleaning compulsions and fears to its conclusion, it leads to these predictions. First, any therapeutic procedure that reduces fears (e.g., participant modeling) should be capable of reducing obsessional-compulsive cleaning disorders. Given comparable degrees of severity and the same therapeutic procedures, the success rates for phobias and for cleaning disorders should be similar. Second, the mechanisms of therapeutic change should be similar in both types of disorder.

In view of the similarities between compulsive cleaning and phobias, it might be best to describe this particular kind of obsessional-compulsive disorder by the term *phobic-compulsive*. Despite some differences, there are important similarities between the two types of disorder: They can be precipitated in comparable circumstances; the subjective and psychophysiological reactions are similar; both give rise to escape and avoidance behavior; and both can be modified by the same behavioral therapeutic procedures.

Although we are hampered by a shortage of critical information, there is some support for the idea of a similarity in the mode of onset of compulsive cleaning disorders and phobias. In both of these disorders, numerous patients give a history of sudden onset. In the case of compulsive *checking* disorders, however, the majority of patients report a history of gradual onset. In passing, it is worth mentioning that examples in which a sudden onset is reported are more easily accommodated within the conditioning theory of fear acquisition (see Rachman, 1977b).

Additional support for the claim that there is a close association between compulsive cleaning rituals and phobias, and a weaker association between checking rituals and phobias, comes from an interesting experiment by Foa and Chambless (1978). They studied the declining course of subjective anxiety during the flooding treatment of 11 obsessional and 6 phobic patients. The only patients who failed to show a curvilinear pattern of habituation were the 3 severe checkers. Although the phobics and other obsessionals shared a common pattern of habituation, the latter patients reported higher overall levels of anxiety.

There are obstacles to reaching firm conclusions about the reasons for the persistence of the accompanying escape and avoidance behavior, but it is likely that in the majority of instances both types of disorder achieve a reduction in anxiety/discomfort. On this basis it can be postulated that the escape and avoidance behavior is usually maintained by virtue of its discomfort-reducing effects.

If we are correct in drawing attention to the importance of the similarities between the disorders and attributing less significance to the differences between them, it is not unreasonable to expect that they might share a common cause.

Obsessional-compulsive disorders can be said to present three major questions: What is the nature of the disorders? How are they generated? Why are they so persistent? Of the three questions, problems relating to the genesis of the disorder are the most difficult to answer. The primary obstacle in the way of arriving at satisfactory explanations of the genesis of these disorders is that one is forced to rely on retrospective information, which is difficult to obtain and almost impossible to verify. Nevertheless, the questions have to be asked even though the answers will be speculative until full-scale prospective studies can be carried out.

Although most people with obsessional-compulsive disorders complain of a mixture of difficulties, clinicians appear to believe that cleaning compulsions are slightly more common. Next most frequent are the checking compulsions, and last come pure obsessions. It is difficult to establish whether this order of frequency is accurate. Certainly, our research on a clinical sample of some 150 patients appears to confirm this frequency, but it may be a reflection of the tendency to seek professional help rather than the occurrence of compulsive cleaning and checking in a representative sample. However, the outcome of a recent study by Stern and Cobb (1978) did resemble our findings. Despite the overlap between compulsive checking and cleaning, the two types of problem will be treated separately for purposes of the present argument.

Compulsive checking rituals are repetitive, relatively stereotyped acts carried out with the expressed intention of (1) ensuring the safety or well-being of oneself, other people, or animals and/or (2) ensuring the security of inanimate objects, appliances, or belongings (e.g., houses, gas taps, fireplaces, ashtrays, etc.) and/or (3) attempts to verify the accuracy or security of situations or information.

Clinical examples of checking rituals include the following: A 28-year-old patient had checking rituals precipitated by a fear of harming others. He was unable to drive his car, as this provoked intolerable thoughts and checking rituals, and he avoided crowded streets for fear of causing harm to others. He repeatedly checked razors, pins, glass, and so forth. A 34-year-old married woman had checking rituals precipitated by contact with other people. Looking at or talking to people, or giving them food, led to checking behavior in order to ensure that no harm came to them. A 36-year-old man had checking rituals focused on excrement; he engaged in prolonged and meticulous inspections of any speck of brown, particularly on his clothes and shoes. A 40-year-old nursery school teacher checked that all rugs and carpets were absolutely flat lest someone trip over them, and spent long periods looking for needles and pins on the floor and in furniture. She repeatedly checked to ensure that all cigarettes and matches were extinguished. A 30-year-old male nurse was incapacitated by repeated checking rituals. He had to ensure that no one had been inadvertently locked in a room or been trapped in a manhole, that no babies had been dumped into dustbins or bushes, and so forth. A 40-year-old man had to retrace many of his automobile trips in order to make sure he had not inadvertently injured anyone. A 28-year-old woman teacher spent up to three hours each night checking doors, gas taps, windows, plugs, and switches before going to bed. A 45-year-old television technician spent up to two hours checking the taps, doors, windows, plugs, and so forth of his apartment before he was able to leave for work. A 35-year-old married woman repeatedly checked with the police to ensure that she had not caused any accidents. A 19-year-old clerk carried out four hours of checking rituals after the other members of his family retired at night. He checked all electrical appliances, doors, taps, and so on and was not able to get to bed much before 3 or 4 o'clock in the morning.

Although our sample of 83 cases is not representative, it nevertheless is of some interest that 50 percent more of the checkers described a gradual as opposed to a sudden mode of onset. In cases of sudden onset, the precipitating event was an accident or near-accident, or an episode of depression. Particular acts of checking can be provoked by leaving a place (e.g., one's home, the kitchen, the bathroom), preparing to leave, preparing for bed, contact with people (especially crowds), traffic, and so on.

Our psychometric and experimental studies, reported in Chapters 10 to 12, produced some additional information about compulsive checking and compulsive checkers. Although the effects of conducting the compulsive rituals most often are discomfort reducing, they tend to be less consistent and less predictable than the effects of cleaning rituals. More checkers than cleaners reject the idea that their adverse mood state prior to starting a ritual can be described as "anxiety." The emotional reactions and rituals of checkers are more strongly influenced by the presence of other people than the reactions and rituals of cleaners. The checkers report comparatively less discomfort when "provoked" in company, and they execute their rituals less slowly in company (these findings indicate the influence of *social factors* in checking compulsive disorders). Checking rituals tend to take longer to complete than cleaning rituals. Checkers more often report feelings of subjective resistance to their rituals, and checking compulsions are correlated with self-doubt. The ratio of female to male checkers is roughly equal, but the ratio of female to male cleaners is in the region of 4:1.

We have suggested that most forms of obsessional checking are predominantly attempts at *prevention* while most cleaning compulsions have, in addition, an important *restorative* element. Most, but not all, checking rituals are intended to forestall some unpleasant event—usually the occurrence of harm to oneself, to one's friends and relations, or even to strangers. Most cleaning compulsions, however, are intended to restore a state of safety (e.g., cleanliness, hygiene) and are preventive in the sense that a failure to restore safety is threatening. If we view checking rituals as attempts to forestall unpleasant events such as harm coming to one's family, how can we explain checking rituals that occur after the event? In the majority of examples, the preventive quality of the checking ritual is obvious. For instance, one secures the gas taps after use or locks the door before leaving one's home. However, it is less clear why one should bother to check whether an automobile accident occurred some days previously. Why bother to check the newspapers for evidence of past accidents? Neither of these last two examples of obsessional checking is capable of forestalling harm to others. The answer may be that the underlying motive in these examples is the attempt to avoid punishment in the form of criticism, either criticism from others or self-directed cirticism (i.e., guilt). Whereas cleaners are trying to avoid coming into contact with danger, discomfort, or fear, checkers often are taking steps to avoid criticism or guilt (which is related to obsessional problems—e.g., Fernando, 1977).

GENESIS

As a first assumption, we have to allow for the possibility that there is some degree of personal vulnerability or excessive sensitivity to criticism (including guilt) in the absence of which the person will not develop obsessional behavior. It has been proposed by a variety of writers that people who are prone to develop neurotic disorders are oversensitive—particularly to frustration and punishment. In some accounts great emphasis is placed on social punishment. Examples of this type of theorizing can be found in the work of Eysenck (1967) and Gray (1971). In their theories, people who are high on neuroticism or high on neuroticism and introversion are presumed to be particularly prone to develop disorders such as obsessions. In Gray's version, "neurotics are assumed to be excessively sensitive to reinforcing events in general" (p. 233). Gray goes on to postulate that increasing degrees of introversion "represent increasing sensitivity to punishment rather than reward."

Making allowance for some constitutional predisposition or vulnerability, we can then speculate about the environmental events that are likely to be involved in the development of obsessional complaints (see Figure 9.1). Taking a look back into the past, it is postulated that the origins of cleaning and checking compulsions share the common factor of excessive parental concern and control, but differ in the nature of that control. Cleaners will emerge in families in which the parents are overcontrolling and overprotective. It is hard to conceive of an independent, coping child developing cleaning compulsions. Checking rituals are most likely to arise in families in which the parent(s) set high standards and are overcontrolling and overcritical. In these cases a parental

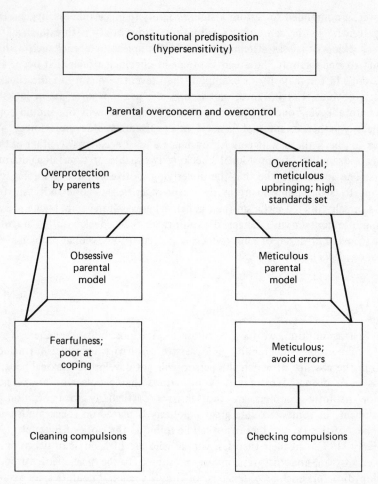

FIGURE 9.1. A hypothetical model of the relationship between type of obsessional problem and parental behavior.

model may facilitate the growth of obsessional troubles in the child, but to a lesser degree than in the case of cleaning compulsions. It is predicted that parents who exhibit cleaning compulsions are more likely to have obsessional children than parents who exhibit checking compulsions. The one small piece of psychometric evidence we collected on parental training (Did you have a strict parent?) was not consistent with our hypothesis of a relation between parental strictness and checking. The claim itself will need to be checked.

For present purposes we will assume that in passive-avoidance training you get punished if you do; in active-avoidance training you get punished if you don't. We will also assume that in the case of passive-avoidance training, and indeed of cleaning compulsions, the person is suffering from fear of an object or situation, in addition of course to the pervasive concern about longer-term events that one has to actively avoid. In the case of checking rituals (and in the present analysis this implies mainly *active avoidance*), the person is motivated largely by fear of criticism or guilt. As mentioned earlier, in clinical practice a strict division between washing/cleaning and passive avoidance, and between checking and active avoidance, is not always apparent. All obsessionals show elements of both passive and active avoidance, just as they often show features of cleaning and checking. The hypothetical relationship between the various types of obsessions and compulsions (and, for additional interest, phobias as well) is illustrated in Figure 9.2.

Most forms of phobia are best construed as instances of passive avoidance; hence, we expect to find an affinity between phobias and compulsive cleaning. There should be less similarity between phobias and compulsive checking, which is construed as largely a form of active avoidance. Following this line of reasoning, one might expect that compulsive cleaners are more likely to have concurrent phobias or a history of earlier phobias. They might also show

FIGURE 9.2.   The overlap between phobias, cleaning, and checking compulsions.

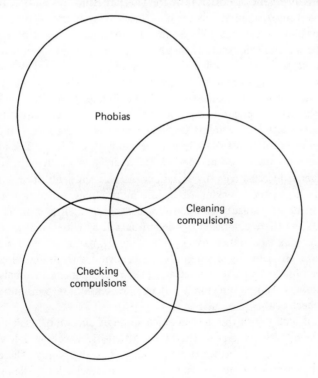

evidence of a wider range of ordinary fears, perhaps at a more intense level than is encountered in the general population.

So far it has been argued that compulsive checking most often is character-istic of active-avoidance behavior, that the fear of criticism or guilt plays an important part in the compulsive behavior, that discomfort frequently is reduced by checking, and that most checking rituals are preventive in intent. Upon clinical observation, the most notable characteristics of obsessional *checkers* appear to include the following: an expressed fear of causing harm to themselves or others, albeit inadvertently; checking occurring mostly in the home, conduc-ted while alone, not necessarily associated with fear intensified when depressed, less intense when responsibility is diminished; and longer rituals, with associated feelings of doubt. How can our present analysis account for these features?

The preventive aspect of checking is explained by the fact that the under-lying concern is to avoid guilt and/or leaving oneself open to criticism. Causing harm to others would be regarded as an important reason for incurring criticism or guilt, and hence would be avoided by repetitively checking to ensure that no errors have occurred and that no safety precautions have been neglected.

The significance of the checkers' feeling of responsibility can be accounted for by the fact that only acts for which they can be held responsible are likely to produce guilt or criticism. If the checker is not responsible for the act or its consequences, then it relieves him or her of criticism for the action and it also helps him or her avoid guilt. So it is, for example, that one of our patients said that she was quite content for the therapists to leave knives, blades, and pins unattended on the ward provided that it was understood that they and not she, the patient, were fully responsible for any adverse consequences. Most checking behavior takes place in the home and can be attributed to the fact that the home usually is the place of greatest responsibility; we can also assume that the fear of criticism is greatest from parents or other members of the family and that we feel most guilt in relation to family members and close friends. The intensifica-tion of checking rituals during periods of depression might be a result of a further increase in sensitivity to social punishment and guilt during periods of low mood. Hence, the checking rituals are more intensive and prolonged. The fact that a small percentage of compulsive checkers report little or no disturbance before or during the commission of their ritualistic activities, unlike compulsive cleaners, may be accounted for by the transformation of active-avoidance behavior into efficient, highly stereotyped behavior with diminishing fear [in the manner observed in Solomon et al.'s (1953) experimental animals]. Some-times the absence of discomfort may reflect a low sense of responsibility for that particular check at that particular time.

The difficulty with the present explanation of obsessional checking is that most of these patients report that their ritualistic checking behavior itself produces a good deal of criticism from members of the family. There are two possible explanations for the persistence of checking behavior in the face of this criticism. In the first place, punishment of active-avoidance behavior can lead to a paradoxical enhancement of the intensity and persistence of the avoidance behavior (Gray, 1971). In the case of ritualistic checking, therefore, the delivery of criticism by members of the family may serve to intensify rather than reduce the checking. Another possibility is that the compulsive checker has gone through a period in which he or she carried out avoidance behavior in order to forestall criticism but that this avoidance behavior then undergoes a transformation into stereotyped active-avoidance behavior that becomes largely independent of its original causes—in a manner similar to that observed in Solomon's experimental animals. More embracing explanations are considered in Chapters 11 and 12.

The present account incorporates the therapeutic effect of behavioral methods, but can it predict which methods are likely to be the most effective? Although there has been a good deal of research carried out since the original attempts of Solomon, Kamin, and Wynne (1953) to extinguish highly persistent active-avoidance behavior in experimental animals, their findings can be restated with little alteration. They concluded that ordinary extinction procedures were virtually incapable of eliminating persistent avoidance behavior. A method that today would be described as response prevention was moderately effective in reducing avoidance behavior, as was a punishment procedure. Neither of these methods was, however, capable of producing extinction in more than one-third of the experimental animals, and as we now know, punishment of avoidance behavior can lead to an increase rather than a decrease in this behavior. However, Solomon and his colleagues found that a combination of response prevention and "punishment for responding" procedures was effective in extinguishing the active-avoidance behavior. Insofar as our modern methods have proved to be effective in overcoming compulsive checking behavior—and they may well be less effective than methods for treating compulsive cleaning rituals—they seem to be based on a combination of modeling, flooding, and response prevention. Clinical experience leads one to believe that response prevention plays a critical part in therapy for compulsive checking. Whether the response prevention part of the treatment is crucial in the management of obsessional cleaning is an open question. Extrapolating from the experimental literature, we can assume that the punishment of well-established compulsive checking rituals may reduce them, but is also capable of exacerbating the condition. We can also be fairly sure that ordinary extinction procedures are unlikely to be of any value.

PREDICTIONS

The present proposals lead to the following predictions:

1. Criticism will increase checking behavior (the intensity can be measured by speed, duration, and total amount).
2. Increases in responsibility will result in increased checking behavior.

3. Insofar as a move to novel surroundings implies a diminution in responsibility, checking will decrease.
4. Increases in guilt feelings, evoked directly or mediated indirectly through depression, will increase checking behavior.
5. Reductions in guilt and/or criticism will result in a decrease in checking behavior.
6. Increases in guilt feelings will result in the spread of checking rituals to a wider range of situations.
7. Reductions in guilt and/or criticism, accompanied by direct behavioral treatment aimed at controlling checking behavior, will decrease checking substantially.
8. Direct behavioral treatment of checking may be accompanied by a temporary increase in guilt.

DIFFERENCES BETWEEN CHECKING AND CLEANING RITUALS

Of the four types of complaints identified, checking and cleaning rituals are the most frequently encountered in clinical practice. They are similar in many respects: There is an internal pressure to execute repetitive and stereotyped actions; they are at least partly irrational; and they are often difficult to resist. In spite of these similarities, there are a number of apparent differences that, if firmly established, would require improved models and explanations, and possibly different methods of treatment. Also, there is some evidence that checkers are slower to respond to treatment than cleaners (Foa and Goldstein, 1978). Consequently, further investigation of the differences between washing and checking rituals appeared to be desirable. The major aim was to pursue the similarities and differences between these two types of compulsion, but we also took the opportunity to test a number of other ideas, such as the relationship between duration of the disorder and feelings of "senselessness."

One of the several ideas we were interested in following up was the role, if any, of indecisiveness in determining or influencing these rituals. Walker and Beech (1969) and Beech (1974) have argued that obsessional-compulsive neurotics suffer from a basic impairment of decision making, and have suggested that this inadequacy applies not only to the decisions that control rituals (i.e., when to start and when to stop them) but to all decisions that involve the risk of high cost (i.e., unpleasant consequences). Without anticipating our full discussion of this theory (see Chapter 13), it can be said that there are reasons for believing that indecision is unlikely to provide a cornerstone for a theory of obsessional disorders. As a start, there are numerous obsessional patients who have little or no difficulty in deciding when to start and when to stop a ritual. To take one clinical example, a closely studied patient of ours who suffered from frequent feelings of contamination carried out her stereotyped hand-washing rituals on many occasions each day. Every time she became contaminated, she promptly washed for a few minutes, displaying considerable decisiveness in initiating and stopping the ritualistic cleaning act. She was incapacitated by the frequency of the rituals, not by doubting or indecisiveness.

In our clinical experience numerous obsessional patients complained of indecisiveness per se, and this complaint was frequently associated with checking compulsions. Hence, we expected that checking rituals take longer and possibly have more discomfort-arousing consequences than cleaning rituals. As they bear little relation to indecisiveness, cleaning rituals should be briefer and more discomfort reducing. Clinically, checking rituals appear to be resisted more often than cleaning rituals. It should be borne in mind that these are generalizations and that there is, of course, variation within groups of checkers or cleaners—some of the patients describe short, discomfort-reducing checking rituals and long, frustrating cleaning rituals.

A questionnaire was designed to test the strength of several notions, including the following: Are checking rituals longer, more often associated with doubts, and more often resisted than cleaning rituals? Are parental criticism and punishment more often implicated in the genesis of checking than in that of cleaning? The full list of questions is reproduced in Table 9.1.

TABLE 9.1:   STUDY 1 QUESTIONNAIRE[a]

1. I spend more than an hour continuously hand washing (or checking).*
2. I feel very tense while hand washing.
3. I feel angry with myself while hand washing.
4. I feel much better after hand washing than before.
5. I have difficulty in deciding when to stop hand washing.
6. I experience doubts about whether I have hand washed properly and have to go back and hand wash again.*
7. I try hard to resist hand washing.*
8. If interrupted while hand washing, I have to start all over again.
9. I can delay hand washing for half an hour without much trouble.
10. I think that something dreadful will happen if I don't hand wash properly.
11. As a child I was frightened of punishment.
12. As a child I was strongly criticised if
    a. I was late.
    b. I was untidy.
    c. I was caught swearing.
    d. I was dirty.
    e. I mentioned sex.
13. My hand washing is sensible/senseless.
14. I think that I can remember a particular incident that started my excessive hand washing. (YES/NO)

[a]This was administered to 17 "checkers" and 17 "cleaners." The first seven questions provided evidence relevant to our primary hypothesis. The response categories for questions 1-13 were ALWAYS, OFTEN, SOMETIMES, and NEVER. Checkers were given a questionnaire in which *hand washing* was replaced by the word *checking*. Asterisks indicate significant differences between checkers and cleaners.

In the preliminary study, 34 patients who were referred for behavioral treatment of obsessional-compulsive problems, and who were easily identified as either cleaners or checkers, were asked to complete the questionnaire. The group of checkers included patients who were compelled to check that they had not harmed others (5 cases) or had not contacted contamination (4 cases) or broken glass (1 case). Six of the patients repeatedly checked that objects were in their correct position, and one patient checked to ensure that the gas was not leaking. All of the patients in the cleaning group were worried by contamination from germs or poisons, and carried out appropriate washing rituals.

We included only patients for whom checking or washing was felt to be the major complaint; the investigation was confined to these two types of rituals, since they are the most prominent, are frequently the reason for seeking treatment, and are easily distinguishable.

RESULTS

A multivariate analysis of variance indicated that the checkers and cleaners differed significantly in their profiles of responses to the first seven questions ($p < 0.02$). The univariate F was significant for questions 1, 6, and 7 (see Table 9.2). The checkers did not differ from the cleaners on questions 8 to 14, duration of symptoms, or age.

It appears that cleaning rituals seldom last as long as an hour (81% of the informants answering no), but checking rituals of this length are not uncommon ($p = 0.004$). More patients with checking rituals doubt themselves and go back to repeat their rituals than patients with cleaning cleaning compulsions ($p = 0.004$), and checking rituals tend to be resisted far more commonly than

TABLE 9.2: STUDY 1 QUESTIONNAIRE ANALYSIS: UNIVARIATE AND MULTIVARIATE ANALYSIS OF VARIANCE QUESTIONS 1 TO 7

VARIABLE	UNIVARIATE F[a]	P LESS THAN
Q1	9.62	0.004b
Q2	1.77	0.193
Q3	0.59	0.448
Q4	0.93	0.342
Q5	0.40	0.533
Q6	9.93	0.004b
Q7	5.31	0.028b

[a]F = ratio for multivariate test of equality of mean vectors = 3.14; $p < 0.02$.
[b]Questions that differentiate "washers" from "checkers."

cleaning rituals (p = 0.028). There is a greater tendency for checking rituals to be accompanied by feelings of anger and tension.

After transforming the relevant data into 2 X 2 contingency tables and chi squares, calculated with Yates's correction, the following findings emerged. The longer the duration of the disorder (more than ten years), the greater the likelihood that the patient considered his or her ritual to be senseless (chi square = 8.37; p = 0.05). Prolonged duration of the disorder was not, however, associated with longer rituals. Shorter duration of the disorder (less than ten years) was associated with greater improvement observed after treatment (p = 0.05). Although early age of onset (less than 20 years of age) was found to be associated with reports of parental criticism during childhood (p = 0.05), it was not associated with fear of punishment during childhood.

The finding that longstanding rituals are more likely to be considered senseless is probably due to the disappearance of the original cognitive element (e.g., fear of disease). Arguing along these lines, Walton and Mather (1963) observed that longstanding rituals appear to run an independent course, to be "functionally autonomous"; they went on to suggest that these rituals appear to be uninfluenced by anxiety reduction. Our evidence on the occurrence of primary obsessional slowness (Rachman, 1974b) is consistent with this view. We might also add that longstanding rituals appear to lack any accompanying psychophysiological or psychological disturbance—and to lack an adequate rationale. Compulsive checking or cleaning degenerates into a way of life, and the term *functionally autonomous* seems entirely apt.

As can be seen from the results, our rudimentary attempt to obtain retrospective information about the potential contribution of childhood experiences to the genesis of these disorders came to grief.

THE SECOND QUESTIONNAIRE STUDY

In an attempt to replicate and extend these findings, a revised questionnaire was given to a new group of cleaners (n = 32) and of checkers (n = 31) drawn from the same pool of patients as those who participated in the first study. This second questionnaire (see Table 9.3) was based on the previous one, revised to take into account our developing ideas about the nature of compulsive rituals. We postulated not only that checkers have longer rituals, more doubting, and more resistance, but also that, relative to cleaners, they more often consider their rituals to be senseless. They also have more trouble remembering whether they have completed the rituals correctly, more often ask for reassurance, and more often are unable to estimate how long a particular ritual will last. Finally, we postulated that cleaners obtain more immediate relief from carrying out their rituals than checkers do.

Since some of the data obtained from Questionnaire 2 were provided by

TABLE 9.3:   STUDY 2 QUESTIONNAIRE[a]

1. I spend more than one hour continuously hand washing.
2. I feel tense while hand washing.
3. I feel angry with myself while hand washing.
4. I feel much better after hand washing than before.
5. I have difficulty deciding when to stop hand washing.
6. I experience doubts about whether I have hand washed properly and have to go back and hand wash again.
7. I try hard to resist hand washing.
8. I can delay hand washing for half an hour without much trouble.
9. I spend more than half an hour continuously hand washing.
10. I have trouble with my attention wandering while hand washing, even though I try hard to concentrate.
11. My hand washing appears senseless to me.
12. After completing my hand washing, I still find that, later, I begin to doubt whether it was done properly and have to hand wash all over again.
13. I count while I am hand washing.
14. If asked at the start of my hand washing how long it will take, I can make a fairly accurate estimate.
15. I go to bed at night worrying that I haven't hand washed properly during the day.
16. I can go for days without hand washing excessively.
17. I have a feeling of relief as soon as I start hand washing.
18. I spend more than two hours continuously hand washing.
19. I seem to have trouble remembering whether I have hand washed properly.
20. If I cannot hand wash right away, then the urge to hand wash tends to pass away.
21. If I cannot hand wash right away, then I try hard to persuade myself that all is well and there is no need to hand wash.
22. If I cannot hand wash right away, then I ask others for reassurance.
23. I can spend hours *just thinking* about whether or not I have hand washed properly.

---

[a]This questionnaire was administered to 31 "checkers" and 32 "washers." The response categories were ALWAYS, OFTEN, SOMETIMES, and NEVER. Checkers were given a questionnaire in which *hand washing* was replaced by the word *checking*.

colleagues working in other hospitals, we did not have an adequate assessment of the age of onset of the main compulsive problem.

RESULTS

The results of a multivariate analysis of variance, presented in Table 9.4, show that the questionnaire differentiated the checkers from the cleaners with considerable success and at a high level of significance ($p = 0.0005$). The univariate tests shown in Table 9.4 indicated that the two groups responded differently to 16 out of the 23 questions, thereby providing support for our belief that the two types of ritual have many dissimilar features. Checkers reported that they more frequently experienced long rituals, doubt and repetition, wandering

TABLE 9.4:   STUDY 2 QUESTIONNAIRE ANALYSIS[a]

VARIABLE	HYPOTHESIS MEAN SQ.	UNIVARIATE F	P LESS THAN	
Q1	5.31	5.83	0.02	*
Q2	10.00	10.05	0.002	*
Q3	6.59	6.90	0.01	*
Q4	3.70	4.13	0.05	*
Q5	3.66	3.88	0.05	*
Q6	7.91	17.39	0.0001	*
Q7	12.08	18.81	0.0001	*
Q8	1.00	1.04	0.3	
Q9	7.14	9.23	0.003	*
Q10	3.83	4.87	0.03	*
Q11	3.80	4.46	0.04	*
Q12	6.13	9.79	0.003	*
Q13	4.03	2.57	0.1	
Q14	12.70	12.88	0.0007	*
Q15	3.15	3.30	0.07	*
Q16	0.32	0.49	0.48	
Q17	10.45	8.18	0.006	*
Q18	1.50	3.91	0.05	*
Q19	1.90	2.58	0.1	
Q20	1.43	2.28	0.1	
Q21	0.26	0.26	0.6	
Q22	0.41	0.53	0.5	
Q23	5.88	9.06	0.004	*

Degrees of freedom for hypothesis = 1
Degrees of freedom for error   = 61

[a]Multivariate and univariate analyses of differences between responses of washers ($n = 32$) and checkers ($n = 31$) to the Study 2 Questionnaire presented in Table 9.3. Questions that significantly differentiated washers and checkers in the predicted direction are indicated by an asterisk.

[b]F ratio for multivariate test of equality of mean vectors = 3.34; d.f. = 23 and 39; $p < 0.0005$.

attention, and difficulty in estimating how long their ritual would take. They also reported a more frequent tendency to be worried by doubts some hours after the completion of a ritual, and to feel that their rituals were senseless. Checkers frequently reported spending hours simply thinking about whether or not they had checked correctly.

By contrast, cleaners reported having shorter rituals, usually felt relief as soon as their cleaning started, and tended to feel better after the ritual than before. As in the previous study, cleaners did not resist their rituals as commonly as checkers did. There were more females in the cleaning group than in the checking group but removing the variable of sex in a multivariate analysis did not alter in any significant way the results presented in Table 9.4 The two groups did not differ in age.

127

TABLE 9.5:   PRINCIPAL-COMPONENTS ANALYSIS OF THE
STUDY 2 QUESTIONNAIRE[a]

First Component (Doubting and Repetition)	*Loading*
2. Tension during ritual	+0.64
3. Anger during ritual	+0.55
5. Difficulty deciding when to stop	+0.76
6. Doubting and repetition	+0.76
10. Attention wanders during ritual	+0.57
12. Delayed doubting and repeating	+0.71
15. Going to bed and worrying about a ritual performed during the day	+0.52
19. Trouble remembering whether a ritual was performed properly	+0.73
23. Spending hours just thinking about whether a ritual was performed properly	+0.65
Second Component (Length of Ritual)	
1. Rituals of more than 1 hour	+0.71
9. Rituals of more than ½ hour	+0.71
18. Rituals of more than 2 hours	+0.64
Third Component (Relief)	
4. Feel much better after ritual	+0.66
17. Relief as soon as ritual starts	+0.60

[a]Questions that have high loadings (> 0.50) on the first three principal components.

The results of a principal-component analysis are displayed in Table 9.5 and the factor scores of checkers and cleaners in Figure 9.3. It is obvious from the displays that cleaners report less doubting and shorter rituals, and obtain relief from their rituals more reliably than checkers do (see also Chapter 12). It is of interest to note the percentages of checkers and cleaners who respond "always," "often," "sometimes," and "never" to each question (see Table 9.6). For instance, 71 percent of the cleaners reported that they *always* feel better after cleaning, and 48 percent feel relief as soon as they start (Q17). The comparable figures for checkers are 44 percent and 19 percent. Eighty-five percent of checkers but only 42 percent of cleaners report that they often or always experience doubts after performing the ritual, and that they then have to go back and repeat it (Q6). Cleaning rituals lasting for more than half an hour are uncommon—74 percent of cleaners report that they never occur (Q8), but only 25 percent of the checkers report that such rituals never occur.

Descriptions of obsessional-compulsive disorders often imply that compulsions are always resisted and always appear senseless to the patient (see Chapter 2). The results of the present study confirm our clinical impression that these features are not always present. Twenty-six percent of the cleaners but only 3 percent of the checkers replied that they never try to resist (Q7); a mere 25

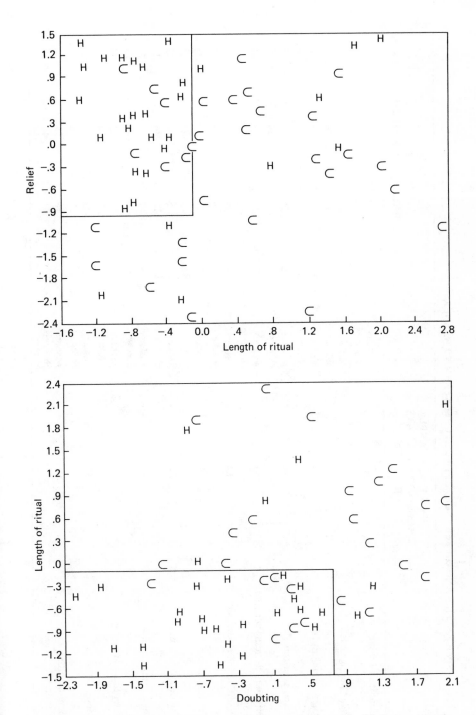

FIGURE 9.3. The position of groups of checkers and cleaners in the factor space described by relief, length of ritual, and doubting.

TABLE 9.6: SIMILARITIES AND DIFFERENCES BETWEEN CHECKERS AND WASHERS[a]

	% OF TOTAL SAMPLE RESPONDING "ALWAYS" OR "OFTEN"	GROUP	ALWAYS	OFTEN	SOMETIMES	NEVER
Q1 More than 1 hour*	22	washers	6	10	3	81
		checkers	9	19	34	38
Q2 Tense during ritual*	65	washers	32	13	29	26
		checkers	47	37	16	0
Q3 Angry during ritual*	54	washers	16	23	35	26
		checkers	31	38	25	6
Q4 Better after ritual*	76	washers	71	16	6	7
		checkers	44	22	28	6
Q5 Difficulty deciding when to stop*	61	washers	29	16	39	16
		checkers	34	41	22	3
Q6 Doubting and repetition*	64	washers	3	39	45	13
		checkers	19	66	15	0
Q7 Try hard to resist*	41	washers	3	16	55	26
		checkers	25	37	35	3
Q8 Can delay for ½ hour	26	washers	13	6	42	39
		checkers	12	19	44	25
Q9 More than ½ hour*	23	washers	6	7	13	74
		checkers	6	25	44	25
Q10 Attention wandering*	54	washers	10	35	23	32
		checkers	13	50	34	3
Q11 Senseless*	51	washers	10	29	42	19
		checkers	25	38	28	9
Q12 Later doubting and repetition*	36	washers	3	19	55	23
		checkers	19	31	47	3

TABLE 9.6 (continued)

	% OF TOTAL SAMPLE RESPONDING "ALWAYS" OR "OFTEN"	GROUP	ALWAYS	OFTEN	SOMETIMES	NEVER
Q13 Counting	36	washers	19	6	10	65
		checkers	28	16	16	40
Q14 Accurate estimate of ritual length*	36	washers	32	26	26	16
		checkers	6	12	41	41
Q15 Worry at night about rituals performed during the day*	19	washers	10	3	32	55
		checkers	16	9	47	28
Q16 Days without excessive ritualizing	13	washers	6	13	10	71
		checkers	0	6	28	66
Q17 Relief as soon as ritual starts*	57	washers	48	23	16	13
		checkers	19	25	19	37
Q18 More than 2 hours*	7	washers	0	7	0	93
		checkers	3	3	28	66
Q19 Trouble remembering whether ritual performed properly	26	washers	3	16	49	32
		checkers	12	19	50	19
Q20 Urge passes away if ritual not performed immediately	10	washers	0	6	23	71
		checkers	10	3	31	56
Q21 Persuade myself that there is no need to perform the ritual	27	washers	13	16	39	32
		checkers	9	16	37	38
Q22 Asking for reassurance	23	washers	3	20	32	45
		checkers	6	19	41	34
Q23 Spend hours thinking whether ritual performed properly*	14	washers	3	0	36	61
		checkers	9	16	47	28

[a]Asterisks mark items in which responses are significantly different.

percent of the checkers and 3 percent of the cleaners report that they *always* try to resist. *For the whole sample, only 14 percent report that they always try to resist.* Only 25 percent of the checkers and 10 percent of the cleaners report that their rituals *always* appear senseless to them (Q11). Some of these findings were confirmed by Stern and Cobb (1978), who found that 46 percent of their 45 patients reported little or no resistance.

It would be unwise to use these findings to reject earlier conceptions of obsessional-compulsive problems. As we pointed out earlier, the concepts of internal resistance and of senselessness are complex in nature and difficult to assess. We also noted that when obsessional patients are asked superficial questions (e.g., "Why do you wash?") they respond with superficial answers. Inevitably, the statements on our short questionnaire were superficial and the answers equally so (e.g., "I sometimes think that my checking is sensible"—detailed interviews would have revealed more than one level of meaning for the word *sensible*). Future investigations of these phenomena should certainly go beyond questionnaire procedures. It remains true nevertheless that internal resistance and insight are not always or universally experienced—far from it.

The following questions failed to discriminate between the cleaners and checkers: Fifty-three percent of the total sample reported that they never count while carrying out a ritual (Q13), and 69 percent that they can never go for days without performing their rituals excessively (Q16). The response to question 20 is particularly interesting. Very few patients reported that their compulsive urges tend to diminish if the ritual cannot be performed immediately; only 9 percent of the total sample responded with "always" or "often" to this question. This result apears to conflict with the experimental findings reported in Chapters 11 and 12. Under experimental conditions, patients who are prevented from carrying out a ritual almost always experience a spontaneous decline in their compulsive urges. However, the main part of this decay takes place during the first 30 minutes after provocation, and after 2 hours there are few urges and little discomfort remaining—so the important time element differs from that implied in the questionnaire (i.e., the *immediate* effect of a delayed ritual). Moreover, the 60 percent who replied on the questionnaire that their compulsive urges never decay spontaneously may well have guarded themselves against ever experiencing the slow "natural decay" of compulsive urges. The deliberate prevention of compulsive rituals that forms an important part of most forms of behavioral treatment may provide patients with their first opportunity to experience the occurrence of spontaneous decay. Indeed, their exposure to this phenomenon may play an important part in altering their expectations regarding the "untreated" consequences of exposure to provocation.

Only 27 percent of the total sample frequently tried to persuade themselves that there is no need to perform their ritual (Q21); 24 percent frequently asked for reassurance (Q22), and only 25 percent said that they can delay the start of the ritual for up to half an hour (Q8).

The questionnaire data support the view that there are some significant differences between checking and washing rituals. The hypotheses embodied in the second questionnaire were to a large extent generated by clinical observations, not by a coherent model of obsessional-compulsive disorders, and some of the new findings require an explanation. For example, we need to understand why cleaning rituals are shorter than checking rituals. Similarly, why are checking rituals more often associated with doubt and indecision?

Our analysis of some of these phenomena rests on the relative distinction between cleaning and checking. Cleaning rituals are construed as involving, in addition to active avoidance, an important element of passive avoidance and/or escape behavior; and in cases of compulsive cleaning, when the patient's (generally successful) passive-avoidance behavior fails to protect him or her from contamination, he or she attempts to erase the contamination by engaging in stereotyped cleaning rituals (i.e., escape behavior). For most cleaners these rituals succeed in bringing some relief (see Q4), and it is usually achieved promptly (see Q17). Longer-term worries are not so readily dealt with, and presumably it is these that contribute to the repetitiveness of the ritualistic behavior. Nevertheless, cleaning rituals are shorter than checking rituals (see Q1); there is less need for prolonged washing rituals, as the chances of obtaining at least a moderate amount of prompt relief are so high. Seventy-one percent of cleaners reported that they always or often achieve relief as soon as they start their ritual, whereas only 44 percent of checkers gave similar answers.

As the immediate purpose of cleaning is to remove the danger and/or discomfort of contamination, the person feels tense (but not particularly angry) while conducting his or her escape (see Q2 and Q3). As the source of the danger/discomfort is already present and usually evident, visually or tactually, there is little reason for excessive doubting (see Q6). Yielding to the urge to clean away some evident contamination is, in the short term at least, understandable, and hence cleaners less commonly report internal resistance (see Q7).

The next problem is that of why checking rituals are so often regarded as senseless (see Q11). We are not in a position to answer this question, but presumably the perceived senselessness of an action such as checking is determined by the factors of appropriateness, likelihood of success, availability of prompt feedback, and so on. The link between touching a dirty object and washing one's hands for some minutes is clear, appropriate, and open to prompt evaluation. On the other hand, spending hours checking ashtrays, gas taps, doors, and windows to ensure that no one will be harmed at some time in the future, however appropriate it might be, is out of proportion to the risks involved, is less likely to be successful, and is virtually impossible to evaluate. It is not checking as such that is senseless, but repetitive, stereotyped acts that bear little relationship to the actual risks involved. As can be seen in Table 9.6, the distributions of answers to the two questions on resistance and senseless are similar. Despite the apparent plausibility of the argument that people resist the compulsions because they are perceived to be senseless, and the distribution of answers just referred to, the correlation between the answers to the two questions was a mere 0.22. This may mean that the argument is mistaken or that the correlational data are misleading. As we have pointed out, the two questions on the inventory were brief and superficial, but the phenomena of internal resistance and insight are complex. In order to resolve the argument, more penetrating questions need to be asked, and experimental analyses are needed.

Checking rituals, we have argued, are best construed as active-avoidance behavior—the person engages in behavior designed to reduce the probability of some future aversive event (e.g., criticism, guilt, pain). Other factors being equal, it is far more difficult to control future threats than to remove present, evident ones. *Final confirmation or disconfirmation is unobtainable.* It is no surprise, then, to find that checking rituals are associated with more doubting and repetition (see Q6) and indecisiveness (see Q5). According to our results (see Q1), they also take longer to complete—how can you tell when you have successfully completed your checking procedures? Checking rituals are accompanied by anger and by tension (Q2 and Q3)—presumably, the anger is a product of the frustration that results from feeling compelled to carry out a task that has no evident solution and yet carries the threat of aversive consequences.

The discomfort-reducing consequences of checking and cleaning rituals are reportedly different (see Q4 and Q13), but as we will see in Chapters 11 and 12, this information is not entirely consistent with the findings from our experiments. As in the case of the spontaneous decay of compulsive urges, the answers given in reply to our questionnaire differ in degree from the behavior observed under controlled conditions. Although the difference in the discomfort-reducing effects of executing a checking or washing ritual reported by our informants (i.e., less relief from checking) was confirmed in the experiments, they underestimated the generality of these effects. Possible reasons for the greater reliability of cleaning rituals as reducers of discomfort include the tangibility of the danger signals emitted by contaminating stimuli. They are present and evident and, hence, more easily controlled. Cleaning rituals can relieve a large part of the discomfort produced by contamination—promptly (Q17) and reliably (Q4). Checking rituals may or may not reduce the probable occurrence of some future unpleasantness, and one's discomfort remains or decreases as a function of these uncertainly perceived probabilities.

Checking rituals are prolonged and associated with excessive doubting because they are designed to anticipate, and indeed to prevent, some future event, and hence can have no end point, no obvious conclusion. Cleaners can stop once they have removed the dirt from their hands—the ritual has a definable conclusion. You know when you have finished the task. A person carrying out preventive checking rituals has no assurance that the task is finished (i.e., that the perceived danger has been removed). At best, the risks are diminished; hence, a checker has the problem of deciding at what point to stop checking and allow events to take their course. There is more uncertainty in preventive activities and, hence, more doubting.

Returning to the question of why checking rituals are more likely to be resisted than cleaning rituals, one answer may rest on the *indecisiveness* that Beech (1974) stresses in his theory. Patients who reported a tendency to resist their rituals (see Q7) also reported that their attention wandered during completion of the ritual (Q10) and that they had difficulty deciding when to stop (Q5). The correlation coefficients are 0.38 and 0.47, respectively. There is also a correlation of 0.52 between Q5 and Q10 (see Table 9.3). If we assume that the experience of indecisiveness is aversive, then people with checking compulsions may be more prone to resist carrying them out. Although this explanation is not entirely incompatible with our own analysis, it is unsatisfactory for the reasons advanced against the theory in general (see Chapter 13). The best construction that can be put on our findings at present is that resistance is a reflection of the person's perception of the senselessness of the activity, of the energy it requires, and the embarrassment it can provoke. The indecisiveness and wandering attention are seen as by-products of the difficulties and uncertainty inherent in attempting to exert control over the probability of *future* aversive events.

Many writers have drawn attention to the prominence of *doubting* in obsessional disorders. As mentioned below, this quality emerged as one of the principal components of our obsessional-compulsive questionnaire and correlated significantly with the checking component. The questions loading highly on the doubting/conscientiousness component of our obsessional-compulsive questionnaire are the following:

I have a very strict conscience.
I am more concerned than most people about honesty.
Even when I do something very carefully I often feel that it is not quite right.
I tend to get behind in my work because I repeat things over and over again.
Neither of my parents was very strict during my childhood (negative loading).
I usually have serious doubts about the simple everyday things I do.
One of my major problems is that I pay too much attention to detail.

Doubting is associated with strict parents and a strict conscience. This is in line with our reconstruction of clinical case histories to the effect that parental criticism produces exaggerated fear of making mistakes and, consequently, lack of confidence in one's own decisions and abilities. The association with a strict conscience suggests that the patients may have internalized high standards of conduct from their reportedly strict parents. As most matters of morality involve questions of the effect of one's conduct on other people, it is not surprising that the content of most obsessional doubts is on the theme of how to prevent harm from coming to other people. If one places an exaggerated value on the importance of one's duty to protect other people, and if in addition one has a disproportionate estimation of the likelihood of harm occurring, it is easy to see how the avoidance of errors can be elevated to a place of primary importance. The weakness of this analysis is that it is almost wholly rational. It does not begin to explain why obsessional checkers repetitively carry out irrational, stereotyped checking activities, often of a trivial nature designed to prevent trivial occurrences, while at the same time neglecting more important social duties.

SUMMARY

The two main types of complaint under examination are checking and cleaning compulsions. They share the common features of an internal sense of pressure, repetitive and stereotyped actions, a commonly experienced feeling of resistance, and partial irrationality, and they are both inclined to produce distress or embarrassment. Checking compulsions usually are oriented to the future, and often are intended to prevent harm from coming to someone. For the most part they can be construed as a form of (preventive) active-avoidance behavior. Cleaning compulsions have, in addition, a significant element of passive-avoidance behavior and, when that fails, escape behavior. The immediate purpose of carrying out a cleaning ritual is restorative; it may also have a longer-term preventive aim. Cleaning compulsions share some important similarities with phobias.Checking rituals more often than cleaning rituals are associated with doubting and indecisiveness, take a long time to complete, have a slow onset, evoke internal resistance, and are likely to be accompanied by feelings of anger or tension. There are disproportionately more females than males in the compulsive-cleaning category, but there is no sex difference in the incidence of checking compulsions. Far less resistance and far fewer reports of senselessness were recorded than traditional accounts of the disorder led us to expect.

Chapter 10

Psychometric Analyses

The traditional psychometric approach to the concept of the obsessional personality and to obsessional-compulsive neuroses incorporates a number of assumptions that range from highly probable to extremely unlikely. Two out of four of the chief assumptions are rejected as being too wayward, and the remaining two are retained for the present even though their validity is uncertain.

In the first place, the construction of obsessional-compulsive behavior as an illness is rejected as being unjustified. Psychometric studies that deal in psychiatric diagnoses of obsessions and compulsions, or regard such behavior as symptoms of illness, seem to us to be misleading. In the second place, Freud's introduction of the concept of the anal personality, and of anal erotism, into considerations of obsessional behavior is and always has been confusing. As the anal concept has never been shown to be of value in studying obsessions and compulsions, we propose to manage without using the term or the concept except where it is employed in the original source material. We agree with Gottheil and Stone (1968) that there is good reason to question "the place of the mouth and anus in the concept and theory of the oral and anal character types" (p. 16).

In their recent review Fisher and Greenberg (1977) reached a favorable conclusion about the validity of the anal concept, but a critical examination of their evidence and arguments fails to persuade us that any of it comes close to demonstrating that the anus or anal erotism has anything to do with obsessional behavior (see Hodgson and Rachman, 1979). At the very best, the findings (interesting though some of them are) show a loose relationship between a desire for cleanliness and/or orderliness and obstinacy. Regarding these findings as

137

supporting the notion of anal traits or anal character is without justification and helps perpetuate unnecessary confusion. Moreover, the associated hypothesis that severe toilet training produces obsessional traits is unfounded. Hence, there is much to be gained in clarity and accuracy once we discard the anal notions and proceed directly with the study of obsessional behavior and personality. Naturally, there is nothing to say that, once we have achieved a better grasp of the concept of obessional traits, attempts should not be made to relate them to anal interests, toilet training, or whatever—but we would not be sanguine about the outcome.

The third assumption, that there is a recognizable and describable entity called the obsessional personality (or, less ambitiously, that there is a collection of obsessional traits that cohere), is the core of much of the psychometric research, and we will proceed on the basis that it is a reasonable idea to investigate.

The fourth and related assumption is of fundamental importance for all psychometric research, and for much else besides. It is assumed that we display stable, consistent, describable patterns of behavior—in Mischel's description, it is a search for "generalized, global, situation-free personality variables" (Mischel, 1977). His critique of such conceptions (see also Mischel, 1968, 1973) has revived serious doubts about the generality of behavior (and the value of the concept of personality) and cannot be ignored. We remain on the side of the mildly optimistic searchers but acknowledge the implications of Mischel's interactionism and the consequent need to devote far more attention to situational variables and behavioral observations (see Mischel, 1977). Nevertheless, most of the available information falls into the generality category, and therefore this chapter proceeds in that mold, albeit uncomfortably and in recognition of its limitations.

Our goal in reviewing the relevant psychometric data is to understand and not to diagnose, so there is no need to discuss the strengths and weaknesses of a psychometric approach to diagnosis and assessment in general. Our intention is to elaborate our psychological model of obsessionality by answering the following questions: What is the relationship between introversion and obsessionality? Is the obsessional personality a valid construct? What are the main types of obsessional-compulsive complaints, and finally, what is the relationship between introversion, the obsessional personality, and obsessional-compulsive complaints? The analysis begins with a discussion of the hypothesized relationship between introversion and obsessionality.

INTROVERSION AND OBSESSIONALITY

The emerging psychological model of obsessional-compulsive behavior is based on the hypothesis that compulsions are essentially learned avoidance responses that are performed in order to avoid unpleasant events and unpleasant emotional states. The obsessional-compulsive person worries and ruminates if his or her compulsive ritual is not performed carefully and systematically. These worries can involve specific events, for example, poisoning one's family if hand washing is neglected, suffocating while asleep if gas taps are left unchecked, and social criticism if tasks are not completed to perfection. Or the worry can simply involve an anticipated increase in anxiety/discomfort. According to this model, the personality type most prone to develop obsessional-compulsive behavior would be characterized by a strong tendency to develop active-avoidance responses as a result of aversive social and personal experiences. The Eysenckian approach to personality is well known, and it is unnecessary to provide detailed exposition of the complex interrelating predictions that have been generated by the theory (see Eysenck, 1967). One postulate that has gained some empirical support and is of significance in any discussion of obsessionality states that introverts learn fear and avoidance responses very easily. In the present context it does not matter whether we accept Eysenck's view that introverts are highly conditionable or the equally tenable view that introverts are more sensitive to punishment (Gray, 1970). Both views lead to the prediction that introverts are more likely to develop fear and avoidance responses and, therefore, obsessional habits and complaints as well as anxiety states. This postulate can be finally resolved by demonstrating, in a longitudinal study, that introverted children are more likely to develop obsessional-compulsive problems than their extraverted peers. Since there is no such evidence to turn to, one has to consider a weaker test of the hypothesis, namely, that the relationship should hold for concurrent measures of introversion and obsessionality. There is a good deal of evidence to support this hypothesis.

Foulds and Caine (1958, 1959), Martin and Caine (1963), and Foulds (1965) have described a successful attempt to quantify the hysteroid-obsessoid dimension derived from the work of Janet and reviewed by Mackinnon (1944). The defining characterisics of this dimension are displayed in Table 10.1; the obsessoid end of this continuum was thought to represent the personality type most likely to develop obsessional complaints (i.e., the obsessional personality). Foulds and Caine (see Foulds, 1965) constructed the hysteroid-obsessoid questionnaire (HOQ) by generating several items from each of the statements in this table. Obsessional symptoms and statements with moral implications were excluded in an attempt to develop a measure of "ego-syntonic" obsessionality. Although this scale was designed to measure obsessionality, a number of investigators have demonstrated that the HOQ correlates as well with introversion as it does with itself. Foulds (1965) reports a correlation of 0.84 between Eysenck's measure of introversion and the HOQ obsessoid dimension; Barrett and his associates (1966) reported a correlation of 0.66; and Forbes (1969) found a correlation of 0.79 between the HOQ and the 16PF second-order introversion factor. So it appears that a valiant attempt to measure the obsessional personality ends up with a measure of introversion. We need not interpret this finding as a failure to identify the obsessional personality; rather, we may consider it evi-

TABLE 10.1:   OBSESSIOD–HYSTEROID TRAITS (FOULDS, 1965)

HYSTEROID	OBSESSOID
1. Exessive display of emotion	Scarcely any display of emotion
2. Vivid daydreams	Inability to indulge in fanciful thinking
3. Frequent mood changes	Constant mood
4. Underconscientious	Overconscientious
5. Given to precipitate action	Slow and undecided owing to weighing of pros and cons
6. Overdependent	Obstinately independent
7. Careless and inaccurate	Stickler for precision
8. Shallow emotionally	Feels things deeply
9. Desire to impress and gain attention	Self-effacing

dence supporting the views of both Janet and Eysenck. On the one hand, Janet (1901) identified the personality characteristics that, in his clinical judgment, were the precursors of obsessional-compulsive complaints, and these clinical impressions were embodied in the Foulds HOQ. On the other hand, Eysenckian personality theory leads to the prediction that obsessional-compulsive behavior is more likely to develop in the introverted personality. The fact that the HOQ "obsessoid" dimension correlates so highly with Eysenck's introversion dimension supports the hypothesis that the introvert is more likely to develop obsessional-compulsive complaints. A weak association between introversion and obsessionality was confirmed by Kendell and di Scipio (1970) in a study using a different measure directed at obsessionality [i.e., the Leyton Obsessional Inventory (Cooper, 1970)]. In a group of patients recovering from depression, they obtained a correlation of 0.3 between introversion and the Leyton Symptom Score. Our own measure of obsessional-compulsive *complaints* (Hodgson and Rachman, 1977), described later in this chapter, also correlated significantly with introversion (0.4) in a group of patients being treated for obsessional-compulsive problems.

According to the Eysenckian model of personality, neuroticism should also contribute to the development of obsessional-compulsive complaints and, in turn, would be increased by them. This association was confirmed by Kendell and di Scipio $(r = 0.5)$. Orme (1965) also found a correlation of 0.5 for both patients and normals using the Cattell Factor O Scale as a measure of neuroticism and "obsessional-symptom" items derived from a factor-analytical study (Sandler and Hazari, 1960). However, there is some evidence (to be discussed shortly) that the Sandler and Hazari items do not measure obsessionality. Of course, an association between neuroticism and obsessional-compulsive complaints is not surprising and would be predicted by most theories.

Further confirmation of the relationship between obsessional problems and neurotic introversion is provided by Eysenck (1959) in the manual of the

Maudsley Personality Inventory and by Eysenck and Eysenck (1964) in the Eysenck Personality Inventory manual. In his review of the relevant psychometric data, Slade (1974) concluded that "there seems to be overwhelming evidence that a strong relationship exists between obsessionality and measures of neuroticism and extraversion-introversion; to put it another way, that the obsessional neurotic patient is a neurotic introvert" (p. 105). We accept this conclusion, but would maintain only that the obsessional neurotic patient *tends to* the neurotic-introvert quadrant.

The hypothesis that neurotic introverts are more likely to develop obsessional complaints can be finally tested only by a longitudinal study, since it is probable that the development of an obsessional disorder is an emotionally disturbing and introverting experience, and therefore elevated neuroticism and introversion scores may reflect effects as well as causes. If these relationships are confirmed in a longitudinal study, it could be maintained that neuroticism and introversion are neither necessary nor sufficient conditions for the development of obsessional-compulsive complaints. They are not *necessary* because other personality types will develop obsessional-compulsive problems if subjected to unusually stressful or frequent learning experiences; they are not *sufficient* because a specific set of learning experiences are presumed to be necessary.

THE OBSESSIONAL PERSONALITY

Any discussion of the obsessional personality and its relationship to obsessional complaints must include the influential study published by Sandler and Hazari (1960). They concluded on the basis of a factor-analytical investigation that *the obsessional personality* refers to people who are exceedingly systematic, methodical, and thorough. They like a well-ordered mode of life; they are consistent, punctual, and meticulous in their use of words. They dislike half-done tasks and find interruptions irksome. They pay much attention to detail and have a strong aversion to dirt. A second factor appears to reflect *obsessional-compulsive complaints* and describes a person

> whose daily life is disturbed through the intrusion of unwanted thoughts and impulses into his conscious experience. Thus he is compelled to do things which his reason tells him are unnecessary, to perform certain rituals as part of his everyday behavior, to memorize trivia, and to struggle with persistent "bad" thoughts. He tends to worry over his past actions, to brood over ideas, and finds himself getting behind with things. He has difficulty in making up his mind, and he has an inner resistance to commencing work. [p. 120]

Brooks (1969) included many of Sandler and Hazari's items in a factor-analytical study and identified similar factors that appeared to be associated with "orderliness" and "doubting."

According to Sandler and Hazari, they identified a cluster of obsessional "traits" and a cluster of obsessional "symptoms" that are unrelated; however, inspection of their data and arguments does not justify such a conclusion. First of all, it should be noted that two oblique vectors would more closely represent their clusters of items, suggesting that there *is* a correlation between the "obsessional traits" and the "obsessional symptoms." Second, a large correlation between obsessional personality and obsessional complaints would not be expected in their sample, even if every obsessional-compulsive person had an obsessional personality. A high correlation would be obtained only if most individuals with an obsessional personality also reported severe obsessional complaints, and no theory would predict such an outcome. Even more troublesome is evidence suggesting that the Sandler and Hazari scales may not in fact be valid measures of obsessionality. Reed (1969a), for example, administered the items to 20 patients with obsessional symptoms, 20 patients with obsessional traits but no symptoms, and 20 controls, and found that the groups did not differ significantly on either the trait or the complaint items. Other attempts at independent verification of the findings have also been unsuccessful. For example, Snaith, McGuire, and Fox (1971) administered the Sandler-Hazari scale to 50 consecutive patients suffering from primary depressive illnesses. Contrary to prediction, patients with obsessional symptoms did not return higher scores on the Sandler-Hazari scale than patients without obsessional symptoms. The patients with obsessional symptoms recorded a mean obsessional-trait score of 26.7, while those without obsessional symptoms returned an obsessional-trait score of 25.7. The patients with obsessional symptoms obtained an obsessional-symptom score on the Sandler-Hazari scale of 14.6, while those without obsessional symptoms obtained a symptom score of 15.9. Along similar lines, Orme (1965) administered the Sandler-Hazari scale to 15 obsessional patients and 15 phobic patients. "They produced almost identical mean scores on both scales" (p. 269). That is, the Sandler obsessional scale failed to distinguish between phobic and obsessional patients. The Orme report contains two additional points of interest. In the first place, Orme found a large and significant correlation between the Sandler obsessional scale and a scale designed to measure emotional stability. Second, when the Sandler scale was reapplied to 22 patients after their discharge from the hospital, it was found that the obsessional-trait score had declined from 13.95 to 10.91—a larger decline than one would expect from a trait scale that should show evidence of greater stability. These three failures to validate the Sandler-Hazari scales force one to conclude that they may not be valid measures of obsessionality, and that the original study neither confirms nor disproves the hypothesized relationship between obsessional traits and complaints.

Kendell and di Scipio (1970) used the Leyton Inventory to assess the relationship between obsessional symptoms and traits in a group of patients recovering from depression. They found a high correlation between the two measures (0.78), confirming the relationship noted by Cooper (1970) for normal women (0.74), normal men (0.79), and house-proud housewives (0.87). Unfortunately, these results cannot be taken at face value, since the division of the Leyton items into trait and symptom categories was made on the basis of subjective judgment and appears to be arbitrary. For example, consider the following items, which are called obsessional symptoms but could equally well refer to obsessional traits:

Do you hate dirt and dirty things?
Do you tend to worry a bit about personal cleanliness or tidiness?
Are you fussy about keeping your hands clean?
Do your armchairs have cushions that you like to keep exactly in position?

Since studies that have utilized the Sandler and Hazari items and the Leyton Inventory cannot help unravel the relationship between obsessional traits and complaints, we are left with the unvalidated evidence from a number of psychometric studies designed to test the psychoanalytical theory of obsessionality.

Elsewhere we have considered Freud's conjecture that there is an anal personality type linked with obsessionality, characterized by a tendency to be parsimonious, obstinate, and orderly, and that its etiological basis can be traced back to infantile anal erotism and severe toilet training (Hodgson and Rachman, 1979). We found no evidence to support Freud's etiological speculations, but did not discount the possibility of an obsessional triad (i.e., a strong relationship among the traits that are considered to be the core of the obsessional personality—parsimony, obstinacy, and meticulousness).

Fisher and Greenberg (1977) present a "brief overview" of the relevant data, concluding that "there is no question but that past studies have almost unanimously found it possible to isolate recognizable clusters of anal traits and attitudes. Repeatedly these studies depict trait patterns quite reminiscent of Freud's anal character" (p. 144). Our assessment of the same data suggests different conclusions. First, there is no evidence that the anal personality, if it exists, is a function of the specific antecedents predicted by Freudian theory. Second, the psychometric studies do not confirm a strong relationship among orderliness, parsimony, and obstinacy. So in the following discussion we will ignore the notion of anality and simply ask whether the evidence supports the hypothesis that there is a particular cluster of traits that is specifically linked with obsessionality.

Barnes (1952) carried out a factor-analytical investigation and concluded that although the Freudian theory of psychosexual development was not supported on the whole, there was some evidence to support an "anal" factor. He concluded that "all the tests with the largest loadings on the unitary trait of meticulousness, such as orderliness, reliability, law abidance, cleanliness and meticulousness are associated with the anal stage of development. Not all the anal tests, however, have heavy loadings on this factor" (p. 163). So although a factor emerged that could be labelled "orderliness," there was no evidence that parsimony and obstinacy were related. The trait of cleanliness correlated with obstinacy to the extent of 0.19, and with meticulousness 0.18. Obstinacy correlated insignificantly with cleanliness, not at all with meticulousness (0.02), and not at all with orderliness (0.01). Meticulousness correlated with cleanliness to the extent of 0.18, with obstinacy 0.02, and with concern over money matters to the extent of 0.06. It is also of some interest, in the light of our earlier discussions on the relationship between depression and obsessions, to notice that depression scores correlated not at all with cleanliness, obstinacy, orderliness, or meticulousness (Barnes, 1952, p. 129).

Beloff (1957) factor-analyzed a questionnaire designed to measure the anal character and then attempted to relate this measure to bowel training experiences. The 28-item scale was administered to 120 Belfast undergraduates, and in addition to answering for themselves, each subject was asked to answer for four other respondents known to him or her. The results were interpreted as revealing a single general factor of "anal character."

The most remarkable feature of this study is that the majority of high-loading items deal with assertive behavior and few of them refer to the classical triad of parsimony, obstinacy, and meticulousness. Insofar as Beloff was successful in constructing a satisfactory questionnaire, it is primarily a measure of assertiveness, not of anal character or of the obsessional personality. Of the ten factor items with the highest loadings, no more than two are related to the anal triad; instead, they are statements such as "Active in family affairs," "A sense of power," "Enjoys criticizing others," "Blames newspapers for distortions," "Irritable," and so on. Beloff comments, "The qualities of parsimony, cleanliness, and collecting . . . contribute less variance than the literature would have led one to predict" (1957, p. 158). As for the qualities of the questionnaire itself, it had a low internal reliability; the split-half consistency coefficient was 0.62. Also, there was considerable disagreement between the subjects' self-rated scores and the scores turned in by their peers. The agreement between subject and peers, correlated for attenuation, was $r = 0.48$. In Beloff's words, "The correspondence . . . was by no means perfect" (p. 158).

The mothers of 43 of the subjects were interviewed in order to gather information on the toilet training experiences of the subject. The correlation between coercive bowel training and anal character, defined by Beloff in terms of the scores recorded on her questionnaire, was precisely 0.05. From this she concluded that, although "the anal character had been shown to exist" in her sample of subjects, "it is not related to bowel training experiences" (p. 165). One could go further. In our view this study failed to demonstrate the existence of the anal character and, hence, could not test the putative relationship between bowel training and anal character traits.

It is interesting to note that Stagner and Moffitt (1956), working at approximately the same time, obtained scant support for the Freudian theory from their statistical study of personality types. They administered a scale to 200 male students and found little sign of the Freudian typology (p. 73).

Finney (1961) analyzed the responses of 50 male and 50 female subjects to a set of 56 short scales and, after rotation to oblique simple structure, found that 5 factors were common to both male and female subjects. The first of these factors contained substantial loadings on 3 experimental scales designed to measure orderliness, parsimony, and obstinacy. The loadings for males and females were, respectively, as follows: Orderliness, 0.61 and 0.61; parsimony, 0.34 and 0.23; obstinacy, 0.40 and 0.21. It is assumed that these experimental scales are valid measures, although the one example of the orderliness scale that is reproduced suggests that orderliness and cleanliness were confounded ("I like to have my clothes clean and tidy at all times"). Given that the scales are valid measures, orderliness, obstinacy, and parsimony appear to be related to some extent—but only for men, since loadings below 0.25 are of little significance. Hetherington and Brackbill (1963) found the obverse to be true (i.e., significant correlations in girls but not in boys).

Comrey (1965) carried out a factor analysis of the responses of 305 "volunteer students and community persons" to 51 scales and rotated to approximate oblique simple structure. One of the factors, labeled compulsion, is of some interest in our attempt to describe the obsessional personality. It is formed from the following subscales: need for order (loading 0.72), love of routine (0.62), drive to finish (0.61), meticulousness (0.55), cautiousness (0.53), impulsiveness (-0.37), and personal grooming (0.35). Although Comrey's study was included in Fisher and Greenberg's overview, it has little bearing on the notion of the anal personality, since parsimony and obstinacy were not assessed.

Further psychometric data were provided by Gottheil (1965) in a paper entitled "An Empirical Analysis of Orality and Anality." A 40-item trait scale was developed from descriptions in the literature, checked by 20 professional judges who agreed that each item referred to the anal character, and also by carrying out an item analysis based on the responses of 179 Army-enlisted male subjects. Thirteen items were found to be unrelated to the total score, but the following items were closely correlated:

When you start a job, does it upset you to stop before you are through?
When you meet people, do you notice whether their fingernails are clean?
When you leave the house, do you check all the lights and gas?
When you finish a test, do you check your answers?
If you come across a word you do not understand, do you look it up in a dictionary rather than ask someone?

These questions appear to be assessing perfectionist and checking behavior, usually linked with the concept of obsessionality. In order to clarify the relationship, if any, among parsimony, obstinacy, and orderliness, we must look at a factor-analytical investigation of the same questionnaire (Gottheil and Stone, 1968). Five factors were extracted in a centroid analysis and then rotated using a quartimax procedure. The fourth factor, defined by the following items, is concerned with parsimony:

> Is not a collector.
> When leaving the house does not check lights and gas.
> Considered free and loose with his/her money.
> Does not keep track of the money he/she spends.
> Is a careless person.
> Does not check price in several stores before buying an item.

However, there is no sign of orderliness and obstinacy in this factor. Factor 3 covers perfectionism, orderliness, persistence, and a critical tendency, and the only question that could be considered to be a measure of obstinacy loads on factor 1 ("Finds it embarrassing to stick up for one's rights"). Since these are uncorrelated factors, this study does not support the notion of an anal triad, although it is of some interest to students of obsessionality.

Another psychometric investigation of the anal character entitled "The Anal Character: A Cross Cultural Study in Ghana," was reported by Kline (1969). A 75-item "anal inventory" was devised from descriptions found in the psychoanalytical literature. In constructing these items an attempt was made to avoid response biases caused by the influence of social-desirability and acquiescent response sets. The responses of 300 students were subjected to an item analysis, and it was found that 30 items correlated with the total score (greater than 0.26), including items pertaining to orderliness (8 items), parsimony (4 items), and obstinacy (5 items). However, the fact that these subscales correlate with the total score is no evidence that they correlate with each other; it is possible that the subscales are unrelated but nevertheless correlate at a low level with the total-scale score. Kline's test appears to have construct validity, since it is related to other tests that supposedly measure obsessional or anal traits (Beloff, 1957; Hazari, 1957; Grygier, 1961), but this cannot be taken to confirm the notion of *anal* character. The Ghanaian sample referred to in the title of Kline's paper turned out to have a mean score that was two points higher than the British sample. However, this statistically significant difference cannot be taken seriously, since for the Ghanaian sample six of the items did not correlate with the total score. This change in factorial structure could easily result in a two-point difference between mean scores and invalidates Kline's conclusion that his Ghanaian sample differed significantly in anal character from their British counterparts.

The studies reviewed by Fisher and Greenberg in support of the anal character do not strongly support the notion that orderliness, parsimony, and obstinacy covary. A study by Lazare and his associates (1966) and a replication (Lazare et al., 1970), taken together, suggest that, at least in female patients, there is a personality type that includes orderliness, parsimony, and obstinacy but is *mainly* characterized by orderliness, overconscientiousness, perseverance, and rigidity. Both studies included female patients at the Massachusetts Mental Health Center and were designed to test the hypothesis that the clusters of personality traits identified in a factor-analytical study would correspond to those described in the classical psychoanalytical literature. Twenty traits covering the "oral, obsessive and hysterical personality types" were derived from the psychoanalytical literature, each being measured by a seven-item questionnaire. Table 10.2 lists these traits, indicates which were expected to load on the "obsessional factor," and gives the "obsessional-factor" loading for both the original and the replication study.

There is sufficient overlap between the defining traits of this factor in the two studies to suggest that the traits do cluster together in a way that confirms, to some extent, the predictions derived from the psychoanalytical literature.

TABLE 10.2:   COMPARISON OF "OBESSIONAL FACTOR" OF ORIGINAL AND REPLICATION STUDIES (LAZARE ET AL., 1970)

Original Study		Replication Study	
TRAIT	FACTOR LOADING	TRAIT	FACTOR LOADING
Orderliness	0.74	Emotional constriction	0.67
Superego	0.62	Orderliness	0.66
Perseverance	0.54	Parsimony	0.63
Obstinacy	0.54	Rigidity	0.61
Rigidity	0.50	Superego	0.55
Rejection of others	0.38	Perseverance	0.50
Parsimony	0.37	Obstinacy	0.37
Emotional constriction	0.35	Passivity	0.18
Egocentricity	0.21	Suggestibility	0.10
Fear of sexuality	0.12	Emotionality	0.06
Self-doubt	0.12	Aggression	0.06
Aggression	0.07	Self-doubt	0.06
Emotionality	0.02	Rejection of others	0.04
Pessimism	0.00	Egocentricity	−0.08
Oral aggression	−0.04	Exhibitionism	−0.08
Exhibitionism	−0.05	Fear of sexuality	−0.11
Passivity	−0.05	Dependence	−0.15
Sexual provocativeness	−0.07	Pessimism	−0.16
Suggestibility	−0.10	Oral aggression	−0.36
Dependence	−0.12	Sexual provocativeness	−0.40

This personality dimension is characterized by orderliness, conscientiousness, perseverance, and rigidity.

Before discussing the overlap between the various psychometric investigations of the obsessional personality, we will summarize some of the negative and contradictory evidence that emerges. First of all, it should be stressed that none of the psychometric investigations of the obsessional personality has been validated. Since items are selected from the relevant clinical literature, the factor-analytical studies may be perpetuating myths or half-truths. Second, the existence of the "anal triad" is called into question, since insignificant or very low correlations are often reported. Parsimony and obstinacy do not always load highly on the orderliness factor. Some researchers conclude that obsessionality is best covered by more than one factor (e.g., Barnes, 1952; Gottheil and Stone, 1968), whereas others have identified a single factor (e.g., Finney, 1961; Lazare et al., 1970). Although there are many inconsistencies, it should be remembered that the obsessional factors that emerge from a study will depend on the range of obsessional traits that are included, and the type of analysis conducted. If only apparently obsessional items are factored, then more than one obsessional factor will probably be identified. If a large number of other items are included, assessing, for example, aggression, dependence, and sporting interests, then there is a greater probability that only one obsessional factor will emerge. Of the studies that factor-analyzed a set of items supposedly tapping obsessional traits (e.g., Barnes, 1952; Beloff, 1957; Sandler and Hazari, 1960; Gottheil and Stone, 1968), three identified a factor that can be called *orderliness*. The studies that include a large range of nonobsessional items have also identified a factor, with orderliness having a high loading (Finney, 1961; Comrey, 1965; Lazare et al., 1966, 1970; Brooks, 1969). The orderly person appears to be tidy and organized, doesn't waste time, is systematic and methodical, does not put things off until the last minute, plans ahead, tends to be clean, is cautious, and is not impulsive.

We still have no evidence to support the hypothesis that orderliness is a precurser of obsessional-compulsive complaints. Is there any evidence of predictive or concurrent validity, the former indicating that orderly people are more likely to develop obsessional complaints and the latter showing that people who have already developed obsessional complaints tend to be more orderly than people who have not developed them?

We found no data that could be construed as a test of predictive validity, but there is some evidence from our own research that is relevant to the question of concurrent validity. Recognizing that the psychometric studies of obsessionality lacked validation data, we developed a questionnaire consisting only of items that discriminated between a group of neurotic patients with obsessional complaints and a matched group with no obsessional complaints. (The questionnaire will be described in the next section.) To our surprise we discovered that items that were included to cover the concept of orderliness did not discriminate between the groups. These items were the following:

I do not get upset if other people accidentally move some of my personal belongings.
I worry a great deal about keeping things tidy.
I tend to be unnecessarily careful when folding clothes and putting things in drawers.
I am not a perfectionist.
I do not spend a long time attending to my hair every morning.
I do not worry too much if I have to leave a job half-finished.
One of my major problems is that I have to keep everything in a set place.

In other words, our obsessional neurotic sample was not more orderly than an equally introverted nonobsessional neurotic sample, suggesting that orderliness may not be specifically associated with *obsessional* complaints. The validation data on the Sandler and Hazari items also suggest the same conclusion (e.g., Reed, 1969a; Snaith et al., 1971; Orme, 1965). It would appear that although orderliness is the main "obsessional trait" to emerge from factor-analytical studies, it should not be labeled obsessional, since it is equally likely to be found in nonobsessional but introverted neurotics. According to Eysenckian theory, the introverted neurotic is more likely to suffer from dysthymic complaints (i.e., anxiety states and phobias) as well as obsessions and compulsions. Could it be that the obsessional personality is actually a precursor of dysthymic states rather than specifically obsessional states and has therefore been mislabeled? Whether this is true or not, the fact remains that there is no evidence to support the custom of referring to the meticulous, cautious, and orderly person as an "obsessional personality."

As it is unlikely that a trait such as orderliness will be equally related to each of the various types of obsessional problem, one needs a rational description of obsessional complaints before proceeding.

OBSESSIONAL-COMPULSIVE COMPLAINTS

The following account of our attempt to investigate types of obsessional-compulsive complaint and to construct a simple questionnaire to assess them includes information about selection of items, principal-components analysis, validity, and reliability (Hodgson and Rachman, 1977).

Item Selection

After surveying the literature, interviewing 30 obsessional patients, and following our hunches about etiology, we assembled 65 items. In order to control for the possibility of an acquiescent response set, the questions were phrased in such a way as to ensure that a totally obsessional individual would respond with equal numbers of true and false replies. Our next task was to eliminate all items that failed to discriminate between a group of obsessional patients and a group of matched neurotics. The questionnaire was completed by 50 obsessional patients referred to the Maudsley Hospital and by 50 nonobsessional neurotic patients who were also recent referrals to the Maudsley. The patients were diagnosed by two experienced clinicians. Those described as psychopathic or hysteric were excluded from the neurotic group in order to match the two groups on dysthymia (Eysenck, 1957). In fact, the groups were matched on all of Eysenck's PQ scales (Eysenck and Eysenck, 1968), namely, the psychoticism, extroversion, neuroticism, and lie scales, as well as age, sex, and percentage of in-patients. (See Table 10.3.) As predicted, the obsessional group was more neurotic and introverted than the general population.

Thirty questions differentiated between the neurotic and obsessional groups on both a parametric and a nonparametric test (t-test and chi square). A new questionnaire was then formed using only these 30 questions. (See Appendix A.) Luckily, the questions in this final version did not have to be altered to control for response set, since a totally obsessional individual would respond with "true" to exactly half of them.

Principal-Components Analysis

A principal-components analysis with oblique rotation was performed on the responses of 100 adult obsessionals, 50 in the original group and 50 more contacted through colleagues working in other hospitals throughout England, Scotland, and Wales.

Patients were selected for the study only if they satisfied the following criteria:

1. They exhibited observable obsessional-compulsive rituals and were not pure ruminators.
2. Their obsessional problems were sufficiently chronic to require treatment.
3. They were not psychotic.

Plotting the slope of the Eigenvalues suggested a 5-component solution. However, component 5 was ignored, since it consisted of only two items that correlated well together (Q2 and Q8). Consequently, a 4-component solution, accounting for 43 percent of the total variance, was considered to be the most appropriate, the 4 components accounting for 17, 11, 8, and 6 percent of the variance. The questions that load on the 4 components are listed, with their loadings, in Table 10.4. They have reasonable face validity and appear to cover four major types of complaint that we have observed in obsessional patients, namely, checking, cleaning, slowness, and doubting-conscientiousness.

TABLE 10.3: CRITERION GROUPS: AGE, SEX, AND EYSENCK PQ SCORES OF OBSESSIONAL AND NEUROTIC GROUPS

| | Obsessional Group (N = 50) | | Neurotic Group (N = 50) | | General Population Norms | | | |
| | | | | | Males | | Females | |
	MEAN	SD	MEAN	SD	MEAN	SD	MEAN	SD
Psychoticism	3.5	2.6	3.9	3.2	3.95	3.28	2.77	2.54
Extraversion	7.0	4.6	7.7	5.5	13.12	4.95	12.95	4.67
Neuroticism	17.3	3.9	17.0	4.2	9.69	5.10	12.73	5.07
Lie scale	8.9	5.1	9.0	4.9	7.22	4.24	8.06	4.14
Age	34.7	11.7	36.6	13.0				
	18 males	32 females	23 males	27 females				

TABLE 10.4:   QUESTIONS THAT LOAD ON THE FOUR COMPONENTS,
               WITH THEIR LOADINGS

Component 1—Checking

6.	I frequently have to check things (e.g., gas or water taps, doors, etc.) several times.	(+.79) H
22.	I do not tend to check things more than once.	(−.66) H
15.	I do not check letters over and over again before mailing them.	(−.63) H
28.	I spend a lot of time every day checking things over and over again.	(+.62) H
20.	My major problem is repeated checking.	(+.60) H
26.	I take a rather long time to complete my washing in the morning.	(+.43) L
14.	Some numbers are extremely unlucky.	(+.38) L
8.	I find that almost every day I am upset by unpleasant thoughts that come into my mind against my will.	(+.37) L
2.	I frequently get nasty thoughts and have difficulty getting rid of them.	(+.33) L

Component 2—Cleaning

17.	I am not excessively concerned about cleanliness.	(−.72) H
21.	I am not unduly concerned about germs and diseases.	(−.70) H
24.	My hands do not feel dirty after touching money.	(−.70) H
1.	I avoid using public telephones because of possible contamination.	(+.62) H
19.	I can use well-kept toilets without any hesitation.	(−.60)
9.	I do not worry unduly if I accidentally bump into somebody.	(−.56) L
5.	I don't worry unduly about contamination if I touch an animal.	(−.55)
13.	I use only an average amount of soap.	(−.53) L
27.	I do not use large amounts of antiseptics.	(−.53) L
4.	I am often late because I can't seem to get through everything in time.	(+.41) L
26.	I take rather a long time to complete my washing in the morning.	(+.43) L

Component 3—Slowness

2.[a]	I frequently get nasty thoughts and have difficulty getting rid of them.	(−.64) H
16.	I do not take a long time to dress in the morning.	(−.63) H
8.[a]	I find that almost every day I am upset by unpleasant thoughts that come into my mind against my will.	(−.62) H
23.	I do not stick to a very strict routine when doing ordinary things.	(−.58) H
29.	Hanging and folding my clothes at night does not take up a lot of time.	(−.52) L
4.	I am often late because I can't seem to get through everything on time.	(+.38) L
25.	I do not usually count when doing a routine task.	(−.34) L

Component 4—Doubting-Conscientiousness

7.	I have a very strict conscience.	(+.61) H
3.	I am more concerned than most people about honesty.	(+.60) H
30.	Even when I do something very carefully, I often feel that it is not quite right.	(+.53) L
12.	I tend to get behind in my work because I repeat things over and over again.	(+.51) L
11.	Neither of my parents was very strict during my childhood.	(−.50) L
10.	I usually have serious doubts about the simple everyday things I do.	(+.48) L
18.	One of my major problems is that I pay too much attention to detail.	(+.44)

[a]Note the two items relating to unpleasant thoughts load on this component but that they do not load in the expected direction. Thus, individuals who take a long time to dress in the morning tend to report that they do not suffer from unpleasant, intrusive thoughts.

Although the compilation of obsessional-compulsive complaints was part of an investigation of the types or dimensions of obsessional behavior, we ended up with a brief questionnaire that can be used as a research tool for assessing the types and severity of obsessional problems. When used as a questionnaire, approximate factor scores can be derived by totaling the number of questions that are answered in the obsessional direction for each factor. The questions that identify each factor are listed in Table 10.4. Using this approximate method, the correlations between factor scores are changed slightly, but not enough to invalidate the simple scoring method. The questionnaire can be used to give a total obsessionality score as well as four factor scores. (See Appendix B for the scoring key.)

Consistency of the Subscales

The alpha coefficients of the subscales are 0.7, 0.8, 0.7, and 0.7. Essentially, an alpha coefficient averages the intercorrelations between all the items in a particular test or subscale to give some indication of the extent to which a scale hangs together as a measure of a single dimension (Cronbach, 1951).

Validation of the Questionnaire

Since we had treated 42 out of the 100 patients in the obsessional sample for cleaning or checking complaints, we were able to validate two of the subscales against our retrospective ratings. It was possible to reach dichotomous ratings of the severity of these two problems (1 = slight or no problem; 2 = moderate or severe problem), but impossible to give satisfactory retrospective ratings on "obsessional slowness" and "doubting." The questionnaire subscale scores were also transformed into dichotomous ratings, scores of 7 and above being rated 2. This cutoff point is approximately two standard deviations from the mean for the nonobsessional neurotic group. The degree of association between therapist and questionnaire ratings was then ascertained by calculating gamma coefficients (Goodman and Kruskal, 1963), and in view of the retrospective nature of the therapist ratings, these coefficients were satisfactory (i.e., 0.7 for the "cleaning" and "checking" subscales). Another method of assessing the validity of the cleaning and checking subscales is to use the scale scores to categorize patients as "checkers" or "cleaners" and compare these with the category assigned by the therapist. This was impossible to do for 7 of the 42 patients, since 4 of them did not differ on the questionnaire subscales and 3 could not be categorized by the therapist. However, for the rest a gamma coefficient of 0.8 was obtained. For 30 obsessionals Leyton Inventory Scores (Cooper, 1970) were available and correlated with our "total obsessionality" score (0.6).

Finally, we were interested in validating the questionnaire by assessing

TABLE 10.5: INTERCORRELATIONS BETWEEN RATINGS OF IMPROVEMENT AND THE QUESTIONNAIRE CHANGE SCORES, WITH INITIAL SCORES ELIMINATED AS COVARIATES (CORRELATIONS BEFORE COVARIANCE IN PARENTHESES)

	THERAPIST 1	THERAPIST 2	PATIENT
Therapist 2	.81 (.82)		
Patient	.74 (.75)	.60 (.61)	
Questionnaire total scores	.67 (.46)	.74 (.42)	.53 (.42)

the extent to which it could pick up changes in obsessional-compulsive complaints. For this purpose the available pre- and posttreatment scores on 40 treated patients were used. The posttreatment scores were obtained during the follow-up period, usually about 6 months after treatment. At this stage of our research, we were piloting different outcome measures and did not have identical behavioral and subjective measures on every person; consequently, both of the therapists and the patient gave independent ratings of the amount of improvement due to treatment (1 = not improved; 2 = slightly improved; 3 = much improved). Table 10.5 displays the intercorrelations between these ratings and the questionnaire change scores. Since the change scores were a function of pretreatment scores, the latter were eliminated as covariates.

First, it should be noted that our subjective ratings were reasonably reliable. Since each patient was treated daily and since treatment included the completion of specific behavioral tasks, it is reasonable to suppose that we obtained some idea of the extent to which a patient improved during treatment. Second, the questionnaire change scores and subjective ratings correlated at a reasonable level. We considered this to be further evidence of the validity of the questionnaire as a measure of obsessional complaints. Volans (1976) found that the MOCQ differentiated between groups of phobic and obsessional patients, even though the groups were small (N = 8).

Test-Retest Reliability

Fifty adult night school attenders completed the 30-item questionnaire on two occasions, one month apart, generating a total of 1,500 response pairs. In the unlikely event of the questionnaire's being totally reliable then the 1,500 response pairs would all be either true-true or false-false. The contingency table (Figure 10.1) indicates that the test was very reliable, since 1,341 response pairs were concordant. Kendell's tau for this data is 0.8.

FIRST OCCASION

		True	False
SECOND OCCASION	True	634	73
	False	77	707

FIGURE 10.1. Fifty subjects completed the 30-item questionnaire on two occasions, generating 1,500 response pairs.

Checking the Consistency of an Individual Questionnaire

In order to develop a method for checking the consistency of an individual questionnaire, six pairs of items that were correlated (r = 0.4) in both the obsessional and nonobsessional samples were selected. A person responding in a consistent way would tend to give the same response to questions 2/8, 7/3, 10/12, and 17/21 and different responses to questions 6/22 and 16/26. By scoring 1 for consistent and 0 for inconsistent responses, we have a measure of consistency that varies from 0 to 6. A person answering entirely at random would be expected to obtain a score of 3. Figure 10.2 displays the distribution of consistency scores for the obsessional and nonobsessional groups, indicating that a consistency score of 3 or less is suspect.

	Consistency Score						
	6	5	4	3	2	1	0
100 obsessionals	24	43	25	6	1	1	0
50 neurotics	12	19	14	5	0	0	0
50 night school students	21	19	8	2	0	0	0

FIGURE 10.2. Frequency of occurrence of the various consistency scores in the obsessional and nonobsessional groups.

Bearing in mind the limited aims of this study, it appears that people who suffer from observable obsessional-compulsive rituals complain of five main types of problem, which we have labeled checking, cleaning, slowness, doubting, and ruminating. These labels refer to types of problems and not to types of people, and a person may suffer from more than one type of complaint. Only two items loaded on component 5, so we decided to ignore it. However, it should be noted that both items described obsessional ruminations. It should be remembered that our sample of obsessional patients did not include those who complained only of ruminations, with no observable compulsive behavior. Since we were able to validate the checking, cleaning, and total-obsessionality scores, we are confident that these scales will be useful research tools; however, the usefulness of the obsessional-slowness and doubting scales remains to be seen. Before discussing other studies of obsessional complaints, a brief description of the first five principal components based on items which have high loadings is provided.

1. *Obsessional Checking.* Repeated checking is a major problem, and a great deal of time is spent every day checking things over and over again (e.g., gas or water taps, doors, letters, etc.). The morning wash takes a long time to complete (possibly because checking is involved). Some numbers are considered to be extremely unlucky, and there is a tendency to suffer from obsessional ruminations. meditating the thoughtfulness.

2. *Obsessional Cleaning.* Obsessional cleaning involves excessive concern about germs, diseases, and cleanliness, and worries about contamination from money, public telephones, toilets, and animals. Soap and antiseptics are used excessively, and washing takes up a lot of time.

3. *Obsessional Slowness.* Dressing and hanging/folding clothes take up a lot of time. A person suffering from this problem is often late because he or she cannot get through everything on time. The person adheres to a strict routine and often counts when doing a routine task. He or she tends *not* to suffer from obsessional ruminations.

4. *Obsessional Doubting-Conscientiousness.* A person suffering from this problem often feels that a job has not been completed correctly even when it was performed very carefully. The person usually has serious doubts about simple everyday events. He or she gets behind with work because things are repeated over and over again and too much attention is paid to detail. The person has a strict conscience and is more concerned than most people about honesty (and probably had a strict parent/s).

5. *Obsessional Ruminating.* Almost every day unpleasant thoughts occur. They are upsetting, come into the mind against the will, and are difficult to remove.

These descriptions are based only on the questionnaire data. A clinician with experience of these complaints would be able to add other significant details.

If the presence of a complaint is defined as a score of two standard deviations above the mean for the nonobsessional neurotic group, then 48 percent of our obsessional sample complained of cleaning/contamination problems and 53 percent complained of checking problems. These percentages are similar to those reported by Stern and Cobb (1978). Slowness was also a common complaint, with 52 percent of our sample obtaining a high score on this component. It is interesting to note that those who obtain a high "slowness" score tend not to suffer from persistent unpleasant thoughts. This is in line with our clinical experience of obsessionals who suffer from slow, repetitive behavior with little or no anxiety and no persistent ruminations. They appear to be complaining of a type of ritual that has been called "functionally autonomous" (Walton and Mather, 1963), the probable basis for "primary obsessional slowness" (Rachman, 1974b). "Doubting-conscientiousness" is our label for the fourth component, which appears to describe a type of obsessional problem commonly seen in clinical practice. Akhtar and his associates (1975) report that obsessional doubting was experienced by 75 percent of their sample of 82 obsessional neurotics, and 60 percent of our sample obtained high scores on this component. The majority of people in our sample had more than one obsessional complaint.

Although our aim was primarily to investigate obsessional-compulsive complaints, we have produced a short questionnaire that may be useful to clinicians and research workers (the Maudsley Obsessional-Compulsive Questionnaire). Unlike the Leyton Inventory (Cooper, 1970), the MOCQ is quick and easy to administer, controls for an acquiescent response set, and includes only items that differentiate obsessional from nonobsessional neurotics.

In summary, our investigation suggests that an etiological model should attempt to explain the development of specific types of complaint and not a unitary obsessional-compulsive neurosis. The major types of complaint are checking, cleaning, slowness, doubting, and ruminating.

A learning theory interpretation of obsessional-compulsive behavior suggests that these five types of complaint could be exaggerations of relatively normal learned behavior. At one end of the obsessionality dimension we have checking behavior (e.g., of doors and gas taps) that might be considered to be prudent, slightly eccentric, or even bothersome, but not an abnormal obsessional-compulsive complaint. At the other end of this dimension are severe checking complaints that are distressing and incapacitating. One way of investigating dimensions of obsessionality is to administer an obsessional-complaints questionnaire to groups of subjects who are not asking for treatment of obsessional problems. Just such an analysis of obsessional behavior in normal subjects has been reported by Cooper and Kelleher (1973) using the Leyton Obsessional Inventory. This Inventory (Cooper, 1970) consists of a card-sorting procedure obtaining yes/no replies to 69 questions, the questions being generated from the lists of obsessional symptoms and obsessional traits displayed in Table 10.6.

Cooper and Kelleher completed a principal-components analysis on the scores of 302 normal Irish and English subjects, divided into subgroups by sex and nationality. Four analyses were inspected, and three components appeared

TABLE 10.6:   AREAS COVERED BY THE LEYTON INVENTORY (COOPER, 1970)

SYMPTOMS QUESTIONS	TRAIT QUESTIONS
1. Unpleasant recurring thoughts	10. Indecision
2. Checking	11. Hoarding ~ *putting away for safe keeping*
3. Dirt and contamination	12. Cleanliness
4. Dangerous objects (bits, splinters, chips, pins)	13. Meanness
	14. Irritability and moroseness
5. Personal cleanliness and tidiness	15. Rigidity
	16. Health (bowels)
6. Household cleanliness and tidiness	17. Regularity and method
	18. Punctuality
7. Order and routine	
8. Repetition	
9. Overconscientiousness and lack of satisfaction	

to be common to all of them, with a fourth component being common to three of the subgroups. The questions that define these components are as follows:

1. *Clean and Tidy*

Do you take care that the clothes that you are wearing are always clean and neat, whatever you are doing?
Do you dislike having a room untidy or not quite clean for even a short time?
Do you regard cleanliness as a *goodness* virtue in itself?
Are you very strict about keeping the house always very clean and tidy?

2. *Incompleteness*

Even when you have done something carefully, do you often feel that it is somehow not quite right or complete?
Do you feel unsettled or guilty if you haven't been able to do something exactly as you would like?
Are you ever overconscientious or very strict with yourself?

3. *Checking*

Do you ever have to check gas or water taps or light switches after you have already turned them off?
Do you often have to check things several times?
Do you ever have to go back and check doors, cupboards, or windows to make sure that they are really shut?
Do you ever get behind with the housework because you have to do something over again several times?

4. *Ruminating*

Do unpleasant or frightening thoughts or words ever keep going over and over in your mind?
Do you usually look on the gloomy side of things?

We can now consider the similarities and differences between this analysis and our own analysis of the complaints of obsessional patients. First of all, it should be noted that the questions defining the first component of the Leyton Inventory confound tidiness and cleanliness, so that we cannot be sure of their relative importance. Bearing this in mind, the component is similar to our "cleaning" component. The Leyton "incompleteness" component is almost identical to our "doubting" component; it refers to an overconscientious type of person who finds it difficult to be certain that a task has been performed properly. The Leyton checking component is certainly the same as our checking component, and the fourth component is the same as our fifth component, consisting of items related to unpleasant thoughts. It is reasonable to conclude that discussions of both obsessional behavior and obsessional complaints should distinguish among at least four types of obsessionality (i.e., checking, cleaning, doubting, and ruminating). The "slowness" component that emerged from our analysis of obsessional patients was not a principal component of the Leyton Inventory. To test the hypothesis that "slowness" is not a principal component of obsessionality in normal subjects, we calculated the alpha coefficients of each of the MOCQ subscales when administered to 50 nonobsessional neurotics and 50 night school attenders. The alpha coefficient gives an indication of the extent to which a scale hangs together as a measure of a single dimension, and the results (see Table 10.7) demonstrate that obsessional slowness does not appear to be a dimension of "normal obsessionality."

The combined MOCQ data on all 100 subjects were then pooled and subjected to a principal-components analysis followed by a varimax rotation of the first 5 components, an exact replication of Cooper and Kelleher's method of analysis. Plotting the slope of the Eigenvalues suggested a 3-component solution, so a further varimax rotation was performed on just 3 components. The components that emerged were very similar to the checking, cleaning, and

TABLE 10.7: ALPHA COEFFICIENTS OF MOCQ SUBSCALES FOR NONOBSESSIONAL GROUPS

	CHECKING	CLEANING	SLOWNESS	DOUBTING
Night school attenders (N = 50)	.8	.7	.3	.7
Neurotics (N = 50)	.7	.6	.0	.7

TABLE 10.8:   THE THREE MAJOR COMPONENTS OF THE MAUDSLEY OBSESSIONAL-COMPULSIVE INVENTORY

Component 1—Checking

1. I frequently have to check things (e.g., gas or water taps, doors, etc.) several times.
2. I do not tend to check things more than once.
3. I do not check letters over and over again before mailing them.
4. I spent a lot of time every day checking things over and over again.
5. My major problem is repeated checking.
6. I find that almost every day I am upset by unpleasant thoughts that come into my mind against my will.
7. I frequently get nasty thoughts and have difficulty getting rid of them.

Component 2—Cleaning

1. I am not excessively concerned about cleanliness.
2. I am not unduly concerned about germs and diseases.
3. I avoid using public telephones because of possible contamination.
4. I can use well-kept toilets without any hesitation.
5. I use only an average amount of soap.
6. I do not use a great deal of antiseptics.
7. I take a rather long time to complete my washing in the morning.

Component 3—Doubting-Conscientiousness

1. I have a very strict conscience. *aware of ones own existence - mentally awake*
2. I am more concerned than most people about honesty.
3. Neither of my parents was very strict during my childhood.
4. I usually have serious doubts about the simple everyday things I do.
5. One of my major problems is that I pay too much attention to detail.

doubting components identified in our previous analysis. The items that have loadings greater than 0.3 in both analysis are listed in Table 10.8.

There is one way in which the present analysis differs from the previous one, and that is the tendency for the doubting-overconscientiousness items to have high loadings on component 1 as well as on component 3.

The picture that is beginning to emerge from the various psychometric studies of nonobsessional and obsessional patient groups is reasonably clear. Checking, cleaning, doubting, and ruminating have been identified as principal components of both normal and abnormal obsessional behavior, whereas obsessional slowness is identified only in an obsessional patient group. It should be noted that tidiness did not emerge as a component of obsessionality in our studies because questions relating to tidiness in our original 65-item MOCQ did not discriminate between our obsessional and nonobsessional criterion groups and were not included in the final version.

We have now discussed introversion, the obsessional personality, and obsessional-compulsive complaints in some detail, but have not yet been able to unravel the relationships among them. However, the development of the MOCQ has enabled us to investigate these relationships, and our findings will be briefly described here.

INTROVERSION, THE OBSESSIONAL PERSONALITY, AND OBSESSIONAL COMPLAINTS

After reviewing the relevant psychometric data, it remains uncertain whether the obsessional personality is a valid construct. It would appear that the label refers to a cluster of traits centering on "orderliness"; however, there is no psychometric support for the notion that this feature of personality is more likely to be present in the obsessional neurotic than in the phobic or anxious person. Introversion is certainly associated with obsessional complaints, but introversion is not the obsessional personality, since it is linked not only with obsessionality but also with other dysthymic complaints (i.e., anxiety and phobic states). The obsessional personality would be a valid construct if it discriminated a group of phobics from a group of obsessionals, if a measure of obsessional personality correlated more highly with a measure of obsessional complaints than introversion and obsessional complaints, and if obsessional personality was a better *predictor* of obsessional complaints than introversion. In order to investigate the first two of these predictions, tests of introversion (Eysenck and Eysenck, 1977), obsessional personality (Lazare et al., 1970), and obsessional complaints (Hodgson and Rachman, 1977) were administered to 62 ex-patients of the Maudsley psychiatric hospital and to 19 other subjects. This study is described elsewhere (Hodgson, Rankin, and Stockwell, 1979), so only the main findings will be presented here.

There was a low but significant correlation between introversion and obsessional complaints ($r = 0.21$) and an equally low but insignificant correlation between obsessional personality and obsessional complaints ($r = 0.18$). In view of the strong relationship between introversion and Foulds's measure of obsessional personality, we were surprised to find no comparable relationship; it would appear that Foulds's HOQ and the questionnaire devised by Lazare and his colleagues are measuring different constructs. The anal triad, which is considered to comprise the three roots of obsessionality, does not seem to constitute the same tree, since obstinacy did not correlate with either orderliness ($r = 0.06$) or parsimony ($r = .06$), and the correlation between orderliness and parsimony was insignificant ($r = 0.17$). The only subscales of the obsessional-personality questionnaire to be associated with obsessional complaints were parsimony ($r = 0.31$) and overconscientiousness ($r = 0.44$); since one of the subscales of the obsessional-complaints questionnaire includes items on overconscientiousness, this high correlation was expected. [Overconscientiousness correlated with parsimony ($r = 0.26$) and also with introversion ($r = 0.25$)].

Human mind and spirit

Furthermore, the MOCQ (Hodgson and Rachman, 1977) discriminated between obsessional and phobic ex-patients who still complained of obsessional and phobic problems, but these two groups did *not* differ on introversion or obsessional personality.

It would seem that "the obsessional personality" either is an invalid notion or has not yet been properly defined; certainly, the obsessional personality is not well represented by the "anal triad," which does not even form a single construct. *while*

Since obsessional complaints are not homogeneous, and since the obsessional-personality subscales do not measure a single dimension, a better picture of the significant relationships is given by the subscale intercorrelations. Considering only correlations that are significant at the .01 level, we find the following relationships, ignoring that between overconscientiousness and the doubting-overconscientious MOCQ subscale:

MOCQ Subscale	Associated Obsessional Personality Subscales
Checking	Overconscientiousness, parsimony
Cleaning	–
Slowness	Rigidity
Doubting/overconscientiousness	Parsimony, Orderliness

In this sample of subjects with a wide range of problems, there was a high correlation between the checking and doubting scales of the MOCQ, so that one possible generalization to emerge is the relationship between checking/doubting complaints and parsimony/overconscientiousness. Whether such a relationship can be replicated or whether it is of any theoretical or practical significance remains to be seen.

We have failed to validate the concept of obsessional personality. The total obsessional-personality score did not correlate significantly with the obsessional-complaints score or with any of the MOCQ subscales, nor did it differentiate between phobic and obsessional patients. Overconscientiousness and parsimony were associated with checking/doubting complaints but not with washing complaints, and it now seems reasonable to conclude that there is no "obsessional personality" that is predisposed to develop an obsessional illness, although there may be more specific personality traits that are associated with more specific obsessional complaints.

SUMMARY AND CONCLUSIONS

We are left with weak evidence to support a loose association among introversion, neuroticism, and obsessional complaints, but neither introversion nor neuroticism can be called the obsessional personality. The link between dimensions of personality and obsessional complaints deserves further comment, since there are arguments in favor of rejecting such general traits (e.g., Mischel, 1968); they are usually based on the notions of response and situation specificity. For example, Sears (1963) carried out a time-sampling study of children's behavior to test the hypothesis that there is a general trait of "attention seeking," but found little or no relationship among the five types of attention-seeking behavior that were recorded. In other words, each child tended to use a specific method of getting attention (response specificity). Hartshorne and May (1928) reached similar conclusions when investigating deceit. There was no relationship between a test of lying given in a classroom situation and deception tests given in other situations. They found that as the situation was progressively changed, the correlations between tests were progressively lowered (situation specificity). To apply the specificity argument in the present context, it would be argued that introverted and obsessional behavior are situation and response specific. A particular person may be introverted in one situation and not in another, and may tend to display one type of introverted behavior but not another.

Mischel points out that the Hartshorne and May data can be interpreted as supporting a weak general factor, since there were small but statistically significant correlations between responses in different situations (see Burton, 1963), and consequently whether one talks about relatively independent specific behavior or a weak general factor will depend on the utility of the two approaches. It is not our intention to discuss the general utility of psychometry in clinical assessment; the available psychometric data have been discussed in order to help in the development of a model of obsessionality. Our conclusion that the loose association of traits called introversion covaries with the loose association of behavior called obsessional-compulsive may have little utility in assessment, but it does have implications for a model of obsessionality, since such a model must be able to explain the covariance. Of course, this relationship probably accounts for only a small portion of the variance in obsessional behavior, but this does not imply that the relationship is not worth knowing. Eysenck (1976) makes this point in a recent discussion of the scientific status of personality measurements:

> It may be worth while to make a final point about the importance of personality and individual differences research, in both theoretical and applied psychology, and to cast doubt on the logic of those who argue that the contribution of such factors to the variance, in many instances, is rather small. If we can agree that human behavior is very complex, and that causal factors in any particular situation are probably multiple, then it is obvious that no single factor is likely to account for much of the total variance . . .
>
> To take an example, let us imagine that we study 1,000 cars that refuse to start. This could be due to an almost infinite number of causes such as a defective starting motor, run-down battery, failure of the ignition system, too thick oil due to cold, etc. An engineer would think it a curious form of criticism to say that none of these multivarious causes were worth

studying because none of them accounted for more than 10 percent of the actual failures observed. What we look for in the first place is a proper understanding of the causal interactions, i.e., the invariances which are involved in the phenomenon we are studying; once this is achieved, we may be able to manipulate one or other of the factors involved. [p. 3]

Mischel (1968, 1977) proposes that psychologists would be well advised to concentrate their research efforts on situational rather than personality variables. In acting on his advice, it is as well for us to be aware of the possibility that measurable situational variables might themselves account for a relatively small proportion of the variance. Sarason and his associates (1975) have surveyed a number of studies in the literature involving the control of both personality and situational variables, and in one comparison they found that 35 percent of the situational main effects accounted for more than 10 percent of the variance, compared with 29 percent for personality indexes. So the predictive power of personality variables can be as high as it is for situational variables. Sarason and his colleagues argue that "the issue of the relative potency of situational and dispositional variables becomes secondary in importance to the question of how they might best be concurrently studied to advance our understanding of behavior" (p. 204). We are aware of the complex interaction of variables that influences the development of obsessional traits and complaints, and that a fruitful approach will probably turn out to involve a multivariate analysis of these interactions. However, we are willing to use any demonstrated invariance that might help us understand obsessionality.

The studies reviewed in this chapter suggest that we should steer the middle course between the idiographic approach, in which every problem-situation interaction is considered to be unique, and the medical model, with its implication that obsessional-compulsive behavior is symptomatic of an illness. We should investigate the relationship among checking, cleaning, doubting, slowness, and ruminating complaints and ask whether they have different onsets and maintaining factors and respond to different training methods. We must also remember that these components do not account for the total variance in obsessional behavior and that in clinical work there is no substitute for detailed behavioral analysis of the individual case.

Chapter 11

The Persistence
of Compulsive Behavior: I

INTRODUCTION

The persistence of obsessions and compulsions is extremely puzzling. There is no obvious reason for people to engage in repetitive, tiring, embarrassing, and unwanted self-defeating behavior. There is no obvious explanation for the persistent recurrence of intrusive, unacceptable, and distressing thoughts. In recognition of these puzzles, Mowrer (1950) spoke of this kind of self-defeating behavior as "the neurotic paradox."

The most favored answer is that compulsive behavior persists because it reduces anxiety. Although this view was proposed in one form or another before the growth of learning theory, it received powerful support from most psychologists who applied learning theory concepts to abnormal behavior. Mowrer's two-stage theory of fear and avoidance (1939, 1950, 1960), stating that successful avoidance behavior paradoxically *preserves* fear, was incorporated into many expositions of obsessional and compulsive behavior and has had a profound influence on the way in which we construe these disorders (e.g., Metzner's, 1963, interesting exposition).

Mowrer's theory of fear, and indirectly of compulsive rituals, served extremely well for a period, but some inadequacies are now apparent (Rachman, 1978d), and the theory cannot provide the basis for a comprehensive account of obsessions and compulsions. Even though Mowrer's original conception and its fruitful development in the hands of Miller, Metzner, Dollard, Wolpe, Eysenck, and others helped clarify the persistence of compulsions, it was never capable of offering an explanation for the occurrence and persistence of *obsessions*. Mowrer's (1960) revised theory, introducing the idea of behavioral persistence based on hope (a positive drive for safety signals) as well as on fear, goes some way toward saving the learning theory account of compulsions (see Chapter 25).

In 1958 Wolpe offered a slightly different account, claiming that there are two major types of compulsive ritual. The first type, which he called "anxiety-reducing obsessions," is easily accommodated by the anxiety reduction theory, but the second type, called "anxiety-elevating obsessions," posed and still poses problems for theories based on the reinforcing value of anxiety reduction. During the past few years, Beech (1974) and his colleagues have proposed another view. Although it is not fundamentally different from Wolpe's two-part classification, Beech attributes far greater importance to the anxiety-elevating obsessions than Wolpe, and with interesting consequences.

Our own view, expressed in an analysis of compulsive checking rituals (Rachman, 1976d), is that "obsessions and compulsions can (1) reduce anxiety/discomfort or (2) increase anxiety/discomfort or (3) leave anxiety/discomfort unchanged" (p. 272). It was argued that the first pattern (i.e., reduction of anxiety/discomfort) is likely to be the most common. Further, it was postulated that compulsive cleaning rituals most often follow the type (1) pattern (i.e., they are discomfort reducing). Obsessions follow the second pattern (i.e., they increase discomfort), and checking rituals follow either the first or the third pattern.

As an introduction to the examination of the problems raised by the persistence of obsessions and compulsions, we have constructed a simple scheme in the hope that it will clarify the major questions. For the sake of simplicity, a number of uncertain assumptions are allowed in this introductory section but are critically analyzed later.

If we assume that all forms of obsessions and compulsions have the same immediate effects, there are four main possibilities:

1. Obsessions and compulsions reduce adverse emotional feelings (e.g., reduce anxiety/discomfort.
2. Obsessions and compulsions increase adverse emotional feelings (e.g., increase anxiety/discomfort).
3. Obsessions and compulsions neither increase nor decrease adverse emotional feelings (e.g., leave anxiety/discomfort untouched).
4. Obsessions and compulsions have irregular effects (i.e., at least two of the three preceding possibilities occur at one time or another).

This introductory scheme assumes uniformity of different kinds of obsessions and compulsions, but as we will argue presently, there is reason to believe that obsessions and compulsions are not uniform in their *effects*.

Another problem with the present analysis is that it is based on the assumption that obsessions and compulsions occur only in the presence of adverse emotional states. Although this assumption is widely made, and despite the fact that often there is an intimate connection among obsessions, compulsions, and mood states, we have contrary evidence showing that obsessions and compulsions can occur in the absence of adverse mood states. For example, certain checking rituals bear little relation to the person's mood before, during, or after the ritual is carried out. Along similar lines, patients suffering from primary obsessional slowness seem to carry out their protracted, meticulous rituals regardless of their prevailing mood (Rachman, 1971). The theoretical consequences of these findings will be taken up later, but for the moment it should be pointed out that they do not exclude possibilities (2) and (3) in the list just presented (i.e., that obsessions and compulsions may be accompanied or followed by adverse emotional reactions). It is also well to remember that obsessions and compulsive activities may be *prompted* by influences other than adverse mood factors but then go on to produce adverse mood changes. So, for example, someone suffering from primary obsessional slowness may begin his or her ritual in an equable mood but experience increasing frustration and/or unpleasantness as the ritual goes wrong.

In pursuing the four main possibilities just stated, relying on a necessary connection between mood and ritual, it should be noted that at present we can say little more about the relation between mood and ritual than that they are frequently observed to covary. We are not in a position to argue that the presence of an adverse mood is either a sufficient or a necessary condition for the occurrence of obsessional or compulsive activities. Having drawn attention to the necessary qualifications of this exposition, we can now examine the evidence pertaining to the four possibilities listed earlier.

THE ANXIETY REDUCTION THEORY

The essence of the theory is that compulsions reduce anxiety. Sometimes this view is qualified by stating that it is the immediate and/or temporary effects that are anxiety reducing (e.g., Metzner, 1963).

The theory has been supported by a majority of psychologists and psychiatrists (e.g., Dollard & Miller, 1950; Chapman, 1976; Metzner, 1963; Nemiah, 1967; Rosen, 1975; etc.), and with good reason, but it is not free of problems. For example, even though it is assumed or stated that the postulated reduction of anxiety reinforces the compulsion, relatively few writers have addressed the thorny problem of the persistence of compulsive behavior. Is there a causal relationship between the reduction of anxiety and the maintenance of the rituals?

Few of the psychologists who subscribe to the anxiety reduction theory have taken up the possibility that the completion of compulsive rituals may have significant psychological effects other than, or in addition to, anxiety reduction. It has also been widely assumed that the unpleasant feeling state that features prominently in obsessions and compulsions is anxiety—rather than, say, tension or discomfort or depression. In our own research on compulsive rituals, we expanded our use of the term *anxiety* to include the *discomfort* that our patients assured us was clearly distinct from the anxiety they might experience in other circumstances. In response to their insistence, almost certainly well founded, we changed to using the awkward compound term *anxiety/discomfort*.

Jaspers (1963), a leading member of the phenomenological school of psychiatry, who left a stimulating account of obsessions and compulsions, relied on an early form of the anxiety reduction theory to account for the persistence of compulsions. He stated that "to get rid of the anxiety, patients must once more carry out the meaningless ritual of harmless acts—when the compulsive urges are surrendered to, there is, as in impulsive action, a vivid feeling of relief. If however they are resisted, severe anxiety arises or other symptoms such as motor discharges" (p. 136). This quotation illustrates the four major aspects of Jaspers's views. In the first place, it is assumed that the obsessional patient is troubled by anxiety. Second, the rituals are carried out in order to reduce this anxiety. Third, the rituals produce relief. Fourth, resisting the compulsive urge leads to an increase in anxiety or its substitute. These four points encapsulate a great deal of psychiatric and psychological writings on the subject, ranging from psychoanalysis through conventional contemporary psychiatry to most forms of psychological theory and therapy, not excluding behavior modification.

In his *Introductory Lectures* Freud (1949) expressed the view that "obsessive acts" are "only performed to escape the feeling of dread" (p. 337). They are acts of defense against the "otherwise inevitable development of anxiety" (p. 337). It follows from this view that "attempts to restrain them from carrying out their obsessive performances, their washing, their ceremonies, etc." (p. 337) lead to anxiety and a compulsion to carry out the act. Although this part of Freud's theory resembles Jaspers's account, greater emphasis is placed on the *avoidance* of anxiety; in Jaspers's construction the major function of the compulsive act is to *remove* anxiety. In contemporary terms, we might say that Jaspers construed compulsions as escape behavior whereas Freud viewed them as instances of avoidance behavior. The widespread acceptance by psychiatric writers of an anxiety reduction explanation is illustrated by the following quotations from two contemporary textbooks; similar examples can be found in most of the textbooks currently in use. Chapman (1976) states that "the performance of the [compulsive] act relieves the person of anxiety he felt prior to the act" (p. 137), and while remaining in the same line, Nemiah (1967) added a volitional element to his account of "the anxiety-allaying function of compulsive acts."

The idea that people troubled by compulsive urges carry out the rituals with a clear *purpose* is illustrated in this extract from a reliable textbook of abnormal psychology edited by London and Rosenhan (1968). The author, De Nike, says that "the compulsive neurotic develops rituals by which he attempts to avoid intense anxiety" (p. 347). This view was also stated explicitly by two pioneers of the learning theory approach to obsessions and compulsions, Walton and Mather (1963). In describing one of their six important cases, they claimed that when the patient was unable to avoid contaminating sexual stimuli, "excessive washing was adopted as a means of anxiety-reduction" (p. 169).

As mentioned earlier, contemporary psychological theorists, particularly those following in the tradition of learning theory, have been greatly influenced by Mowrer's writings on the two-stage theory of fear and avoidance (Mowrer, 1939, 1960). According to him, "Fear is a decisive causal factor in avoidance behavior" (1960, p. 97), and insofar as one regards obsessions and compulsions as a form of avoidance behavior (most theorists do), it follows that fear is a decisive causal factor in compulsive behavior. The influence of this point of view is clearly shown in one of the earliest and most successful attempts to apply some of the ideas of experimental psychology to psychopathological behavior.

Dollard and Miller (1950) argued that "the compulsion is reinforced in exactly the same way as the avoidance response in the phobia" (p. 163). Following Mowrer, they argued that intense fear motivates avoidance responses and that whenever these responses are successful they are reinforced by a reduction in the strength of the fear. "A reduction in any strong drive, such as fear, serves to reinforce the immediately preceding responses," and hence, "any response that produces successful avoidance . . . will be learned as a strong habit" (Dollard and Miller, 1950, p. 158). Although they firmly supported the notion that completing a compulsive act reduces anxiety, they qualified their views by saying that such reduction was of a temporary character. Thus, "the compulsive act produces only a temporary reduction in the anxiety . . . after a relatively short time, the anxiety starts to increase again so that the patient is motivated to repeat the compulsive act" (p. 164). Like Jaspers, Dollard and Miller believed that if a compulsive act is "interrupted by a command or physical restraint, the subject experiences a marked increase in anxiety . . . As soon as the compulsion is resumed, the anxiety disappears" (p. 163).

In their influential text on behavior therapy, Meyer and Chesser (1970) follow the view that compulsive rituals are secondary to fear and go on to state that it is "these secondary symptoms [i.e., the rituals] which appear to be anxiety-reducing responses" (p. 64). Although Wolpe shares the view of most writers about the role of anxiety ("It may be stated almost as dogma that the strength and frequency of evocation of obsessional behavior is directly related to the amount of anxiety being evoked in the patient," 1958, p. 90), he proposed a more complex view of obsessions and compulsions. He distinguished between two major types of "obsessional behavior." According to him, the first type "appears to be part and parcel of the immediate response to anxiety-evoking stimulation and has secondary effects entirely in the direction of increasing anxiety" (p. 90)–the anxiety-elevating obsession. The second type "occurs as a reaction to anxiety, and its performance diminishes anxiety to some extent, for at least a short time" (p. 91).

Wolpe's clinical distinction has now been supported by experimental analysis, but the theoretical problems posed by the first type of obsession/compulsion remain to be overcome. In accounting for the second type of obsession/compulsion, the anxiety-reducing variety, Wolpe explained its persistence in this way: "Its maintenance depends upon the reduction of anxiety it is able to effect at each performance" (p. 92). Although his views share some important characteristics with those of earlier writers, most notably the emphasis on the temporary reduction of anxiety achieved by rituals and the role of anxiety reduction in maintaining the rituals, the importance of the anxiety-elevating obsessions was neglected until Beech's work of the late 1960s. While accepting the validity of Wolpe's distinction, Eysenck and Rachman (1965) pointed out that "there are no figures available on the relative frequency of the anxiety-elevating and the anxiety-reducing obsessional illnesses but on the basis of clinical impressions, we feel that the latter type is far more common" (p. 139). Recently collected evidence is consistent with these early clinical impressions (Chapters 11, 12, and 14).

In sum, then, proponents of the anxiety reduction theory assume the presence of anxiety and assert that the compulsive ritual achieves a reduction in this anxiety. Several writers qualify their views on the anxiety-reducing effects of rituals by noting that the effects are temporary, and most agree that the reduction of anxiety strengthens the compulsion. In the view of some writers, this anxiety-reducing tactic is carried out as a matter of deliberate purpose. Most writers who comment on the matter appear to believe that interruption of a compulsive ritual leads to an increase in anxiety.

THE EVIDENCE

Although most of the evidence on which these views are based consists of unsystematic clinical impressions, the degree of unanimity among writers is impressive. Unfortunately, little has been attempted in the way of methodical experimental research. Virtually no tests have been made of the assumption that anxiety is always present, nor of the claim that the rituals are carried out with the deliberate intention of reducing anxiety. The other three aspects of the anxiety reduction hypothesis have been investigated to some extent.

As we will see, what little research has been conducted on the question of primary importance, the postulated anxiety-reducing effects of rituals, is generally supportive of the hypothesis—but there are some important, albeit infrequent, exceptions. The effects of interrupting a compulsive ritual have also been studied in small samples, but little is known about the duration of the anxiety-reducing relief that is said to be achieved by completing the appropriate ritual. The relevant evidence is of four kinds. In the first place, we have what patients report either in treatment or during assessment. In our experience the large majority of patients give an account of their ritual that comfortably fits into the anxiety reduction theory. Some of them, however, give explanations that are contrary to this hypothesis. The second source of information about the effects of rituals, their purpose, the consequences of interruption, and so on is what psychologists observe their patients doing and what the family and friends of the patients report. Third, information is also systematically gathered from answers to standardized questions, and the final source of evidence is experimental analysis of ritualistic acts and their consequences.

Our clinical impression is that the large majority of obsessional patients who engage in ritualistic cleaning activities give an account that is consistent with the anxiety reduction hypothesis—provided that one extends the concept, as we do, to include anxiety/discomfort reduction. Although a majority of our patients with checking rituals gave comparable accounts, considerably more of them were exceptions, or apparent exceptions, to the theory. That is, more checkers than cleaners averred that the effects of their rituals were not necessarily, or consistently, anxiety reducing or discomfort reducing. Moreover, it is our impression that a larger minority of the checkers disavowed the idea that the adverse emotional state present before commencing their rituals was anxiety. Our experience with the small number of patients who suffer from what has been described as primary obsessional slowness is that anxiety plays a smaller role here than in the cleaning or checking disorders. Going down the scale, cleaners are more likely to complain of anxiety (or discomfort) than checkers, and checkers are more likely to complain of anxiety than obsessionally slow people. Similarly, cleaners are more likely to attribute anxiety-reducing effects to their rituals than checkers, who in turn are more likely to attribute anxiety-reducing effects to their rituals than the obsessionally slow. The same ordering applies with respect to the declared intention of carrying out the rituals.

We are not aware of any obvious differences in the effect that interruptions produce on the various rituals. Although many patients complained that interruptions were aversive, a substantial minority denied that this was the case. In summary, our clinical impression is that a majority of obsessional-compulsive patients give an account that is consistent with the anxiety/discomfort reduction hypothesis; a small but significant minority give an account that is not consistent with the theory.

✳As far as the relatives of patients are concerned, an unsystematic analysis of their reports is broadly consistent with the patients' assessments. However, it is our impression that relatives tend to give a lower estimate of anxiety than the patients and to report considerably more in the way of adverse reactions to the interruption of an ongoing ritual.

The greater part of our research effort, however, has been directed toward the experimental analysis of obsessions and compulsions. To this end we have conducted a series of connected experiments over the past few years. These will be described in chronological order.

EXPERIMENTAL ANALYSES

✳In the first experiment we investigated the effects of contamination and washing in a group of 12 obsessional-compulsive patients (Hodgson and Rachman, 1972). We were interested in the empirical qualities of these phenomena and had an overriding theoretical interest in examining the effects of executing a (washing) ritual. The second experiment had similar aims but was conducted on a different sample of patients, this time comprising patients whose primary problem was obsessional-compulsive checking (Röper, Rachman and Hodgson, 1973). The third experiment was an attempt to replicate the experiment on obsessional checkers while at the same time seeking to overcome one of the limitations that emerged in the first experiment on checkers (Röper and Rachman, 1975). As before, we were interested in the empirical properties of exposure to a provoking type of stimulation and the effects of carrying out the appropriate compulsive ritual. The fourth experiment, on compulsive cleaners, investigated the role of situational factors and is described here for the first time. The fifth experiment dealt with the decay of compulsive urges (Rachman, de Silva and Röper, 1976).

In all five experiments we were interested in finding out whether the urge to carry out a compulsive ritual can be provoked in a deliberate and controlled manner under experimental conditions, the nature and extent of any disturbance experienced by the patient under these circumstances, and most important, the psychological consequences of carrying out the appropriate ritual.

Early in our research on the general subject of obsessions and compulsions, we reached the conclusion that discussions of these disorders that are restricted to changes in *anxiety* may be unduly limiting. As mentioned earlier, we settled on the compound term *anxiety/discomfort*, which appeared to suffice for our purposes and at the same time to be acceptable to a wider range of our patients. In all five experiments we encountered patients who did in fact experience feelings that could reasonably be described as those of anxiety; this was particularly evident in the experiment conducted on patients with compulsive washing rituals but was less clear among the obsessional checkers.

The first experiment was carried out on a group of twelve patients with moderate to severe disorders who displayed clear-cut washing rituals arising out of fears of dirt or contamination.

The detailed results are given in Hodgson and Rachman (1972), but the main effects may be seen in Figure 11.1. Subjective anxiety/discomfort was significantly increased by contact with a contaminated object and was significantly reduced after completion of the washing ritual. When, after the provocation of discomfort by the contaminating event, execution of the hand-washing ritual was postponed for half an hour, a slight (spontaneous) decrease in discomfort was observed. The contrast in the speed and extent of discomfort reduction achieved by hand washing or achieved spontaneously is shown in the part of the figure that describes the effects of a delayed wash and an interrupted wash (i.e., the two graphs on the bottom line of the figure).

Contrary to what we expected, there was no evidence that the interruption of the washing ritual increased anxiety/discomfort, nor was it felt by the patients to be a particularly frustrating experience. At least in the short run, Jaspers was wrong, Freud was wrong, Dollard and Miller were wrong; and Mandler and Watson (1966) may have been wrong.

We concluded from this experiment that touching a contaminated object does produce an increase in subjective anxiety/discomfort and that there is a trend for pulse rate variability to increase. The completion of a washing ritual after such contamination does produce a reduction in subjective anxiety/discomfort and a tendency for pulse rate variability to decrease. The interruption of the washing ritual after such contamination produces neither an increase nor a decrease in subjective anxiety/discomfort, nor an increase or decrease in pulse rate variability (Hodgson and Rachman, 1972, p. 115).

As far as they go, the subjective effects of contamination and washing observed in this experiment offer some support for the contention that compulsive rituals succeed in reducing discomfort. The pulse rate data were consistent but not confirmatory. In no case did we find that anxiety/discomfort was increased after completion of the ritual. With the work of Walker (1967) in mind (see Chapter 13), we asked 10 of our 12 patients whether they had difficulty deciding when to terminate their ritual. Eight of them reported no difficulty; one experienced occasional difficulty; and the other one found it to be a major problem.

We also discovered, incidentally, that there was a significant order effect indicating that three repetitions of the experimental exposure to the contaminating object were sufficient to produce a significant decrease in subjective estimates of anxiety/discomfort. This could be a reflection of habituation to the contamination object and/or a result of a cognitive reappraisal of the situation. After experiencing the first experimental exposure, patients presumably were

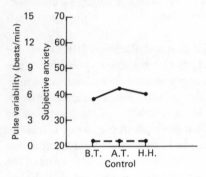
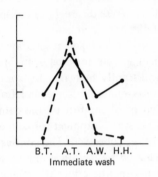
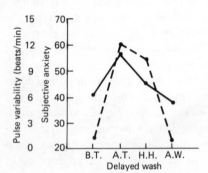
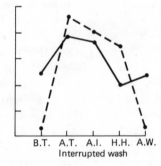

FIGURE 11.1. Means for subjective anxiety/discomfort (broken line) and pulse rate variability (continuous line) under the four conditions. B.T. refers to measurements "before touching"; A.T. refers to measurements "after touching"; A.W. refers to measurements "after washing"; H.H. refers to measures "after half-hour interval"; and A.I. refers to measures "after an interrupted wash."

reassured that the experimental requirements were not demanding and contained no surprises. Less anxiety or discomfort is evoked when the patient recognizes during the course of the experiment that he or she is to undergo a controlled, albeit slightly disturbing experience.

Our results were uniformly unlike some of the findings reported by Beech and his colleagues, and we speculated that this might be attributable to differences in composition of the samples of patients involved. "It may turn out that the anxiety reduction model is suitable for attempting to account for obsessional-compulsive acts of the ritualistic type associated with fears of contamination but that it will prove to be less suitable when attempting to account for obsessional doubting or compulsive checking" (Hodgson and Rachman, 1972, p. 116). With this possibility in mind, we undertook a replication of the experiment with a different sample of patients.

An Experiment on Obsessional-Compulsive Checking

Although Beech's (1974) views were an important stimulus for this replicated study, by the time the experiment was organized we had two additional reasons for suspecting that compulsive checkers might display different patterns of behavior than compulsive cleaners. We had by now gathered more clinical experience of treating obsessional patients and were beginning to pick up signs that cleaners and checkers sometimes responded differentially to exposure and response prevention treatment (see Rachman, Hodgson, and Marks, 1971). Also, by this time we had compiled the preliminary results from our psychometric study of checkers and cleaners (Chapter 9). This evidence, showing some significant differences between compulsive cleaners and compulsive checkers, made it desirable to carry out a replication of the first experiment.

Once again our major aims were to determine whether moderately to severely disturbed obsessional-compulsive patients experienced an increase in discomfort when required to carry out what they considered to be a potentially harmful act. Moreover, would they, like the compulsive washers, experience a reduction of discomfort (relief) when permitted to carry out their checking rituals? In all of the twelve patients who participated in this experiment, checking rituals were the main clinical problem or a major feature of the main clinical problem.

The results are shown in Figure 11.2 and follow the pattern of the first experiment, but in a significantly muted key. Detailed analysis of the results (see Röper, Rachman, and Hodgson, 1973) showed that provoking the urge to check was followed by a significant increase in anxiety/discomfort, although the degree of discomfort was noticeably smaller than that observed in the experiment on compulsive cleaners. Execution of the appropriate checking ritual was followed by an immediate decline in discomfort, in the same way as in the first experi-

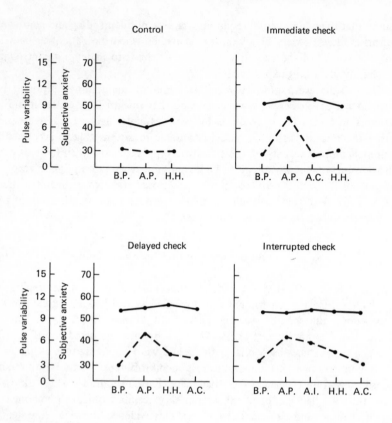

FIGURE 11.2. Means for subjective anxiety/discomfort (broken line) and pulse rate (continuous line) under four conditions. B.P. refers to measurements before provocation; A.P. refers to measurements after provocation; A.C. refers to measurements taken after check; H.H. refers to measures after half-hour intervals; and A.I. refers to measures after an interrupted check.

ment. A significant but not very large amount of discomfort was dissipated spontaneously when the patient was asked to postpone his or her checking rituals for half an hour. During this delay period reductions of up to 25 percent of the discomfort were observed. Once more, contrary to expectations, interruption of the checking ritual did not lead to an increase in discomfort.

Upon obtaining these results we decided to carry out a more detailed statistical comparison of the results obtained in the two experiments (see Röper, Rachman, and Hodgson, 1973, pp. 274-75). This comparison showed that patients with a washing compulsion reported more anxiety/discomfort when provoked than patients with checking rituals. The major difference between the groups occurred immediately after provocation, but nonperformance, of the ritual.

Although the mean scores in the checking experiment indicated that checking rituals were followed by a reduction in subjective anxiety/discomfort, five of the patients reported an increase in discomfort after checking on at least one out of three possible occasions. This is in contrast to the patients with washing compulsions, none of whom reported any increase in discomfort after completion of their washing ritual.

It proved rather difficult to elicit discomfort in subjects with checking compulsions. The most probable explanation for this relative failure was offered by some of our subjects. The presence of another person, especially someone in a responsible position, apparently inhibits the arousal of discomfort, and the experimenter was always present or very easily accessible throughout the experiment. What seems to happen is this: The subject reasons that the experimenter is unlikely to allow the gas taps (or whatever) to be left on, and even if he or she did, then the responsibility for ensuring harm from this act of carelessness would rest with the experimenter and not the subject. If the obsessional subject is divested wholly or partly of responsibility for the act, he or she experiences little discomfort.

With this unforeseen difficulty in mind, the experimental findings were stated in a modified way:

(1) Obsessional-compulsive checkers experience an increase in anxiety/discomfort after carrying out what they consider to be a potentially harmful act.
(2) Completion of the appropriate act of checking is usually followed by a decrease in anxiety/discomfort.
(3) Interruption of the checking ritual does not provoke a significant change in anxiety/discomfort.
(4) Overall there is a significant decline in anxiety/discomfort during a half-hour period of response prevention.
(5) None of the above findings were associated with significant changes in pulse rate variability.
(6) Both checking and washing produced a significant reduction of anxiety/discomfort. In spite of this overall trend, significantly more checkers than washers indicated increased anxiety/discomfort, after checking on at least one occasion. Increases in discomfort were observed on 7 out of 36 occasions of testing in the group of checkers but never in the group of washers. [Röper, Rachman, and Hodgson, 1973, p. 275]

Two qualifications should be noted in determining the significance of these results. As has already been mentioned, we found it relatively difficult to provoke the appropriate discomfort in the sample of patients. One possibility is that the results are atypical representations of naturally occurring checking rituals. The second qualification was that the findings represented short-term effects and may, to that extent, have been misleading. Our clinical observations had suggested that, for some patients at least, the urge to check increased with the passing of time. A person might feel safe and satisfied about the state of the gas taps after checking them at lunchtime but then be overwhelmed by uncertainty and fear when attending the theatre in the evening. This may result in a return of the desire to go home and repeat the check.

The possibility that our experimental situation might have introduced a serious distortion as a result of its artificiality was raised in Beech's appraisal of this work (Beech and Liddell, 1974, pp. 153-54). [The other query raised by these writers, to the effect that our patients might have been less disturbed than those described by Walker and Beech (1969), is unfounded; the patients had comparably severe disorders.] As we were dissatisfied with the inconclusiveness of some of the results, especially those of the second experiment, it was decided to carry out a replication and development of the study on compulsive checkers.

Obsessional-Compulsive Checking: Replication and Development

Our main concern in this replication and development study (Röper and Rachman, 1976) was to exclude, if possible, and certainly to reduce the potentially distorting effects of experimental artificiality. In addition, we decided to make allowance for the possibility that compulsive *checking* urges might show a different time course from that of other urges, by extending the duration of our experimental observations. Lastly, in response to critical suggestions from Beech (1974), we decided to include a wider range of subjective measures than subjective anxiety/discomfort.

Twelve patients with moderate to severe disorders, whose main problem was compulsive checking, were selected. All the testing was conducted either in the patient's home (8 cases) or in a therapeutic community (4 cases). For each patient we took measurements of subjective discomfort and mood before the patient entered the provoking situation, after the provocation of compulsive urges, again after the performance of the checking ritual, once more an hour later, and then finally two hours later. In all, these measurements were taken on five occasions. In addition, the time taken to repeat the ritual was recorded.

The compulsive urges were successfully provoked. Both when the experimenter was present and when he was absent, the provocative act was followed by a significant increase in subjective discomfort. The execution of the checking ritual produced a reduction in discomfort, and there was a tendency for this discomfort reduction to be greater when the experimenter was present. The detailed analysis of these results is given in Röper and Rachman (1975).

On three of the six measures of mood, the patients showed significantly higher negative scores in the absence of the experimenter after the provocation of compulsive urges. They felt tenser, more anxious, and more worried when they experienced the compulsive urges in the experimenter's absence.

Only two of the twelve patients reported an increase in discomfort/anxiety *after the performance of the ritual*, and at that, they did so only when the experimenter was present. The influence of the experimenter's presence is seen most clearly in the time taken to complete the checking ritual—it took an average of 3.5 minutes when the experimenter was present but fully 12 minutes when the patient was alone. During the extended period of response prevention, discomfort and other negative feelings decreased. The observation that patients receiving direct behavioral treatment for compulsive checking may experience undue discomfort in the period after the conclusion of a treatment session was not borne out in this experiment. In general, the mood scale scores followed the same pattern as those of the subjective-discomfort scale but were less pronounced. The patients reported an increase in worry, tension, and anxiety after the provoking act, followed by reductions in all three of these measures after completing the checking ritual. These changes were more pronounced when they occurred in the absence of the experimenter.

The major result of the present study was that the patients' feelings of anxiety/discomfort increased when they were placed in situations that provoked the urge to carry out one of their compulsive checking rituals. This reaction was strongest when the patients were alone in the provoking situation. Execution of the checking ritual reduced both anxiety/discomfort and negative feelings. The patients took longer to terminate the checking ritual when the experimenter was absent. Compulsive urges to check seldom reappeared after completion of the checking ritual.

The responses to provocation showed a pattern comparable to that observed among both the cleaners and the checkers in the earlier experiments. As in those earlier studies, we observed an increase in discomfort after exposure to provocation and a decrease in discomfort after performance of the compulsive ritual. However, the changes in level of anxiety/discomfort were less pronounced in checkers than in washers. Our earlier interpretation of the difference between washers and checkers received some support from the findings of this third experiment, in that the discomfort and relief scores observed when the experimenter was absent were more similar to the pattern observed in compulsive *washers*. The earlier observations on compulsive checkers might have been inadvertently distorted by the presence of the experimenter. In addition, the provoking items in this experiment had to have a minimal rate of occurrence in the patient's natural environment—and these items turned out to be more provoking than the laboratory-based items used in the earlier experiment on compulsive checkers.

The results confirmed that Beech's (1974) reservations about the generality of our findings on compulsive washers were well taken, but that he was wrong about the *direction* of the presumed distortion. The anxiety-reducing effects of checking rituals are *more* pronounced, not less pronounced, when the patient is alone at home. As we will see presently, a small study designed specifically to check this point showed that in cases of compulsive *cleaning* there are no significant differences in feelings or behavior when the ritual is provoked and executed at home or in the laboratory situation.

In general, the results of our third experiment provide further support for the view that executing the compulsive ritual does reduce anxiety/discomfort. Checkers and washers show the same result—reduced discomfort after performance of the ritual. The results run contrary to the hypothesis proposed by Walker and Beech (1969), which is based on the assumption of a deterioration in mood state as a result of performance of the ritual (see Chapter 13 for a full discussion). Prior to the completion of this experiment, we were of the opinion (Hodgson and Rachman, 1972; Röper, Rachman, and Hodgson, 1973) that Beech's hypothesis might well be applicable to compulsive checking behavior even though it was not usually applicable to compulsive cleaning behavior. In a minority of instances, the execution of the checking ritual was in fact followed by an *increase* in discomfort. In the light of the results obtained in this third, improved experiment, it now seems that deterioration in mood state after the performance of rituals is likely to be too unusual an occurrence to be of great importance in explaining the *maintenance* of ritualistic behavior. Nevertheless, regardless of their infrequency, such occurrences cannot be ignored.

In the response prevention part of the experiment, we had expected to observe a spontaneous reappearance of some compulsive urges or subjective discomfort during the two-hour prevention period. This expectation was not confirmed. The data obtained on occasions 4 and 5 give some slight indication of minor increases in discomfort or declines in mood state. In general, however, the results of the experiment show that a steady course of declining discomfort is far more common than the reappearance of the unpleasantness or urge.

Our clinical impression is that large numbers of obsessional patients, especially checkers, conduct their compulsive activities predominantly in solitude. For some of them it is essential that they protect themselves from observation and possible interruption, and this may provide the main reason for the peculiar hours they keep. It is not uncommon to find that the greatest part of the checking ritual is carried out late at night. For clarification, we have set out the five differences that emerged in the present experiment. (See Table 11.1.) It should, however, be borne in mind that there were far more similarities between the rituals (and associated feelings) carried out at home and those

TABLE 11.1:   CHECKING RITUALS—AT HOME AND IN THE LABORATORY

ALONE AT HOME	IN LABORATORY, EXPERIMENTER PRESENT

Provocation causes:
  great anxiety/discomfort.
  considerable tension and worry.
Rituals are:
  slower.
  less effective in reducing anxiety/
    discomfort.
	Provocation causes:
	  moderate anxiety/discomfort.
	  moderate worry and tension.
	Rituals are:
	  quicker.
	  more effective in reducing anxiety/
	    discomfort.

performed in the laboratory than there were differences. If we were to summarize the observed differences in one statement, it appears that the *checking rituals and associated mood are muted in the presence of another person* but are not fundamentally altered.

When alone, the obsessional-compulsive checkers were more disturbed (i.e., felt more discomfort, greater worry and tension) and took longer to carry out their rituals, which were in any event less effective. All of these differences may be attributable to the reassuring presence of another person. In addition (but not incompatible with this possibility), the presence of another person may serve to reduce the obsessionals' sense of responsibility for the act and, hence, allow them to experience less discomfort when someone else is present. As a consequence they are able to carry out the appropriate ritual more effectively and quicker. Our observation that some slight increase in discomfort occurs after completion of a ritual when the experimenter is present was not confirmed in the home environment. If this finding is repeated, and particularly if the effect is shown to be more marked than it was in our experiment, it will require incorporation into a comprehensive explanation of compulsive behavior.

In addition to our interest in the two major questions tackled in this experiment, we predicted, largely on the basis of clinical experience, that compulsive checkers would be able to terminate their rituals more quickly in the presence of the experimenter than when they were alone. This prediction was, of course, supported by the results. The effects of the presence or absence of the experimenter may well have clinical implications, and may provide the basis for a specific form of treatment (what inhibits checking?). As the presence of the experimenter appears to damp the reactions of compulsive checkers, it is to be expected that generalization of improvement during treatment sessions will require a larger step for checkers than for washers. It may be crucial for the patient to carry out a wide variety of self-directed and self-monitored tasks outside the treatment sessions (e.g., Emmelkamp and van Kraanen, 1977). In treating obsessional checkers, it may be even more important than usual to take steps to facilitate the generalization of improvements from the clinical situation to the patient's natural environment. In the course of our therapeutic work, we frequently make use of "telephone control," in which the therapist's instructions are relayed directly into the patient's home. The patient, in turn, carries out the required tasks and, when necessary, reports back immediately by telephone.

Contamination and Ritualistic Cleaning—
At Home and Away

As we have seen, Beech's (1974) reservation about experimental artificiality was well taken in the case of compulsive checkers, even if the distorting effects were in the direction opposite to those that he appeared to expect. For the sake of clarification and completeness, we decided to search for distorting effects of experimental artificiality among compulsive cleaners—in addition to the study on compulsive checkers just described.

We made a simple comparison by asking each of ten obsessional-compulsive cleaners to touch a contaminating item and then conduct a suitable ritualistic wash on two occasions. Using a balanced-order design, each patient had to carry out decontamination and washing procedures (1) at home and (2) in the clinic.

There were no significant differences between the effects observed in the two situations although slightly more discomfort was experienced when contaminating oneself at home. The mean discomfort score was 74 (out of a maximum of 100) at home and 66 in the clinic.

The major conclusion is that it is unlikely that any significant distortion entered into the first experiment, and therefore the findings and conclusions drawn from that experiment can be taken at face value. One can also conclude that the effect of social influences on the provocation of compulsive urges and the execution of compulsive rituals differs slightly between cleaners and checkers. As we have already seen, the checkers experienced less discomfort when there was another person present, and their rituals were muted when they had company. The presence of another person appears to have little effect on the discomfort experienced by patients who are worried by contamination and feel a compulsive urge to carry out repetitive cleaning rituals.

We are of course aware that there are at least two differences in the experimental conditions used in this little study. In the clinic situation the person was being observed by the experimenter, while at home he or she was alone. In other words, both the situation and the presence of another person were varied. There was little difference in the results from the two situations.

To what extent have these findings been supported or confirmed by independent reaearch? In the course of conducting their research into the psychophysiological concomitants of obsessional-compulsive disorders, Boulougouris, Rabavilas, and Stefanis (1977) obtained incidental evidence of the effects of contamination and ritual execution. Their findings, coming from an independent source and from research that had a different purpose than ours, are of some interest. They measured the psychophysiological effects (and incidentally the subjective reactions) of exposing obsessional-compulsive patients to relevant contaminating or provoking material. Four different types of presentation were used: fantasy material, real material, short presentations, and long presentations. Each of their 12 patients was presented with material in these 4 variations, using a balanced-order design. Although their major interest was in the psychophysiological reactions, Boulougouris and his colleagues asked their patients to rate their reactions at each stage on an anxiety scale that ran from 1 to 5 (maximum). As in our experiments, the patients' reactions to the provoking stimuli were compared to their reactions when they were presented with neutral stimuli. The findings are clear-cut and of striking magnitude. When provoked by the relevant stimulus, the patients showed a rapid and large increase in anxiety. The physiological and subjective effects of carrying out the appropriate ritual were not examined in this experiment.

Lipsedge (1974) investigated the effects of 3 variations of behavioral treatment on compulsive rituals. In the course of carrying out this pilot clinical study on 12 patients, he recorded their feelings during real or imagined contact with a contaminant (all the patients complained of having been troubled by compulsive hand-washing rituals for at least one year prior to the experiment). He reports that "although Walker and Beech (1969) reported that compulsive rituals are not always preceded by anxiety, in the present study all the patients reported feeling anxious during real or fantasied contact with a contaminant, and this is reflected in the rating scale scores" (p. 52). Summing up the major part of her research project, Walker (1967) conceded that "there are two kinds of rituals . . . One kind improves mood: when mood is bad it is longer and produces more improvement . . . in fact it conforms exactly to the anxiety-reduction theory" (p. 147). In this category could be included the rituals of 4 of the 7 patients studied.

Although it is not an independent study, an experiment that was carried out subsequent to the four described earlier (Rachman, de Silva, and Röper, 1976), and for a different purpose, incidentally yielded some information that is of direct bearing on the present questions.

Exposure to the provoking stimulation resulted in large and significant increases in subjective discomfort; execution of the appropriate checking ritual was followed by virtual elimination of the discomfort and urges (see Chapter 14 for a full account). The independent and external findings are scanty but give little cause for concern about the trend of our own studies; there are no inconsistencies discernible so far.

recognized.

THE EXPERIMENTAL FINDINGS

We now have data from 5 connected experiments involving a total of 55 different patients (12 + 10 cleaners, 10 + 11 + 12 checkers), and the results are consistent. The important exceptions account for less than 10 percent of all test instances and less than 10 percent of all subjects.

The results can be summarized in this way: Touching a contaminated object produces an increase in subjective anxiety/discomfort, and there is a trend for pulse rate variability to increase. Completion of a cleaning ritual after such contamination produces a reduction in subjective anxiety/discomfort and a tendency for pulse rate variability to decrease. Interruption of a washing ritual after such contamination produces neither an increase nor a decrease in subjective anxiety/discomfort, nor an increase or decrease in pulse rate variability. A significant but markedly slower rate of decline in subjective discomfort takes place during an enforced delay in washing. The arousal of anxiety/discomfort by contamination is unaffected by the presence of other people or by situational context.

Leaving aside the significant but infrequent exceptions, the following findings emerged from the experiments on obsessional/compulsive checking: Obsessional checkers experience an increase in anxiety/discomfort after carrying out what they consider to be a potentially harmful act. Completion of the appropriate act of checking is followed by a decrease in anxiety/discomfort. Interruption of the checking ritual does not provoke a significant change in anxiety/discomfort. There is a small but significant decline in anxiety/discomfort during a half-hour period of response prevention (i.e., when execution of the ritual is delayed). None of these findings was associated with significant changes in pulse rate variability. Apart from some infrequent but significant exceptions, provocation of compulsive urges follows the same pattern in both checkers and cleaners, and most important of all, the reported effects of carrying out the cleaning or checking ritual appear to be similar. The extent of subjective discomfort produced by the provoking action is similar in both types of disorder but of greater magnitude among the compulsive cleaners; similarly, and perhaps because of the originally greater discomfort, cleaning rituals are followed by a steeper decline in anxiety/discomfort. Compulsive rituals, cleaning or checking, are followed by a decline in discomfort that is far more rapid than the "spontaneous" decline.

Interruption of checking or cleaning rituals is not followed by any marked change in discomfort. After provocation, the postponement of the compulsive ritual—be it checking or cleaning—is not followed by any change in discomfort. Compulsive checking rituals appear to be influenced to a slight but significant extent by social and contextual influences, unlike cleaning rituals, which appear to be less affected by these factors. Checking urges and rituals appear to be muted by the presence of another person and by an inappropriate context.

Before concluding this chapter it is worth taking up the question of interruptions. It is widely believed that interrupting a compulsive ritual produces short-term distress, usually in the form of anxiety, and that if the interruptions are frequent and prolonged they may in the long run lead to serious consequences. In clinical seminars, hospital ward rounds, and the like, the view is expressed that if obsessional patients are prevented from carrying out their rituals it may precipitate a psychotic reaction or force them into suicide. On the basis of these beliefs, relatives and friends of obsessional patients have been advised by psychiatrists and psychologists that it is inadvisable for anyone to interfere with the patient's ritualistic behavior. In our clinical experience, we have observed some patients who appear to experience adverse effects in the short term if their rituals are interrupted, but have not come across any lasting adverse effects as a result of such curtailment. The longer-term prevention of compulsive behavior, far from having adverse effects, is a crucial element in modern treatment methods (see Chapters 21 to 24).

On the theoretical side, there are many explicit statements asserting that interrupting compulsive behavior is likely to produce an adverse reaction. For example, Jaspers (1963) says that if the compulsive urges are resisted, "severe anxiety arises or other symptoms such as motor discharges" (p. 136). Freud (1949) regarded obsessional-compulsive activities as defense mechanisms whose function was to ward off anxiety, and consequently he believed that any serious interruption of this defensive activity is bound to lead to a show of anxiety or to the emergence of some substitute symptom or difficulty. The view expressed by Walker and Beech (1969) is in sharp contrast. They have argued that there are at least two kinds of rituals and one of them "causes greater deterioration in mood" the longer it lasts. It follows from their analysis that "artificially curtailing them has a beneficial effect" (p. 1268), at least in the short term.

The experimental evidence gathered in our studies shows that interrupting a ritual produces no significant effects either in the form of anxiety/discomfort or on the subsequent course of the ritual. Neither the subject's emotional state nor the execution of the ritual are significantly altered by interruptions. It remains possible that the artificial constraints implicit in our experimental situation suppressed some effects that might arise in the patient's natural environment. It may turn out that the relevant emotional reaction is something other than anxiety/discomfort (perhaps a sense of frustration?). However that may be, the current evidence gives no support for the predictions derived from theories such as those proposed by Freud and Jaspers, by Mandler and Watson, or, on the other side of the fence, by Walker and Beech. Interruptions neither increase nor decrease anxiety/discomfort—in the short term. There is one escape clause: Perhaps the artificiality of our experiments muted some of the adverse reactions to interruption.

Theories that postulate some form of hydraulic flow from a reservoir of emotion receive no encouragement from our results. Blocking the execution of a ritual temporarily, as in our experiments, or permanently, as in therapy that involves response prevention, is not followed by emotional or motor discharges.

REPETITIVENESS

The repetitive quality of many compulsions, often the most striking aspect of a ritual, has attracted little attention. Phenomenologically, three explanations are commonly offered. The most frequent explanation is that the task (of checking or cleaning) has to be carried out *to perfection*; otherwise it will not achieve its purpose, be that preventive or restorative. Perfect prevention is unattainable. Insofar as the compulsions are forms of active avoidance aimed at preventing some future unpleasantness, they cannot secure their goal. As confirmation of the effectiveness of the compulsion is unavailable at the time of its execution, the person can never be fully satisfied that the ritual will suffice, hence, perhaps, the tendency to repeat it again and again in the hope of increasing the chances of preventing the anticipated unpleasantness from occurring. Preventive rituals necessarily include uncertainty of outcome.

A second explanation for the repetitiveness of compulsive acts is the need, which numerous patients report, to carry out the preventive or restorative actions in an unbroken sequence and/or in the presence of a "good thought." If, during the execution of the compulsion, something goes wrong (e.g., an interruption or a bad thought), the ritual has to be repeated. A third, compatible explanation is that the rituals have to be carried out in a predetermined style and frequency (e.g., in fours) in order to achieve their aims.

Explanations that do not rest on phenomenology include the following:

1. The rituals are repeated because most executions are at best only partially successful. If the compulsive act produces only a *partial and/or fleeting relief from discomfort* (a likely outcome for most checking compulsions and many cleaning compulsions), then repetitions are called for. The less effective rituals should be especially prone to repetitions (this can easily be tested). Wholly ineffective rituals will extinguish and highly successful rituals will be less prone to repetition (this also is easily testable).
2. Rituals associated with undue doubting will be prone to frequent repetitions. As argued earlier, preventive rituals are incapable of immediate confirmation; obsessions that are difficult to subdue with reasonable

certainty will require repeated preventive rituals. Similarly, compulsive acts that have an uncertain or weak preventive value are likely to demand frequent repetitions. Or, to look at the matter positively, compulsions that have a high perceived probability of achieving their aim (less room for doubting) will be less prone to repetition.

3. Rituals are repeated in order to postpone or reduce the anticipated aversiveness of stopping. This curious paradox is suggested because of the irrational quality of some compulsions. The person may give clear expression to the view that his or her compulsive behavior is senseless and then regret the need to carry it out in the face of this irrationality. "I know that it is senseless, and cannot influence the safety of my family, but I must carry out 4 X 10 sets of touching rituals and whisper 4 X 10 'Ave Marias' before commencing a new task." Despite the longer-term disadvantages and embarrassment, in the short term carrying out the rituals is relieving or, if not actually relieving, less aversive than stopping. During the rituals the unpleasant failure threats are subdued, but they may well return once the ritual ends. One patient in whom this balance between immediate and future unpleasantness was resolved by repeatedly carrying out tidying rituals gives an unusually clear illustration of the phenomenon. In early adulthood her chronic social anxiety underwent a steep increase and she had several panics when encountering people in public places. Her movements became increasingly restricted, but she had great difficulty rationalizing or justifying her housebound behavior. She slipped into progressively more exacting, time-consuming, repetitive cleaning and tidying household tasks. Finally she had no time left for outdoor excursions or activities. Despite the embarrassment, fatigue, and irritation she had to endure as a result of her compulsive behavior, it was relatively less aversive than completing her repetitive tasks and leaving the safety of her home.

To conclude, phenomenologically the repetition of rituals can be explained in various ways. They might be repeated because, as active-avoidance responses, they cannot achieve certain prevention of future unpleasantness. Second, some rituals are repeated because of the need to complete them in a prescribed style and frequency (e.g., in groups of six). Third, some rituals are repeated because of the need to complete them in an unbroken sequence or in the presence of a "good thought."

The nonphenomenological possibilities include the following: Rituals are repeated if they are only partially and/or transiently effective in reducing discomfort. They are prone to repetition if they are associated with doubting and ruminations, and lastly, they may be repeated in order to avoid the unpleasantness associated with stopping.

Chapter 12

The Persistence
of Compulsive Behavior: II

In the light of the contemporary research on obsessions and compulsions, we can now reexamine the main points extracted from the writings of anxiety reduction theorists. The first point is that anxiety reduction theorists, with the exception of Wolpe (1958), appear to have made no allowance for compulsive rituals that are not followed by a reduction in anxiety (i.e., they left no room for exceptions). The fact that exceptions do occur, albeit infrequently, poses problems for the theory. It must be said, however, that on the whole the theory looks healthy. With few exceptions, it is possible to provoke subjective anxiety/discomfort in these patients quite readily. As noted earlier, confining the description of their emotional reactions to the term *anxiety* can be misleading, and we have therefore substituted the compound *anxiety/discomfort*. Almost all of the evidence supports the central part of the hypothesis, namely, that execution of the compulsive ritual is followed by a reduction in anxiety. None of the recent experimental evidence bears on the subhypothesis that claims that the *purpose* of ritual execution is to reduce anxiety. Similarly, none of the research looked specifically at the question of whether the anxiety reduction achieved by compulsive acts is temporary or not. However, during the course of carrying out our experiments we had ample opportunity to observe how readily the anxiety can be re-evoked. One has merely to ask the subject to come into contact with the situation or contamination once more. The hypothesis that interruption of a compulsive ritual is followed by an increase in anxiety has not been confirmed.

The empirical evidence obtained from the questionnaire replies given by a group of our patients shows that, in their view, completion of rituals is usually followed by a reduction in discomfort, but there were a significant number of exceptions in which completion of the ritual was said not to be followed by a reduction in discomfort. Our investigations of patients suffering from intrusive, unacceptable obsessions show that the most common consequence of having one of these unpleasant thoughts is an elevation of anxiety rather than a reduction of it. Along similar lines, our research on patients with primary obsessional slowness shows that compulsive rituals can persist for a very long time even in the apparent absence of anxiety or its reduction.

If our experiments and clinical evidence are reliable and our interpretation of these results valid, then the anxiety reduction theory (and its competitors) needs to accommodate three different effects of the execution of compulsive rituals: a decrease in anxiety/discomfort (most common), an increase in anxiety/discomfort (least common), or no change in anxiety/discomfort.

THREE VARIATIONS

In a sense, recognition of the three variations in anxiety/discomfort that follow the execution of compulsive rituals (and on present evidence we appear to have no alternative) marks the opening of a new problem. Plainly, matters cannot be left in this unsatisfactory state.

In attempting to account for the three variations, we can decide that they reflect three differing types of ritual, each of which requires its own explanation. Or we can retain the hope that they are essentially similar phenomena and try to discover what maintains all ritualistic behavior and why we observe the three variations in anxiety/discomfort. In pursuing this second possibility, that the rituals are essentially similar, complete reliance on an anxiety reduction explanation seems bound to fail.

There is no need to suppose that these two possible approaches are necessarily incompatible. So, for example, one could envision an explanation along these lines: Rituals are prompted by noxious stimulation; such stimulation gives rise to varying reactions, and those that are followed by an escape from the stimulation or an avoidance of further such stimulation will be maintained (i.e., repeated). The noxious stimulation may be experienced as anxiety/discomfort, and the reduction of these feelings on completion of the ritualistic activities may strengthen the tendency to repeat the ritual upon subsequent exposure to the stimulation. However, the noxious stimulation may also be experienced as something other than anxiety/discomfort (e.g., gloom). If the pertinent mood state is improved after carrying out the ritual, this may lead to a strengthened tendency to repeat the ritual—even at the expense of tolerating increased anxiety/discomfort.

It is also conceivable that people persist with their rituals in the face of increasing anxiety/discomfort in order to reduce or avoid some more threatening future anxiety/discomfort or unpleasantness. A compulsive hand washer tolerates the discomfort of aching hands and stinging skin in order to avoid the threat of greater unpleasantness in the future (e.g., venereal disease). Although we can recruit a good deal of clinical evidence to support this idea, it is an uncomfortable solution because it can turn into an infinite regress.

Explanations that depend on a division of rituals into three types are likely to be disappointing because of their lowered level of generality. Moreover, if they succeed it will necessitate changes in nosology, diagnostic practices, and therapeutic approach. It will also lead to a narrower and more precise use of the terms *obsession* and *compulsion*.

It has to be said that the derivation of the anxiety reduction theory is a cause for some concern. The modern version of this theory was derived from the two-stage theory of fear and avoidance originally proposed by Mowrer (1939, 1960) to account for the neurotic paradox, among other problems. It proved to be of considerable value over at least three decades, but some weaknesses are now apparent (Rachman, 1976b). Contrary to the theory, persistent avoidance behavior can arise and continue in the absence of fear evocation.

This problem is discussed at length in Chapter 25, where it is suggested that Mowrer's extension of the theory to include the concept of "hope" can rejuvenate the anxiety reduction theory. Turning now to what we might call "small-theory" considerations, in the opening exposition of the anxiety reduction theory it was assumed that all forms of obsessional-compulsive behavior have the same immediate effects. Spelled out, the assumptions are that the execution of a compulsive ritual always produces the same effect and, secondly, that there is a uniformity of effect across different kinds of compulsive rituals. It is difficult to sustain these assumptions. As we observed in our two experiments on checking rituals, the same patient experienced different anxiety/discomfort-reducing effects on different occasions. Comparing the results of the first experiment with those obtained in the second and third shows that the assumption of uniformity across different types of ritual is not always borne out.

MOOD CHANGES

The observed irregularity of the effects of compulsive rituals can probably be traced to the fact that the connection between ritual and mood is more complex than we have so far allowed. Most theorists have confined themselves to a consideration of the anxiety-reducing effects of compulsive rituals, but there is little reason to restrict the discussion in this way. In particular, Beech (1974) has been insistent over the past few years in his assertion that the connection between mood and ritual is intimate and that mood states other than anxiety are involved. We already know from clinical observation that there is a close and complex relationship between depression and obsessional disorders. It is also our clinical impression that many patients experience what can best be described as psychological tension before, during, and after the execution of various rituals. Beech himself has made a start in exploring the role of mood states other than anxiety (e.g., hostility, depression, etc.), but thus far most of these additional measures appear to correspond closely to anxiety. Our view is that useful clarification will follow once experimenters widen their research to include other mood states besides anxiety—bearing in mind, of course, that these various mood factors will not necessarily work in the same direction.

So far, this analysis of mood states in compulsions has assumed that the putative mood changes are a once-and-for-all phenomenon. For example, if anxiety is reduced shortly after the ritual begins, we assume with insufficient basis that the anxiety remains low throughout. It may well be the case, however, that more than one mood change occurs during and after a ritual, particularly when it is a lengthy one.

Even if we could satisfy ourselves about the particular mood states involved in a specified compulsive ritual, and if we had good grounds for believing that it showed little variation during the course of the ritual, we would nevertheless need to be cautious in concluding that the relationship between the mood and the ritual is unvarying. For example, it need not follow that the same mood(s) is involved in some regular connection with a particular compulsive ritual. A prominent feature of mood changes is their volatility, and consequently one has to be cautious in drawing conclusions about regularities and uniformities between rituals (which tend to be unchanging and stereotyped) and mood states (which tend to fluctuate and can even be volatile).

Easily influenced

DISCOMFORT ELEVATION

Why, then, do some rituals persist even though they are not followed by a reduction in anxiety/discomfort? And why do others persist even though they are, on occasion, followed by an increase in anxiety/discomfort?

The first point to bear in mind is that these exceptions are generally irregular (see experiments 2 and 3, pages 177 and 178). That is, the same compulsive ritual is sometimes followed by an increase in discomfort and on other occasions followed by a decrease. This irregularity (which contrasts with the greater regularity of discomfort-reducing effects, as in the first experiment of this series), coupled with the fact that some compulsions persist regardless of the level of discomfort present before or after completion of the particular ritual, suggests that in these exceptions we need to look beyond the concept of anxiety/discomfort.

Anxiety elevation occurs in a minority of instances; furthermore, our experimental evidence shows that patients who report this postritual elevation of anxiety on other occasions describe a *reduction* of anxiety after carrying out the same ritual. That is, in our experiments the elevation of anxiety was *neither common nor consistent*. However, the results cannot exclude the possibility that some patients consistently experience anxiety elevation.

If these compulsions persist and vary independently of changes in anxiety/ discomfort, then presumably some other affective and/or motivational factor is involved (a view expressed by Beech and his colleagues). Two prominent possibilities are that (1) the compulsions persist because they alleviate guilt or (2) they persist because they alleviate remote worries (i.e., they reduce the person's concern about some distant possibility, such as the occurrence of a burglary). If either or both of these psychological states contributes to the persistence and fluctuations of the exceptional compulsions, then the manipulation of anxiety/discomfort (as in our experiments) should produce irregular changes, or no changes at all, in the course of the rituals. These experimental manipulations are largely or wholly irrelevant.

The two alternatives raised here, and others of a similar kind, are of course open to investigation. On encountering a person whose compulsions are not followed by anxiety/discomfort reduction, a detailed study of his or her psychological state should produce hints about the possible consequences of executing the ritual, and the patient's rationale can then be subjected to testing by the simple maneuvers adopted in the series of experiments already completed.

A third major possibility is that, in the exceptions at least, the person's behavior is under more than one affective influence. So he or she might persist in carrying out the compulsive rituals—despite the fact that occasionally they are followed by increasing anxiety/discomfort—because they successfully reduce his or her guilt or because they reduce (or delay) the probability of some remote unpleasantness. In this way *the person purchases longer-term "safety" at the expense of short-term increments in anxiety/discomfort*. This analysis, which we tend to favor, has intuitive appeal and is compatible with our clinical impressions. Unfortunately, it runs the risk of becoming an open-ended hypothesis. It is not easy to identify the postulated longer-term influences, and it will not be easy to capture them in a laboratory; moreover, it will be difficult to ensure that all of the contributing influences have in fact been identified. Hence, negative results might be irredeemably inconclusive. If this loophole is not closed, we will be left in Popperian limbo.

Leaving this complication on one side, the three possibilities can be developed. To begin with, they are not exclusive. A compulsive checker may be motivated by an affective state, or by the anticipation of an affective state, other than anxiety/discomfort. If his or her checking rituals are unsuccessful, the (presumably aversive) affective state develops (or continues). This in turn leads to escape behavior. In the more common case, the checking rituals are successful and the affective state is reduced or avoided. In order to reduce the possibility of experiencing this (aversive) affective state again, the checker carries out his or her rituals—even though the immediate consequences sometimes are uncomfortable.

So if we observe a discrete episode of compulsive checking, the person may well report an immediate increase in discomfort. However, further study should reveal that this discomfort is tolerated in the hope of forestalling or delaying the occurrence of a more remote, but potentially more distressing, event or experience. According to this analysis, if a checker who follows the exceptional pattern deliberately refrains from carrying out his or her compulsive rituals, as in response prevention treatment, he or she will experience little or no immediate anxiety/discomfort. Instead, the person should experience increasing *worry* about the longer-term consequences. Repeated therapeutic blocking of checking responses enables him or her to sample repeated disconfirmations of the anticipated consequences.

It would appear that a comprehensive explanation for the maintenance of compulsive ritualistic behavior, one that incorporates cleaning *and* checking compulsions, is unattainable as long as the search is confined to the immediate effects of the ritual. At least on some occasions, compulsive checkers experience no (immediate) relief from carrying out their rituals, a conclusion supported by their replies to our questionnaire.

Rather than proliferate explanations for the continuance of compulsive behavior, we hope to show that despite the obstacles, checking compulsions may yet be incorporated within a discomfort-reducing model. In order to do so, however, it may be necessary to be reminded of Bandura's (1977) skillfully argued demonstration that "most human behavior is maintained by anticipated rather than by immediate consequences" (p. 109). (We suspect that only psychologists or philosophers would admit that there was ever a problem to be resolved here.) If we are correct in supposing that the primary purpose of most checking rituals is to reduce the likelihood of aversive events taking place at some time in the future (i.e., they are preventive), then the occasional occurrence of short-term discomforts is submerged in service of the larger aim. For example, "I will tolerate the irritation, discomfort, and effort involved in repeatedly checking the security of the doors and windows—in order to reduce the threat of a robbery or assault taking place in the future." Checking compulsions are influenced by "anticipated consequences" to a larger extent than cleaning compulsions. In the latter case the immediate consequences, in the form of discomfort reduction, are more regularly and reliably observed to follow the completion of the appropriate cleaning ritual.

The influence of immediate consequences on current compulsive behavior can be seen in a case illustration. Taylor (1963) provided a detailed description and accompanying analysis of a compulsive hair plucker. The patient claimed to derive (prompt) pleasure of a mildly erotic kind from plucking her hairs but complained of the social criticism she received because of this activity and the effect it had on her appearance. According to Taylor's interpretation, the delayed social punishment was not strong enough to cancel out the immediately pleasurable effects of hair plucking. Taylor went on to suggest that in cases in which this type of temporal sequence occurs, the punishment may be experienced by the patient as guilt or remorse (common complaints made by obsessional patients) but have little effect on the strength of the compulsive behavior.

A person might be willing to tolerate an increase in anxiety/discomfort *in order to avoid or delay some even more unpleasant possibility*, such as profound and debilitating feelings of depression. One could, for example, envision a person repeatedly carrying out a "senseless" ritual of checking the taps six times in six batches of six, even at the expense of increasing discomfort and embarrassment, if the person felt that doing so would prevent harm from coming to his or her child. The anxiety-elevating ritual may persist because it is the less aversive of two unpleasant options. Although there are experimental data that might provide a basis for an analog that would be suitable for testing this hypothesis (e.g., Herrnstein, 1969), and the hypothesis seems to fit well with explanations offered by obsessional-compulsive patients, little attempt has so far been made to explore and develop the idea.

This neglect may not be accidental; the hypothesis presents some difficulties. If one fails to detect the putative secondary source of discomfort, does that mean that the hypothesis is incorrect or does it mean that we are inept searchers? How do you demonstrate the *absence* of something—especially if it is something that is intrinsically difficult to grasp? In short, it may be an irrefutable hypothesis.

Secondly, it assumes the correctness of the anxiety reduction hypothesis and helps conserve it from disproof. A third problem with this plausible hypothesis is that it can be applied equally to anxiety-reducing rituals. Perhaps these rituals are also being maintained by the avoidance of some other unpleasant option.

When, in the course of behavioral treatment, the checking rituals are blocked, the anticipated consequences are repeatedly disconfirmed. This should lead to a decline in anticipatory worrying. If we construe checking rituals as active-avoidance behavior (which, like these types of compulsive rituals, is highly resistant to extinction), then the Seligman-Johnston (1973) theory of avoidance learning is applicable. This theory leads one to predict that avoidance behavior is best tackled by arranging for the person to experience repeated disconfirmations of his or her anticipation of future unpleasantness.

It can be argued that avoidance responses, such as repetitive checking to avoid future unpleasantness, persist because they are seldom if ever exposed to disconfirmation. If Seligman and Johnston are correct in attributing the weakening of avoidance behavior to the occurrence of disconfirmatory experiences, then many checking compulsions are preserved from extinction because they are rarely open to such disconfirmation.* For example, the young man who carried out rituals to protect his parents from violent assault never experienced disconfirmation of the efficacy of his ritualistic actions—his parents were never attacked. The same reasoning is applicable to the many cases in which the anticipated unpleasantness is mainly subjective.

Returning, then, to the original problem, the persistence of cleaning compulsions (regarded as passive-avoidance and escape behavior) is largely explicable in terms of the anxiety/discomfort reduction theory. Checking compulsions (regarded as active-avoidance responses) are partly explicable in these terms but can be comprehensively accounted for only by including a safety signal analysis or some related explanation.

NECESSARY AND SUFFICIENT CONDITIONS

The status of the anxiety reduction hypothesis can now be assessed in a different way. Is anxiety reduction a necessary and sufficient condition to account for the persistence of compulsive rituals? In our view anxiety/discomfort reduction is a sufficient, but not a necessary, condition for the persistence of compulsive rituals.

Anxiety reduction is not a *necessary* condition because some compulsive rituals persist even in the apparent absence of anxiety reduction or indeed even in the absence of anxiety arousal. To press the point, we can cite examples of compulsive rituals that persist despite the fact that their execution is followed by anxiety *elevation*. Broadly speaking, the cleaning rituals fit neatly into an anxiety reduction theory, but the checking rituals are irregular in their effects. There are experimental and clinical examples of checking rituals that persist despite the fact that they are followed, on occasion, by an increase in anxiety/ discomfort. Patients suffering from primary obsessional slowness continue to carry out prolonged, meticulous, compulsive rituals in the apparent absence of anxiety arousal. People whose main complaint is the repetitive, intrusive occurrence of unwanted thoughts generally experience an elevation of anxiety/ discomfort—and persistence of the obsessions. The reduction of anxiety is not a necessary condition for the persistence of obsessional-compulsive behavior.

There are two arguments that can be advanced against this conclusion. First, it could be argued that our clinical examples are not typical instances of genuine obsessions and compulsions. While this objection might succeed against some of our examples, say, those of primary obsessional slowness, it cannot be sustained in the face of examples such as the (common) anxiety-elevating obsessions. A second argument against the conclusion that anxiety reduction is

*At the time of its execution, the efficacy of a preventive act is unknowable—the act is infused with uncertainty.

not necessary could be based on the fact that the intermittent reduction of anxiety might well sustain persistent responding (e.g., Hilgard, 1956). So the finding that rituals persist even though on occasions the execution of the ritual is not followed by anxiety reduction creates no difficulty.

Although intermittent reinforcement may well contribute to the persistence of obsessions and compulsions, one cannot rescue the anxiety reduction theory on this basis. The contribution of intermittent reinforcement is unlikely to account for the persistence of anxiety-elevating obsessions and compulsions, or for the persistence of obsessionally slow ritualizing, and it allows no obvious explanation for the differences between types of ritual. For example, why are washing rituals so consistently followed by anxiety reduction while checking rituals have less consistent consequences? In all, it seems safe to conclude that anxiety reduction is not a necessary condition for the persistence of obsessions and compulsions.

Theoretically, there are two methods by which we can determine whether anxiety reduction is a *sufficient* condition for the maintenance of rituals. One could attempt to synthesize the phenomenon (i.e., produce a persistent, compulsive ritual by arranging for each occurrence of the ritual to be followed by anxiety reduction, while excluding alternative influences). This method is ethically untenable. The second possibility is to select a stable, well-established ritual and then systematically strip down and exclude all recognizable influences other than anxiety reduction (e.g., delete all consequences other than anxiety reduction). The drawbacks to this method are that doubts will arise over whether all the possible influences have been identified and excluded. In addition, practical constraints would make it difficult to achieve adequate experimental control for a sufficiently long period to permit tests of the long-term persistence of the ritual.

In the absence of information gathered in tightly controlled experiments of this character, we are bound to put the most probable interpretation on the available evidence. Our construction of the experimental evidence, supplemented by the verbal and written information provided by our patients and their behavior before and during treatment, plus the published clinical reports, is that anxiety reduction is indeed a sufficient condition for the maintenance of compulsive rituals. In reaching this conclusion greatest reliance is placed on the experimental evidence, which shows that there is a close temporal connection between rituals and anxiety reduction. As we have tried to show, this connection is especially clear in the case of compulsive cleaners and slightly less so in compulsive checkers. We also lean on evidence gathered in our controlled clinical trials, which shows, indirectly, that when this close temporal connection is broken, the most common outcome is a decline or disappearance of the compulsive rituals. Our clinical impressions and the reports of our patients provide general reassurance.

Next we turn to the question of how to identify the circumstances in which anxiety reduction is a sufficient condition for ensuring the persistence of rituals (it being allowed that anxiety reduction is not a necessary condition). One cannot be sure at such an early stage of research, but it seems probable that completion of a ritual is sufficient to increase persistence if (1) the compulsive urge is elicited by circumscribed anxiety/discomfort-provoking stimulation and (2) the execution of the ritual is followed by a noticeable reduction in anxiety/discomfort.

There are of course other conditions that might lead to the persistence of compulsive rituals, including some examples in which anxiety plays no part. It seems highly probable that rituals can be, and are, strengthened not only by the reduction of anxiety but also by the successful *avoidance* of anxiety (i.e., by avoidance training as well as by escape training). The avoidance training paradigm seems to us to provide a better fit for many types of checking ritual than the escape training paradigm, which is often the most suitable for explaining cleaning rituals. Stated formally, the completion of a ritual is sufficient to ensure persistence if (1) the compulsive urge is elicited by stimuli that are premonitory of anxiety/discomfort and (2) execution of the ritual is followed by a decrease in the probability of the anxiety/discomfort's occurring.

More distant from the anxiety reduction hypothesis, we share the view that compulsive rituals can be strengthened by positive reinforcement. Examples of this type are provided by Taylor (1963) in his description of a compulsive hair puller, and by Ullmann and Krasner (1975). We go further and propose that compulsive rituals can be initiated and maintained by the *transmission of information* in the same way that fears can be acquired (Rachman, 1977b). In the simplest example of this kind, a person can learn to carry out repetitive rituals involving fifty applications of disinfectant because he or she has been told to do so by a powerful, dominating parent. The cleaning ritual can be maintained in the same way that it is started, by the transmission of information, say, to the effect that repetitive cleaning is essential in order to avoid disease and death. It is probable that the occurrence of rewarding consequences contingent on the completion of the compulsive ritual can be a sufficient condition for ensuring persistence of the behavior.

Still confining our discussion to the postulated anxiety-reducing rituals, we also need to ask why the particular compulsions become fixed. Why this particular method for reducing discomfort? Why not pill taking or prolonged bed rest? The answer probably consists of two parts. In the first place, the rituals generally match both the provoking stimulation and the consequent anxiety/discomfort. If the discomfort is provoked by touching dirt, removing the dirt by cleaning oneself is the appropriate action to take. In this restricted sense the rituals are functional and appropriate.

In the second place, there is an element of prepared learning in the types of obsession and compulsion that arise. The cleaning and checking rituals observed in clinics across the world are far too similar to be regarded as a random phenomenon, and one can conceive of many of the common rituals as having a biological-evolutionary significance in the sense in which Seligman (1971) uses these concepts (see Chapter 25).

To conclude, it seems that a comprehensive resolution of the problem of the persistence of compulsive activities is unlikely to be achieved without taking two preliminary steps. Although we are assuming that compulsive activities are best construed as forms of avoidance behavior, the recommended steps are not contingent on acceptance of this conception.

First, it has to be recognized that avoidance behavior can be generated and maintained in the absence of anxiety or its reduction. Contrary to Mowrer's view (1960, p. 491), fear is not "an essential intermediate cause or variable" of active and passive avoidance behavior. The second preliminary step that we recommend is the working assumption that the observed elevation of anxiety plays no part in maintaining the obsession or compulsion but is better conceived of as some sort of co-effect. When one comes across compulsive activities that are followed more than rarely by an elevation of anxiety, it is doubly necessary to search for sources of reinforcement, probably longer term, that might be maintaining the compulsive behavior.

To sum up, it would appear that most compulsive rituals are followed by a reduction in anxiety/discomfort. This is particularly true in the case of cleaning rituals, but there is a small, significant minority of instances (especially checking rituals) in which anxiety/discomfort is unaffected by, or increases after, completion of the ritual. Overall, the results are consistent with the anxiety/discomfort reduction theory, but there are important exceptions. The reduction of anxiety is not a necessary condition for the continuation of compulsive rituals, but it can be a sufficient condition. Although several explanations to account for the persistence of anxiety-elevating obsessions and compulsions have been proposed, none of them appears to be entirely satisfactory. It can be assumed, however, that a comprehensive explanation will rest on the recognition of longer-term influences that exceed the immediate discomforts produced by executing the compulsion.

Chapter 13

Adverse Mood and Indecisiveness: Beech's Theory

The prolific and provoking writings of Beech (Beech, 1971, 1974; Walker and Beech, 1969) offer an unusual and stimulating alternative perspective on obsessional-compulsive behavior. Beech has written extensively on this and related subjects, both alone and in collaboration with his colleagues (Walker, Liddell, Perigault, Milner), and it has become difficult to distill the essence of his point of view. In this account we have given preference to his latest writings on the subject, contained in *Obsessional States*, which he edited in 1974. For the sake of simplicity, what we consider to be his main propositions are set out in the following statements.

1. The anxiety reduction theory is criticized as being mechanical and over-simplified.
2. Instead, it is proposed that the execution of compulsive rituals most often leads to a deterioration of mood.
2a. Longer rituals are likely to produce greater disturbances of mood.
2b. The interruption or curtailment of a compulsive ritual has no adverse effect on mood and may help reduce the unpleasantness that accompanies the ritual.
3. Adverse mood plays a central part in the production of obsessional-compulsive thoughts and behavior.
3a. Obsessional patients are especially vulnerable to disturbances of mood.
3b. The obsessional's predisposition to adverse mood states is an enduring attribute.
4. The obsessional patient's rationale for his or her disordered behavior is offered after the event in an attempt to explain the disturbances of mood that he or she has experienced.

5. The adverse mood states involved in obsessional disorders are complex, and may or may not include anxiety.
6. Difficulties in making decisions constitute a central problem for obsessionals.
6a. Disturbances of mood result from the difficulties experienced in making decisions.

With regard to the first statement, Beech has argued that it is "a common misconception that rituals serve to reduce anxiety and are preserved on this account" (Beech and Liddell, 1974, p. 146). Later in the same article, it is argued that "we must disabuse ourselves of any simple-minded notion that the ritual serves the function of reducing anxiety as it certainly does not do so on many occasions and, indeed, as often as not leads to incrementation of the adverse mood state" (p. 147). On the same lines, it is argued that "the performance of a ritual often leads to deterioration rather than improvement in mood state" (p. 148). It is also proposed that the likelihood of a deterioration in mood is increased with the duration of the ritual—"Some rituals cause mood to deteriorate, and this deterioration is more marked the longer the ritual" (Walker and Beech, 1969, p. 1268).

From this hypothesis it is but a short step to the next statement: "Artificial curtailment of such rituals has a beneficial effect on mood" (p. 1268). Repeated interruptions should produce enduring benefits. It is worth mentioning that for a considerable time precisely the opposite claim was made. It is fair to say that until experimentally minded psychologists began to address the problem of obsessions and compulsions it was widely believed, especially among psychologists and psychiatrists influenced by the work of Freud, that interference with compulsive rituals was likely to lead to seriously adverse consequences, and even to suicide. This gloomy prediction was made on the grounds that compulsive rituals constitute an important form of defense activity and that, consequently, suppression of this safety valve might lead to unrestrained emotional disturbance.

Beech and his colleagues place a great deal of importance on the predisposing role of adverse mood. "It seems to us that our observations and findings strongly suggest the *primacy* of mood in the causal chain which culminates in ritualistic behavior" (Beech, 1971, p. 419, emphasis in original). Furthermore, "A predisposition to states of pathological arousal and some mechanism by which such a state leads to morbid thoughts and aberrant behavior" are two important features of Beech's theory (Beech and Perigault, 1974, p. 115). Or, in slightly different words, the theory "postulates an unusual state of arousal . . . and some means by which these emotional states, which in the theory have primary importance, became attached to certain cognitive events" (p. 136).

Obsessional patients are "characterized by a tendency to an exaggerated state of arousal" (Beech, 1971, p. 420), and there is a critical level of arousal at which incrementation, rather than decline, occurs. This tendency to a pathological level of overarousal is "seen by us as being relatively enduring so that . . . the basic vulnerability of the unstable arousal system is constantly providing further opportunities for pathological connection-forming" (Beech and Perigault, 1974, p. 116). In consequence, although attempts to overcome ritualistic behavior may be greeted by temporary success, "the continuing vulnerability . . . rapidly leads to renewed associations of the same or a similar kind" (Beech, 1971, p. 420).

The crucial determining factors in obsessional disorders, and the manner and sequence in which they operate, are, from the patient's point of view, obscure. In order to make sense of the "massive, unsolicited mood changes" to which he or she is subjected, the patient "will create a fiction or pathological idea (such as that concerning some source of contamination) and abnormalities of overt behavior (e.g., rituals or avoidance behavior) which are consistent with these ideas" (Beech and Perigault, 1974, p. 115). Elsewhere, Beech (1971) has written that "the cognitive component of the abnormal behavior exhibited in rituals probably reflects post-hoc accounts given by the patient to explain his subjective experience of disturbance" (p. 419).

The adverse mood state associated with ritualistic behavior comprises (at least?) three "important components . . . hostility, depression and anxiety" (Walker and Beech, 1969, p. 1268). These components "vary together" (p. 1266), and they show some relationship to the length of the ritual (i.e., longer rituals are associated with greater deterioration of mood). According to Beech (1974, p. 160), Walker's elaboration of the adverse feeling states is a useful advance over the earlier view that anxiety is the central and indeed the only pertinent mood state involved in compulsive rituals.

In his later work Beech attributed increasing importance to the obsessional patient's postulated difficulty in making decisions—what Maudsley (1895) described as "terrible and incredible . . . petty vacillations and paltry irresolutions" (p. 165). Drawing on the work of Reed (1968), Beech points out that among the nine categories of difficulties complained of by obsessional patients, one was decision making. Reed suggests that they might have trouble in reaching a decision and/or might suffer from lack of conviction about the conclusions reached. He also makes the point that the difficulties in decision making are not necessarily related to the importance or emotional significance of the problem. As Beech points out, "Indeed often the greatest agonies of mind are experienced when handling quite trivial issues" (Beech and Liddell, 1974, p. 144). It is further argued that difficulties in decision making "result in a state of unpleasant high arousal which is reflected in the measures of mood states of hostility, depression, and anxiety" (p. 149). This view was also proposed by Reed (1968), who observed that most of his patients felt that the unpleasant emotional reactions that they experienced were a result rather than the cause of their repetitive doubting and indecisiveness.

While recognizing the provocative value of Beech's writings, it has to be conceded that the supporting evidence for his views is limited. The postulates regarding mood and the central role of indecisiveness are especially in need of buttressing. "Clearly the data we have provided are extremely limited, both in terms of number of patients and important controls. Only further intensive effort in collecting evidence will inform us of the value of the theoretical formulation outlined above" (Beech and Perigault, 1974, p. 141). This part of Beech's work is at too early a stage to permit a thorough evaluation. With regard to the remaining research, some of the findings are supportive; other evidence appears to contradict some of his propositions; and yet other findings are inconclusive. In any event there are some problems inherent in the theorizing itself.

Beech's writings provoked, and in turn were influenced by, two main research projects, both of them doctoral dissertations carried out under his supervision: Walker (1967) and Liddell (1976). Both projects have novel features and contain interesting findings, but from Beech's point of view they must be regarded as insufficiently positive. A few of the propositions received support, but a majority of the predictions were not confirmed and some were discomfirmed. For example, Walker (1967) found that the patient she studied most intensively experienced a reduction of depression on 11 out of 13 occasions when completing her washing ritual. Also contrary to prediction, there was no relation between mood state before the ritual and the time taken to carry it out.

In discussing her results Walker (1967) concluded that "the most interesting finding here was that, directly contrary to prediction, all three mood states showed significant improvement after this (final) wash" (p. 122). Although some evidence (regrettably not entirely consistent) was obtained in support of the idea that at least part of the ritual (i.e., the hair-combing section) led to or was accompanied by a deterioration in mood, the argument is weakened by another observation: that "contrary to prediction, a significant deterioration in both hostility and depression scores occurred *during the delay before washing* in the experimental period" (p. 133, emphasis added). In other words, a significant deterioration in the patient's mood occurred even during periods when she was not engaging in the ritualistic behavior. These alterations in mood make it difficult to attribute the observed deteriorations, or indeed the improvements, to the execution of her rituals.

In interpreting her observations Walker was obliged to rely on incomplete information, all of it of unknown reliability. Even the specially devised short questionnaire, designed to measure hostility, depression, and anxiety, is of unknown reliability (and, for that matter, validity).

In all, she concluded, in keeping with Wolpe's (1958) analysis, that there are two types of rituals—one that leads to mood improvement and another that leads to mood deterioration.

The second part of Walker's research consisted of an attempt to test seven predictions about how obsessional patients would behave in an experimental task requiring them to make decisions on a shape discrimination task. Great emphasis is placed on the conclusion that "obsessionals tend to postpone terminal decisions longer than controls" (Walker, 1967, p. 173). In practice this means that the obsessional patients made more requests for the test items to be repeated than the control subjects did. However, the value of this finding is brought into question by the failure to replicate it in the subsequent experiment. Here it was found that "it is the normal group whose number of 'requests' tended to be higher than those of the other two groups" (i.e., obsessionals and neurotics) (p. 247).

Continuing her search for some correlates of adverse mood, Walker examined the relation between initial mood and the tendency to postpone decisions. "On 15 out of 16 correlations computed, no significant effect was found and thus no confirmation is found for the prediction" (p. 252).

In summary, Walker found slight but inconsistent support for the hypothesis that rituals on occasion lead to a deterioration in mood. She also found some evidence from the case studies indicating that the execution of the ritual as often, or more often, is followed by an improvement in mood state. The attempt to relate mood and the length of the ritualistic activity was unsuccessful. The exploration of the proposition that obsessionals have difficulty reaching decisions produced a negligible amount of supporting evidence and a number of disconfirmations.

Later, Liddell (1976) attempted to recruit support for the decision-making theory of obsessional disorders proposed by Walker and Beech (1969) and Beech (1974), and elaborated by herself. As we have seen, the theory places considerable reliance on the importance of mood state in determining obsessional-compulsive behavior. An immediate difficulty arises from the fact that mood states show larger and more frequent fluctuations than compulsive rituals. They are often out of key. Walker's (1967) attempt to confirm that obsessionals postponed decisions excessively yielded inconsistent results, but on the other hand, the study reported by Milner, Beech, and Walker (1971) showed that a group of two obsessional patients and four depressed patients with some obsessive features (Milner, 1966) made significantly more requests for repeated trials in a tone detection task than a comparable group of eight depressed patients. As there were only two diagnosed obsessionals in the study and it was possible that the experimenter was aware of which group each subject belonged to, a replication is needed.

Liddell set out to test a selection of hypotheses derived directly or indirectly from the position established by Beech and Walker. She administered questionnaires and conducted some small-scale experiments on 60 subjects: 20 obsessional patients, 20 nonobsessional neurotic patients, and 20 nonpsychiatric subjects. She found no difference between the obsessionals and the neurotics with respect to reported difficulty in reaching decisions. The matter was then pursued by summing the scores of the neurotic and normal samples in order to compare these scores with those of the 20 obsessional patients.The difference between the combined group and the obsessionals reached statistical significance. Examination of the raw data shows that 7 out of the 20 obsessionals scored positively on only 2 of the 4 selected items. On the other hand, 7 out of the 20 neurotic subjects replied affirmatively to 3 out of 4 of the items that were said to be particularly indicative of decision-making difficulties. Moreover, 5 of the normal subjects replied affirmatively to 3 out of the 4 items. In all, the distinction between the groups on these 4 items of the questionnaire was not clear-cut.

Contrary to prediction, the obsessionals were found not to differ from the neurotic sample on any of the seven indexes of hostility used in this study (see also Fernando, 1977, who found no correlation between hostility and obsessionality). Moreover, they were not even different from the normals on four of the same seven indexes. "All comparisons of general hostility scores failed to reach significance" (Liddell, 1976, p. 96).

In part, the results of an interesting experiment by Volans (1976) are consistent with the view that some obsessional people are poor at decision making, but the author was careful to avoid overconcluding from her study. Compared with eight phobic and eight nonpsychiatric subjects, eight obsessional checkers showed poorer inferential ability in a task involving estimates of probability. However, Volans was unable to find any relation between their performance on this laboratory task and the decisions made by her subjects in real-life situations. Moreover, the decision-making "deficits" were evident on only one of two forms of the task. According to Shackleton (1977), it is unclear how the observed deficits might relate to the specific fears, discomforts, and rituals that characterize obsessional disorders. In her full critique of the study, Shackleton correctly argues that the experiment has weaknesses in matching (e.g., the depression variable is not controlled) and, more important, that there is no reason to conclude that the decision-making deficits are *primary*. It should also be added that the generality of the deficit is questionable. The obsessional group showed a deficit on one form of the test but not on the other one, and as already noted, there was no relation between test deficits and real-life decision making.

Even if the results were more encouraging for Beech's view than they are, it would be necessary to bear in mind that they refer only to checkers. As we have suggested, compulsive cleaners appear to have little or no difficulty reaching decisions—especially about the source of their contamination, or indeed about the need to clean themselves. Our psychometric evidence indicates that excessive doubting/conscientiousness is one of four separable obsessional factors. It does not lend support to the view that indecisiveness is the primary deficit in obsessional disorders.

It is doubtful whether this information, coupled with the discouraging inability of the specifically designed experiments to obtain adequate supporting evidence, can fully justify confidence in Beech's view that difficulties in decision making constitute the central problem of obsessional neuroses. At present there is insufficient reason to expect that indecisiveness will turn out to be more than one of several characteristics observed with greater frequency among obsessional patients, as indeed is the case in depressive patients. Levitt and Lubin (1975), for example, report that 80 percent of 500 depressed patients complained of indecisiveness. There is no reason for assigning primary importance to indecisiveness as opposed to many of the other features described elsewhere in this book. Our psychometric findings are in keeping with the work that gave impetus to Beech's theorizing. Like Reed (1968), we concluded that obsessional disorders are multifactorial. Indecisiveness is one of these factors, but there are no grounds for assuming that it is primary.

The importance that Beech attaches to rituals, which are followed by a deterioration in mood, receives some slight support from external sources. As Wolpe (1958) pointed out, some patients suffer from what he described as anxiety-elevating obsessions. The report by Solyom and his colleagues (1971) is consistent with this in showing that some obsessional patients (40% in his sample) report that on at least some occasions they experience a deterioration in mood associated with their obsessions or compulsions.

Our own research, both experimental and psychometric, provided confirmation that in a small minority of instances completion of the ritualistic activity is followed by an increase in discomfort. The occurrence of compulsive rituals that are followed by an increase in some adverse mood state is not at issue. Contrary to Beech's view, however, this consequence of ritualistic activity occurs far less often than the discomfort-reducing type. Consequently, it may be inadvisable to elevate the less frequently observed effects of ritualistic activity into the central fact requiring explanation. Even as subsidiary and relatively infrequent phenomena, they provide sufficient difficulty for anyone struggling to make coherent, comprehensive sense of obsessional-compulsive rituals.

At this point a small digression is required. The interest in decision making has spilled over to the related matter of risk taking, and Carr (1974) has taken a special interest in the subject. On the basis of his psychophysiological studies on compulsive neuroses, Carr (1974) concluded that "*in all* situations the compulsive neurotic has an abnormally high subjective estimate of the probability of occurrence of the unfavorable outcome" (p. 315, emphasis in original). However, the research findings provide an inadequate basis for sweeping conclusions. In keeping with the conclusions of Kogan and Wallach (1967), Steiner, Jarvis, and Parrish (1970) could find little support for the idea of a general factor of risk taking. As a small part of her larger study of obsessional behavior, Liddell (1976) asked her subjects four questions about their risk-taking attitudes. The scores of the obsessional patients did not differ from those of the neurotic control group (p. 111).

Another proposition contained in the model elaborated by Carr (1974) states that "because the compulsive neurotic *always* makes an abnormally high subjective estimate about the probability of the undesired outcome, then all such situations that have a potentially harmful outcome, however minimal, will generate a relatively high level of threat with its consequent anxiety" (p. 316, emphasis in original). In her exploration of the role of decision making in obsessional-compulsive disorders, Walker administered two questionnaires to groups of obsessional patients, neurotic patients, and normal subjects. On neither of these questionnaires, which related to the probability of unpleasant events and their effects and were both relevant to Carr's proposition, did the obsessionals give any sign of having special problems. "There are no significant differences between the means of the groups . . . on either the unpleasantness or probability questionnaire" (Walker, 1967, p. 233). The propositions incorporated in Carr's model have yet to be subjected to direct test, but as can be seen from the few results that are now available, the prospects are not encouraging.

Returning to the original propositions distilled from Beech's writings, the available evidence can be summarized in this way: It is correct that some compulsive rituals are not followed by a reduction in adverse mood. It is also correct that some rituals are followed by a deterioration in mood state—however, the relative frequency of mood-improving and mood-deteriorating rituals postulated by Beech appears to have been incorrect. In all but a few instances, the completion of a compulsive ritual is followed by a decrease in discomfort (or other adverse mood state). Despite their appeal, it has not been possible to confirm the claims that adverse mood states are associated with longer rituals or, in turn, that longer rituals are more likely to produce adverse mood states.

There is some slight evidence that obsessional patients are especially vulnerable to unpleasant events, such as criticism, and even a hint that they might have a persistently elevated level of physiological arousal. In neither instance is the evidence compelling, and equally important, there is as yet no indication that obsessionals differ in either of these respects from other neurotic patients. A high level of psychological arousal is not a distinguishing feature of obsessional disorders. Beech's view that the obsessionals' particular sensitivity is an enduring quality and, hence, leaves them open to the likelihood of relapse has not yet received any experimental support. The relapse rate after behavioral treatment is not high (see Marks et al., 1975).

The argument that the patient's explanation for his or her obsessional-compulsive behavior is offered *post hoc* has not received support so far and is unlikely to be borne out because it assumes what Seligman (1970) has described as the "generality of laws of learning." According to this view, *what* the person or animal learns is a matter of irrelevance. The weakness of this position was demonstrated in Seligman's critical analysis. Applied to the present question, Beech's argument about *post hoc* rationalization appears to assume such generality (i.e., the content of the compulsive behavior is irrelevant). What is important, Beech would argue, is the person's attempt to account for his or her postulated disturbance of mood. Beech's argument so far leaves no room for the possibility that compulsive rituals are a prepared form of learning, and subject to development, his theory does not further our understanding of the remarkable and puzzling similarity among the rituals displayed by various patients. It is stretching matters too far to assume that the exceedingly common occurrence of ritualistic hand washing is a matter of coincidence. Equally, why do so many patients choose similar *post hoc* rationalizations?

Beech's emphasis on the complexity of the adverse mood states that appear to be involved in obsessional-compulsive behavior is well taken. Certainly, the older view that it was necessarily and exclusively anxiety that was involved in the genesis or maintenance of ritualistic behavior is difficult to support. As we have pointed out, many of our patients firmly resisted the idea that the adverse feelings that they experienced were akin to anxiety. For this reason, among others, we chose to distinguish between anxiety and discomfort or the more vague but less misleading term *psychological tension*. Having identified a weakness in present approaches to the psychological analysis of obsessions and compulsions, we hope that Beech's view will lead to some fruitful explorations of the nature and role of mood states in this disorder. As a cautionary note, however, Kringlen (1965) found more adverse mood swings among nonobsessive patients.

Is Beech's insistence on the importance of decision-making difficulties well founded? There is little doubt that many patients complain of indecisiveness and that for some of them it appears to be the major problem. Although it is more than likely that for some patients extreme indecisiveness is a cause of emotional disturbance, this is not to say that this attribute is of central significance in obsessions and compulsions. As mentioned earlier, indecisiveness is also a prominent feature of depression (e.g., Levitt and Lubin, 1975; Woodruff et al., 1967). At present there is no reason to suppose that indecisiveness is the primary dysfunction—particularly in the light of the discouraging outcome of the two research programs with which Beech was associated—nor are there satisfactory grounds for concluding that the adverse mood states associated with many compulsive activities are the consequences of decision-making difficulties. Lastly, indecisiveness is not peculiar to obsessional disorders.

Reed (1976) shares the view of Beech and his colleagues that indecisiveness is decisive, but interprets the phenomenon in his own manner. He argues that the indecisiveness is a manifestation of attempts to impose structure, and expresses surprise at the failure of Hodgson and Rachman (1972) to acknowledge the importance of indecisiveness. While we are inclined to agree with his description of the relation between indecisiveness and ill-defined tasks (especially anticipatory, checking tasks), his dismissal of our earlier report (1972) on the *decisiveness* of eight out of ten obsessional patients is difficult to follow. This finding is, he states, "open to several interpretations" (p. 444), and the one that he prefers is that obsessional patients are "unable to act upon" their decisions; "this is the cause of their anguish and why they reproach themselves for their lack of determination" (p. 444). Even if we accepted that the putative inability to act on their decisions is both universal and of special significance (we do not), this would not support the claim that *indecisiveness* is of paramount importance. Reed appears to concede that it is not indecisiveness per se but, rather, inability to carry out decisions already made—in his words, "It is not so much *decisions* that cause difficulties for obsessionals as *decisions about decisions*" (p. 444, emphasis in original). The idea is worth considering, but it should not be confused with Beech's hypothesis that obsessionals have a basic impairment in ability to make decisions. The decisiveness displayed by many obsessional patients is not predictable from the views advanced by Reed or Beech.

Some of the deductions that might legitimately be made from Beech's writings are consistent with the results obtained in recent clinical trials of behavior modification. In particular, the observed effects of techniques that incorporate response prevention are fully compatible with Beech's view on the emotional consequences of long rituals. It will be recalled that he predicted that curtailment of rituals, especially those of long duration, might lead to an improvement rather than a deterioration in mood. On the other hand, the alternative view, which we support, is more closely connected with the newly successful behavioral treatment methods than Beech's account. So, for example, his emphasis on the importance of indecisiveness has limited practical implications, and significant clinical results can be achieved without reference to indecisiveness. By contrast, some alternative views, such as those presented in this book, are interwoven with practical clinical procedures and consequences.

Turning now to a general appraisal of the theoretical work of Beech and his colleagues, there is no doubt that it has played an important part in stimulating research into obsessional-compulsive disorders. The theorizing has also served the useful function of drawing attention to the importance of mood states and to the fact that the mood states are more complex than was formerly believed to be the case. Beech's insistence on the importance of rituals that lead to a deterioration of mood, although in our opinion exaggerated, has been a useful corrective for theories based on the assumption that all rituals serve to reduce anxiety. Beech's writings have also helped restore Wolpe's (1958) analysis of the two different types of "obsessional behavior" to the prominence that it deserves.

It must be conceded, however, that part of Beech's theorizing is not satisfactory. The emphasis placed on the importance of mood-deteriorating rituals runs contrary to the evidence; although these effects are observed, it seems certain that they are far less common than Beech's theorizing requires. The emphasis placed on this kind of ritual, as opposed to the far more frequent type in which the execution of the ritual is followed by an improvement in mood, makes it difficult to achieve a balanced view of the putative function of these rituals.

The theory suffers from lack of specificity. At its most successful, it provides a reasonable explanation for certain kinds of neurotic behavior, but it adds little to our understanding of the specific characteristics and mechanisms of obsessional-compulsive behavior. To take two examples: Elevated levels of arousal have been implicated in the genesis of other neurotic disorders as well, and indecisiveness is not a distinctive feature of obsessions. Furthermore, on the critical question of how the adverse mood states "become attached to certain cognitive agents" (Beech and Perigault, 1974, p. 136), the theory provides insufficient guidance.

There is another difficulty in the role attributed to adverse mood states. In different parts of the theory these mood states are made to play two different roles. In one part adverse mood states are described as the major predisposing factor in ritualistic behavior. Elsewhere, however, adverse mood states are described as being one of the major *consequences* of ritualistic behavior. There is no reason why adverse mood should not operate in the two ways suggested, but one should not lose sight of the fact that adverse mood state is regarded as both a cause and an effect. In these circumstances it is important to achieve clarity in presenting the theory and to specify with care whether one is referring to the effects or to the cause.

On the empirical side, the main weakness of the theory is the number of predictions that have not been confirmed. In the two projects generated by the theory, several predictions were not confirmed. Moreover, some parts of the theory appear to be contradicted by evidence gathered independently (Chapters 11, 12, and 14). Indeed, some of the predictions have been disconfirmed by the research conducted by Beech and his colleagues themselves. So, for example, Beech and Perigault (1974) say that "the position adopted by us was that obsessionals are characterized by a tendency to exaggerated arousal . . . Individuals who are susceptible to high arousal and slow recovery from stimulation might also be expected to show an increased number of spontaneous fluctuations of arousal state, thus creating more opportunities for special conditioning effects" (pp. 115-16). However, in Liddell's research, described by Beech and Liddell (1974), it is reported that "the general level of spontaneous fluctuations among obsessionals is *lower* than that found in the other two groups . . . in both . . . conditions and over the four kinds of decision-making tasks employed" (pp. 156-57, emphasis added). Another example, dealt with earlier, concerns the prediction that obsessionals postpone their decisions to a greater extent than either neurotics or nonpsychiatric subjects. In the second experiment carried out by Walker (1967, p. 247), it was the nonpsychiatric group of subjects who postponed their decisions longest.

As far as the development of Beech's stimulating theorizing is concerned, the most profitable lines to follow may be intensive investigations of mood factors before, during, and after ritualistic activity and continuation of the search for an explanation of why rituals that are followed by a deterioration in mood do not extinguish. Clarification and development of the mechanism by which, it is postulated, pathological arousal leads to aberrant thoughts and behavior are also awaited with interest.

Chapter 14

Compulsive Urges

Urges are defined as impelling forces, and usually it is implied that they are directed towards a goal. It is also implied that the source of the prompting is internal, even if the urge itself was originally provoked by some external event (e.g., a discarded cigarette may provoke an urge to check in susceptible people). An urge may or may not provoke internal resistance, but if we follow conventional practice (Lewis, 1936), the presence of resistance would be regarded as an essential characteristic of a compulsive urge. As we have already seen, although insistence on the occurrence of internal resistance is semantically correct, there is a significant minority of patients who in all other respects would undoubtedly be described as having an obsessional-compulsive disorder but persuasively deny that they experience such resistance—either consistently or at all. With this reservation noted, the remainder of this discussion is based on a definition of compulsive urges as internal, goal-directed promptings that encounter subjective resistance to the execution of the appropriate behavior.

We construe compulsive urges as the psychological activity that lies between an obsessional thought and the execution of a compulsive act. If the urge is suppressed, it is unlikely that the compulsive act will be executed (possible exceptions will be discussed shortly). Just as a compulsive urge can be experienced without leading to a compulsive act, so compulsive urges can arise in the absence of a clear obsessional thought. Usually there is a close connection between thought and urge.

The following extracts from clinical cases illustrate the nature of the relationships among obsession, compulsive urge, and ritualistic action. These brief case illustrations are intended to convey something of the quality of compulsive urges and, at the same time, illustrate six of the primary features of compulsive urges: (1) Urges are related to obsessions;(2) they impel toward action;(3a) they can be internally prompted or (3b) externally provoked; (4) they frequently are related to compulsive rituals; (5) they generally are met with internal resistance; and (6) their translation into compulsive behavior can be suppressed.

A clear connection among obsessions, urges, and compulsions was evident in the 20-year-old student who complained of the repeated intrusion of disturbing thoughts and images in which his parents were in danger of being sexually assaulted. The appearance of the obsession usually provoked a strong urge to protect them from harm by carrying out (preventive) hand-washing rituals. Although he recognized the senselessness of repeatedly washing his hands and was embarrassed by this ritualistic behavior, his ability to resist the urges was weak and intermittent.

While this connection is most commonly encountered, any one of the three components in this chain can occur in apparent isolation. For example, a young computer clerk came to us complaining of "mental paralysis" caused by intrusive, disturbing thoughts concerning an incident that had occurred in her middle childhood. She was obsessed by the sudden death of an old woman whom she had visited occasionally. The patient spent days pondering the circumstances of the death and whether or not she was in some inexplicable way responsible for killing the old woman. These obsessional ruminations were not accompanied by urges or rituals. The same patient also complained of sudden, unsignaled urges to expose herself when she approached any group of men. These urges, which were successfully resisted, were not preceded by obsessional ideas.

The occurrence of compulsive rituals, unconnected with obsessions or urges, is illustrated by the case of a 40-year-old bookkeeper who was handicapped by primary obsessional slowness. Each day he spent many hours cleaning and dressing himself. Each part of the process had to be carried out meticulously and in the correct sequence. The rituals were not preceded by obsessions or compulsive urges, and the substantial modification of his ritualistic behavior that was achieved during therapy was not followed by the emergence of urges or obsessions. He provides a clear exception to the usual sequence in which suppression of the urge is followed by the failure to execute the compulsive act.

During the course of our clinical research into the modification of behavior disorders, particularly those in which anxiety plays a prominent part, we gradually came to realize that people are considerably more resilient than we had assumed. Initially, we were reluctant to use flooding treatment (Rachman, 1969) because it was anticipated that many patients would find it intolerable. To our surprise we slowly learned that most patients are capable of tolerating considerable discomfort and/or anxiety for short periods; not only capable, but quite willing to do so. In our clinical work anxious patients were routinely offered a choice between the slow, gradual, and mildly uncomfortable method of desensitization or the quicker but uncomfortable method of flooding. A majority chose flooding, seemingly because of its promise of rapid clinical improvement.

As flooding methods were used more frequently, it became evident that patients rapidly recover their composure after being exposed to anxiety-provoking stimulation. Within minutes of experiencing considerable anxiety, they were able to speak and act calmly—and then quietly drink their tea. Reassured by our experiences with the effects of flooding (and later with participant modeling), we were in a position to advise our early obsessional patients that although their treatment sessions might make them feel extremely uncomfortable, they could look forward to an early restoration of calmness after each session. Naturally, some exceptions were encountered, but on the whole obsessional patients do recover their composure soon after the completion of each session.

We then became curious about the time course of this recovery from anxiety/discomfort and, in the case of obsessional patients, the relation between declining discomfort and declining strength of the associated compulsive urges. Although we now have some information about how the urges and discomfort decline, as yet there is little understanding of why they decay.

THE SPONTANEOUS DECAY
OF COMPULSIVE URGES AND DISCOMFORT

For both theoretical and therapeutic reasons, it was decided to gather information about the spontaneous decay of compulsive urges and about the relation between urges and discomfort. Our primary aim, however, was to study the time course of compulsive urges. For example, we were interested in knowing what happens when an obsessional-compulsive checker undergoes an experience that provokes the urge to check but is then prevented from carrying out his or her normal ritual.

On the theoretical side, it was hoped that an investigation of the time course of urges and discomfort might help clarify some of the differences in experimental results obtained by Beech and ourselves. On the ground that some of these differences might be attributable to variations in the time course of the experiments, we felt that it might be useful to make an extended study of the course of compulsive urges during a long period of response prevention. A third reason for undertaking this investigation was our growing interest in the relationship between subjective reports of discomfort and the course followed by compulsive urges. For most purposes, in company with other workers, we have tended to assume that subjective discomfort and compulsive urges covary or, indeed, to assume that they refer to the same phenomenon. For various reasons it was necessary to distinguish between these two concepts, and it therefore became a matter of some interest to trace the interrelationships in question, especially during a period in which the compulsive urges were undergoing a process of spontaneous decay.

Our experimental plan also put us in a position to assess the possible occurrence of so-called displacement activity. It has been proposed that ritualistic behavior serves some important purpose. It follows that failure to carry out ritualistic acts will be followed by some displacement activity. It is suggested that in this way the person is able to discharge his or her aggression or other pent-up emotion. In addition to this old theory, one of the modern interpretations of learning theory might also lead to a prediction that prevention of the ritualistic activity will be followed by some displacement activity:

> Following from Gray's theory (1971), it is possible to set up some testable predictions about the course of checking behavior. If checking is indeed maintained by the achievement of safety signals, then blocking the checking behavior should lead to a loss of comfort and perhaps, but not necessarily so, even to an increase in discomfort. Perhaps a feeling of frustration is the most likely consequence. It is also reasonable to expect the person to search for other safety signals. At the conclusion of a response-blocking period, we might expect him to resume working for his safety signals, i.e., to start checking once more. [Rachman, 1976b, p. 275]

Along the same lines, it is not unreasonable to suppose that if the checking ritual is blocked, the person might seek out other signals of safety by carrying out seemingly unrelated ritualistic checking behavior. With these several ideas in mind, we sought evidence of displaced checking behavior during the period when the appropriate checking response was blocked (i.e., during the response prevention period).

Finally, we were looking for evidence of the differences and similarities between the *spontaneous* decay of compulsive urges and the *truncated* decay of the same urges following the execution of the ritualistic behavior shortly after the emergence of the urge. In summary, we wanted to observe the provocation of compulsive urges and discomfort, and their decay, under two conditions: (1) attendant upon the execution of the appropriate checking ritual and (2) spontaneous decay during a period of response prevention. While plotting the course of the spontaneous decay of these compulsive urges and of the patient's discomfort, we also looked for evidence of the occurrence of displaced checking rituals. In order to carry out this study, the simple method of provoking compulsive behavior developed in our earlier investigations of the effects of executing compulsive rituals was used. The subjects were eleven adult obsessional-compulsive patients whose condition was moderate to severe and whose main compulsive activity comprised checking rituals.

The results and analysis are given in Rachman, de Silva, and Röper (1976).

As can be seen from the figures, exposure to the provoking situation led to a significant increase in both urges and discomfort. The execution of the ritual led to a significant reduction in both of these measures. During response prevention the urges and discomfort aroused by the exposure dropped significantly by the time the session had ended (in this analysis up to 2½ hours after provocation). In fact, a significant reduction in both measures was observed by the end of the first half-hour period after provocation; thereafter, the urges and discomfort both underwent significant declines by the end of the session. In the case of urges, the significant drop occurred between the first and second measurement occasions (i.e., during the second half-hour period). In the case of discomfort, this decline occurred more slowly. After the large initial drop, neither urges nor discomfort showed a significant upsurge (i.e., there was no significant resurgence *Coming - Returning.* of urges or discomfort).

Although the results of the full statistical analyses confirmed the patterns shown by the main scores plotted in Figure 14.1, there were individual cases that did not conform to this pattern. In one of the eleven subjects, carrying out

FIGURE 14.1.   Mean ratings for urge and discomfort across occasions (n=11). The measurement occasions plotted on the horizontal axis are: BE, before exposure to provoking stimulus; AE, after exposure; AR, after ritual; AE, after second exposure; and half-hourly intervals up to 3 hours.

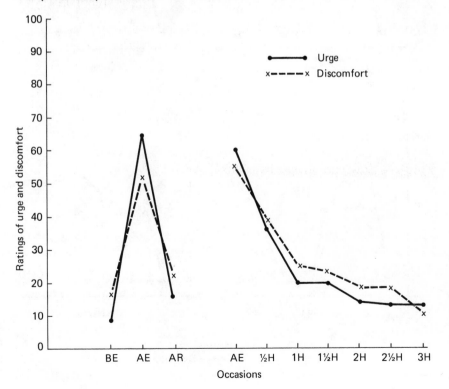

the ritual did not lead to a reduction of urge and discomfort; the discomfort increased. In another, the execution of the ritual had no effect on either urge or discomfort (see Figure 14.2, subject 9). In a third subject, the drop in discomfort was negligibly small (see Figure 14.2, subject 4). There were also individual

FIGURE 14.2.   Ratings for urge and discomfort, of 4 selected subjects. Subjects 5 and 8 illustrate the typical course of urge and discomfort, while subjects 9 and 4 illustrate exceptions to this pattern. Subject 9 displays no reduction of urge and discomfort after ritual, and also shows resurgence of these in the response prevention period. Subject 4 displays a wide discrepancy between urge and discomfort—she complained of high, unremitting anxiety throughout the experimental period.

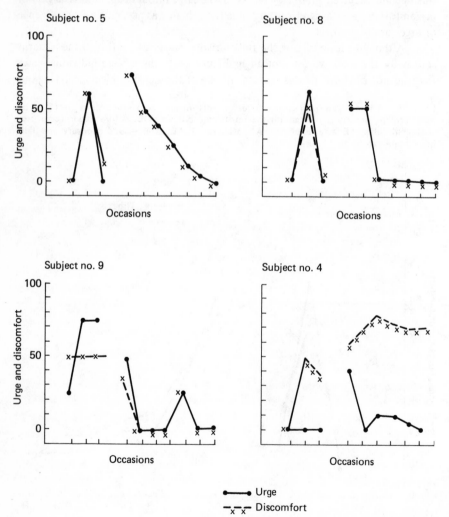

cases showing a temporary slight recurrence of urge and discomfort after initial reduction in the response prevention part of the experiment.

In sum, the results show encouraging uniformity; in only 2 of the few exceptions noted was there a recurrence of urge and discomfort of any magnitude, and these were the subjects who inadvertently encountered other provoking stimuli. In all, increases were recorded on only 5 out of 62 measuring occasions for discomfort, and on 5 occasions out of 62 for urges.

THE RELATIONSHIP BETWEEN URGE AND DISCOMFORT

As expected, the urge to check and feelings of discomfort tended to run parallel and close to each other (see Figure 14.1). Correlation coefficients calculated between the two sets of measures for 10 out of the 11 subjects varied from near-perfect ($r = 0.991$) to high ($r = 0.796$), all being significant at the .01 level. The one subject (no. 4 in Figure 14.2) in whom the measures were not significantly correlated was in an agitated state, and in her case the lack of a close relationship between urge and discomfort was due to the high level of general discomfort, while her urge remained at a low level. The parallel course of urges and discomfort was recently confirmed in the treatment trial described by Foa and Goldstein (1978).

However, the valuable observations reported by Mills, Agras, Barlow, and Mills (1973) prove that the relationship between urges and rituals can be more complex. In a series of five case studies, they neatly explored various aspects of this relationship while at the same time testing the power of the response prevention method. The investigations were not complete and therefore are regrettably inconclusive. Apart from their tentative findings regarding the strength of response prevention, these investigators also picked up some interesting data on compulsive urges. At the risk of introducing some slight oversimplification, the findings can be summarized as follows: In the "natural state" (i.e., before any interevention takes place), compulsive rituals and urges do follow a parallel course. The introduction of response prevention instructions successfully suppresses the rituals, but the urges continue unchanged or even show a transient *increase*. Most interesting of all, in three of the four relevant cases the enduring reduction of ritualistic behavior achieved by response prevention was (more slowly) followed by a corresponding decline in urges. It seems that the pretreatment concordance between rituals and urges can be broken up by a high demand treatment. Thereafter, desynchronous changes will take place, with urges changing more slowly than rituals—but concordance between urges and rituals will return if the treatment succeeds. Given the purpose and power of the response prevention method, this pattern of change is unsurprising—but the experimental demonstration of the pattern is useful and the enduring decline of urges and rituals is a source of encouragement for therapists.

Our experimental findings on displacement of checking rituals were inconclusive. In assessing the information we were hampered by ambiguity over the question of whether activities that were normal for the person under study but were provoked by accidental exposure to trigger stimuli during the response prevention period should be considered displacement activities. We decided to exclude these as irrelevant and to consider as displacement checking only rituals that were not normal, in the circumstances, for the subject. There were three subjects who displayed such checking. One engaged in the solitary act of checking to see whether or not she had knocked over a stool; another carried out many intense rituals in her kitchen for up to two hours. A third, who was in an agitated state, kept checking repeatedly and indiscriminately. The numbers are too small to make any useful analysis of the possible differences between these and the other subjects, but inspection of the data revealed no obvious correlates of this displacement checking.

In passing, it may be mentioned that two of the subjects volunteered the information that they mentally "went over" the exposure experience and, hence, decided not to worry about the prevented response during the response prevention period. They claimed that this was helpful. Whether such mental "going over," or rehearsal, can be considered a displacement activity or an indirect search for "safety signals" is open to debate; our own view is that it does not constitute displacement activity.

DISCUSSION OF RESULTS

Insofar as this experiment was a replication, the results were consistent with our earlier findings. With minor exceptions, obsessional-compulsive patients experience a marked increase in anxiety/discomfort when exposed to an appropriate provoking situation. Exposure to provocation also produced a marked increase in urges to carry out the appropriate ritualistic activity. Further, execution of the ritual reduced both discomfort *and* urges. These reductions were achieved promptly and left a minimal amount of residual discomfort, if any. As before, the results run contrary to the views proposed by Beech and Liddell (1974) and by Walker (1967). The exceptions, in which execution of the compulsive ritual was followed by an increase in discomfort, provide support for their emphasis on this phenomenon, but they occurred so infrequently as to make it exceedingly unlikely that Beech's theory can achieve comprehensiveness.

The results of this experiment are also consistent with our earlier findings in showing that the arousal and reduction of anxiety/discomfort and compulsive urges follow strikingly similar patterns in obsessional checkers and obsessional cleaners. The only differences between checkers and cleaners are that the discomfort-reducing effects of cleaning rituals are generally larger (and more reliable?) than those of checking rituals, and that the exceptions referred to earlier are occasionally observed in compulsive checkers but rarely seen in compulsive cleaners.

The fact that, with minor exceptions, compulsive checking rituals are followed rapidly by marked reductions in discomfort *and* urges is consistent with an anxiety/discomfort reduction hypothesis. It need hardly be repeated that it does not necessarily follow that the reduction of anxiety/discomfort is responsible for maintaining the compulsive behavior.

The course of the compulsive urges and anxiety/discomfort, provoked by exposure but not followed by the appropriate ritual, was examined over a three-hour period. In this way it was possible to trace what we call the *spontaneous decay* of compulsive urges and discomfort. Using a three-hour observation period made it possible to trace the complete time course of this spontaneous decay.

Some reduction of discomfort and urges occurred within the first 30 minutes after the provoking action, and a further reduction occurred during the subsequent 30 minutes. At the end of one hour, the greatest part of the discomfort and urges had decayed. In addition to their theoretical interest, these results provide support for behavioral methods of treatment that employ response prevention periods. The theoretical significance of the spontaneous decay of the urges presents no difficulties either for the anxiety/discomfort reduction hypothesis or for the views proposed by Beech and his colleagues.

It is of some interest to notice that the successful completion of the appropriate ritual produces an almost immediate reduction of urges and of discomfort. During a response prevention period, discomfort and urges dissipate *spontaneously, but noticeably more slowly.* Needless to say, the experimental reduction of compulsive urges and discomfort, whether achieved "spontaneously" or by executing the appropriate ritual, was not permanent; they could easily be re-evoked by exposure to the provoking stimulus situation.

Some minor resurgences of urges and discomfort were observed during the three-hour observation period. They were fewer in number and smaller in magnitude than might have been anticipated. Moreover, they were provoked more by external stimulation than by internal changes. The "spontaneous" return of compulsive urges to repeat check was extremely uncommon; rather, these resurgences were provoked by inadvertent exposure to other sources of provocation. It should be remembered that many obsessional checkers report that their urges are provoked by numerous, pervasive types of stimulation. We also have some evidence that the background level of anxiety has an influence on the patient's reaction to provocation and on the success of his or her compulsive rituals in dealing with the discomfort and urges. In the one case in whom high anxiety was present, it overshadowed the otherwise uniform reaction to provocation and the otherwise uniform consequences of executing the appropriate ritual. A replication of this finding would be of some interest.

⚓Contrary to expectation, we found little evidence of displacement checking. As mentioned earlier, recurrences of checking behavior or of urges to check were provoked by inadvertent exposures to provoking stimuli and not by internally generated discomfort or compulsions.

PROPERTIES OF COMPULSIVE URGES

On the basis of our findings, particularly in the experiment just described, complemented by our clinical observations and those reported by other workers, a tentative picture of the nature of compulsive urges can be constructed.

As described earlier, compulsive urges are construed as the psychological activity that generally lies between an obsessional thought and the execution of a compulsive ritual. However, many and perhaps most compulsive urges are not translated into compulsive rituals; compulsive urges probably can arise in the absence of obsessional thoughts. The main features of compulsive urges are shown in this tentative list:

1. Compulsive urges can be provoked by external stimulation or arise "spontaneously."
2. Under most conditions anxiety/discomfort and compulsive urges run parallel courses.
2a. Desynchronous changes in the relation between urges and rituals can occur and
2b. are readily provoked by high-demand therapy (including strict response prevention).
2c. In these conditions the compulsive acts typically decline earlier than the compulsive urges.
3. The strength of the urge is usually related to the strength/frequency of the pertinent compulsive act (i.e., they usually covary).
4. Compulsive urges are subject to spontaneous decay.
4a. The maximum rate of decline in the spontaneous-decay curve occurs within one hour of the appearance of the urge.
4b. The spontaneous-decay process approaches completion within two hours of the appearance of the urge.
5. During the course of successful therapy, the frequency and strength of the compulsive urges decline (usually more slowly than the rituals).
5a. This decline generally occurs after the compulsive behavior has been modified.
6. Repeated extinction trials (here taken to mean spontaneous-decay trials) are followed by permanent reductions in the strength of compulsive urges.

While there is little doubt that this composite account of compulsive urges will be altered as further information becomes available, it may serve a useful purpose in concentrating and clarifying current knowledge of this phenomenon.

Anxiety/discomfort and compulsive urges generally run a closely parallel course. This may mean that they are parallel coeffects or that there is a causal relationship between the two. The most obvious interpretation is that the discomfort gives rise to the compulsive urge rather than the other way around. As our research was not carried out with this particular question in mind, we are not yet in a position to attempt an answer. However, the fact that during one period of the response prevention part of the experiment described earlier, the urges dissipated slightly (but not significantly) sooner than the discomfort, might be incompatible with this view. If there is a desynchronous relationship between discomfort and urges, one might expect that the discomfort would dissipate first and then the urge to check would diminish. In due course we hope to examine the relations between these two variables in sufficiently microscopic detail to trace the precise time relations between them. Only in this way will it be possible to approach a determination of whether there is a causal link between them.

Some evidence of desynchrony between compulsive urges and rituals was uncovered by Mills, Agras, Barlow, and Mills (1973) in their five case studies. Their four hand-washing patients (the fifth engaged in self-care rituals that are irrelevant for present purposes) recorded the daily frequency of their hand-washing rituals and their compulsive urges under varying experimental conditions. In the baseline condition the urges and rituals ran parallel courses in three out of the four patients, but when the hand-washing rituals were suppressed, the urges increased temporarily in two cases, decreased in one, and remained unchanged in the fourth.

In these case studies, as indeed in our own treatment research, repeated response prevention trials were followed by an enduring decline in the ritualistic behavior (and, when measured, by an enduring decline in compulsive urges as well). While it must be noted that compulsive urges can be reduced by other methods, the repeated provocation of compulsive urges, which are then allowed to decay spontaneously, will probably lead to the cumulative growth of a general inhibition (i.e., an enduring decrement in compulsive urges).

In keeping with this hypothesis, Wilson (1977) reports having achieved useful therapeutic results by encouraging obsessional-compulsive patients to delay the execution of their rituals. After the therapist and the patient have agreed on an attainable first goal, the duration of the delay period is gradually extended. Presumably, this method allows the postulated urges and discomfort to undergo spontaneous decay repeatedly and for increasingly long periods.

Finally, we come to the question of the nature of the spontaneous decay of urges. Plainly, it is not "spontaneous" in the sense that it is uncaused. The dissipation of discomfort and urges might be a result of a process of fading (in a similar way, perhaps, to the spontaneous dissipation of pain) after the withdrawal of a provoking stimulus, or it might indicate a more active process of inhibition (the more likely to these two alternatives). The distinction between fading and inhibition has of course been made before in many debates on the nature of the extinction that can occur after learning. The information we have so far does not allow us to attempt an answer to this question. Nevertheless, it is our feeling that, whatever the nature of the spontaneous-decay process, it can be facilitated by the deliberate introduction of competing activities (for example, vigilance tasks, conversation, etc.). We are also of the opinion that the spontaneous-decay process will be unduly prolonged if the person is maintained in an isolated environment after provocation of the anxiety/discomfort and the compulsion urges. We anticipate that the absence of external stimulation will "preserve" the discomfort and urges for slightly longer than might otherwise be the case. Another question that will have to be addressed is the relationship between the temporary reduction in discomfort and urges observed during a circumscribed response prevention period and the more lasting reduction of discomfort and urges achieved in successful therapy that incorporates many response prevention periods. At what point and in what manner does the transition from a temporary reduction to a permanent reduction occur? Is it, we have assumed a cumulative effect? That is to say, does the repeated dissipation of compulsive urges, in the absence of ritualistic behavior, give rise to the growth of permanent extinction or inhibition of the unwanted behavior?

One last observation is worth mentioning. In view of the *relative* slowness with which the urges and discomfort decay, it is perhaps easier to understand why compulsive rituals develop in the first place. They produce quicker relief.

Chapter 15

Primary Obsessional Slowness

Although slowness is a prominent feature of obsessional-compulsive disorders, it has attracted little interest in its own right. Most writers appear to assume that the slowness reflects other, more profound aspects of the disorder. The assumption is probably justified in the majority of cases. There seems little doubt that slowness is generally a result of repetitive checking or some other kind of compulsive activity. Our purpose here is to draw attention to a type of obsessional slowness that is a *primary* dysfunction, not merely a secondary consequence of other difficulties (Rachman, 1974b).

Our interest in primary slowness was aroused by close observation of a young man with a severe and crippling obsessional disorder who required admission to a psychiatric hospital. He arose each day at about 8 o'clock in the morning, but finally appeared washed and dressed between 4 and 6 o'clock in the afternoon. The greater part of his day was devoted to searching for and disposing of body hairs. As he was a particularly serious case of obsessional slowness and at the same time an articulate person, close daily observation of his abnormal behavior was desirable and possible. In the course of a series of investigations into different aspects of obsessional disorders, other and equally severe cases of slowness had been observed, but with this patient the circumstances made it easier to carry out the detailed observations that we felt to be necessary.

Although the patient's search for hairs was plain to see for part of the time, there seemed to be long periods during which he was motionless and time itself seemed to slow down. We began to wonder whether the patient's explanation of his own slowness (i.e., that he was checking for hairs) was sufficient. Recalling some previous patients whose slowness had resembled life as seen in a slow-motion movie, the possibility of a primary dysfunction began to seem worth considering.

The problem of whether to regard obsessional slowness as a basic dysfunction in its own right was soon followed by other questions. Does the slowness persist even when the checking or washing rituals are excluded temporarily or filtered out? Is the slowness a general or specific feature? Is it unvarying? If not, can a connection be found with mood states or other variables? How difficult is it to modify this slowness? Do attempts to increase the patient's speed lead to untoward reactions?

In an attempt to approach some of these problems, we carried out an investigation on ten patients with severe obsessional disorders characterized by incapacitating slowness. The study consisted of a structured interview and a number of simple experimental tasks that had to be carried out under standard instructions and then under speeded-up conditions. Finally, three short tests were carried out to assess the patient's estimation of time. The tasks and tests were also carried out on ten nonobsessional neurotic patients. Details of the procedure and results are given in Rachman (1974b).

All of the obsessional patients complained that the simple tasks of daily living absorbed a vast amount of their time. They spent hours getting ready in the morning, washing themselves, brushing their hair, cleaning their teeth, shaving, and so on. Two of the female patients had enormous difficulty performing simple kitchen tasks such as replacing the cutlery and crockery in drawers and cupboards or setting pots correctly on the stove and so on. Few of the patients found it easy to explain *why* they took so long to complete the simplest of tasks. In the main it seems to be a desire to do things precisely and correctly— a need to be fanatically meticulous. Each task has to be done in the correct manner, in the correct order, using the correct instruments, in an unchanging fashion from day to day. Slow motion of the limbs seems to play no part in the patients' overall slowness. Some of them felt, however, that if they were distracted during the conduct of their everyday tasks they might appear to stare into space while preoccupied with some thought other than the task at hand. The predominant impression was that the major determinant of their slowness was a meticulous concern for the manner in which they carried out their tasks. Full descriptions of their behavior are given in Rachman (1974b).

In view of their potential therapeutic importance, it was of interest to observe the reactions of these patients when someone attempted to speed them up. All but two of them felt that they would carry out their tasks more quickly if prompted to do so by someone else. Four of the ten said that they had experienced adverse reactions when placed under a time pressure by someone else, but of these, only two felt that their reactions had been more than moderate in intensity. The most common adverse reactions described were increased tension or irritability and loss of concentration. In view of our earlier therapeutic experience with patients of this kind, the present obsessional patients were asked whether they felt that they could increase their speeds equally satisfactorily in the presence of a prompter or merely when the prompter provided instructions. With two exceptions, the patients felt confident that they would be more successful in speeding up their activities when the prompter was present.

In regard to the generality of their slowness, all of the patients felt that they were slower than most people on most tasks. However, they were all able to give at least one example of a task that did not require excessive time. The most common examples were walking at a normal pace or talking or eating at normal speeds. An interesting point raised by some of the patients was their claim that there were some activities that they could carry out a little less slowly when in company (e.g., eating). It is summed up in an amusing example provided by one of our patients, who related that when he rowed in a team he did so quickly, but when he rowed alone he was extremely slow. Although all of the patients agreed that there were some fluctuations in their speeds from day to day, the general impression was one of comparatively unvarying slowness. They all acknowledged, however, that there were some periods during their life when their activities had become excessively slow even by their own standards; in a number of instances, this was attributed to the onset of depression.

As mentioned earlier, all of the patents complained of some difficulty in the simple but unavoidable tasks of daily living. For example, the *average* time taken by the patients to clean their teeth each day was 14 minutes, with a range from 3 to 30 minutes.

As can be seen in Figure 15.1, the patients were moderately successful in speeding up their performance on the real-life task when given external monitoring and time checks. Although this group trend is clear and statistically significant ($p = 0.05$), it should not obscure what might be a clinically important fact. Two of the ten obsessional patients took slightly *longer* under the speeded-up condition than under the non-speeded-up instruction. The ratings of discomfort were not high under the non-speeded-up condition, either before or after completion of the task. Perhaps surprisingly, under the speeded-up condition only three of the patients had discomfort ratings of more than 50, and in all but one case relatively little discomfort was reported upon completion of the task. The one exception was a patient whose discomfort score increased from 0 to 90 under the speeded-up condition. These large variations in individual responsiveness to speeding up need to be borne in mind when examining the group effects.

On the cancelation and arithmetic tasks, the obsessionals were slower under the non-speeded-up condition but approached the performance of the control subjects when speeded up (see Figures 15.2 and 15.3), and reported little discomfort.

The three small tests of time estimation failed to produce anything re-

Real-life task

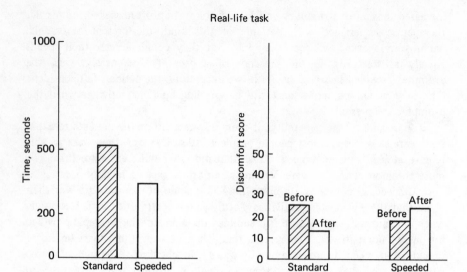

FIGURE 15.1. The times taken by 10 slow obsessional patients to complete selected, everyday tasks under standard and speed conditions, with a measure of discomfort associated with each condition.

FIGURE 15.2. Times taken to complete a simple cancellation task under standard and speed conditions: obsessional vs. neurotic subjects.

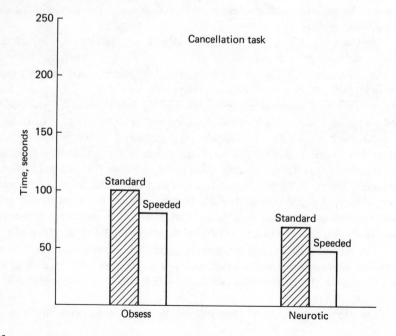

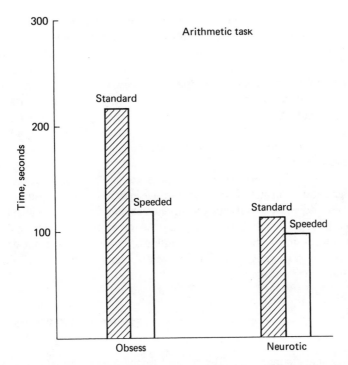

FIGURE 15.3. Times taken to complete simple arithmetic problems under standard and speed conditions: obsessional vs. neurotic subjects.

remarkable. With perhaps two exceptions, the time sense of the obsessional patients was no different from that of the neurotic patients and probably no different from that of a normal population. This failure to observe any important distortion of time is of some interest to clinicians because it is not uncommon to find that obsessional patients who are plagued by problems of slowness complain that they "lose all sense of time" when they are carrying out their daily tasks.

THERAPEUTIC IMPLICATIONS

Although the findings from our limited investigations need replication and confirmation, it might be worth while to draw together some clinical impressions, the main findings, and their therapeutic implications. Obsessional slowness may appear as a basic dysfunction. This slowness occurs even in the absence of repeated checking or other ritualistic behavior—although it should be remembered that an association with repeated checking is extremely common. Primary obsessional slowness appears to be a general dysfunction affecting most, but not all, aspects of the patient's life. It is a relatively unvarying dysfunction characterized by minor fluctuations over a short period, with slightly larger changes observed over periods that span many years. The extent to which it persists in a relatively unchanging form, its chronicity if you will, is a marked feature. It would seem that in the majority of cases the excessive slowness can be modified without much difficulty—seemingly the simplest way is by the provision of an external monitor who remains present for at least part of the performance, prompting and shaping. The most common reactions of an untoward nature (luckily, not too frequent) are an increase in tension, irritability, or loss of concentration.

Although it has been shown that increases in the speed of execution of simple tasks can be achieved with comparative ease, the larger question remains. Is it possible to bring about worthwhile increases in speed that will *persist* for prolonged periods? A firm answer to this question must await larger-scale therapeutic investigation. It may be of some interest, however, to present data from two patients with primary obsessional slowness who showed at least a degree of therapeutic responsiveness.

THERAPEUTIC POSSIBILITIES

Our feeling that flooding had little to contribute to the treatment of these slow patients was confirmed in clinical practice. Therapeutic modeling (Rachman, 1976c) was found to be of some help, but the most useful method seems to be a combination of prompting, shaping, and pacing. After providing the necessary instructions and modeling (where appropriate), the therapist prompts more reasonable, quicker behavior while the patient is carrying out the task. Shaping instructions are used to encourage improvements and discourage errors or persisting slowness. External pacing is provided. Once some progress has been achieved, the patient is shown how to monitor his or her own performance.

This *prompting, shaping, and pacing* method is illustrated by the case of S.N., a 38-year-old man suffering from a chronic and severe obsessional disorder in which excessive slowness was the main feature. Although he had been admitted to psychiatric hospitals on several occasions, the present course of treatment was carried out on an out-patient basis in the hope that his social and occupational behavior might improve as he achieved greater control over his daily tasks by means of the prompting/shaping program. At the start of treatment, the patient was taking roughly 3 hours each morning to prepare himself for work, confining his teeth brushing to late at night because it took, on the average, 45 minutes to complete; he bathed irregularly because he needed between 3 and 5 hours to complete the process.

This illustration of the treatment method is confined to the management of the patient's teeth brushing. Initially, he was advised and instructed on how to brush his teeth in a reasonable length of time. This produced a small improvement (see Figure 15.4), but a plateau was soon reached (a typical feature). The patient was then asked to carry out the brushing process in front of the therapist on a few occasions. It was evident that the slowness resulted from his wish (need?) to brush each small group of teeth in turn in an astonishingly meticulous, unchanging manner. He was given a demonstration of brushing at normal speed and then was asked to imitate the therapist. Some improvement was obtained immediately. Lastly, the patient was asked to brush his teeth on a number of occasions during which the therapist set a speeded-up goal and provided time checks each 30 seconds. This produced further improvement, but the patient found it hard to break the 5-minute barrier—the agreed-upon goal. Nevertheless, his overall improvement in bathing, washing, teeth cleaning, and dressing is satisfactory and stable. His progress has been maintained over 6 years so far.

A second patient suffering from a similar disorder was so incapacitated as to require repeated admissions to a hospital over a 20-year period. He took up to 8 hours to prepare himself each morning and was seldom ready for lunch

FIGURE 15.4. Treatment progress with one aspect of S.N.'s obsessional slowness, cleaning his teeth. Large early improvements were followed by slower and smaller changes, interspersed with plateaus.

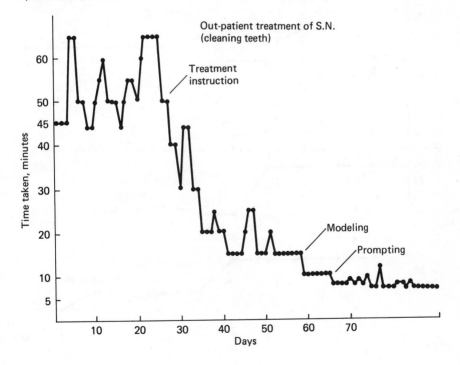

before 5 P.M. The patient, T.N., was readmitted for prompting/shaping treatment. A selection of the major measures of change and their course over treatment is shown in Figure 15.5, with follow-up data shown in Figure 15.6. Overall, he made sufficient improvement to return home and to full employment. His improvement was maintained reasonably well for over 4 years, but he had to return to the hospital for 2 successful courses of booster treatment. Throughout the 4-year follow-up period he managed to retain his post despite the creeping return of some of his slow habits. It is interesting to notice the specificity of the treatment effects; each problem required separate, direct management, and this is reflected in the stepwise sequence of improvements.

Experience with these and other patients indicates that this type of treatment intervention produces large, early improvements in most patients, followed by a long period of slow, steady gains interspersed with plateaus. Although most of the patients became able to deal far more satisfactorily with their everyday tasks, they remained, as they began, socially isolated.

FIGURE 15.5.   The effects of treatment on T.N., a chronic and severely incapacitated obsessional patient. Notice the specificity effects, reflected in stepwise sequence of changes and the size of the early improvements.

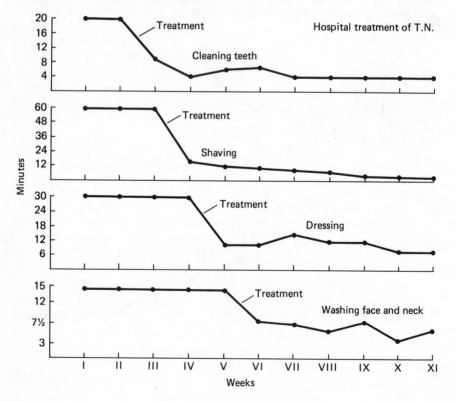

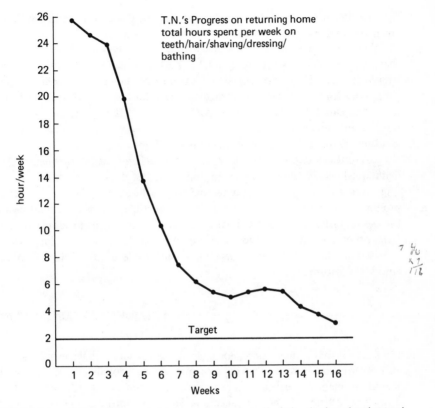

FIGURE 15.6. T.N.'s progress: total hours spent on teeth, hair, shaving, dressing, and bathing.

THEORY AND PRACTICE

The data and arguments presented here urge the recognition of a type of obsessional dysfunction that is real but rare: primary obsessional slowness. The origin of the dysfunction is obscure, but all ten patients in our study had meticulous habits, approaching those of the so-called obsessional personality, unlike many obsessional checkers or washers. Although the possibility that this slowness reflects a more fundamental dysfunction, excessive meticulousness, it cannot be ruled out, but it will not be pursued here. In all cases the disorder was present in early adulthood and took a chronic and unvarying course, usually leading to increasing degrees of incapacitation. All ten patients were socially isolated. The relation of the dysfunction to mood is not known, but its chronicity argues against an intimate connection, at least as far as maintenance of the abnormal behavior is concerned. Incidentally, these patients tend to give underestimates of the time taken to complete their daily tasks, and direct behavioral observations are an essential part of the assessment of the problem.

The interview and test data show that in the majority of cases prompting, shaping, and pacing will lead to quicker performance and only minimal disturbance, if any. There are occasional exceptions, however, in which external prompting leads to slower performance and mild distress. Observations on the ten cases, supported by clinical experience, led to the prediction that "burnt-out" cases will respond easily and well, but those who are under stress or are emotionally disturbed will respond neither well nor easily.

A critical question is the extent to which quicker performance can be maintained when the external prompter fades from the scene. The case fragments presented here encourage the hope that at least part of the therapist-prompted improvement will persist. Where possible, provision should be made for the requisite support in the patient's home environment to supplement long-term psychological supervision and support. One suspects that improvements achieved in and after treatment remain vulnerable to psychological stress or emotional disturbance.

THEORETICAL CONSEQUENCES

If we accept that primary obsessional slowness is an identifiable disorder and if we also accept that it falls into the category of obsessional-compulsive disorders, several problems arise. As we have seen, execution of these slow (mainly self-care) rituals is not preceded or accompanied by a significant amount of anxiety/discomfort or followed by changes in anxiety/discomfort; only one of the ten patients experienced a clear increase in discomfort. The main result of the study is that these rituals bear little relation to anxiety/discomfort. Hence, an explanation of their great persistence cannot rely on fluctuations of anxiety/discomfort. In particular, the anxiety reduction hypothesis is inapplicable.

Rather than use these rare, though clear, exceptions as a sufficient reason for rejecting the well-supported anxiety/discomfort hypothesis, it seems preferable to regard them as poorly understood exceptions to the general rule. As yet, we have little idea about the nature of this disorder and even less understanding of why it persists.

An alternate way of dealing with the problem would be to reject either or both assumptions stated at the opening of this discussion. We can reject the notion that primary obsessional slowness is an identifiable disorder and thereby automatically reject the second assumption, that it is a form of obsessional-compulsive neurosis. Or we can accept the first claim but deny that the disorder is correctly classified as an obsessional neurosis.

It is difficult to obtain universal agreement about the identity of any psychological disorder, and in the face of the current hostility to unrestrained (sometimes incorrect) classification, any proposal that we recognize a new and rare bird is bound to meet opposition. It is our view, notwithstanding, that these are people who have a recognizable problem that shares certain properties with obsessional-compulsive disorders and yet has some important distinctive features. Like the large majority of obsessional-compulsive patients, they engage in persistent, protracted stereotyped activities while acknowledging that, in some sense at least, their behavior is irrational. They rarely describe full resistance to the entire behavior pattern involved; rather, they generally state that they would like to complete the acts more quickly but are incapable of doing so. As we have already noted, their slowness is not secondary to compulsive checking or other rituals (hence the adjective *primary*), and they rarely complain of intrusive and unacceptable thoughts (i.e., obsessions). Some support for these views was recently reported by Stern and Cobb (1978).

Our psychometric investigations produced some support for the view reached on the basis of our clinical observations, even though we have yet to administer our scales to an adequately sized sample of patients with this disorder. We expect that when the information is gathered it will confirm the identity of this rare but distinct subgroup of obsessional-compulsive patients.

Returning to the theoretical problem posed by this subgroup, at present we can do little better than note that they cannot be accommodated within anxiety reduction explanations and that the reasons for the persistence of their ritualistic behavior are unknown. Regrettably, the theorizing of Beech and his colleagues, with its emphasis on mood disturbances, is not of obvious assistance in dealing with this problem.

The idea that seems to us to come closest to matching the patients' accounts of the course of the problem is an analog, not an explanation. Primary obsessional slowness recalls the precise, meticulous, effective, and unemotional avoidance jumping behavior displayed by the dogs used by Solomon, Kamin and Wynne (1953) in their famous experiments on the effects of aversive conditioning. In the early stages of training, the animals displayed intense emotional reactions, which then diminished and finally disappeared as their escape and avoidance jumping became more meticulous and, hence, more effective. They continued to jump smoothly and unemotionally for hundreds of trials, even in the absence of further exposures to the UCS. This is the analog (and most of the patients we have seen do give a story of an intensely disturbing period in their earlier lives), but as is well known, the Solomon-Wynne research posed insoluble problems for the available theories of avoidance learning (see Rachman, 1976b). So even if we are correct in drawing attention to some important similarities between primary obsessional slowness and Solomon's persistently meticulous dogs, a satisfactory explanation for the extraordinary persistence of such senseless, bizarre behavior in normally intelligent, rational people still eludes us.

Presumably, these slow rituals serve some function. Because they are so time-consuming, they effectively prevent the person from undertaking other activities. Although half the patients retained some form of employment, they were, without exception, social isolates. It is not inconceivable that profound social (and other?) difficulties result in their increasing avoidance of social situations—their endless repetition of these tedious rituals necessarily takes place mainly in isolation. Hence, once the compulsions take hold, the person is bound to spend more and more time away from other people. In this way the rituals serve to prevent exposures to potentially aversive situations. Another, but more remote possibility is that the slow, repetitious rituals prevent the occurrence or formation of obsessions—we found a negative correlation between primary slowness and obsessions (see Chapter 10).

Chapter 16

Psychophysiological Aspects of Obsessions and Compulsions

⚹In our introductory chapter we grouped the phenomena of obsessions and compulsions under four headings: nature, genesis, maintenance, and modification. Ideally, psychophysiological research should contribute to our understanding of each of these aspects of the disorder. However, as the psychophysiological information collected so far is limited, an attempt has been made to extract from it the questions (there are few answers thus far) that are most pertinent and offer the hope of providing some answers in the future. In order to facilitate matters, a framework within which new research can proceed is proposed.

In pursuit of these two aims, we have reviewed and evaluated the available evidence and drawn attention to some of the psychophysiological assumptions, explicit and implicit, that are embedded in this analysis of obsessions and compulsions. Before embarking on the main task of reviewing current evidence, some preparatory comments on general features of the published work may be helpful.

As is the case with a good deal of psychophysiological work in abnormal psychology, most of the research is confined to two or three measures chosen largely on grounds of convenience and with insufficient regard to the significance of the phenomenon being recorded. For example, skin conductance recordings feature in most studies, even though the significance of such information is often obscure. There is even less justification for including some of the other measures (e.g., respiratory rate). It is known in advance that even if such recordings produce statistically interpretable data, which is by no means assured, one would be at a loss as to how to deal with the information. Certainly, we are unaware of any hypotheses that are based on, or even incorporate, the respiratory patterns of obsessional-compulsive patients. Obviously, it would be preferable to have some advance ideas, even if they do not aspire to the status of hypotheses, before undertaking this type of psychophysiological research. If the structure of this chapter has merit, it should help guide people away from the purposeless collection of data and towards the framing of specific questions and answers—and especially answers of potential theoretical significance (e.g., do these psychophysiological findings contradict the anxiety reduction hypothesis?). In short, the psychophysiological measures should be selected for their potential significance rather than on grounds of practical convenience.

Our second comment is of a more general character. There is a tendency for research workers (and psychophysiological studies of obsessions and compulsions are still at the stage of research rather than service work) to regard psychophysiological data as secondary, blunt information. The recordings are rarely the core of the investigation. They are almost always included as an extra—usually, it would seem, in the hope of confirming the "emotional intensity" of the behavior and/or the reduction in the "emotional intensity" observed after a course of therapy. Most often they attempt to obtain some reassurance about the validity of other, primary data. Although there is nothing wrong with this approach, and some of the information already collected is of considerable interest, more useful data could be gathered if specific psychophysiological predictions based on psychophysiological arguments were prepared before selecting the measures and tasks.

THE NATURE OF OBSESSIONS AND COMPULSIONS

To begin, what are the defining characteristics of obsessions and compulsions? As the subjective components of obsessions and compulsions are of central importance, it is inadvisable to seek a psychophysiological definition of these disorders. In any event current psychophysiological concepts lack the specificity required for precise definition. A more profitable approach would be to determine what type of psychophysiological patterns, if any, are characteristic of obsessions and compulsions, and the extent to which these characteristics help distinguish these disorders from other types of problems, such as depression. If, however, it turns out that obsessions and compulsions show distinctive psychophysiological attributes, then the search for similarities and differences between them and disorders such as anxiety will become more complex. Instead of asking whether obsessions and compulsions are similar to, say, agoraphobia, it might be wiser to analyze the psychophysiological qualities of each disorder separately. It may, for example, confirm our claim that there is a significant similarity between cleaning rituals and circumscribed phobias (see Rachman, 1976d) and that the degree of *this* similarity exceeds the degree of similarity between cleaning rituals and obsessional ruminations. The demonstration of an identity between circumscribed phobias and obsessional-compulsive worries about contamination would strengthen the claim that similar processes are involved in maintaining and modifying both.

Instead of confining ourselves to searching for supposedly reassuring evidence of parallel, correlated psychophysiological changes consequent on subjective and/or behavioral modifications, attention could be turned to the conditions and circumstances in which desynchronous (and synchronous) changes occur in the three components (Hodgson and Rachman, 1974). In addition to filling out patchy views of the nature of these disorders (and there is reason to expect different patterns of desynchrony in obsessions and compulsions), research of this kind would help clarify the maintaining conditions of these disorders—it being remembered that the major competing theories all invoke psychophysiological changes as a basis for explanation.

GENESIS

Psychophysiological research into the genesis of obsessional-compulsive disorders is handicapped in the same way, and for the same reasons, as other types of research. Practical and ethical constraints preclude most types of prospective research into the onset and growth of such disorders. Even though they are confined to retrospective analyses, psychophysiological studies can nevertheless contribute to a clarification of the problem of genesis. If, for example, it is postulated that obsessionals are especially prone to states of pathological arousal and, hence, to obsessions and compulsions, psychophysiological investigations become essential. To give a specific example, Beech and Perigault (1974) postulated that obsessionals have "a predisposition to states of pathological arousal and [to] some mechanism by which such a state leads to morbid thoughts and aberrant behavior." In addition, obsessionals "are characterized by a tendency to exaggerated arousal" (p. 115).

If it is argued—and several writers have done so—that obsessional-compulsive patients are unduly sensitive, then psychophysiological analyses can help test this assumption. To take a third example, if the accumulation of new information confirms the significance of a hereditary component in determining obsessions and compulsions, again psychophysiological studies may help provide a basis for studying this contribution.

MAINTENANCE

The most popular explanation for the maintenance of obsessional-compulsive behavior is one or another version of the anxiety reduction hypothesis. Most of these versions are based implicitly on the "lump" theory of fear, which assumes a close and necessary connection among the subjective experience of fear, the associated avoidance behavior, and an underlying psychophysiological disturbance. However, an anxiety reduction theory can be based solely on the fluctuations of the subjective component without reference to putative psychophysiological events. Such an explanation need not demand psychophysiological parallelism. Nonetheless, the study of the psychophysiological events that occur before, during, and after the execution of compulsive acts is of potential value. In the case of pure obsessions, those that have no behavioral referents, psychophysiological recording may well prove to be crucial in studying both the genesis and the maintenance of the obsessions.

In the short term, however, psychophysiological studies of the maintenance mechanism are likely to be most useful for refuting incorrect hypotheses.

MODIFICATION

Conventional studies of the outcome of behavioral-modification techniques applied to obsessional-compulsive disorders, including those that we have conducted, were all based on an overly simple model of synchronous change. An absence of correlated changes in the outcome measures was, on the whole, regarded as unfortunate, and steps were taken to guard against this sort of result. Our present view is that this strategy is misguided and tends to distort the phenomenon being studied.

In the past, measuring instruments were excluded if they failed to correlate with other indexes of therapeutic outcome (e.g., if a psychometric test failed to correlate with the degree of clinical improvement as judged by a generalized clinical rating, then it was likely to be deleted in subsequent studies). So, in the case of psychophysiological measures, if at the conclusion of a course of treatment the patient's heart rate response changes failed to correlate with behavioral improvement, this was taken as a disappointment—a failure to validate the behavioral changes.

When the problems of outcome research are recast in terms of synchronous and desynchronous changes, doors begin to open. If the major components of obsessional-compulsive disorders are imperfectly coupled, and if they also change at varying speeds, we predict *low* correlations between some outcome indexes at specifiable measurement points. If a method of treatment such as flooding produces desynchronous changes, as predicted by Hodgson and Rachman (1974), then the behavioral improvements observed shortly after treatment should *not* correlate highly with subjective-discomfort or heart rate responses. Derivations from the lump conception of fear lead to a prediction of correlated changes occurring shortly after successful treatment, while derivations from a desynchronous model lead to predictions of low or zero correlations, depending on the particular method of treatment employed.

Proponents of the lump theory would regard low posttreatment correlations as disappointing. Repeated findings of this kind did in fact lead some workers to abandon psychophysiological assessments—precisely because they seldom correlated with clinically rated outcomes. In turn, the systematic exclusion of psychophysiological (and other) measures on the ground of their low correlation with clinical ratings will perpetuate a one-sided and ultimately false view of the nature of the changes achieved by behavior therapy or other techniques.

This argument in favor of the inclusion of rationally selected psychophysiological measures of assessment does not express a wish to return to past practices. Poorly chosen measures merely obscure the processes that are of central interest.

PSYCHOPHYSIOLOGICAL INFORMATION ABOUT THE NATURE OF COMPULSIONS

As none of the research reported to date was planned to fit into the present framework, there is a certain amount of overlap and some minor misclassifications in our arrangement of the evidence. The following statements are a summary of the present evidence pertaining to the nature of compulsions (see Chapter 17 for obsessions). These statements should be regarded as tentative, as the number of methodological problems almost equals the number of findings.

1. Provocation by exposure to a relevant stimulus or event is followed by increase in heart rate, pulse rate variability, and skin conductance (maximum deflection), and sometimes by increased frequency of skin conductance fluctuations.
1a. These increases occur in response to presentations of real or imagined stimulation.
1b. These increases occur in response to provocation by compulsion-relevant stimuli and by instructions to obtain relevant obsessional thoughts.
2. After such provocation, execution of an appropriate ritual is followed by a prompt decline in heart rate and pulse rate variability, and possibly in the electrical conductivity of the skin.
3. The pattern and course of psychophysiological responses to provocation is similar to the pattern and course of subjective anxiety/discomfort observed in comparable circumstances (especially in patients complaining of compulsive cleaning rituals).
   Incidentally, there is no direct evidence of the occurrence of exceptions

of the type referred to in Chapter 12. For example, it is not known whether obsessional-compulsive checkers show the pattern of psychophysiological responses described in statements 1 and 3 of this list.

4. After provocation, heart rate variability decreases even if no ritual is executed—these decreases may be slower than the type observed to occur after the execution of the appropriate ritual.

5. While there are some differences, the general pattern of psychophysiological responses to provocation displayed by obsessional-compulsive patients is strikingly similar to those observed among phobic subjects.

The formulation of these statements was shaped by our own experiments and clinical experience as well as by the research carried out by Boulougouris, Rabavilas, and their colleagues in Athens, and by the work of Carr (1970). The essential findings of the Athenian workers are reported in papers by Boulougouris and Bassiakos (1973), Boulougouris, Rabavilas, and Stefanis (1977), and Rabavilas and Boulougouris (1974). The style of working adopted by this group is uniform across studies. Measurements were taken before and after the provision of behavioral treatment for moderately to seriously disturbed obsessional-compulsive patients. The studies by Boulougouris and his colleagues are based on the following samples of psychiatrically disturbed obsessional-compulsive patients—the 1973 study was a pilot containing 3 patients, the 1975 study was carried out on 8 patients troubled primarily by obsessional ruminations, and the 1977 study was conducted on 12 patients complaining of compulsions and obsessions. The psychophysiological measures were heart rate, maximum deflection of skin conductance, and number of spontaneous fluctuations in skin conductivity (supplemented by verbal reports of subjective anxiety). During each assessment session the experimenters presented neutral and relevant material to the patient by verbal instruction or by the presentation of tangible objects, where appropriate. The evidence accumulated in their connected series of experiments provides clear support for statements 1, 1a, 1b, 3, and 5. The part of statement 1 that refers to increases in pulse rate variability after provocation is drawn from the experiment reported by Hodgson and Rachman in 1972. It should be said that the results showed evidence of a clear trend, but this did not reach statistical significance; moreover, the replication experiment (Röper, Rachman, and Hodgson, 1973), conducted this time on compulsive checkers rather than compulsive hand washers, failed to produce evidence of significant heart rate variability at any stage of the experimental procedure. At most, the evidence from these experiments is suggestive and is confined to compulsive hand washers.

The evidence to support statement 1a, that increases occur in response to real or imagined stimulation, comes from the research of Boulougouris and his colleagues, as does the evidence for statement 1b.

The evidence supportive of statement 2, however plausible, is based on scanty evidence. Although Hodgson and Rachman (1972) found a clear trend toward decreasing pulse rate variability after execution of the appropriate ritual, it failed to reach a satisfactory level of statistical significance. Nor is the supporting evidence obtained by Carr (1970) free of problems. Carr obtained evidence of a decrease in blood pressure and in skin conductance after execution of the ritual, but this pattern was not evident in the findings on pulse, blood pressure, or respiratory rate. Moreover, the collection, scoring, and analysis of the skin conductance data were not satisfactory.

Having set up several hypotheses, Carr subjected them to experimental test by recording the psychophysiological reactions of seven obsessional patients under four types of stress. The three major hypotheses were that (1) obsessional-compulsive patients exhibit stereotyped patterns of response to stress; (2) their responses to neurotic stimuli are similar to, but greater than, responses to normal stress; and (3) compulsive rituals are accompanied by decreases in activation, while the performance of the act returns autonomic activity to nonstressful levels. Each of the seven patients had a motor compulsion: three were hand washers; two compulsively shook dust off themselves; one checked figures; and one prayed repetitively. Three of them had undergone a leucotomy, and three were on drugs at the time of the experiment.

Regrettably, the experimental procedures failed to control for order effects or for initial levels, or indeed for the effects of the drugs. The scoring procedures were unsatisfactory (e.g., the GSR data were scored by the extent of the deflection of the recording pen). Because the data are presented and analyzed in terms of "inches deflected," it is not possible to relate them to those of other workers. It also precludes the possibility of making corrections for the effects of the initial level of responding or the extent to which the recordings obtained from each of the seven patients were comparable. The experiment was not designed in a way that permits an adequate test of hypothesis 1 or 3, and as we have seen, methodological problems make interpretation of the data pertaining to hypothesis 2 rather difficult.

Evidence in support of statement 3, that the psychophysiological responses to provocation are similar to the subjective reactions, comes from Rabavilas and Boulougouris (1974), Boulougouris and his associates (1977), and Hodgson and Rachman (1972), and indirectly from the treatment trial described by Lipsedge (1974). In Lipsedge's study subjective anxiety/discomfort was seen to increase after provocation and to decrease upon completion of the appropriate ritual. Increases in subjective discomfort occurred in response to real or imagined stimulation and upon presentation of concrete stimuli or verbal instructions to imagine such stimuli. Although he made no psychophysiological measurements, Lipsedge did carry out pre- and posttreatment assessments. He says that "although Walker and Beech (1969) reported that compulsive rituals are not always preceded by anxiety, in the present study all of the patients reported feeling anxious during real or fantasized contact with a contaminant" (p. 52).

In our replication study, carried out on 12 obsessional-compulsive checkers (Röper, Rachman, and Hodgson, 1973), we found no evidence of significant change in heart rate variability after provocation. Indeed, there was only a slight increase in subjective discomfort under these conditions. In a third study, by Röper and Rachman (1975), we discovered part of the reason for the low responsiveness of the 12 subjects who participated in the first experiment on checking (i.e., Röper et al., 1973): The reactions of compulsive checkers are muted when the provocation takes place in the contrived conditions in a laboratory.

The limited support for statement 4 is drawn from the experiment by Hodgson and Rachman (1972), in which we found that there was a discernible decline in subjective discomfort and in heart rate variability during the half-hour delay period that was introduced in one of our experimental conditions. The suggestion that arose from that experiment—that a spontaneous decline in reactivity occurs more slowly than the decline achieved by executing the appropriate ritual—later received some support from the experiment (described earlier) designed specifically to test the course of the spontaneous decay of discomfort.

The evidence to support statement 5, that there is a general similarity between the psychophysiological reactions observed among phobic and obsessional/compulsive patients in these experimental conditions, comes from two sources. The evidence on the effects of exposing phobic subjects to relevant stimuli was lucidly reviewed and analyzed by Mathews (1971), who concluded that the effects of phobic imagery are consistently different from those of neutral imagery. Presentation of phobic stimuli is consistently followed by increased autonomic responsiveness; moreover, repeated presentation of such stimuli results in a "characteristic decrement" (p. 73). Among the more important experiments contributing to this conclusion were those of Lang, Melamed, and Hart (1970), Geer (1966), and Paul (1966). By comparison with this by now well-documented evidence gathered on phobic subjects (e.g., Lader, 1975), the current evidence on obsessional/compulsive patients is disappointingly meager. Nevertheless, the similarities are quite striking. As in the case of exposure to phobic stimuli, the work of Boulougouris and his colleagues has shown that the psychophysiological (and subjective) responses to stimuli that provoke obsessional-compulsive reactions are consistently different from those observed after exposure to neutral stimulation. Moreover, they are consistently different in the same way that phobic and neutral stimuli produce consistently different reactions (i.e., presentation of obsessional-compulsive stimuli produces a range of increments in autonomic responsiveness). Unfortunately, we still do not have any sound information about the effects of repetitive presentation of an obsessional-compulsive stimulus, but there is every reason to expect that habituation occurs.

Without losing sight of the thin evidential basis for statement 5, it does seem likely that there is an important identity between the psycnophysiological nature of phobic disorders and that of obsessional-compulsive disorders (at least for those characterized by compulsive cleaning behavior). Phobic and obsessional-compulsive disorders also appear to share another important characteristic: Prior to any therapeutic intervention, there is a high concordance between subjective and psychophysiological reactions to provocation. It remains to be seen whether phobic and obsessional-compulsive disorders also display similar patterns of habituation and of desynchronous changes consequent upon specified treatment interventions. Lastly, we await with great interest investigation of the possibility that under certain circumstances anxiety does not dissipate between stimulus presentations but, rather, appears to summate (Wolpe, 1958). As Mathews points out, this clinical observation has received support from only one experiment so far—"Response increment would seem to be the exception rather than the rule, and its occurrence may depend on relatively high anxiety in a subject or on the frequent application of high intensity stimulation" (1971, p. 87). As we have already seen, an elevation of anxiety/discomfort after the execution of a compulsive ritual is the exception rather than the rule insofar as rituals are concerned. If a connection can be demonstrated between these unusual increments in psychophysiological responsiveness and the unusual increments in anxiety/discomfort, it might provide the initial step toward an explanation of the puzzling type II rituals, which persist in spite of their uncomfortable consequences.

PSYCHOPHYSIOLOGY AND GENESIS

Although all theories about the genesis of the disorder seem to require the assumption of some special sensitivity among obsessional-compulsive patients (e.g., Beech, 1974; Liddell, 1976; Rachman, 1971; Carr, 1970, 1974), little progress has been made in identifying the nature of this predisposition. As quoted earlier, Beech and Perigault (1974, p. 115) postulate that obsessional-compulsive patients are predisposed to states of "pathological arousal" and that this provides the foundation for development of the disorder. In an early attempt to account for the persistence of obsessional ruminations, it was postulated that patients who suffer from this disorder fail to adapt to the unwanted thoughts because of an underlying mood disturbance that "facilitates sensitization" (Rachman, 1971, p. 229). A comparable suggestion was proposed by Teasdale (1974) in his learning theory account of the disorder. Carr assumed that obsessional-compulsive patients exhibit a characteristic (and exaggerated) reaction to stress.

It is a matter for regret that, despite the recurrent theme of these hypotheses, there is virtually no evidence on which to judge their usefulness. So, for example, Beech and Perigault (1974, p. 141) had to concede reluctantly that the data are extremely limited in terms of number of patients and important controls.

Even if agreement were reached on the form of this postulated predisposing sensitivity, and if the agreed-upon signs of sensitivity were found in a group of obsessional-compulsive patients, the presumption that this state was present at the time (or over the period) that the disorder developed would remain tenuous. Moreover, once some form of excessive sensitivity is demonstrated, it remains to be shown how this predisposition, if that is what it is, is triggered into an obsessional-compulsive disorder (remembering that usually the onset of the disorder is gradual).

The construction and testing of retrospective hypotheses is so difficult and risky that the practical obstacles to carrying out a prospective study can be overlooked. Ideally, one would like to be present when it all happens. A high-risk sample could be gathered and their psychophysiological and other predispositions studied prior to the onset of the disorder.

The identification of *distinct* psychophysiological responsiveness among obsessional-compulsive patients would be a useful advance, especially if it could be related to a general theory of genesis, but we are not sanguine about its existence. Although the demanding task of mounting a prospective study should not be ruled out, there is a less awkward, if less satisfactory, alternative.

In any group of patients selected for inclusion in a controlled clinical trial, a certain percentage of those who respond successfully to the course of treatment subsequently experience a return to their original (or some similar) difficulty. If the pre- and posttreatment assessment procedures include a suitable psychophysiological measure (and if the recordings are repeated at, say, three-monthly intervals), we will then be in a position to observe the onset, or rather the return, of an obsessional-compulsive disorder, albeit in a nonrandom group. This strategy might provide vital information about the presence or absence of a specially predisposing psychological state as the obsessions and/or compulsions emerge. Presumably, different results will be obtained from sudden-onset and gradual-onset cases.

It will be evident that this strategy is bound to encounter difficulties in pinning down the temporal connection between the postulated state of excessive sensitivity and the precise time of onset of an acute disorder, and even more in the case of disorders that have a gradual onset. These are serious but not insuperable obstacles, and among other things, they serve to emphasize the inevitable crudity of retrospective studies of the genesis of this kind of disorder.

PSYCHOPHYSIOLOGY AND MAINTENANCE

Psychophysiological research can contribute to analyses of the maintenance of obsessional-compulsive disorders in two respects: by studying habituation and incrementation rates, and in testing aspects of the anxiety reduction hypothesis.

Just as all theorists appear to feel obliged to postulate the presence of some predisposing sensitivity in obsessional-compulsive patients, they also seem bound to theorize about the extraordinary persistence of this disorder. Why do obsessions and compulsions fail to extinguish? Beech and Perigault (1974) postulate that in states of pathological arousal obsessionals "are characterized by a tendency to exaggerated arousal" and that "instead of decrement being observed, additional stimulation may produce increased arousal" (p. 115). This extract illustrates the postulate of impaired habituation, coupled with the suggestion that in certain circumstances abnormal incrementations may occur. In theorizing about the persistence of obsessional ruminations (Rachman, 1971), we were led to postulate that ruminative patients display an unusual failure to habituate to noxious stimulation. A similar view was proposed by Teasdale (1974), and Eysenck (1977) has attached great importance to the occurrence of "incubation" in the genesis and maintenance of neurotic disorders as a whole. As habituation theory has been useful in clarifying certain aspects of fear and its modification, there is every reason for confidence that the analysis of certain aspects of obsessional-compulsive disorders in terms of the habituation model may prove fruitful. Regrettably, there have been no studies of the habituation rate of obsessional-compulsive patients comparable to the research on phobics. Insofar as there are similarities between phobias and compulsions (and as we have argued, some of these are of significance), it is to be expected that the habituation rate among obsessional-compulsive patients will be slower than that observed in a nonpsychiatric population, and will approximate to that of phobic subjects.

The allied possibility, that obsessional-compulsive patients may also exhibit a tendency to experience increments of responsiveness rather than decrements, offers a possible basis for explaining the undue persistence and growth of obsessional-compulsive problems. Research into response incrementation or, as the associated concept is called, incubation, is likely to prove fruitful. Our strong expectation is that research of this kind will help clarify the persistence and growth of obsessional ruminations.

Of our five statements covering present knowledge of the psychophysiology of obsessional-compulsive disorders, three have a direct bearing on the problem of maintenance, and on the anxiety reduction hypothesis in particular. Statements 2, 3, and 5 are all relevant—they refer to the observations that execution of the ritual is followed by a decline in physiological responsiveness, that this pattern corresponds to subjective reports, and that the general pattern of physiological and subjective changes is similar in phobic and obsessional patients.

As argued earlier, it is perfectly possible for an anxiety reduction hypothesis to survive even if it is confined to one of the three major components of fear (i.e., subjective apprehension). It should be remembered, however, that the classical exposition of the anxiety reduction hypothesis (Mowrer, 1939, 1960) incorporated the assumption that execution of the appropriate avoidance response would be followed by declining psychophysiological reaction as well as subjective relief. It follows, therefore, that if we can demonstrate that execution of the appropriate ritual is followed by a decline in psychophysiological responsiveness, and that this decline is associated with comfortable subjective changes, then we have good grounds for continuing to give the theory serious consideration. It is also worth bearing in mind that despite the serious weaknesses in the two-stage theory of fear and avoidance (Rachman, 1976), it retains useful explanatory value for certain aspects of fear and its modification. Once again, insofar as phobias and obsessional-compulsive disorders share important similarities, it should follow that the two-stage theory retains some explanatory value in dealing with the latter disorders. With respect to the problem of why compulsions persist, the psychophysiological evidence summarized in statements 2, 3, and 5 is consistent with a two-stage theory. We have tentative evidence that execution of the ritual is indeed followed by a reduction in psychophysiological responsiveness and that these decrements are in reasonably close association with the decrements in subjective discomfort reported after execution of the ritual. Thus far, the only piece of contrary evidence, summarized in statement 3a, was our failure to obtain evidence of declining psychophysiological responsiveness after execution of the appropriate *checking* ritual (Röper, Rachman, and Hodgson, 1973). As we have pointed out, however, this experiment cannot be regarded as definitive, and the follow-up experiment by Röper and Rachman (1975) confirmed the presence of a confounding effect in the experiment on compulsive checkers.

It is nevertheless true that any comprehensive theory proposed to account for the maintenance of obsessional-compulsive disorders needs to take into account the exceptions described in Chapters 11, 12, and 15. Psychophysiological investigations of patients who fall into this group of exceptions are bound to prove useful. As a first step, it would be extremely interesting to know whether patients who persist in carrying out their obsessional-compulsive acts despite *increases* in subjective discomfort also display increments in psychophysiological responsiveness at the relevant times.

PSYCHOPHYSIOLOGY AND MODIFICATION

Following the style introduced in evaluating the evidence on the nature of obsessional-compulsive disorders, we have listed the major findings in formal statements. Once again, we should caution that these statements are to be regarded as tentative because the amount and quality of the supporting evidence is not satisfactory. Before considering these statements, however, it is necessary to recall two observations referred to earlier. In the first place, there are pretreatment signs of excessive reactivity to relevant obsessional-compulsive stimuli, and second, these excessive reactions follow on provocation from real or imagined relevant stimuli.

1. After successful treatment, as judged on the basis of clinical ratings, the excessive psychophysiological reactions to obsessional-compulsive stimuli (real or imagined) diminish.
   This statement is based primarily on the evidence provided by Boulougouris and Bassiakos (1973), Rabavilas and Boulougouris (1974), and Boulougouris, Rabavilas, and Stefanis (1977), who have described the pre- and posttreatment assessments of patients treated by behavioral methods. In their third study 4 of the 12 patients were troubled predominantly by compulsions, 4 suffered mainly from obsessions, and the remaining 4 had a mixture of both problems. As before, they used three psychophysiological measures—heart rate, maximum deflection of skin conductance, and spontaneous fluctuation of skin conductance. All three measures showed evidence of a steep decline upon completion of treatment, but these decreases did not always reach a statistically significant level. Nevertheless, the overall pattern is clear and relates reasonably well to the comparably steep decline in subjective anxiety reported after treatment.
2. The psychophysiological decrements observed after treatment are correlated with declines in subjective discomfort. The evidence for this statement is again provided by Boulougouris, Rabavilas, and their colleagues.
3. The same pattern of declining psychophysiological responsiveness is observed after the treatment of both compulsive and ruminative disorders (see the 1974 and 1977 reports of Rabavilas, Boulougouris and their colleagues).
4. The pattern of declining psychophysiological responsiveness and the associated decline in subjective discomfort are both similar to those reported after the treatment of phobic patients.
   The basis for this last statement is provided by comparing the results discussed here with those reviewed and evaluated by, among others, Mathews (1971) and Lang (1969). It is particularly noticeable when comparisons are made between the heart rate responses of phobic and obsessional-compulsive patients. In both instances exposure to the relevant noxious stimulus reliably produces an increase in heart rate. There is, furthermore, a convincing degree of evidence indicating that heart rate responsiveness declines with successful treatment. For these reasons we feel that at present the most productive psychophysiological index for this kind of research is the heart rate response.

Turning to some conclusions of a more general character, psychophysiological studies of the modification process also point to the similarities between phobias and obsessional-compulsive disorders. People with these disorders not only show similar psychophysiological reactions to relevant stress stimuli but also display comparable patterns of therapeutic change; the similarities are so evident that one is tempted to describe these people as suffering from *phobic compulsions*.

The findings of Boulougouris and his colleagues on the psychophysiological reactions provoked by obsessional *ruminations* are of considerable interest.

In particular, they are consistent with the view that these intrusive thoughts can usefully be construed as (internal) noxious stimuli (Rachman, 1971). They also illustrate a potentially important similarity among ruminative, compulsive, and phobic reactions.

The psychophysiological findings add little new to current theories of how behavior therapy acts in this disorder, but they do appear to be compatible with a habituation theory or an extinction theory. As far as the habituation theory goes, the research has uncovered two bits of evidence that seem to fit comfortably into this theory. Boulougouris and his associates (1977) found a clear order effect in their psychophysiological studies (i.e., there was a declining responsiveness with repetition of the pertinent stimuli). This finding arose from the treatment section of their research and is consistent with their observation of an overall decline in psychophysiological responsiveness during repeated *assessment* sessions, even including a decline in responsiveness to neutral instructions and imagery. In other words, the patients who participated in these studies showed declining psychophysiological reactions *to both neutral and relevant stimuli*, and they showed these decrements in sharp relief during the various types of treatment that were used—hence the clear order effect.

Rabavilas and Boulougouris (1974) found some signs of greater concordance between measures during intense reaction patterns. As they say, "The maximum concordance after treatment between the three autonomic measures was obtained during exposure to the most threatening stimulus" (i.e., flooding in practice), supporting the hypothesis "that the concordance between response systems is likely to be high during strong emotional arousal" (Boulougouris et al., 1976). Less directly, Boulougouris and his colleagues (1977) found a few signs that after *in vivo* flooding the heart rate responses showed greater (and perhaps quicker) decreases than subjective reactivity. Our prediction on this matter, admittedly with respect to phobic rather than obsessional-compulsive patients, was that flooding treatment is more likely to produce desynchronous changes in which behavioral and psychophysiological changes occur in advance of subjective improvement (Rachman and Hodgson, 1974). Research aimed at analyzing the nature of the relationships (and especially the *changing* relationships between the major components of obsessional-compulsive disorders) requires different experimental designs, and will be followed with interest.

On the practical side, Boulougouris's evidence reinforces the view that the deliberate evocation of anxiety during flooding treatment is *not necessary* in order to produce significant clinical improvement. Boulougouris and his associates (1977) concluded that "pulse rate and subjective anxiety ratings," although they discriminated between obsessional and neutral stimuli, "predicted [neither] good [nor] poor prognosis." This conclusion follows their earlier claim that "clinical observations during the treatment sessions support the notion (Rachman and Hodgson, 1974) that the deliberate arousal of anxiety is not a prerequisite of therapeutic success" (Boulougouris, Rabavilas, and Stefanis, 1976).

Lastly, Boulougouris and his colleagues have provided some tentative prognostic indicators of therapeutic success. Unfortunately, as this study contains a large amount of complex statistical information, 67 clinical and physiological variables assessed on 2 occasions, it is difficult to reach unequivocal conclusions. Their major findings, a little surprising in view of earlier experience with phobic patients, was that "the patients who are most clinically and physiologically handicapped" do best. With certain variations of treatments, such as long practice *in vivo*, the presence of high anxiety was correlated with a good outcome. On the contrary, however, the presence of high anxiety was negatively correlated with the effect of flooding treatment presented by imaginal stimuli. None of the biographical variables in their patient sample correlated with therapeutic outcome. To give some idea of the difficulty of interpreting the findings, it was found that skin conductance fluctuations correlated positively with response to *in vivo* flooding treatment, while on the other hand heart rate response was negatively correlated with outcome. It will be evident that these findings do not provide a satisfactory basis for making prognostic statements.

Despite some methodological shortcomings and confusing results of the kind to which we have referred, there is every reason to be grateful to Boulougouris and his colleagues for leading the way in exploring these aspects of obsessional-compulsive disorders, and for gathering some valuable information.

CONCLUSIONS

Psychophysiological research into obsessional-compulsive disorders is limited and is replete with methodological and technical problems. Under the circumstances, it is surprising that so much interesting information has been accumulated.

The heart rate response is at present the most useful index to include in this kind of work because it is responsive to the presentation of noxious stimulation. Moreover, it is subject to modification, and in a magnitude that enables one to study it in detail before and after treatment interventions. In addition, it is relatively resistant to rapid and premature habituation. Measures of skin conductance are of restricted value, partly because of their tendency to habituate rapidly and, even more important, because of their obscure psychophysiological significance. They are not without value, but seem to be more suitable for carrying out studies in which the relevant stimuli are unlikely to be repeated on many occasions. The inclusion of EMG and respiratory measures has not been justified by the returns.

It is to be hoped that future research will be directed toward psychophysiologically significant problems and not restricted merely to "secondary problems." An attempt should be made to avoid the purposeless accumulation of secondary psychophysiological data; rather, questions should be selected on grounds of theoretical significance. Finally, we hope that the four-part structure presented in this chapter—nature, genesis, maintenance, and modification—will provide a helpful framework for posing relevant questions and organizing the evidence that accumulates.

Chapter 17

Obsessions

Obsessions are intrusive, repetitive *thoughts, images,* or *impulses* that are unacceptable and/or unwanted and give rise to subjective resistance. The person finds them difficult to dismiss or control. The necessary and sufficient conditions for defining a thought, impulse, or image as obsessional are intrusiveness, internal attribution, unwantedness, and difficulty of control. The most important confirmatory indicators are internal resistance, and rejection of the idea or impulse as alien and/or unrealistic. Unlike mere preoccupations, obsessions generally are tormenting and produce distress. Obsessions may take one of three forms—thoughts, impulses, or images—but we have little knowledge about the distinctive properties of each form. Consequently, for most of this analysis, and pending new information, it will be assumed that the three forms of obsession are essentially similar.

A combination of thoughts and impulses is most common, followed by thoughts only and then impulses only, and finally, by images only. Most obsessions occur in association with compulsive behavior; pure obsessions unrelated to overt behavior occur in a small minority of cases. We also have information indicating that more than half of all obsessional patients are troubled by a single obsession rather than by multiple obsessions. The content of an obsession is repugnant, worrying, blasphemous, obscene, nonsensical, or all of these, and frequently takes the form of doubting.

Obsessions and compulsions are intimately related, and the nature of this association is discussed in Chapter 2. The most characteristic sequence is for an obsession to lead to a compulsion. Perhaps in recognition of this close associa-

251

tion, many writers use the terms *obsessional* and *compulsive* interchangeably. Strictly speaking, they refer to distinct phenomena. Recognition of the distinction between compulsions and obsessions is, comparatively speaking, a recent development. As mentioned in our historical notes, the earliest descriptions appear to have been confined to obsessions. The recent shift in emphasis from thoughts to (compulsive) *behavior* is attributable to the growing interest shown by psychologists in studying the phenomenon.

"NASTY, VEXATIOUS, AND BLASPHEMOUS THOUGHTS"

In early writings on the subject of religious melancholy, the occurrence of these poisonous thoughts was afforded a prominent place. It was observed that deeply religious people were particularly prone to such thoughts, and William James (1942) noted that "the lives of the saints are full of such blasphemous obsessions, ascribed invariably to the direct agency of Satan" (p. 167). He argued that when people "of tender conscience and religiously quickened" become unhappy, they experience "moral remorse and compunction of feeling inwardly vile and wrong . . . This is the religious melancholy and 'conviction of sin' " (p. 167). These people of tender conscience were well described in 1660 by Jeremy Taylor: "They repent when they have not sinned, and accuse themselves without form or matter; their virtues make them tremble and in their innocence they are afraid" (quoted by Hunter and Macalpine, 1963, pp. 163-64). Describing the obsessions of a famous religious personality of the time, Taylor said that "his thoughts revolved in a restless circle, and made him fear he knew not what." Taylor also noted the incessant doubting that is characteristic of this kind of problem, ("It is a trouble where the trouble is over, a doubt when doubts are resolved") and attributed it to "indisposition of body, pusillanimity, melancholy, a troubled head, sleepless nights, the society of the timorous, from solitariness, ignorance, or unseasoned imprudent notices of things, indigested learning, strong fancy, and weak judgment." Anyone suffering from this catalog of woes and inadequacies may perhaps be excused for having thoughts that revolve in a restless circle.

"Pollution of the Mind"

One of the most famous sufferers was John Bunyan, who used the striking phrase "pollution of the mind" to describe his intrusive, unacceptable, blasphemous thoughts—and in so doing, knowingly or unknowingly, made the connection between obsessional ruminations and the fear of contamination more usually associated with cleaning compulsions. (An excellent clinical illustration of "pollution of the mind" was recently provided by a patient who was tormented by the fear that she might unwillingly say "God" while in the lavatory.) After a dissolute early life, Bunyan turned toward nonconformist religion and became a powerful and popular preacher. *A Pilgrim's Progress* is of course one of the finest allegories in the English language.

According to the account given in his autobiography, Bunyan experienced several periods of intense guilt and remorse before devoting himself to a religious way of life. During one of these intense spiritual experiences, he lived through an "obscure night" that was "wide, vast, and lonely," and at times he felt that the Devil was "pulling at his clothes." He described several episodes of intense despair during which he was afflicted by "whole floods of blasphemies."

He continued: "A very great storm came down upon me which handled me twenty times worse than all I had met with before. It came stealing upon me, now by one piece, then by another. First, all my comfort was taken from me, then darkness seized upon me, after which whole floods of blasphemies, both against God, Christ and the Scriptures were poured on my spirit, to my great confusion and astonishment" (p. 134). On another occasion he was "fiercely assaulted" with the temptation "to sell Christ ... The wicked suggestion ... was running in my mind—'sell him, sell him, sell him, sell him,' as fast as a man could speak. Against which also in my mind, as at other times, I answered 'No, no, not for thousands, thousands, thousands,' at least twenty times together" (p. 135). His attempt to put matters right by repeated incantation, a phenomenon that we describe mundanely as neutralization, is discussed later.

When assailed by these unacceptable, intrusive, alien thoughts and impulses, Bunyan fell deeply into despair "at the sight of my own vileness," for he believed that "none but the Devil himself could equalize me for inward wickedness and pollution of mind" (p. 134). In another extremely interesting passage, he describes how he experienced a sudden onset of relief from one of these periods of despair and vileness. He heard a noise like wind rushing through a window, and a voice came to reassure him and "made a strange seizure upon my spirit" (p. 136). The voice "brought light with it, and commanded a silence in my heart of all those tumultuous thoughts that had used, like masterless hellhounds, to roar and bellow and make a hideous noise within me" (p. 136).

Although none of our patients described quite as dramatic a release from their unacceptable obsessions, or described it so vividly, some of their experiences are of a similar character. In a number of instances, considerable relief has occurred over a short space of time, with or sometimes without any evident alteration in external circumstances. One of our moderately severe compulsive checkers, whose disorder had lasted for two years, made a well-nigh complete recovery over a weekend after learning that he had inherited a large sum of money. His improvement continued for at least a year and possibly longer.

Even more interesting is Ray's (1964) report on 42 New Delhi patients, to the effect that improvements were observed after intense religious experiences.

In 3 of the patients "with strong religious tendencies . . . visits to places of pilgrimage where expiatory rites were performed . . . were followed by dramatic improvement" (p. 182).

CONTENT

As might be expected, the content of obsessions has changed over the centuries. Nowadays, religious obsessions appear to be encountered less frequently whereas ideas of dirt/disease contamination, aggression, and sexual preoccupations have become more common. In their analysis of the content of obsessions reported by 44 obsessional patients, Akhtar and his colleagues (1975) reported the following distribution. Dirt and contamination was the most common theme (59% of cases), followed by aggression (25%), "impersonal/orderliness" (23%), and religion (a mere 10%). Sexual obsessions were relatively uncommon, being found in 5 percent of the cases. In London, Stern and Cobb (1978) confirmed that dirt/contamination themes were most common (35%) in their 45 patients. Sexual themes occurred in 9 percent of the cases.

Using the classificatory system described by Akhtar and his associates, we analyzed the themes reported by our 83 early cases, with the following results. Dirt/disease contamination themes were the most common (55%), followed by impersonal/orderliness in 35 percent of the cases, aggressive themes in 19 percent, sexual themes in 13 percent, and religious themes in 10 percent. It can be seen that the results are surprisingly similar, bearing in mind that the samples were drawn from populations in New Delhi (Akhtar et al.) and southeast England (our patients). Religious obsessions are uncommon, and dirt/disease contamination is most prominent.

Our English sample showed rather more aggressive, impersonal, and sexual themes than the Indian sample. It is also worth mentioning that we confirmed the distribution of single and multiple obsessions reported by the Indian research workers. In their sample 75 percent of the patients had single obsessions predominating, and in our sample 73 percent had a single dominant theme. Similarly, we confirmed their finding that the great majority of patients who complain of obsessions also show compulsive behavior—in our sample 93 percent of the patients displayed associated compulsive behavior.

By contrast, it would appear that patients whose primary disturbance is a depressive disorder show a different pattern of obsessional themes. In 124 patients who experienced obsessions during depression, just over 50 percent reported aggressive themes, mainly of a homicidal or suicidal character (Gittelson, 1966d). This preoccupation with aggression among depressed patients is confirmed by the findings of Kendall and di Scipio (1970) and Videbech (1975).

Despite some important similarities, obsessional ideas can be distinguished from morbid preoccupations (Rachman, 1973). The important similarities are impairment of concentration, intrusiveness, repetitiveness, expressions of guilt, and dysphoria. However, morbid preoccupations are different in that the themes are more likely to be rational, contemporary and realistic, ego-syntonic, and provoke little resistance. As we have seen, obsessions are irrational, ego-dystonic, unrealistic, and repugnant in content. The differences between obsessions and delusions, including the presence or absence of insight and internal versus external attribution, are analyzed in Chapter 17 and will not be reiterated here. Obsessions resemble the repetitive thoughts characteristic of morbid jealousy in being intrusive, unwanted, dysphoric, hard to control, and disruptive of normal concentration.

ILLUSTRATIVE CASE MATERIAL

In Chapter 2 we provided brief examples of each of the three forms of obsession—ideas, impulses, and images. In order to convey the quality of the disorder more fully, we have selected four patients whose troubles were predominantly obsessional. These cases not only illustrate the phenomenology of the disorder but also show how great an impact obsessions can have on the style of a person's life. The first patient, a young student, sought help because he was finding it increasingly difficult to concentrate on his studies and was avoiding attendance at classes for this reason. He was a timid, anxious young man who was excessively dependent on his mother, an overprotective and emotionally reactive woman. His problems provide a clear example of the functional connection between obsessional ideation and compulsive behavior. According to the patient, he was troubled almost all day by unwanted and unacceptable violent and/or sexual thoughts in which prominent people, relatives, and his parents were the victims of sexual or aggressive attacks. In addition to impairing his concentration, they made him unhappy and tense. He was unable to identify any precipitating stimuli other than letters from or talk about his parents or close relatives. Although the duration of each obsession varied according to "the mood of the moment," we discovered during an extensive baseline study period that the most common duration of a single obsession was 30 minutes. The patient had developed a number of tactics for dealing with the thoughts and concluded that the two most effective methods were hand washing or repeating an action *after* constructing a "good thought." So, for example, if an obsessional thought intruded while he was preparing a sandwich, he would discard the bread, strive to achieve a good thought, and then remake the sandwich. During the baseline period we found that he was carrying out an average of 80 brief hand washes per day. Evidently, this technique was not always successful, and therefore the ritualistic behavior exceeded the frequency of obsessions. Some of the patient's less successful techniques included violently shaking his head or other parts of his body, changing the names of places or characters, or intense concentration on some distracting thought or activity. He explained the effectiveness of the hand-washing ritual as achieving a "symbolic cleansing of the bad or unwanted thought." According to him, the hand washing reduced tension and sometimes was successful in eliminating the bad thought. Once the bad thought had been canceled, he was able to proceed with whatever activity he had been engaged in when the obsession intruded.

The second patient, a 35-year-old mother of three children, complained of an extremely disturbing obsession that was a mixture of rumination and impulse. She feared that she might harm her children and, in particular, that she might blind them with a sharp instrument. She had a secondary fear of harming their ears by shouting at them. As a result of these obsessions, she was constantly anxious and, not surprisingly, depressed as well. She continually sought reassurance from her husband that the children were safe, and strictly avoided being left alone with any of them. She also insisted that all sharp objects that could not be discarded (many were) should be stored in a secure and inaccessible place. She was extremely reluctant to handle sharp objects even in the presence of a trusted person, and was totally incapable of handling them when she was alone. As a result of her disorder, the three children were taken into the care of the maternal grandparents. The patient was an anxious, shy, reserved, and pessimistic person who related having had a moderately severe phobia at the age of 18. Shortly after the birth of her first baby, when she was 24, she began compulsively cleaning the infant's diapers. This compulsive behavior gradually declined, possibly as a result of moderately successful pharmacological treatment of the associated depression. Later the patient had two years of unsuccessful psychotherapy, and finally, at the age of 30, she was admitted to a psychiatric hospital, complaining of the obsessional fear that she might harm her children. Once again she achieved some relief from antidepressant medication, until the birth of her third child, when she was 33 years of age. The obsessional ruminations and impulses restarted in greater intensity shortly after the birth of this last child, and she then received a variety of psychiatric treatments, including two complete courses of EST and five different types of medication. Thereafter, three attempts were made to treat her by intravenous infusions of three different types of sedating drugs, without success.

The obsessions were very easily provoked by placing the patient in a dangerous situation (i.e., alone with one of her children, particularly the youngest). The thoughts and impulses could, however, arise spontaneously, and she was not free of them even when she was entirely alone. They tended to continue in an unchanging manner whenever she was close to the youngest child; when she was alone, the obsessions lasted, on the average, for approximately an hour. Although she reported some subsidiary obsessions, her life was dominated by the single major obsessional idea/impulse that she might harm her children. Having failed to develop satisfactory techniques of self-regulation of the obsessions, she adopted widespread and psychologically paralyzing passive-avoidance behavior.

The third patient, a newly married young computer programer, sought help in overcoming a single tormenting obsessional rumination that had plagued her for years. It fluctuated in intensity and appeared to be fueled by recurrent depression. She spent many long hours ruminating over whether she had or had not murdered a solitary old lady whom she had visited regularly. This troublesome thought intruded repeatedly, seriously impaired her concentration, and provoked considerable discomfort and guilt. Repeated enquiries, including several visits to the local police station, failed to satisfy her that the woman had in fact died of natural causes some days after the patient had last seen her.

The thoughts were abhorrent, intolerable, and decidedly alien to this highly moral, religious young woman, but they remained exceedingly difficult to dismiss by the normal methods of reassurance. After her depression had been successfully reduced through drugs, she was given a course of habituation training—the ruminations having survived intact the reduction of depression. She formed the rumination with ease but had trouble removing it at the end of each trial. After an unpromising start the frequency, duration, and intensity of the rumination finally underwent a significant decline after some 12 sessions. Her rumination was reasonably well controlled in the 4 years of follow-up, despite recurrent episodes of depression that responded favorably to drugs.

The fourth case, a young married woman, suffered from repetitive and intrusive images of an abhorrent nature, and provides one of the clearest examples of an obsessional problem that took the form of intrusive images rather than ideas or impulses. One of the patient's most distressing images consisted of four people lying dead in open coffins in an open grave. Once this image intruded she was unable to continue with her normal activities unless and until she put matters right by having one or more images in which she saw the same four people standing and walking about, seemingly healthy. Although the images appeared for the most part to be spontaneously (i.e., internally) generated, they could be provoked by exposure to violent or aggressive material of one sort or another—books or television programs. The images were extremely distressing and were capable of provoking her to tears in a matter of minutes.

INVESTIGATIONS

Almost all of our current knowledge about the nature of obsessions is drawn from epidemiological and phenomenological studies. Fortunately, the few studies carried out so far have yielded a disproportionately large amount of interesting information. As we will see, the psychophysiological experiment

✗carried out by Rabavilas and Boulougouris (1974), despite some methodological shortcomings, contains valuable information. The research by Horowitz and her colleagues on the deliberate provocation of intrusive thoughts has also been fruitful. Before examining these experimental investigations, the results of a study by Rachman and de Silva (1978) will be recounted.

In the first version of the theory of obsessions proposed here, it was necessary to assume that "everybody experiences distasteful and unacceptable thoughts" (Rachman, 1971, p. 231). It was further assumed that "the difference is that obsessional patients experience them repetitively and are greatly disturbed by them." Obsessions were construed as noxious stimuli that "resist" habituation. In due course it became essential to test the validity of these suppositions, and three small exploratory studies were therefore conducted (Rachman and de Silva, 1978). Our aim was to ascertain the incidence and character of obsessional experiences among nonclinical subjects. We were also interested in determining the extent to which "normal" and "abnormal" obsessions are comparable phenomena. For these purposes 124 nonclinical subjects and 8 obsessional patients were assessed.

NORMAL AND ABNORMAL OBSESSIONS

Notwithstanding the exploratory nature of the studies, some tentative conclusions are permissible:

1. Obsessions, in the form of thoughts and/or impulses, are a common experience. A large majority of people report experiencing obsessions; it is unknown why the small minority fail to do so. There are no age- or sex-related differences in occurrence.
2. The form, and to some extent the content as well, of obsessions reported by nonpsychiatric respondents and by obsessional patients are similar.
3. So-called "normal" obsessions are also similar to "abnormal" obsessions in their expressed relation to mood and in their meaningfulness to the respondent.
4. Despite some similarities of form and content, normal and abnormal obsessions differ in these respects:
   a. The threshold of acceptability is higher for abnormal obsessions.
   b. Normal obsessions are easier to dismiss.
   c. Abnormal obsessions last longer both overall and in particular instances.
   d. Abnormal obsessions are more vivid.
   e. They produce more discomfort.
   f. They are more frequent.
   g. They are more ego-alien.
   h. They are more strongly resisted.
   i. They are more likely to be of known onset.
   j. They provoke more urges to neutralize.

Broadly speaking, normal and abnormal obsessions are similar in form and content but differ in frequency, intensity, and consequences.

5. Obsessional patients are more likely to exhibit associated compulsions.

6. The execution of neutralizing behavior, overt or covert, reduces discomfort and urges in both clinical and nonclinical subjects.

7. (a) Most obsessional patients can form their obsessions to instruction; a large number of nonclinical subjects are unable to do so. (b) The obsessions are formed within less than a minute in both groups.

8. The obsession produces discomfort; the level is greater in the abnormal instances than in the normal ones.

9. Overall, abnormal obsessions formed to instruction are moderately intense, while normal ones are of mild intensity.

10. With repeated instructed trials of four-minute duration, the following statistically nonsignificant, but predicted, short-term changes were observed:
    a. The latency to obsession formation increases.
    b. The duration of the obsession decreases.
    c. The accompanying discomfort decreases.
    d. The intensity of the obsession may decrease.

11. There was evidence, in two of our nonclinical subjects, of sensitization rather than habituation.

The extent to which these findings are consistent with the theory will be assessed presently. Here it need merely be noted that we cannot explain at present why some people apparently do not experience obsessions. Nor do we know why nonclinical subjects find it more difficult to form their obsessions—perhaps they lack the necessary practice, and this can be tested easily.

The findings relative to the habituation postulates of the theory are reassuring but wholly insufficient at present. Experimental analyses of the effects (short- and long-term) of habituation training on normal and abnormal obsessions are essential before this part of the theory can develop.

INTRUSIVE THOUGHTS

Horowitz and her colleagues have for some years been carrying out systematic investigations into the nature of intrusive thoughts and images. The experimental methods that they have been obliged to develop in coming to grips with these difficult phenomena are as interesting as the findings themselves. In successive studies they have employed the same experimental paradigm. After taking baseline measurements from their subjects, a brief film, either neutral or stressful, is shown to the audience. The pretest measurements are then repeated, and the subjects are asked to report the occurrence of visual images and the degree to which they were intrusive. Other assessment measures have included a signal detection task, self-rating of affect, and "mental-content reports" in which the subjects were asked to report any mental content (such as thoughts, feelings, images, etc.) that occurred during the performance of the detection task. The fundamental experiment has now been repeated on a range of different subject populations and with movies that vary in length and content. The findings are reassuringly consistent.

> *The results support the hypothesis, based on clinical observation, that persons tend to experience intrusive and stimulus-repetitive thoughts after a stress event . . . . The tendency to intrusive and repetitive thought is general in that it occurs in a large proportion of populations not designated as psychiatric patients; and it is general in that it occurs even after the comparatively mild or moderate stress of witnessing an unpleasant film. In other words, compulsive repetitions are not restricted to major stresses or traumas but occur in milder forms after lesser degrees of stress. [Horowitz, 1975, p. 1461]

Among some of the more interesting subsidiary findings are the following: "In the stress condition, persons who rate themselves high on negative emotions tend also to report high levels of intrusions" (p. 1460). It is especially interesting to notice that there is a small but highly significant correlation between sadness and frequency of intrusive thoughts. (See also the study recently reported by Teasdale and Rezin, 1978). Incidentally, Horowitz found no relationship between anger and frequency of intrusive thoughts. Even though the stressful experiences were, as Horowitz and her colleagues agree, comparatively mild, the subsequent increase in intrusive and task-irrelevant thoughts was considerable. Horowitz and her associates have replicated the main findings on short and long threatening films, and on a thirty-minute film about the separation of an infant from its mother that is capable of inducing sad affect. In this study by Wilner and Horowitz (1975), 19 university students who saw the depressing film experienced similar frequencies of intrusive thoughts (and negative affect) as the subjects who participated in the earlier experiments. Comparable increases in the incidence of intrusive thoughts as a result of provocation occur in patients with mild neuroses or personality disorder (Horowitz, Becker, Moskowitz, and Rashid, 1972).

The information obtained about the relation between intrusive visual images and intrusive thoughts is unique (Horowitz and Becker, 1971). They found that after exposure to a stressful film the frequencies of visual images, intrusive thoughts, and task-irrelevant thoughts were all positively correlated. However, they also obtained evidence of independent variation of certain aspects of these visual images. The degree of intrusiveness of the visual images was found to be unrelated to the frequency of intrusive images or to the frequency of intrusive or task-irrelevant thoughts. In the case of visual images at least, frequency and intrusiveness appear to be independent variables. It will be interesting to discover whether the frequency and intrusiveness of unwanted and task-irrelevant thoughts are similarly independent. The small amount of information obtained so far appears to support the supposition that intrusive thoughts and images are closely related; it remains to be seen whether intrusive impulses also share important characteristics.

Although the work reported by Horowitz and her colleagues has been productive, there remains some doubt about whether their experimental paradigm is a satisfactory model for "clinical" obsessions. It is not clear, for example, that they have made a satisfactory distinction between obsessions and preoccupations. It seems unlikely that the intrusive thoughts they are studying have the quality of repugnance so characteristic of naturally occurring obsessions. Another potentially important difference between obsessions and the intrusive thoughts provoked in their experiments is the personal significance of a true obsession. Thirdly, their experimental approach has made no allowance for intrusive thoughts of the *anticipatory* type, for example, "I *might* expose myself or kill someone." Closely related to this is the question of obsessional impulses; so far Horowitz and her associates have not included this type of obsession in their investigations. Next, it seems that their definition of *intrusive* thoughts is unduly wide, including as it does, not merely resistance to "entry" but also attempts at removal: "Briefly, an *intrusive thought* is any thought that implies nonvolitional entry into awareness, requires suppressive effort or is hard to dispel, occurs perseveratively, or is experienced as something to be avoided" (Horowitz, 1975, p. 1458, emphasis in original).

Nevertheless, their findings are enlightening and their evolving methodology most helpful.

In summary, the main findings are as follows:

1. Exposure to threatening or depressing films (Wilner and Horowitz, 1975) is followed by an increase in intrusive thoughts, intrusive images, and task-irrelevant thoughts (Horowitz, 1975).
2. There is a positive correlation between experienced stress and amount of intrusive thoughts and images (Horowitz, 1975).
3. People who score highly on self-reported "negative emotions" report higher levels of intrusive activity (Horowitz, 1975).
4. Self-reports of sadness correlate positively with high levels of intrusive activity (Horowitz, 1975).
5. After stress, women report higher levels of intrusive thoughts than men (Horowitz and Becker, 1971).
6. Degree of intrusiveness of visual images does not correlate with incidence of these images, or with the incidence of intrusive thoughts (Horowitz, 1975).
7. Incidence of intrusive visual images correlates positively with frequency of intrusive and task-irrelevant thoughts (Horowitz, 1975).

As we will argue presently, some of these findings can profitably be construed in terms of a central filtering theory. Independent incidental findings (apart from clinical observations) that support the postulated relation between stress and intrusive thoughts include the following examples. During World War II, airmen reported significant increases in intrusive thoughts, apparently as a direct result of combat exposures (see Rachman, 1978d). In addition, Bandura, Adams, and Beyer (1977) discovered that their snake-phobic experimental subjects had many snake-related intrusive thoughts and dreams—and most fascinating of all, the frequency of these thoughts and dreams declined significantly when their fears were reduced by participant modeling.

PSYCHOPHYSIOLOGICAL DATA

In an admirably clear experimental study, Schwartz (1971) demonstrated that "specific thoughts can act as potential stimuli of autonomic responses" (p. 462). When his subjects generated affective thoughts to instruction, an increase in heart rate was observed (see also Mathews, 1971). As we will see, more direct and clinically significant results, although less precise, have since been obtained from obsessional patients. They are consistent with Schwartz's experimental findings and interpretation. In passing, we might mention that these researches support the view that obsessional material can have stimulus properties (see Rachman, 1971).

During the course of a moderately successful therapeutic experiment on eight obsessional patients (without accompanying compulsions), Rabavilas and Boulougouris (1974) accumulated some valuable information about the psychophysiological accompaniments of obsessional thoughts. They took recordings of heart rate, spontaneous fluctuations of skin conductance, and maximum deflection of skin conductance during exposure to neutral fantasies, obsessional fantasies, therapeutic thought stopping, flooding talk, and flooding in practice. For our purposes the most important results are those that point to the existence of a remarkable similarity in the psychophysiological reactions that accompany deliberately provoked obsessional and *phobic* responses. When obsessions are provoked by direct instruction, they are accompanied by significant increases in heart rate and skin conductance, reactions similar to those observed after the elicitation of phobic reactions. Another similarity has been noted during *in vivo* flooding practice—exposures to phobic and obsessional material both produce significant increases in heart rate and spontaneous fluctuations and maximum deflection of skin conductance.

From the point of view of a three-system analysis (see Rachman and Hodgson, 1974; Hodgson and Rachman, 1974), the psychophysiological results of this experiment are predictable. In their analysis Rachman and Hodgson postulated that concordance between the components of fear increases as a function of the increasing intensity of the reaction. That is, at high levels of fear one should observe a high degree of concordance. This analysis of fear can be applied to obsessions.

According to Rabavilas and Boulougouris, at low levels of stimulation the intercorrelations between psychophysiological measures were minimal. However, "using more intense stimuli, as during flooding in practice, a highly significant difference was obtained in all autonomic measures" (p. 243). The failure to find significant correlations between *clinical ratings* and psychophysiological measures can probably be attributed to the fact that flooding is a high-demand treatment, and it has been argued elsewhere that increases in therapeutic demand lead to desynchrony (Rachman, 1976b).

Leaving aside the details, the most important finding to emerge from the Rabavilas study is that psychophysiological reactions to obsessional stimuli and phobic stimuli are comparable. Earlier we drew attention to the similarity in the psychophysiological reactions to phobic and "compulsive" stimulation. The Rabavilas study shows that this similarity extends to the psychophysiological reactions to "obsessional" stimulation as well. Although the information is revealing and, as far as it goes, is consistent with the argument that there are fundamental similarities between phobias and obsessions, the psychological significance of what are after all comparatively superficial phenomena should not lead to hasty conclusions. Moreover, the sample size was small ($n = 8$), and we also have some information that is not entirely consistent with that obtained by Rabavilas. In the course of their preliminary trial of the therapeutic value of thought stopping, Stern, Lipsedge and Marks (1973) surprisingly found that the psychophysiological reactions to obsessional and neutral thoughts did not differ. There were, however, significantly different *subjective* reactions to the neutral and obsessional thoughts, with the latter producing more anxiety. As the authors point out, the absence of elevated physiological activity during induced obsessive thoughts in this study may have been due to the use of tape-recorded instructions—it having been shown elsewhere that physiological changes "have been absent when instructions were given by tape-recorder" (Stern et al., 1973, p. 662). Rabavilas and Boulougouris (1974), relying mostly on heart rate data, interpreted their findings as supporting the notion that "ruminative thoughts can be considered as being like noxious phobic stimuli" (p. 243).

CLINICAL MATERIAL

In addition to the evidence collected in the investigations described, and the defining characteristics of obsessions discussed in Chapter 17, some other important features of the phenomenon include the following. (The information has been arranged according to source—clinical descriptive material is followed by clinical surveys, our clinical experiences, and experimental evidence.)

Clinical accounts consistently describe a close association between obsessions and depression, and there is some independent confirmation from clinical surveys. There is consistency, too, in the claim that obsessions are distressing and that often they are accompanied by uncomfortable feelings of guilt. The consequences of these obsessions are mostly undesirable and include serious disruptions of concentration, loss of self-confidence, and interference with social and occupational aspects of living. People troubled by these obsessions frequently request reassurance and often engage in extensive avoidance behavior, overt and covert (neutralizing rituals). The people who are affected by obsessions are said to be "of tender conscience" or, in modern terms, "introverted and oversensitive." They rarely act on their obsessional ideas or impulses or engage in antisocial or aggressive activities.

During depressive episodes the incidence of obsessions increases. In Videbech's (1975) study of depressed patients who also had obsessions, the percentage of patients with one or more obsession rose from 23 to 60. Although Gittelson (1966c) also found evidence of the *loss* of some obsessions during depression, the overall pattern was similar to that reported by Videbech. In view of the report from Welner and his associates (1976) on the frequency of the transition from obsessions to depression (three times more common then from depression to obsessions), the phenomenon is more accurately reflected by saying that during periods of heightened obsessional activity the incidence of depressive symptoms increases—at least in a sample of *obsessional* patients. Depressing thoughts can engender depressive moods (Teasdale and Bancroft, 1977).

In simple terms, it can be said that obsessional patients are prone to develop depression and (less frequently) depressive patients are prone to develop obsessions.

Evidence from clinical surveys indicates that people are generally troubled, at any particular period, by a single dominant obsession. There is a negative correlation between obsessions and slow, repetitive rituals (are they a way of controlling the thoughts?) We can add a few clinical observations. Obsessions tend to be moderately stable, and when the patient has more than one, they occasionally show shifts in the hierarchy of dominance. People affected by obsessions engage in a wide range of behavior that can reasonably be interpreted as escape or avoidance behavior, and this includes not only the obvious forms of avoidance but also covert, neutralizing types and repeated calls for reassurance. Most of these attempts to deal with obsessional activity can be regarded as equivalent to overt compulsive rituals.

Experimental evidence shows that although the majority of naturally occurring obsessions appear to be internally generated, obsessions can be *provoked* promptly and with ease. They are responsive to, and partly under the control of, external stimulation. There is experimental evidence to support the clinical observation that the emergence of obsessions produces subjective distress and serious interference with concentration.

In the next chapter we will attempt to impose some order on this information.

Chapter 18

An Anatomy of Obsessions

With the exception of psychoanalysis and the recent papers of Beech (1974) and Teasdale (1974), the theoretical analysis of obsessions has been neglected. In recognition of this gap, we have been moving toward a comprehensive theory of obsessions during the past few years (Rachman, 1971, 1976d). Although the present account aims at comprehensiveness, a number of matters remain unexplained. (See Figure 18.1.)

At each of the three stages of our theorizing, the emphasis has moved from one aspect of obsessions to another, and we now find that the nature of obsessions can be integrated most satisfactorily by applying a three-systems analysis of the kind introduced by Peter Lang (1970), which we have previously found to be useful in construing fears (Rachman, 1978d; Rachman and Hodgson, 1974; Hodgson and Rachman, 1974). Like fear, obsessions can be said to comprise three major but loosely coupled components: cognitive, behavioral, and psychophysiological. The cognitive component is probably the most important—obsessions are by their nature a predominantly cognitive phenomenon—and can be broken down into two aspects. The first is a loss of control of specific thoughts, ideas, or impulses; the person's usual powers of (1) exclusion and (2) removal are weakened. The second aspect of the cognitive component is the familiar subjective report of discomfort or distress. The psychophysiological component is apparently similar to that observed during fear—it is responsive to provocation, probably habituates with repeated stimulation, and is well indexed by the heart rate response. The behavioral component is more complex than the kind involved in fear because, in addition to the more usual forms of

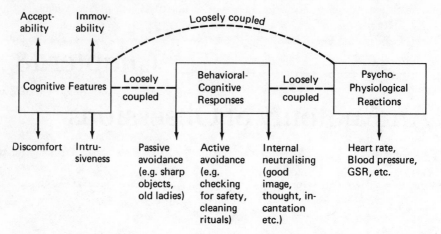

FIGURE 18.1. An Anatomy of Obsessions. The 3 major components—cognitive, psycho-physiological, and behavioral-cognitive—are said to be loosely coupled. The major features of each component are also illustrated.

escape and avoidance behavior, many obsessions are associated with neutralizing behavior (Rachman, 1976a).

GENESIS

Given the predisposing factors of an inherited tendency to neuroticism and the acquisition of high standards and self-critical habits from an excessively controlled home environment, certain thoughts, impulses, or images become frequent, discomfiting, intrusive, and adhesive during and/or after periods of dysphoria and/or exposure to stress. These ideas, impulses, or images have secondary effects in which they take on the properties of noxious stimuli; they are resistant to habituation. The occurrence of these noxious experiences may contribute a sensitizing effect, which, in turn, may add to the dysphoria and/or stress already present. Incubation, as described by Eysenck (1977), may take place.

Despite appearances, it is not self-evident that the incidence of obsessions is greater in people suffering from obsessional-compulsive disorders than in other people. Clinical experience, supported by the exploratory studies discussed earlier, seems to confirm that obsessional patients do experience more obsessions than nonobsessional people. It is, however, necessary to bear in mind that nonobsessional people experience obsessions and that the content of their ideas is broadly comparable to that reported by obsessional patients. The elevated incidence in an obsessional sample is attributable to five related factors.

First, for reasons as yet unclear, dysphoric mood states appear to contribute to an increase in obsessions. This statement is based on our clinical observations of the fluctuations of obsessional activity and on the evidence of increased obsessional activity in depressed patients—see Chapter 6 for an account of "gainers." Perhaps the withdrawal from social and other sources of external stimulation that characterizes depressive states results from an increased frequency of internally generated stimulation, especially of the kind that feeds obsessions—there is always more melancholy in the cloister than in the market-place.

A second and possibly major contributor to the increased incidence of obsessions is exposure to stress. The research completed by Horowitz and her colleagues suggests, in addition, that the nature of the stressful event or material plays an important part in determining the content of the intrusive activities. Threatening material is likely to be followed by (mostly) threatening ruminations. As we observed earlier, this research cannot be applied unquestioningly. The problem of obsessions that are *anticipatory* rather than reflective (e.g., obsessional impulses and fear of future events) remains to be considered, and the studies throw no light on the provocation of obsessions that are unrelated to stress (e.g., ruminative doubting about trivia, the meaning of unimportant words or events, etc.). Perhaps these obsessions are more closely related to mood factors than to stress.

A third determinant of the elevated incidence of obsessions is to be found in the affected person's definition of unacceptability. We have argued that people who suffer from obsessions, those of "tender conscience," tend to have high standards of conduct and morality; hence, they regard a large percentage of their thoughts, impulses, and images as unacceptable. (Many obsessions have "immoral" connotations, with aggressive and sexual themes predominating.) In an interview, one of our nonobsessional subjects described many aggressive and promiscuous ideas and images, but felt that none of them were unacceptable or unwanted (Rachman and de Silva, 1978). Her tolerance for thoughts and impulses that many people would regard as antisocial or immoral was seemingly unlimited.

Along the same lines, if we use research on student populations as a guide, it seems that all but a small minority of young adults find intrusive *sexual* thoughts acceptable (Eysenck, 1976b). Only 3 percent of the respondents endorsed the statement "I consciously try to keep sexual thoughts out of my mind." Bearing in mind that three-quarters of them said that they had sexual thoughts every day, the unacceptability rate is tiny. The male respondents who were disturbed by sexual thoughts had higher scores on a questionnaire assessing neurotic tendencies, and the females had higher scores on questions relating to a strict conscience.

The fourth and closely related determinant is based on our assumption that people who are especially sensitive to external signals of danger or threat will suffer provocation from a wider range of stimuli and, hence, will experience more obsessional impulses, ideas, and images. This is analogous to the extensive range of stimuli capable of provoking fear in a generally *timid* person. We have also mentioned, and will argue later, that obsessional people probably are slower to habituate to emotional stimulation. The obsessions persist, and may accumulate. Failure to habituate is assumed to be, in part, a function of the disturbing properties of the stimulus.

The fifth determinant is to be found in the personality of obsessional patients. As we have seen, they tend to be dysthymic, neurotic, and introverted. This combination of heightened sensitivity to disturbance and greater attention to internal stimulation are predisposing factors that favor the development of obsessions. Extraverted obsessionals are, we suspect, rare.

EXTERNAL PROVOCATION

A somewhat different way of approaching the problem of genesis, one that borders on the question of maintenance as well, is to regard the obsessions as reflecting, in the main, a response to provoking stimulation. The intrusive idea, image, or impulse is provoked by external stimulation (mainly) and persists in the face of continuous stimulation or, as in the Horowitz experiments, lingers for some time after exposure to the provoking stimulus. In our study of normal and abnormal obsessions, we found evidence of a significant amount of external provocation (Rachman and de Silva, 1978), and even this is likely to be an underestimate. (Extensive interviewing may reveal some formerly unacknowledged external trigger.) The occurrence of external provocation was especially evident in obsessional impulses. If confirmed, it would suggest a fuller use of *in vivo* exposure treatment procedures for this disorder.

If we settle for a view of obsessions as responses that are generated by external factors the problem of persistence is largely resolved. The obsession persists because of the presence of external stress stimuli or because of the continuing influence of such external stressors for a period after their removal (as in Horowitz's research). They are resonating responses.

The arguments against this analysis are fourfold. First, it fails to encompass obsessions that have no external trigger (see Rachman and de Silva, 1978). Second, it fails to mesh satisfactorily with some clinical accounts; numerous patients insist that their obsessions arise independently of external events or variations in mood state. Case examples that do not fit into this analysis include patients whose obsessions are enduring, stable, and widely generalized—"The obsession is always there." Third, the analysis encounters difficulty in accounting for anticipatory obsessions ("Will I do it?") and obsessions of a nonsensical, repetitive kind. Fourth, any explanation that rests mainly on the role of external provocation needs tailoring in order to explain the constancy of obsessions. Often the content of the obsession is unchanging, even though major environmental changes take place. For example, the patient described earlier, who worried about whether she had killed the old lady, experienced this intrusive thought at home, at work, on vacation, in London and Brighton, and so forth. In other cases, however, the relative constancy of the obsession *can* be accounted for (e.g., the woman who had obsessional fears of blinding her children experienced the thought whenever she encountered any sharp object—a common occurrence).

Despite the problems just enumerated, the explanatory value of an analysis based on resonating responses to external stressors should not be underestimated. More obsessions can be accounted for by this analysis than might be expected on first inspection. Lastly, obsessional *impulses* seem to be particularly closely related to external cues and stresses; it is also likely that they are of significantly shorter duration than obsessional thoughts.

MAINTENANCE

Cognitive Aspects

The intrusiveness and immovability of obsessional thoughts, impulses, and images are sufficient proof of inadequate cognitive control. Their entry and persistence imply that the person finds it exceedingly difficult to exclude obsessions and, once they have arrived, even more difficult to remove them. The evidence supporting the proposition that obsessional patients have weak control over this kind of mental activity comes from two sources. First, their inability to remove the obsessional material is generally the major complaint made by these patients. Second, in our study on nonobsessional people we found that their ability to remove obsessions distinguished them from the clinical sample. In a sense this inadequate cognitive control is the heart of the problem, and it must be admitted that at present we are unsure why obsessional patients are deficient in such control. Perhaps the answer to this question must await progress in our understanding of the regulation of thought processes in general, thereby recalling Lewis's (1936) remark that the problems of obsessional illness "cover so wide a field that it is difficult to examine them without examining also the nature of man" (p. 325).

Presumably, the deficient control of obsessional patients is specific. We have no reason to suppose that obsessional patients have difficulty removing neutral thoughts, impulses, or urges (this is easily tested). Hence, their difficulties would appear to rest on the nature of the specific obsession and, presumably, on its power to disturb them. The more emotionally disturbing the obsession, the less control the person can exert—except, of course, when for clinical or experimental purposes the person forms the obsession to instruction. They surpass nonclinical subjects in this skill (Rachman and de Silva, 1978). Incidentally, attempts to discover whether obsessional patients retain the general ability to control *nonobsessional* thoughts could well be supplemented by an investigation into the cognitive controls exerted by obsessional patients during an obsessional episode and then again during a period of *remission* (Shackleton, 1977). If the person's control is already weakened by dysphoria, the intrusion of a disturbing impulse or idea might well contribute to a sense of helplessness.

Although we are ignorant about the reasons for their deficient control, we do know that the characteristic attempts at control made by obsessional patients are ineffective in the long run. Their neutralizing behavior, overt or covert, may achieve temporary relief. However, the obsessions generally persist. Even if the duration is truncated, the frequency seems unaffected. Compulsively washing one's hands to remove a bad thought is ultimately as self-defeating as compulsively washing away disease or dirt contamination. Covert counting rituals, restorative images, ritualistic incantations, and the rest may become useful methods of control, but in the long run they generally fail. The addition of compulsive rituals to the unwanted thoughts is a poor solution. It is just possible, however, that some rituals do provide a long-term "solution." Some rituals undoubtedly succeed in controlling obsessions, and the negative correlation between slow repetitive rituals and obsessions referred to earlier suggests that these rituals *may* achieve long-term control.

What, then, are the satisfactory methods of control? Judging from our introspections and the results of our experiments, the best controls can be summarized as *dismissal* and *distraction*. As with other types of unwanted mental activity, external stimulation can inhibit obsessions—see Slade (1976), for interesting observations on the external inhibition of hallucinations, and Teasdale and Rezin (1978) on negative thoughts. Dismissal, the deliberate rejection and removal of the thought, refers to control of an obsession that has made its entry, while distraction includes, in addition, preventing the entry of an obsession. This distinction may be of some value in designing (self-control) treatment procedures. When the problem is mainly one of *frequency*, then a distraction procedure of some form may be preferable. If the problem is the *duration* of the obsession, then a technique for dismissal is to be preferred.

It is to be expected that in a comparison of the effects of predominantly dismissive and predominantly distracting techniques, the former will reduce duration more satisfactorily and the latter will reduce frequency more satisfactorily. In both methods the therapist needs to consider how the patient is likely to use the newly available "space." Applying Seligman's (1975) theory of depression to the phenomenon of uncontrollable obsessional thoughts and impulses, it can be predicted that obsessions are bound to produce learned helplessness and, hence, dysphoria. No doubt this sequence can and does occur, but it is essential to make allowance for the reverse sequence of events (i.e., dysphoria leading to obsessions). Horowitz's (1975) research is consistent with such a possibility.

Moreover, many patients develop obsessions during a depressive episode (e.g., the "gainers" described earlier). In addition, in the clinic one often observes what appears to be a progression from dysphoria to obsessions. Recognition of this sequence (depression leading to loss of cognitive control) need not be seen as contradicting Seligman's theory. Dysphoria can arise from learned helplessness induced by any number and variety of experiences of noncontrollability, not merely by uncontrollable obsessional thoughts. There is nothing in the theory that opposes the possibility of dysphoria in its turn promoting uncontrollable obsessions.

Psychophysiological and Subjective Aspects

It is assumed that obsessions (i.e., the thoughts, images, and impulses themselves) are capable of acting as stimuli. Insofar as they cause distress, they can be regarded as noxious, and in our view they bear some resemblance to the more familiar noxious stimuli such as phobic objects, images, or thoughts. Like phobic stimuli, obsessions may provoke extensive avoidance behavior. In twelve cases analyzed recently, avoidance behavior was always present even though it did not always take familiar forms. While some patients were as housebound as the most classic agoraphobic patients, others engaged in uncommon avoidance behavior such as keeping their hands in their pockets whenever approaching or passing other people. The covert forms of avoidance behavior—neutralizing activities— will be discussed shortly.

Like noxious phobic stimuli, obsessions are accompanied by comparable psychophysiological disturbances, particularly increased heart rate. Even if we grant that there are important similarities between obsessions and phobic stimuli, they cannot be regarded as identical. Two differences that may prove to be of significance are that (1) obsessions have a larger endogenous element than phobic stimuli and (2) obsessions are most likely to be associated with depression than with anxiety. Having noted these differences, we can now concentrate on the similarities between phobias and obsessions.

In the same way that Lader and Wing (1966) argued that phobic stimuli are resistant to habituation, it is proposed that obsessions too (regarded as noxious stimuli) are resistant to habituation (see Rachman, 1978d for a full discussion). (See Figure 18.2.)

Behavioral Aspects

In addition to the more familiar forms of escape and avoidance behavior, people who are troubled by obsessions also engage in some distinctive forms of neutralizing behavior. These may include overt avoidance behavior or attempts to "put matters right" internally. The patient tries to neutralize or make amends for the

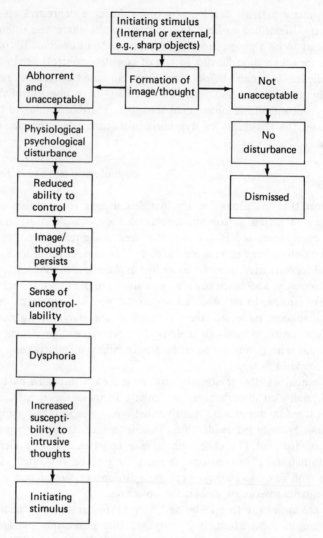

FIGURE 18.2. The Spiral Effect of Obsessions. It is postulated that the sequence of events depicted here can lead to perpetual recurrency of the obsession.

unacceptable thought, impulse, or image. It is not uncommon for the person to feel that the unacceptable idea, if left unaltered, may cause harm to other people. The patient feels obliged to repeat the entire action that was interrupted by a bad thought, but only after he or she has substituted a *good* thought. A portion of the repetitive behavior exhibited by obsessional patients can be attributed to these attempts to complete an action in the presence of a good thought.

While in their calmer moments patients often are able to recognize the irrationality of their fears about danger to other people or the pointlessness of carrying out ritualistic neutralizing acts, such recognition does not strip the obsessions of their power to disturb. Attempts at "putting right" may take many forms. They may be amendatory, neutralizing, reparative, corrective, preventive, or restorative, but as the word *neutralize* appears to cover most cases, it has been introduced to signify the attempt at "putting right." The patient sometimes attempts to form a satisfactory counterthought or counterimage, utter words or numbers of special significance, form an image of the people who feature in the obsession restored to a state of safety, form a virtuous thought, utter an incantation, or have a releasing thought or image. It is contended that these methods of putting matters right (i.e., neutralizing behavior) are equivalents of compulsive checking rituals or repetitive requests for reassurance. When the requests for reassurance are met, they produce temporary relief—and enduring increases in the tendency to seek reassurance.

If this view is correct, it follows that the method for treating obsessions should be patterned on the successful methods of treating other forms of compulsive rituals. The ritual equivalent should be subjected to a period of response prevention or response blocking in the same way that a patient with compulsive checking rituals is first exposed to the provoking situation and then instructed to refrain from carrying out the pertinent checking ritual (Hodgson and Rachman, 1976). So the obsessional patient should be exposed to the provoking trigger—the disturbing thought or image or impulse—and then instructed to refrain from carrying out the checking ritual (i.e., refrain from putting things right).

We have next to address the question of why obsessional patients engage in this neutralizing behavior. Presumably, nonobsessional people seldom engage in compulsive-equivalent neutralizing behavior because there is little need for them to do so. The simpler and less demanding methods of dismissal (escape behavior) and distraction (escape or avoidance behavior) are sufficient to control most unwanted, intrusive thoughts. As we know, however, obsessional patients experience great difficulty in preventing or removing certain ideas and impulses. When the simpler methods fail, they may resort to neutralizing activities and by these means achieve temporary relief, in a similar manner to the temporary relief achieved by compulsive patients when they execute their compulsive cleaning or checking rituals. If the neutralizing activities begin to fail (e.g., requests for reassurance are ignored, positive images fade, the impulses persist despite clean hands, etc.) the person ceases to use them and has to endure prolonged periods of obsessional activity—at least until a new method of neutralizing the obsession is developed.

This analysis of the response to obsessions rests of course on the two-stage theory of avoidance behavior, which, despite its weaknesses (Rachman, 1976b), seems able to accommodate this phenomenon. The discomfort/disturbance engendered by the obsession promotes escape and/or avoidance behavior in the form of neutralizing activities. Neutralizing acts that are followed by a reduction in discomfort are strengthened. Incidentally, viewed in this way the commonly observed tactic of obtaining a "good thought" before undertaking some activity can be regarded as a form of active-avoidance behavior. The person constructs his or her own internal safety signal.

Although the escape and avoidance behavior of people suffering from obsessions shares many properties with that displayed by phobic people, there is one potentially important difference of emphasis. For the most part, phobics are intent on avoiding or escaping from tangible external fear-provoking stimuli—enclosed spaces, heights, social gatherings, snakes, and so forth. Hence, their escape and avoidance tactics are relatively straightforward, although not always easy to execute.

Obsessional patients, on the other hand, are attempting to escape from or avoid disturbing stimuli that are largely internalized. The obsession can of course be triggered by an external stimulus such as a sharp object, in the same way that a phobic stimulus provokes fear. But many obsessions appear to arise with little or no external precipitation. Hence, the problem of controllability is somewhat different for obsessions than for phobias.

In all of this one should not lose sight of the fact that many obsessional patients engage in extensive, observable avoidance behavior (e.g., avoiding sharp objects, defenseless infants, etc.) as well as internalized avoidance. Incidentally, the majority of obsessional patients do in fact develop compulsive rituals (estimates range from 75% to 93%). The figure of 75 percent is probably an underestimate because it does not include covert neutralizing rituals and compulsive requests for reassurance. As we have argued, these activiities can be regarded as equivalent to compulsions.

To sum up, given certain predisposing factors, intrusive, immovable, unwanted thoughts are generated by stress and/or mood disturbances. Specific thoughts, images, or impulses can be initiated by external precipitants (e.g., sharp objects) or arise without reference to any discernible external trigger. Obsessions take on the properties of noxious stimuli and may in turn contribute to a further deterioration in mood and increased sensitivity to stress. Obsessions persist because of a continuing failure of cognitive control coupled with the undue resistance of the obsessional material to normal patterns of habituation. In attempting to achieve relief from the subjective discomfort that accompanies obsessions, the person engages in avoidance behavior, overt and/or covert. Avoidance activities that are successful in achieving at least a temporary release from discomfort are strengthened and may acquire compulsive properties.

Our account leaves several points unexplained. For example, it provides little enlightenment about silly, insignificant obsessions such as number sequences, nonsensical phrases, and the like. Also, it does not tell why, of all the possible themes, certain ideas or images or impulses become repetitive—the selectivity of obsessions is unexplained. In addition, the incidence of clinically significant obsessions falls short of theoretical expectation. Why are there so few ruminators? Stress or dysphoria ignites *clinical* obsessions in a few predisposed people—presumably those who by upbringing and temperament are hypersensitive to the unwanted thoughts to which we all are subject.

Chapter 19

The Theory and Practice
of Modifying Obsessions

Pursuing the present analysis leads to a broader view of treatment strategy. Ideally, the main features of all three components of the obsession should be dealt with—the cognitive components (subjective discomfort, definition of acceptability, intrusiveness, immovability), the behavioral components (overt avoidance behavior, neutralizing activities), and psychophysiological disturbances. These components, and the primary and secondary treatment tactics that appear to be most suitable, are illustrated in Table 19.1.

To achieve the ideal outcome in every case, one would need to use an appropriate combination of the following tactics, depending on the nature and requirements of the particular case—it must be borne in mind that the role and prominence of each of the major components will vary from one case to another. Matching the treatment to the presenting difficulties may require the skill of an experienced therapist. As a general guide, Table 19.1 presents a list of treatment possibilities, with the secondary tactics given in parentheses under the primary methods.

In the first stage of developing the present theory (Rachman, 1971), the satiation technique was proposed as a means of reducing subjective discomfort and psychophysiological disturbance by expediting habituation. The second stage of the theory (Rachman, 1976a) drew attention to the behavioral components of obsessions and stressed the importance of reducing this unadaptive behavior, both the easily recognized forms and the obscure neutralizing types—by means of the robust and tested method of response prevention. It was emphasized that the overt patterns of avoidance behavior should not be ignored.

TABLE 19.1 THE COMPONENTS OF OBSESSIONS AND THEIR RELATION TO TREATMENT TACTICS

| | *Cognitive* | | | | *Behavioral* | | PSYCHO-PHYSIOLOGICAL DISTURBANCES |
| | | | *Cognitive Controls* | | | | |
	DISCOMFORT	ACCEPTABILITY	INTRUSIVENESS	IMMOVABILITY	OVERT AVOIDANCE	NEUTRALIZING	
Direct treatments (plus secondary tactics, given in parentheses)	habituation training (cognitive restructuring, dismissive, desensitization, modeling)	cognitive restructuring	distractive (desensitization, modeling, stress reducers)	dismissive	response prevention after exposure (direct instruction, satiation)		habituation training (cognitive restructuring, dismissive)
Current methods—primary action	drugs, counseling	paradoxical intention, counseling	counseling ("occupy yourself")	thought stopping	paradoxical intention	nil	drugs, leucotomy

As the latest elaboration of the theoretical analysis of treatment deals primarily with the nature and modification of the cognitive components of obsessions, it will be presented first and in greatest detail.

As described earlier, our investigation of the obsessions of a nonclinical sample of people revealed that they had a greater tolerance for aggressive or sexual ideas than obsessional patients did; moreover, their very definition of what constitutes unacceptable impulse or thought appeared to be more tolerant. Implicit attempts to change the person's evaluation of the content of the obsession feature in many nonspecific forms of counseling and psychotherapeutic support (and indeed in paradoxical intention; see Gertz, 1966). In terms of the present analysis, we should consider the introduction into behavioral-modification programs of specific, deliberate, and measurable attempts to modify the person's definition of and tolerance for unacceptable thoughts and impulses. If it can be shown that measurable changes in the definition of and tolerance for the obsession are followed by significant improvements in ability to *control* the thoughts, especially the ability to remove them, we will have made some progress toward understanding the nature of this type of self-control and why it sometimes fails. Measuring the consequences of changing the patient's appraisal of the content of his or her obsession is a potentially fruitful line of investigation.

Some obsessional patients report that repeated clinical discussion of the content of their thoughts, impulses, or images—and more often, repeated therapeutic instructions to form the thought or image—results in a significant loss of their meaning. The thoughts lose some of their horrifying or bizarre or dangerous qualities, in a way that suggests a process of psychological detoxification. The unpleasant cognitive implications of the obsession are diluted, and we presume that this cognitive change facilitates habituation. The methods of cognitive behavior therapy (e.g., Beck, 1976) are likely to be helpful here. Detoxification may facilitate *and* be facilitated by habituation training, in which the person is repeatedly instructed to form the thought or image and then to hold it for a prolonged period. Among some other possibilities, it seems to us that the therapeutic instruction and the praise given contingently upon formation and retention of "evil and unacceptable" thoughts helps deflate the patient's guilt, shame, or fear of the thoughts. The treatment context and procedure implicitly and explicitly change the psychological and moral connotations of the obsessions—they help to detoxify. When the significance of the obsession is so deflated, habituation can proceed expeditiously. The paradoxical-intention method, among others, may well have similar detoxifying effects.

Another compatible possibility is that habituation training helps restore the person's sense of control. With practice the person learns to form the obsession to instruction. He or she is also taught to retain the obsession for prescribed periods and, lastly, to stop having the thought when instructed to curtail it. In achieving these skills the patient is of course gaining *control* over the obsession, albeit incidentally. By this analysis habituation training incorporates thought stopping *and* two other control skills. Assessing the effects of habituation training on the ease of formation, maintenance, and dismissal of an obsession will be an easy matter.

Attempts to control the immovability of the thoughts or, to put it another way, improved ability to remove them have so far taken the form of thought stopping (e.g., Taylor, 1963; Wolpe, 1958; Stern et al., 1973; Yamagami, 1971; Kumar and Wilkinson, 1971), aversion relief (e.g., Solyom et al., 1971), and aversion therapy (e.g., Bass, 1973). If the present analysis of obsessions is even partly correct, it may help explain the indifferent and unpredictable results of thought stopping and other "removal" tactics. For patients in whom neutralizing activities and undue resistance to habituation are of little importance, thought stopping and other removal methods may well be sufficient to achieve valuable, if incomplete, improvements. They are, however, unlikely to be sufficient for helping people whose obsessions produce marked subjective discomfort and/or psychophysiological disturbance and are followed by unadaptive neutralizing and avoidance behavior. "Removal" methods do not deal with these aspects of the problem, at least not directly.

The other cognitive difficulty involved in obsessions, intrusiveness, appears not to have been dealt with as a problem in its own right. It is true that attempts to prevent the entry of intrusive and unacceptable thoughts have featured in nonspecific counseling and psychotherapy, mainly in the form of advice to undertake distracting activities such as social events, more demanding employment, and so on. A thorough psychological analysis of distracting and other preventive tactics, in which the incidence of obsessions would feature as the dependent variable, is overdue.

Before going on to consider the tactics that appear to be most appropriate for dealing with the behavioral and psychophysiological aspects of obsessions, some comments on the loosely coupled functional connections between the components are in order. It would be useful to know how an attack on one component of an obsession (e.g., the control element) affects the other components (e.g., subjective discomfort). A hint of the differential effects of these various tactics is contained in the psychophysiological experiment reported by Boulougouris and his associates (1977). As might be expected from the present analysis, both thought stopping and flooding treatments produced increased heart rate responses, but habituation occurred only after flooding.

This result is consistent with our view that when thought stopping succeeds, it does so by improving the person's cognitive control (enabling him or her to remove the thought more easily), and any habituation that takes place is incidental. Flooding, on the other hand, is more likely to reduce subjective discomfort (after an initial increase) and to facilitate habituation at the same time. Psychophysiological and psychological studies of the relations between these components should produce interesting results. It can be predicted, however, that regardless of whether the cognitive improvements are achieved by habituation training, counseling, or paradoxical intention, it may be necessary to supplement this treatment with special methods designed to deal with the remaining psychophysiological and behavioral problems.

It was postulated that "the patient's inability to habituate to these ruminative stimuli can be overcome by presenting the noxious stimulation in attenuated form under conditions which favor habituation or by effecting a direct improvement in mood state" (Rachman, 1971, p. 234). This analysis assumes, of course, that obsessions, like other noxious stimuli, are subject to habituation, and Foa's (1977) work on habituation during the treatment of obsessional patients gives ground for encouragement.

TREATMENT TACTICS

A new theoretical analysis (Rachman, 1978) leaves us with five related treatment techniques. The predicted effects, both primary and secondary, of each treatment tactic are given in Table 19.2.

We have little new to say about dismissal-training techniques, such as thought stopping, aversion therapy, and so on; their practical utility is uncertain, but we hope that the present theoretical analysis will help make better sense of how, when, and why thought stopping and other dismissal techniques achieve some effects. It also suggests that the search for dismissal tactics should be widened. Music, conversation, work, mental arithmetic, compiling lists, recalling poetry or songs—all are potentially useful dismissal activities. As far as distraction training is concerned, we have not yet carried out any research into this subject, and our practical experience is limited to general counseling. The potential importance of cognitive restructuring became apparent recently, and we hope to investigate the utility of this method before too long. In considering the treatment outline given here, it is necessary to remember that the present emphasis on habituation training and response prevention may require some alteration as information on the newer tactics begins to accumulate. We anticipate the need for a revision within a few years.

In addition to the direct treatment tactics described so far, any procedure —from drugs to desensitization—that reduces the person's stress reactions may well have beneficial secondary effects on obsessions. For example, Bandura, Adams, and Beyer (1977) report that the snake-related ruminations of their snake-phobic subjects declined markedly when their fear of snakes was successfully reduced by participant modeling.

HABITUATION TRAINING	RESPONSE PREVENTION (AFTER EXPOSURE)	DISTRACTION TRAINING	DISMISSAL TRAINING	COGNITIVE RESTRUCTURING	FEAR REDUCTION (MODELING, DESENSITIZATION)
Primary Effects					
Reduced psychophysiological disturbance	Reduced frequency of overt avoidance	Reduced frequency of obsessions	Reduced duration of obsessions	Increased acceptability	Reduced fear
Reduced subjective discomfort	Reduced frequency of neutralizing activities	Reduced duration of obsessions		Generality of changes	Reduced discomfort
Specificity of changes					
Secondary Effects					
Increased acceptability	Cognitive restructuring	Reduced discomfort	Reduced discomfort	Reduced discomfort	Reduced frequency and duration
Reduced duration of obsessions			Reduced frequency	Reduced avoidance and neutralizing	
Reduced frequency					
Reduced intrusiveness					

*The patient is given full instructions before treatment begins. He or she is told that many people experience unpleasant, unwanted, and unacceptable thoughts, impulses, or images. It is explained that under normal mood conditions most people can dismiss these unwelcome thoughts without difficulty. However, when they are associated with a depressed mood or stress it can be difficult to eliminate the unwanted thoughts. The treatment technique is then described, and the patient is told that he or she will be required deliberately to form the unwanted thoughts and retain them for prolonged periods. The concept of response prevention is explained, and the patient is instructed to refrain from carrying out any neutralizing activities, internal or external. At the same time, he or she is warned that the formation of the unpleasant thoughts and the exercise of response prevention will be accompanied by some discomfort, especially in the early stages. Throughout the explanation and the conduct of the program itself, great emphasis is laid on the necessity for self-management. Patients are told that we are attempting to teach them a technique for dealing with unwanted ideas and that, as in any successful training, they should take their new skills with them when they leave the clinic. The need for accurate and regular recording of the pertinent aspects of the behavior is stressed, along with some examples. Patients are also warned that even after they have succeeded in modifying their obsessions the recurrence of serious disturbances of mood or stress might herald a return of the obsessions, but that they can then reapply the control techniques that form the most important part of the training program.

The program begins with the collection of baseline data. The person is required to record the occurrence of each obsession—its content, its duration, any associated disturbance, and the strength of any accompanying urge to carry out neutralizing rituals. Once an adequate baseline has been established, the troublesome obsessions are subjected to habituation training in ascending order as for desensitization, (i.e., repeated and prolonged formation of the obsession itself, usually under relaxation). The therapist records the latency to form the obsession and the number of times that it fades during each trial period. When satisfactory progress is made, the latency to form the idea begins to increase and the obsession shows a tendency to fade during the trial period. (The recording of the requisite data sometimes presents problems, and of course self-monitoring not infrequently produces changes in the behavior being studied.)

Once the habituation training is under way, the response prevention instructions are introduced. The person is reminded of the need to refrain from carrying out any avoidance behavior or neutralizing acts. Throughout each session and between sessions, the recording of the relevant data must be continued. Once good progress is evident in both aspects of the program, the therapist should begin to fade out of the picture. The patient is instructed to continue practicing the two techniques, habituation training and response prevention, even in the absence of the therapist. Depending on the needs of the particular case, the therapist may decide to place greater emphasis on the habituation part of the treatment or on the response prevention part. As we gain greater understanding of the other cognitive treatment techniques described earlier, they will need to be incorporated in the overall retraining program. It should be remembered, however, that, depending on the nature of each problem, it may be unnecessary to employ treatment tactics that address all three components of the obsessions.

This brings us to considerations of selection of the appropriate treatment technique for each patient. First and foremost, the habituation and response prevention treatment seems appropriate for those people whose obsessions are associated with or followed by strong urges to "put matters right." In the assessment that always precedes satisfactory behavioral treatment, special attention should be paid to this aspect of the person's complaint. It is essential to get the person to describe in detail the nature and content of the obsession and its effects. One of the key questions is, "How do you attempt to deal with the discomfort you experience during and after obsessions?" Useful follow-up questions include the following: "How do you bring the obsession to an end?" "How long does the obsession last?" "What helps to shorten the duration of the obsessions?" "What is so unacceptable about the image?"

If the person frequently engages in avoidance or neutralizing behavior, it is quite likely that he or she will respond best to habituation training and response prevention. If, on the other hand, the patient engages in neither internal nor external neutralizing rituals, repeated prolonged presentations of the obsessional content may be sufficient. If the patient is troubled by a wide range of unacceptable thoughts and has little accompanying avoidance behavior, cognitive restructuring might be called for. For obsessions that are unduly persistent and have little accompanying avoidance behavior, some form of dismissal training will be required.

As in other behavior-modification programs, some patients find the program distressing, particularly in the early stages. If such distress occurs, it is best dealt with by providing encouragement, comfort, and social reinforcement for persisting in the face of uncomfortable conditions. The patient can be reassured that the discomfort produced by the provoking experience is likely to dissipate within a reasonably short time. Recovery from the distress provoked by the training experiences can be facilitated by congenial and supportive company and/or strongly distracting tasks.

It is important for the person to take an active part in the planning, recording, and execution of the treatment as soon as possible. Once the patient has gained the rudiments of the treatment and is carrying out the program satisfactorily in the presence of the therapist, he or she should be encouraged to undertake increasing amounts of practice alone. This is particularly important because obsessions probably occur more frequently and more disturbingly when a person is alone. Even more than in other behavior-modification programs, full and accurate recording of the interventions and their effects is of great importance. This is because the major treatment instructions and manipulations are not immediately accessible to the therapist, and in order to assess the effects of the intervention it is essential that therapists have access to detailed day-by-day records compiled by the patient. After each training session the patient should if possible record his or her discomfort and compulsive urges, if any, at 15-minute intervals for up to 2 hours. In this way it is possible to determine whether the decay of the urges and discomfort is following the predicted pattern.

If the problem is mainly one of *duration* of the unwanted thoughts, then one of the thought-stopping tactics referred to earlier might prove to be most efficacious.

effective

COMMENTS

It will be obvious from most of this chapter that in our attempts to understand and modify obsessions we are hampered by a scarcity of experimental data. The conceptual and phenomenological development of the subject probably is just sufficient to permit a move toward a period of experimental analysis. There is no shortage of questions (indeed, this chapter introduces well over a dozen).

As far as analysis and modification are concerned, we hope that the "anatomy of obsessions" set out here has a clarifying value. In describing the "anatomy" we have tried to build our scheme on a three-systems analysis and, from the treatment point of view, to integrate it into current methods of modifying compulsions and phobias. We can now turn our attention to some of the fundamental properties of obsessions and of intrusive ideas generally.

Chapter 20

Obsessions: Theoretical Analyses

This concluding discussion ranges rather widely and sometimes extends beyond traditional boundaries, but there is no alternative when facing a problem as complex as unwanted mental activities. It is predominantly an exercise in formulating questions: Why do obsessions persist? How are they formed? How are thoughts concluded? Why is their content so often aggressive and/or sexual? How do these unwanted images and thoughts evade the postulated central filtering mechanism? Although we have no firm answers, our impression is that many of the questions point to the desirability of carrying out research into the nature of emotional processing in general. Also, we feel that the introduction into the study of obsessions of some of the experimental methods that have been developed for the study of cognitive functions would put us in a position to analyze certain aspects of obsession in a newly precise manner.

Why do obsessions persist despite their obnoxious and self-defeating properties? Are obsessions mere flotsam, or do they serve some psychological function? With regard to the first possibility, that they are mere flotsam, one can regard obsessions as comparable to indigestible material of the kind that features in anxiety dreams; the function of these dreams, if there is one, remains obscure. We have already suggested that obsessions can be construed as noxious stimuli that are resistant to the normal processes of habituation. The existence of other types of stimuli that are similarly resistant to habituation (e.g., certain intense stimuli) makes this a plausible possibility.

Obviously, the description of obsessions as peculiarly resistant flotsam is unsatisfying even if it is accurate. Even if we can discern no functions that are served by obsessions, it is desirable to get to the bottom of their persistence and their resistance to habituation. Earlier we made a first attempt to specify the conditions under which persistence occurs (i.e., dysphoric mood, stress, unacceptability, hypersensitivity, and dysthymia). From there we need to ask how and why normal habituation occurs and what function that process serves. So although we have very little idea at present what function obsessions may serve, the alternative of viewing them as mere flotsam remains unsatisfying. Nevertheless, the assumption that all obsessions are functional is exceedingly difficult to accept—especially when one considers repetitive obsessional trivia such as repeating meaningless phrases or number sequences.

The next problem has to do with the content of obsessions. Why are they so commonly aggressive or sexual in nature? Here we can only speculate that these themes, sexual and aggressive, must have been subjects of particular concern and disapproval to the parents of these vulnerable people. The hypothesis that habituation to these already sensitized ideas is further impeded during dysphoric states (e.g., Foa and Goldstein, 1977) can be evaluated in a way suggested by Shackleton (1977): by testing depressed patients who complain of obsessions, both during and after the depressive episode. Presumably, these patients should be less sensitive to sexual and aggressive ideas when they are no longer depressed; also, they should habituate to these ideas more readily after the depressive period has passed. It is here assumed that dysphoria raises the person's sensitivity and, hence, that ideas that might otherwise be absorbed become "indigestible."

The problem of how to reduce the frequency of obsessions raises matters of considerable complexity and wide significance. In one sense it can be seen as merely one example, admittedly "abnormal," of the larger inquiry into the nature of self-control of thought processes. Although the tendency is to think of obsessions as entering consciousness from "somewhere out there" (they are after all, *intrusive*), it may be preferable to avoid this construction. While it is undoubtedly true that obsessions are easily provoked by external prompts, such as threatening stimuli (e.g., sharp objects), or by instructions given in a laboratory, the obsession proper is an "internal product." As we have argued earlier, obsessions differ from the "ideas of influence" reported by schizophrenic patients. There is no suggestion of the thoughts being inserted by some external agent or force; obsessional patients describe their obsessions as their own property, as it were.

In his analysis of the psychology of imagery, Pylyshyn (1973) criticizes the prevailing conception of images as "pictures in the head" and emphasizes instead their propositional qualities. Developing this alternate view, Lang (1977) writes that "the emotional image is re-created as it is evoked, and propositions may be added or subtracted from this protean cognitive structure as it unfolds over time" (p. 867). Contrary to the way in which we tend to think of unwanted, intruding obsessions, an "emotional image is not always processed as a complete unit, nor does it impact on behavior in the abrupt fashion of an external stimulus" (p. 876).

If we apply this conception to the problem of intrusive obsessions (leaving aside for the moment the question of whether we will ultimately need separate explanations for obsessional images, thoughts, and impulses), then our therapeutic problem changes from one of finding a suitable barrier to prevent the *entry* of unwanted thoughts to one of a need to find ways to stifle emergent obsessions. If obsessions are, like emotional images, unfolding sets of propositions, then we need to find techniques for inhibiting the process of image formation rather than erecting more effective barriers to prevent their entry. In practical terms that would presumably mean self-control techniques capable of stifling the emerging obsession. This is close to, but not identical with, our suggested strategy for removing well-formed persisting obsessions, that is, by using dismissive techniques (e.g., thought stopping).

If this speculative analysis of obsessions, influenced by the writings of Pylyshyn and Lang, has any merit, it will lead to a shift in therapeutic strategy of the kind alluded to, and if so, we may find that the term *distracting tactics* will need to be replaced—by *stifling tactics*, perhaps?

For the reason referred to earlier, as well as more general considerations, at some more fitting stage of development it will become necessary to determine whether there are significant differences among obsessional thoughts, images, and impulses. (The important similarities—alien content, unwantedness, intrusiveness, immovability, etc.—were dealt with earlier). At first inspection it seems probable that obsessional thoughts and images have a good deal in common and that obsessional impulses, by virtue of their drive properties and implications of action, may be distinctive. The superior response of "horrific temptations" to Sookman and Solyom's (1977) treatment supports the possibility that obsessional impulses may differ in at least some respects from obsessional images or ideas. Cognitive research emphasizing the distinctions between verbal and "imagistic" types of memory may undermine the assumed affinity between obsessional images and thoughts.

THOUGHT CONTROL

The problem of how to assert greater control over one's thoughts is of course an ancient one. Most contemporary methods appear to be derivatives of one or another system of thought substitution relying on autosuggestion. Their merits remain to be determined, and sad to say, none of them is backed by a rationale that can be repeated in scientifically respectable company. The thought substitution method recommended by Alexander in 1928 is an illustrative example. It may indeed be effective for removing thoughts on some occasions, but it is unlikely that this simple method will prove capable of denting a robust obsession, and no serious explanation of its proclaimed effectiveness was ever offered:

> When disturbing thoughts enter your mind, switch them aside *instantly*; it is fatal to dwell on them. Oppose them at once with thoughts opposite in character. Oppose poverty thoughts with money thoughts, dismal thoughts with cheerful thoughts, failure thoughts with success thoughts. Let there be no parleying with these disturbers of your peace of kind; switch on instantly to helpful thoughts. Daily practice like this in putting aside thoughts you do not wish to think about will help you . . . in dealing with the more powerful class of thoughts . . . that are so difficult to control. [pp. 111-12, emphasis in original]

Alexander also recommended distracting tactics. "An excellent way to divert attention from the disturbing thought is to engage in some form of activity—taking a brisk walk, or playing some game involving skill" (p. 113).

Many, perhaps most of us, practice thought substitution even without the benefit of spiritual uplift or instruction. In an experiment on psychological stress carried out by Bandura and Rosenthal (1966), some of their subjects described what might be called the natural recourse to thought substitution. They said, for example, "I tried to be cool. I thought about Latin verbs and about Latin compositions." Another subject "tried to think of other topics; general elections in Britain, will Wilson become Prime Minister; academic problems; planned trip to New York. I was not able to keep thinking on any topic too consistently and my thoughts rather broke down after a while" (p. 60).

The fact that both the initiated and noninitiated use thought substitution methods with at least occasional success suggests that a rational investigation may prove worth while. The substitution method, like other attempts to assert self-control over one's thoughts, is of course predicated on the belief that we are capable of what has been called "multiple processing" (Neisser, 1967).

CONCLUDING A THOUGHT

If obsessions are examined from the point of view of Bartlett's (1958) analysis of thinking, a distinction can be drawn between intrusive, ruminative thoughts on the one hand and images or impulses on the other. As we will see, this definition of thinking excludes images and impulses but comfortably encompasses ruminative thoughts and, at the same time, provides a neat match between such thoughts and the process that Bartlett described as "interpolation."

It will be recalled that many obsessional thoughts take the form of attempts to reassure oneself that one's actions have not and will not cause harm to other people. In order to achieve this reassurance, the person quite commonly will rehearse in his or her mind a sequence of events, attempting to recall with great precision each of his or her actions. So, for example, a young truck driver spent hours ruminating over whether or not he might accidentally have harmed someone while driving his vehicle. In his mind he retraced many of his journeys, paying particular attention to the parts of it that he was unable to recall with sufficient clarity. Another patient spent many hours trying to recall and retrace her movements on the day in her childhood when an elderly friend had been found dead. She rehearsed the day's events in a vain attempt to achieve reassurance about her innocence. A third patient, an attorney with considerable responsibility, spent many hours ruminating over whether or not he might inadvertently have written something that would prejudice the trial of a man whom he had charged. Like the other patients, he spent many hours retracing his movements on the day in question and on subsequent occasions when he might have had access to the relevant case material. He needed to reassure himself that he had not carried out an injudicious action in one of his unguarded moments. In all of these examples, and in others not quoted here, the ruminative activity can be seen as a persistent, usually unsuccessful search for missing pieces of information that, if secured, would provide the desired reassurance.

According to Bartlett:

> The important characteristics of the thinking process . . . can now be stated: the process begins when evidence or information is available which is treated as possessing gaps, or as being incomplete. The gaps are then filled up, or that part of the information which is incomplete is completed. This is done by an extension or supplementation of the evidence, which remains in accord with the evidence (or claims to do so), but carries it further by utilizing other sources of information besides those which started the whole process going, and, in many instances, in addition to those which can be directly identified in the external surroundings. Between the initial information and the terminal stage, when the gaps are alleged to be filled, or completeness achieved, theoretically there are always a succession of interconnected steps. [1958, p. 75]

In Bartlett's terms, the patients are attempting to fill in the critical gaps. If we approach the problem in this manner, the relevant question, or questions, can be rephrased. We might begin to ask, for example, why obsessional patients find it so hard to obtain or retrieve the missing piece of information. Another way of looking at it is to ask why, even if they have the missing piece of information, obsessional patients fail to bring the thought process to what Bartlett may have called its "inevitable" conclusion. They seem incapable of achieving completeness. Remember, too, that the provision of missing information by an outside party will not necessarily bring an obsessional thought to a conclusion. Unfortunately, Bartlett's writings provide little guidance on this question, since he devoted most of his attention to the initiation and course of thought processes rather than to their conclusion.

We are suggesting that an improved understanding of the manner in which a thought process is brought to its inevitable conclusion, or is completed, might have a direct bearing on both the persistence of obsessional thoughts and ways in which *they* might be brought to a quicker and satisfactory conclusion. As a first step in this direction, it might be useful to determine whether the difficulty of completing obsessional thoughts is attributable to a difficulty in obtaining the missing pieces of information or whether for some unknown reason these people are unable to complete the thought even when all the pieces of information are available. The latter possibility seems the better approximation to obsessional difficulties.

THE RELEVANCE OF COGNITIVE PSYCHOLOGY

There have been regrettably few attempts to integrate our knowledge of obsessions into contemporary work on cognitive psychology. This discussion is offered more in the hope of providing a stimulus for integration than in the expectation that it will contribute to improved understanding of the phenomena of obsessions. Here we will consider the relevance of two selected themes in contemporary cognitive psychology: the need for a constructionist approach to thought and image formation and the need to postulate some kind of central filter mechanism.

The essence of the constructionist approach, in large part a reaction against the so-called reappearance hypothesis, is that each thought and image is a new construction. A prominent advocate of the constructionist hypothesis, Neisser (1967, 1976), argues against the notion that stored information "consists of ideas suspended in a quiescent state from which they are occasionally aroused" (1967, p. 281). He criticizes the idea that a thought or an image can disappear and reappear over and over again, or that it is stored in its original form and is available for retrieval under ordinary circumstances. He points out that precise repetition of any thought or image "is extremely difficult to achieve" and is a rare occurrence (p. 282). On the contrary, most thoughts and images "are not copies but suitably constructed originals . . . Verbal memory contains new rhythmic organizations rather than copies of stimuli . . . The words and sentences or normal speech are hardly ever duplicates of anything said earlier . . . Verbatim recall of a story occurs very rarely, while reorganization in line with the interests and values of the subject must be expected" (p. 282). Along similar lines, Pylyshyn (1973) has criticized the use of pictorial metaphors to describe images. He argues that images are propositional, not pictorial, and that they too are reconstructions rather than retrieved originals. The criticisms briefly noted here are substantial and persuasive, but it must be admitted at the outset that the weaknesses of the reappearance hypothesis are more evident than the strengths of the constructionist alternative (e.g., how can it account for "internal rotations"?).

Neisser (1967) proposes that stored information "consists of traces of previous constructed mental or overt actions" (p. 303). The construction of thoughts and images is a primary process in which crudely formed thoughts and images are briefly experienced, unless they undergo "elaboration by secondary processes." These secondary processes of "directed thought and deliberate recall are like focal attention in vision. They are serial in character, and construct ideas and images which are determined partly by stored information, partly by the preliminary organization of the primary processes, and partly by wishes and expectations. The executive control of thinking in the secondary process is carried out by a system analogous to the executive routine of a computer program" (p. 304).

There is nothing in this account that contradicts what we know of obsessions, but neither is it particularly enlightening. Also, the construction hypothesis encounters problems, many of them acknowledged by Neisser himself. For example, it is not clear what the raw materials of the constructive process are or how they are stored, and the important concept of the executive agency is left uncomfortably vague.

Neisser's treatment of imagery, despite its intrinsic interest, is rather disappointing from the point of view of the analyst of obsessions. Neisser argues that there are two main types of imagery, the first dealing with unrealistic, unpredictable and novel formations and the second consisting of practical images. These are characteristic of the secondary process of construction and serve normal adaptational functions, especially the provision of information at the time of recall. The function of the first type of image is left obscure. According to the hypothesis, images tend to be "tangential" to purposeful, anticipatory thinking (Neisser, 1976, p. 130). "Images are not reproductions or copies of earlier percepts, because perceiving is not a matter of having percepts in the first place. Images are not a picture in the head, but plans for obtaining information from potential environments" (Neisser, 1976, p. 131).

Even if Neisser is correct in describing images as tangential and anticipatory, neither adjective appears to accommodate the qualities of obsessional images. They are scarcely tangential, but occupy the center of the stage and tend to be irresistible. Nor is it possible to see how obsessional images can be regarded as plans for obtaining information. In the clinical example quoted earlier, one of our patients suffered from the repeated intrusion (or formation?) of an "internal picture" of a group of corpses lying in open coffins. Another patient suffered from repeated images of damaged fetuses. In neither case were the images tangential or anticipatory. Rather, they were characterized by their intrusiveness, unwantedness, and immovability—regrettably, the constructionist's interpretation adds little to our understanding of these qualities. If thought and image formation are constructive as opposed, say, to reproductive, then as far as obsessions are concerned it would appear to be a largely passive form of constructive activity—contrary to the implications of Neisser's view. Obsessional patients tend to suffer from their thoughts and images; they constitute an affliction rather than a constructive achievement. Obsessions are unwanted and, as we have seen, are experienced by most people at one time or another. Moreover, their intrusive quality leads one to think in terms of barriers, gates, or more specifically, filter theories.

Another slight difficulty with the constructionist view is that obsessions not only are intrusive but also have what might be called motion (i.e., they flow). In order to "clear one's mind," as for example in yoga, it appears necessary to practice assiduously and to exert considerable effort in an attempt to remove or exclude all unwanted thoughts in the hope of obtaining or retaining only the "shining light." The putative constructive processes have to be inhibited by active effort. It turns out to be far more difficult to achieve a thoughtless state than most teachers of unmotivated youths would have believed possible.

Some phenomenological aspects of obsessions are more easily accommodated in a filter theory of cognition. Broadbent's (1958) theory posits a central filtering mechanism that relays relevant messages but blocks irrelevant ones. Under stress the mechanism is disrupted (Broadbent, 1971), but (perhaps in compensation?) the filter itself becomes biased or selective. The complexities of filter theories were analyzed by Triesman (1969), who concluded that filtering decisions are based on the origin, amount, and quality of the incoming signals. The fact that obsessions are unwanted signifies a failure of the filter to block these images and thoughts. Before proceeding with this analysis, a major obstacle must be mentioned. Filter theories were designed to apply to the regulation of external stimulation; strictly, they are relevant to obsessions that are initiated by external stimulation. However, for our purposes this impediment will be bypassed even though it requires the further assumption that internally initiated obsessions can also be filtered. The assumption of internal initiation, although indispensable, is of course difficult to test satisfactorily. (Internal initiation of obsessions, and similar processes, remain mysterious—regrettably, we have little to offer as yet.) Nevertheless, even if the present analysis is found to apply mainly to externally initiated obsessions, it is worth remembering that clinical obsessions at least, whether internally or externally initiated, can be provoked at will and with ease. The main aim of analyzing obsessions in terms of a filter mechanism is the hope that by doing so we will achieve some clarity about the nature of the intrusiveness of these images and thoughts; it can tell us little or nothing about their immovability.

If we now proceed to regard the occurrence of an obsession as indicative of a biased filter, it becomes necessary to specify the conditions under which such biasing occurs. We know from the work of Broadbent that at least two kinds of stress, sleeplessness and noise, can produce such disruptions. We are now suggesting that dysphoria and psychological stress (anxiety?) are similarly capable of producing bias in the central filter.

Let us assume that this extension can be supported experimentally. We would then be left with a need to explain why the filter is paradoxically biased *toward* obsessional material rather than against it. In plain language, why should we become preoccupied with *unwanted* thoughts, especially during periods of stress? At present we can do little more than remind ourselves that highly significant material has easier access through the filter. In our terms, we might observe this as an increase in sensitivity to scenes of death, the sight of sharp objects, and so forth—especially during periods of dysphoria or psychological stress. If we are correct in postulating that obsessions traverse the filter because of their significance, and if we are also correct in postulating that under stress the bias of the filter moves toward significant material such as obsessions, then the question of psychological function reasserts itself. Why should significant material such as obsessions be "favored," and why should the bias increase under stress? As before, it all points, however uncertainly, towards some form of emotional processing. The filter mechanism facilitates the preferential processing of emotional material, including obsessions. It takes precedence.

In order to explore these notions, it will be necessary to extend the filter analysis of disruptive influences to include other stresses in addition to sleeplessness and noise, and to include the effects of various kinds of emotional factors on the filtering process. For example, is the capacity to exclude unwanted messages impaired in dysphoria? Does a frightening experience bias the filter towards or against fearful stimuli? Is the selective transmission of emotional messages a general attribute, or does it take place only under or after stress? Assuming that emotional messages do in fact take precedence under stress conditions, is it perhaps because they set up some form of tension and the organism then works to reduce it? We know from the work of Lang (1977) and others that exposure to stress may result in increased emotional processing. When a suitably predisposed person undergoes stress, his or her filter assumes a bias toward the emotional (including obsessional) material.

These and related questions are of course open to investigation, and established laboratory techniques such as the dichotic listening procedure can be utilized. For example, the emotional connotations of competing messages (including obsessions) can be manipulated and/or the same message can be relayed under varying mood states or varying stress experiences.

With regard to the constructionist view, it is not clear why or how dysphoria should affect the formation of images or thoughts. There is nothing in this view to preclude an explanation of dysphoric affects, but they have not so far featured in the theorizing in any significant manner. The intrusiveness of obsessions would be construed differently by constructionists and by proponents of a filter theory (unwanted formations versus unwanted messages), and presumably they would lead to different remedies. For a constructionist the task would be one of stifling the formation of an image or thought, while for a filter theorist the task would be one of improving the efficiency of the central filtering mechanism in blocking messages that produce obsessions.

MULTIPLE PROCESSING

Before considering the therapeutic implications of applying some of these cognitive concepts to the modification of obsessions, it is essential to take up the question of whether or not we are capable of having simultaneous thoughts and/or images. As Neisser (1967, 1976) points out, this ancient question can be reformulated. It seems certain that what Neisser calls "multiple processing" does occur; our processing capacities, however limited, do extend this far. In addition to compiling experimental evidence demonstrating the occurrence of multiple processing, Neisser draws attention to a number of everyday examples that appear to confirm the matter. For example, experienced drivers can carry on complicated discussions while shifting gears and steering; skilled pianists can shadow prose while reading from their music sheets; and so forth. Closer to our topic, Teasdale and Rezin (1977) have shown that negative thoughts can persist even through a flow of external information. Our capacities are limited, and multiple processing seems to require the inclusion of at least one highly practiced skill, but the sheer occurrence of multiple processes is of interest. From our point of view, acceptance of the view that people are capable of multiple processing is *essential* if we are to continue our exploration of the self-control of obsessional or other thoughts. Any attempt to achieve self-regulated control of thoughts or images, as opposed to externally controlled regulation, must be predicated on the belief that multiple processing can occur. All techniques for the self-control of thoughts involve the need to superimpose one cognitive activity upon another (i.e., the preferred activity over the unwanted activity). To state it positively, we can say that the successful accomplishment of a degree of self-control over an obsession demonstrates not only the occurrence of multiple processing but also its deliberate and purposeful manipulation.

Whether one construes obsessions within a constructionist framework or from the point of view of a filter theory, an obvious and relatively easy way to stifle the formation of obsessional images that are triggered by external cues is to cut off the stimulus. This can be achieved by blocking the cues (e.g., "Avert your eyes"), by removing them (e.g., "Hide the sharp objects"), or by removing oneself. If we assume that, multiple processing notwithstanding, we are capable of holding only one thought or image with high clarity at any particular moment, then the problem of dismissing an obsessional idea or image becomes one of *substitution*. (Naturally, blocking an internal cue is an altogether more difficult task.)

Leaving aside for the moment the possibility of producing a mental vacuum, an obsession has to be replaced rather than removed. The problem becomes one of arranging for the domination of thought A over thought B. As obsessions are essentially dominating, the question becomes one of dethroning the unwanted thought or image. As suggested earlier, the initiating and (possibly maintaining) stimulus can be removed. Also, a neutralizing activity or ritual (such as washing) can be carried out. Everyday possibilities include engaging in conversation, listening to music, watching television, and so on. What these methods have in common is the substitution of some new activity, either by excluding the provoking conditions or by introducing new intrusive conditions. Redirecting one's activities is perhaps the best tactic to adopt, and certainly the most obvious. The experimental redirection of obsessional activity using dichotic listening devices and other experimental methods is worth exploring.

As mentioned earlier, some therapeutic tactics are available; of these, habituation training and thought stopping are most pertinent. In passing, it is worth noticing that neither of these tactics rests on the assumption of an inherent limitation on multiple processing or on the assumption that nature abhors a mental vacuum.

THOUGHT CONTROL AND MEDITATION

Theoretically, the successful use of habituation training or thought stopping to *dismiss* an obsession could result in a period of relative blankness. Although these notions themselves border on the ruminative and pose apparently insoluble measurement problems, they are not entirely unrestrained. It is, for example, established that during states of meditation the electrical activity of the brain is altered and becomes distinct from either a normal sleep pattern or a normal resting, conscious record. Subjectively, we are told, the person is aware of a sense of tranquility and a stable but diffuse visual sensation (the shining light?). [The state of consciousness sometimes achieved by a period of intense meditation has been described as "a void," "blankness," or "no-thingness" (Tart, 1975).]

Either way, these meditative states, plausibly described as states of wakeful rest, are accompanied by distinct physiological changes (Wallace and Benson, 1972). There is a marked decline in oxygen consumption, an increase in the electrical resistance of the skin, an increase in the intensity of slow alpha EEG waves, a marked decline in heart rate, and so on. According to Koestler he meditative state achieved by practiced yogis can be induced by various means, including respiratory and muscular maneuvers, repetitive invocations, drugs, and so forth. Whichever method is used, the process appears to be powerfully facilitated by the guidance of a guru and by extensive practice. As a possible source of information about how to prevent or remove unwanted obsessional ideas, yoga, Zen, and other meditative exercises are worth reconsidering. In this connection the emphasis placed on the exclusion of external stimulation is particularly interesting, bearing in mind the discussion of distracting tactics based on the introduction of external stimulation. Koestler quotes Gandhi as saying that "virtue lies in being absorbed in one's prayers in the presence of din and noise" (p. 141). Naturally, one would not wish to encourage an obsessional patient to remain absorbed in his or her obsessions—it is the improved self-control of thoughts that is of interest here.

Certainly, the description of and research into states of meditation show that, given the correct training, at least some people are capable of exerting a great degree of control over the frequency, duration, and content of their thoughts and images. It is not outlandish to suppose that knowledge of the nature and induction of meditative states will prove helpful in achieving improved control over the intrusive, unwanted thoughts that we define as obsessions.

SECTION C

Chapter 21

Psychological Modification: Developing a Method

It is pleasing to record that during the past five to ten years significant advances have been made in coming to grips with the intractability of these disorders. For the first time psychologists are in possession of a treatment program—exposure and response prevention—that is demonstrably successful in reducing the difficulties of most, but by no means all, obsessional patients. On average, the improvements are moderate to marked, but a significant minority of people are free of obsessional problems at the conclusion of their training program. The outstanding questions can be grouped into two broad categories: How can the failures be averted, and what is the mechanism of change?

Despite this welcome turn of events, the style of research carried out so far is disquieting, and we are apprehensive about the consequences of continuing along the same path in the future. Almost all of the research (including our own) was based on three major but unstated assumptions that we now regard as dubious: (1) that the medical model is suitably applied to obsessional-compulsive disorders; (2) that generalized measures of outcome, usually based on the first assumption, are suitably applied to assessing outcomes; and (3) that obsessional disorders are appropriately construed within a "lump model."

If these assumptions are set aside, as we would prefer, then the formulation, delivery, and assessment of psychological methods of modification can be improved. We are, however, bound by the available information and the methods currently in use; rather than reject what we have, the results of current, conventional research and clinical practice are taken at face value and evaluated on their own terms. However, after we have concluded this conventional analysis of the evidence, the three assumptions will be described and their weaknesses identified. An alternate frame of reference that will, we hope, prove more fruitful and more satisfactory will then be presented.

Although there is a significant spontaneous-remission rate in obsessional-compulsive disorders, it probably is lower than that observed in other neurotic disorders (Rachman and Wilson, 1979). In practical terms this means that the majority of people who develop obsessional-compulsive disorders need professional assistance in overcoming their problems. While psychotherapy often is recommended as the "treatment of choice," there is little evidence on which to base such advice. Physical treatment methods, ranging from the radical (psychosurgery) to the benign (e.g., tranquilizers), have been tried with varying success (see Chapter 8).

The psychological approach to modifying obsessional-compulsive disorders has much to recommend it. First, there is growing evidence of its therapeutic value. Second, it is acceptable to the majority of patients. Third, it produces few unwanted changes (so-called side effects). Fourth, the steps are clearly specifiable and, hence, can be taught and replicated. Fifth, it is continuous and congruent with similar forms of treatment that have been used with success in dealing with similar disorders. Sixth, while the approach still lacks a comprehensive and satisfactory theory, the working rationale is plausible and capable of further development.

Rather than follow the customary pattern of cataloging all the earlier clinical work in chronological sequence, we hope to make it easier for readers to learn about the roots and nature of the current work by adopting a different style of presentation. Although the bulk of the clinical and research work on the subject has been carried out in the short space of the past twenty years, assessing its significance is made difficult by the mass of small details already reported and by the variety of treatment methods used. Comparisons between reports on the effects of different methods of treatment are awkward, and deliberate replications are rare. In an attempt to facilitate an examination of the data, we have provided a frame of reference within which the accumulation of details can be contemplated. Recognizing that this course might lead to a distorted presentation of the evidence, we have provided a good deal of detail and a full reference list. After the frame of reference has been presented, short descriptions of the major methods of treatment and some case illustrations are given. We then trace the growth of the methods and give the results of our own connected series of controlled studies. These findings are then related to those reported by workers in various parts of the world, and some theoretical and practical conclusions are offered. Ignoring chronology, we then turn to the rich store of case studies, most of them reported in the period from 1960 to 1970, with a view to interpreting them in terms of our newly available knowledge. The sequence of these treatment chapters is as follows: the frame of reference, current methods, case illustrations, antecedents, our controlled trials, other trials, conclusions, and reinterpretation of older case studies.

A FRAME OF REFERENCE

For many years psychological analyses of *fear* were conducted in the belief that fear can best be construed as a unitary phenomenon. This "lump theory" is now being replaced by a more complex conception, originally proposed by Lang (1969), according to which fear can be thought of as comprising a set of loosely coupled components.

Although the Langian conception has thus far been applied mainly to fear and pain (Philips, 1977), it has wider implications that include the nature of obsessions and compulsions. The most immediate extension of this new conception of fear to the analysis of obsessions and compulsions comes into the examination of what we earlier called phobic compulsions, but it does not stop there. Although most of the reasoning involved in our use of Lang's conception is based on the phenomenon of fear, much of it can be applied with success to obsessional-compulsive behavior. If, like phobias, obsessions and compulsions are construed as comprising three major components, we can then ask which of the three is most (or least) affected by any particular treatment. Secondly, we can observe whether therapeutic changes in the three components occur synchronously or desynchronously. Instead of asking whether a particular treatment X produces a therapeutic change, we can begin to ask what types of changes it produces and whether they are synchronous or not. When the question of effectiveness is altered in this way, the immediate answer is that cognitive treatments should produce the largest and quickest changes in the cognitive component; direct behavioral treatments should produce the largest and quickest change in overt behavior; and so on. Further discussions of the three-systems approach are given in Hodgson and Rachman (1974), Rachman and Hodgson (1974), and Rachman (1978d).

The application of a three-systems analysis to the problems of obsessions and compulsions leads to the following expectations: Treatment methods that place greatest emphasis on direct modification of behavior will produce the largest and quickest changes in the frequency, rate, and intensity of compulsive behavior. Treatments, such as drugs, that are directed mainly at the psychophysiological disturbance fall outside the present discussion, but one can predict their effects. The successful damping of the physiological disturbances reported by a majority of obsessional-compulsive patients should produce secondary reductions in discomfort and avoidance, but these may well be dependent on continued drug use. The third option, treatments that are aimed at modifying the patient's cognitions about the disorder, should, of course, result first in cognitive improvements; these are likely to be followed by changes in the other two major components. Broadly speaking, cognitive treatments can hope to achieve one, preferably both, of the following aims. The treatment can attempt to change the informational (warning) value of the relevant obsessional-compulsive stimuli and/or increase the person's perceived self-efficacy or coping skills.

THE TREATMENT/TRAINING METHOD

The method that we have helped to develop places greatest emphasis on direct behavioral change and comprises two major elements: (1) exposure to the provoking stimuli followed by (2) response prevention. Where possible, the exposure to the provoking stimuli is preceded by therapist *modeling*, and the whole process is done as rapidly as the patient can tolerate it without undue discomfort. The response prevention instructions are repeatedly emphasized. At all stages of the treatment, considerable encouragement and praise are provided, and the patient is required to take an active part in the planning and timing of each stage of the program.

All training (treatment) programs are of course preceded by clinical interviews, data collection, and behavioral analysis. On the basis of this information, the content and timing of the exposure sessions are determined in consultation with the patient. After watching the therapist and at least one other model engage the provoking situation or stimuli, the patient is encouraged gradually to imitate their behavior. Neither the model nor the patient should carry out any undoing (neutralizing) compulsive rituals (e.g., washing their hands) on completion of the exposure experience. Whenever appropriate, the models explain to the patient that coming into contact with the provoking stimuli provokes some discomfort but that the required behavior is completed despite this uneasiness.

Although the response prevention instructions are emphasized, no external supervision is provided unless this is essential (in our experience it is rarely necessary). The treatment briefly described so far is applicable to patients who display at least some overt compulsive behavior. Different methods are required for dealing with problems of primary obsessional slowness and obsessions unaccompanied by behavioral difficulties.

Treatment sessions last an average of approximately thirty minutes, with the earlier sessions being longer than the concluding ones. As the patient begins to make progress, more and more of the responsibility for planning and conducting the exposure and response prevention is handed over to him or her. Moreover, the treatment maneuvers are almost always carried out not only in the clinic but also in the person's own home. Indeed, in some cases (notably obsessional checkers) the greatest part of the treatment is carried out in the patient's home environment. Wherever possible, the cooperation of members of the family and close friends is recruited. However, we do not favor the active involvement of spouses and close relatives in executing the most difficult and distressing parts of the treatment; these most often occur early in the treatment program. A guide to treatment is provided by Hodgson and Rachman (1976).

The method used by Meyer and his colleagues (e.g., Meyer, Levy, and Schnurer, 1974) incorporates the same two elements of exposure and response prevention—but with different emphases. Their patients are given far more extensive training in response prevention, almost always under direct supervision. Other methods that have been attempted include thought stopping (e.g., Hackmann and McClean, 1975) and aversion relief (e.g., Solyom et al., 1971).

The therapist should promote therapeutic changes in all three components, where applicable. An ideal therapy is one that is capable of inducing therapeutic changes in all three components.

CASE ILLUSTRATIONS

A 37-year-old engineer complained of elaborate, time-consuming, and occasionally bizarre cleaning rituals accompanied by extensive and distressing avoidance behavior. He had an abhorrence (and possibly fear) of semen that compelled him to carry out prolonged and meticulous cleaning rituals whenever he ejaculated. All of his sexual activities had to be confined to a "sterile" room that was never used for any other purpose. The patient and his sexual partner had to undress and wash before entering the room and, of course, clean themselves immediately upon leaving it. The patient avoided entire suburbs of London and some coastal towns because they had at one time or another been contaminated. His difficulties had arisen in early adulthood and continued unchanged for fifteen years.

As is customary, the patient was given an explanation of obsessional-compulsive disorders and their course. The rationale of modeling-exposure treatment and response prevention was explained again (even though he had been given a similar explanation in the out-patient clinic before deciding to enter the treatment program). During the first two sessions, he passively observed the therapist touching test tubes containing semen specimens and objects of clothing containing semen stains. While it was explained that engaging in these maneuvers produced some slight discomfort in the therapist, the "contamination" was disseminated by the therapist rubbing the contaminated garments and test tube semen specimens on his clothing and hands. As usual, the therapist said that, for purposes of the treatment, he would refrain from cleaning away the contamination and would not diverge from his normal washing patterns.

In the third session the patient was encouraged to imitate as much of the therapist's contaminating behavior as possible, beginning by touching and then holding the test tube specimens. By the fifth session he was gingerly wiping the contaminated objects over his belongings and helping to spread the contamination into various parts of the ward. During the second week of treatment, the therapist model was gradually faded out and the patient was encouraged to accept increasing responsibility for designing and executing the next steps in his program. During the final sessions of treatment, he was given two contamination-spreading sessions in his own home, including the sterile room, and encouraged to carry a semen-contaminated handkerchief with him on all occasions and excursions. He was told to use every reasonable opportunity to spread the contamination from the handkerchief into his natural environment. It was emphasized that this was especially important whenever he felt a resurgence of abhorrence or fear, or an urge to carry out cleaning rituals. If, for example, he found himself reluctant to touch a "clean" object, he was to contaminate it with his semen handkerchief immediately. His treatment program included visits to places and people he had been avoiding for many years.

The response prevention part of the treatment program was explained and introduced during the first session. The patient was asked to refrain from all abnormal cleaning and washing and to restrict himself to "normal" washing, which for him meant washing his hands before meals, after urinating or defecating, and cleaning his hands, face, and teeth in the mornings and evening. He had a brief bath or shower each day.

The patient appeared to derive some benefit from the modeling demonstrations, and the transition to participant modeling was smooth, even though he experienced considerable anxiety and abhorrence during his early contacts with semen. Despite his apprehensions about the difficulties of coping with semen in his own home, the domiciliary part of the treatment proceeded uneventfully. Not surprisingly, it took a little while for him to achieve a relaxed state during contaminating sexual activities. After one or two minor failures, he gradually overcame his compulsion to avoid various geographic areas in and out of London.

Although no psychophysiological recordings were made, the patient displayed marked decrements in observable emotional reactions to contamination; his avoidance behavior was eliminated; and he expressed confidence in his ability to deal satisfactorily with both the subjective and the behavioral aspects of his problem. All three systems were successfully modified.

This program for treatment of a "phobic compulsion" was comparatively uneventful, helped no doubt by the fact that the patient was intelligent and highly motivated to change.

Our second illustration is of a 55-year-old man who complained of elaborate, repetitive, prolonged stereotyped checking behavior that seriously interfered with his life and threatened to result in his dismissal from a job that he had held for many years. Before leaving his apartment each day, he had repeatedly to carry out hundreds of stereotyped checking rituals designed to ensure that the windows were securely shut, that the taps were not dripping, that the stove was off, that the front door was secure, and so on. It took him up to four hours to complete these checks before leaving the apartment. Consequently, he had to rise very early on workdays and, because of the strain and effort involved, was extremely reluctant to leave the apartment on other days. As his checking compulsions were confined mainly to his own home, the treatment was carried out on a domiciliary basis. The therapist made several visits to the apartment and repeatedly demonstrated how to prepare to leave in less than ten minutes, explaining each action and its rationale as she did it. The patient was then encouraged to model the therapist's behavior. After expressing surprise and even dismay at the therapist's style and speed, he gradually approximated the desired behavior. As usual, he was told to refrain from carrying out any ritualistic behavior after completing the necessary preparations for leaving. He made steady and rewarding progress and learned how to keep his checking to an acceptable minimum and how to leave his apartment within 15 minutes. However, during the closing stages of the treatment and in the follow-up period he needed a good deal of prompting, monitoring, and praise from the therapist. For practical reasons most of this was provided by conversations on the telephone. The general therapeutic outcome was good, and the patient was able to continue living an independent, productive life instead of requiring long-term institutional care.

Our third case illustrates a failure. This patient, a 36-year-old cobbler, had been carrying out repetitive checking rituals over a period of eight years. He felt compelled to inspect any speck of brown, especially on his clothes or person, in order to confirm that it was not excrement. All brown and dark objects and materials provoked intense and prolonged bursts of checking. His rituals were intrusive, pervasive, agitated, and intolerable and had come to dominate his life. Each day he carried out hundreds of checking rituals, many of them purely visual. Despite repeatedly watching the therapist come into contact with excrement contamination and many dubious brown spots, his abhorrence and anxiety were not abated. Although he was able to reduce the frequency of his checking behavior for comparatively short periods of an hour or so, he never succeeded in preventing the compulsive behavior—even when provided with considerable additional support from the therapist. At the completion of the experimental period, he was unimproved and was therefore given a great deal of further treatment. Regrettably, this also proved to be ineffective.

These brief treatment reports illustrate the two main elements in the treatment (i.e., modeling-exposure and response prevention). The method used by Dr. Meyer at the Middlesex Hospital incorporates both of these elements, but with different emphasis. Meyer's patients are required to participate in a prolonged period of supervised response prevention. The aim is to suppress all of the compulsive rituals, if possible. This response prevention period is continuous, and close supervision is provided throughout the day and, when needed, during the night as well. At the same time (or afterwards), the patient is exposed to provoking stimulation, be it contaminated material or activities that ordinarily provoke strong urges to check. During these exposure periods the therapist emphasizes the importance of not resuming the checking or other compulsive rituals—and in order to ensure that no retreat occurs, close supervision is provided until such time as it is felt that the danger has passed. It is fair to say that the emphasis in Meyer's treatment is on the response side, while our treatment lays more stress on the stimulus input.

Meyer, Levy, and Schnurer (1974) give this description of their method: "The treatment itself involved continual supervision during the patient's waking hours by nurses who were instructed to prevent the patient from carrying out any rituals . . . As soon as the total elimination of rituals under supervision was achieved, the therapist increased the stress where appropriate by confronting the patient with situations which normally elicited rituals" (pp. 246-47). Their case 9, a middle-aged woman who had a fear of contamination by dust, was treated according to this plan. "Restriction of rituals was attempted in the usual way. She was given a single room and made responsible for keeping it clean but was only allowed to spend a few minutes a day to do so. She was then gradually exposed to dust, made to shake a duster out of her window and eventually in her room" (p. 254). "In order to control the dust, she had developed elaborate rituals which involved extensive house-cleaning, dusting and the fanatical use of a vacuum cleaner which was employed to free both herself and her husband of dust."

As these extracts show, Meyer's method and our own share at least two important elements—exposure and response prevention. However, Meyer places greater stress on the response prevention aspect (hence the use of continual supervision), and his treatment sequence sometimes is the reverse of ours.

DEVELOPMENT OF THE METHOD

The important progress achieved by behavior therapists in treating phobias, beginning with Wolpe's pioneering work in the 1950s, was not matched by comparable advances in our ability to modify obsessional-compulsive disorders. In particular, the most widely used antiphobic weapon, desensitization, proved to be unwieldy and not satisfactory for dealing with obsessions and compulsions. In the early 1970s, however, a significant change occurred. Now, for a majority of people suffering from obsessional-compulsive disorders, participating in a program of behavioral treatment will help them achieve substantial relief and benefits.

This advance occurred as a result of a combination of several events and influences. In the first place, there was a shift in emphasis in treatment programs provided for phobics, from imaginal presentations to *in vivo* exposures. This change in emphasis, in turn, was influenced by claims that *implosion* was capable of producing large and rapid clinical improvements (Stampfl, 1967; Rachman, 1969). Several research workers and therapists, such as Marks, experimented with *in vivo* presentations of "implosive" stimuli and obtained some encouraging results. At approximately the same time and for some common reasons, research workers began to show renewed interest in the therapeutic possibilities of flooding (i.e., relatively prolonged exposure to high-intensity stimulation). This growing interest was boosted by the methodical animal research carried out by Baum (1970) on the effects of response prevention. Before long, attempts were being made to reduce people's fears by exposing them to intense stimulation for prolonged periods while discouraging attempts at escape.

Bandura's (1969) revival of the concept of imitation and his development of social-learning theory were soon followed by the appearance of therapeutic modeling procedures (see Bandura, Blanchard, and Ritter, 1969; Rachman, 1976c)—one of the first methods to produce a result that exceeded the fear-reducing effects of desensitization (Bandura, Grusec, and Menlove, 1967). Like flooding, therapeutic modeling is almost always carried out *in vivo*.

Bearing in mind the now-evident similarities between phobias and certain types of obsessional-compulsive disorders, it was inevitable that these new fear-reducing techniques would be recruited in a fresh assault on unyielding obsessions and compulsions. Therapists also drew valuable encouragement and advice from Meyer's (1966) instructive report of his success in treating two seriously handicapped patients.

Meyer explained his results in this way:

> The favorable outcome in both patients is consistent with the . . . rationale . . . adopted. Two aspects of the treatment are deemed as important: the realization by the patients that persistent nonperformance of rituals did not lead to the immediate experience of unchecked arousal of anxiety; the patients' expectations of "disastrous consequences" were not fulfilled. The main purpose of the treatment was the modification of the patients' expectations and some evidence, admittedly based only on the patients' verbal reports, indicates that this was achieved to some degree. One may assume that a completely successful modification of expectations would lead to a complete elimination of ritualistic behavior. [p. 280]

In conclusion, he emphasized that the "therapeutic approach adopted here requires that the treatment be intensive and a strict control over patients' behavior exerted" (p. 280).

This therapeutic injunction does not necessarily follow from his rationale, and despite the lukewarm interest shown in the rationale, the method was copied. Ironically, Bandura's (1977) theory of behavior change comes close to Meyer's early but undeveloped explanation. Although Meyer argued that his treatment was not uneconomical in terms of time, he nevertheless expressed the hope that the method might be refined and made more efficient. His desire that research workers and other practitioners "will consider and take up this method of treatment" has of course been fulfilled in part, but that part has proved unusually rewarding.

Our own interest in the modification of obsessions and compulsions antedated the developments described here, but like other clinical research workers we had had scant success with the traditional behavioral-treatment techniques. While engaged in conducting research into the fear-reducing mechanisms of flooding and implosion (Hodgson and Rachman, 1970), we decided to test the value of these methods during the course of our protracted attempts to help three severely disabled obsessional-compulsive patients.

The first, a married woman in her mid-30s, feared contamination by dirt and engaged in extremely extensive avoidance behavior, even to the extent of being unable to visit entire regions of the country. We constructed a hierarchy in the usual way and attempted to treat her with conventional systematic desensitization. She made little progress, so we decided to present the contaminated objects *in vivo* while the patient was in a relaxed state. At last she began to make progress, but at such a slow rate that the prognosis for her eventual recovery was scarcely altered. In an attempt to accelerate the therapeutic process, we started to use modeling procedures. This did achieve a slight increase in the patient's rate of improvement, but it was still inadequate, considering the intensity and extent of her problems. As she was unwilling to participate in *in vivo* flooding sessions, we tried imaginal presentations. She found these too distressing, and little progress was made. Under direct instructions from us, she was able to reduce the frequency and intensity of her cleaning rituals to some extent, but the reduction was not sufficient to be of value as a step toward full rehabilitation.

The second patient had been severely disabled for the greater part of her adult life by an extremely intense fear of cancer. In order to protect herself and others from contamination, she engaged in prolonged and intensive washing and disinfecting rituals. In particular, she washed and disinfected her hands hundreds of times each day—and this pattern persisted despite the marked excoriation and occasional bleeding of her hands. The fact that the water in which she was washing her hands was bloody was no deterrent; it was more important for her to disinfect herself, and all the objects that she touched, in a way that ensured protection from cancer.

Both of these patients had undergone leucotomies, from which they appear to have derived slight but transient benefits. In both patients systematic desensitization proved ineffective. Imaginal flooding and imaginal implosion scenes were similarly ineffective. When we turned to *in vivo* modeling and exposure, however, the cancer-phobic patient began to show signs of progress for the first time. Because of the intense anxiety that contact with "cancerous" (but safe) items provoked, her progress was slow and laborious. Contact produced so much agitation that she was left with extremely powerful urges to carry out her cleaning rituals. With a great deal of encouragement and support, she was able to reduce her ritualistic behavior markedly—but unfortunately she finally decided that the whole procedure was too stressful to endure, and we reluctantly agreed that it was not suitable for her. From this case study, however, we drew the tentative conclusion that whereas exposure with modeling and response prevention was capable of producing changes in an intractable disorder, imaginal presentations, implosive or gradual, were relatively ineffective.

The third member of this severely disturbed trio, a man in his early 20s, was frightened of dirt and engaged in excessive and extensive cleaning rituals. He had already undergone a modified leucotomy (with some resulting reduction in tension), but a mere six months later he was being considered for a second operation. Although we made false starts with this patient, as we had with the other two, the eventual outcome was satisfactory (Rachman, Hodgson, and Marzillier, 1970).

The results obtained with these patients, and the poor results obtained with earlier methods of treatment, encouraged our belief that modeling-exposure and response prevention might prove to be a sufficiently powerful combination to overcome even such an unyielding disorder as obsessional-compulsive disturbances. We were reinforced in this view by successes achieved with additional patients who had similar but less severe difficulties, and began to feel a growing optimism. At this stage we joined forces with Dr. I. Marks, who had already made important progress in the application of flooding procedures to phobic disorders, and later we were joined by Dr. G. Röper, who played the major part in the fourth experiment.

Chapter 22

Psychological Modification: Controlled Studies

Four connected experimental studies were carried out in the following sequence. In the first place, we compared modeling and flooding treatments (Rachman, Hodgson, and Marks, 1971). The next stage was to compare the effects of each of these methods acting separately with a treatment program that combined modeling and flooding (Hodgson, Rachman, and Marks, 1972). The third experiment (Rachman, Marks, and Hodgson, 1973) was an attempt to replicate the major findings obtained in the first two studies. The fourth experiment was designed to determine the extent to which passive and participant modeling experiences contributed to the therapeutic outcome (Röper, Rachman, and Marks, 1975). The fifth and largest experimental trial, a Medical Research Council project directed by Marks and Rachman and now in the follow-up stage, is intended as a replication and development of these earlier studies. In addition, we are investigating the supplementary value of prescribing an antidepressant drug, clomipramine.

THE FIRST CLINICAL STUDY

Our first trial (Rachman, Hodgson, and Marks, 1971) was designed to test the therapeutic value of behavioral treatments compared to a relaxation control treatment. A second aim was to make a preliminary comparison of the effects of participant modeling treatment and flooding.

The study was carried out on 10 moderately to severely incapacitated chronic obsessional-compulsive patients who had been in serious difficulty for at least 1 year and had already received psychiatric treatment of one kind or another. In this first study, as in subsequent ones in this series, we included patients who displayed overt compulsive behavior; those who complained of obsessions unaccompanied by compulsions (a small minority) were investigated separately. Six of the 10 patients in the first trial were unable to work, and two others were severely disabled. The remaining 2 were able to work, but only with considerable difficulty. As a measure of the seriousness of their difficulties, in half of the cases consideration had been given to the possibility of carrying out a leucotomy. In addition to the 10 patients included in our trial, another 7 were interviewed but excluded for the following reasons: Two of them were unwilling to accept a 7-week stay in a hospital; 2 had disorders that were too mild to warrant admission to a hospital; 1 discharged herself within 12 hours of admission; 1 had no overt compulsions; and 1 became severely depressed before entering the trial. The average duration of the problem for our group of 10 patients was 10 years, and their mean age was 35.

The basic plan of the study, followed in the succeeding investigations, was as follows: After selection at an out-patient interview, arrangements were made for a person to be admitted to the hospital. In the first week of their stay in the hospital, detailed observations and measurements were taken. During the next 3 weeks, they were seen every weekday for approximately 45 minutes per session. During this stage of the study, they received relaxation control treatment. Before entering the next 3-week stage of the treatment, they were assessed. Each patient was then allocated randomly to one of two behavioral treatments (i.e., flooding or participant modeling). At the conclusion of this 3-week period of treatment, they were reassessed. Those who required further treatment at the end of the experimental period received it. Hence, the reassessments carried out after the 3-month, 6-month, and 2-year follow-up periods do not give a direct indication of the effects of the control and experimental treatments uncontaminated by additional treatment.

Further information about the treatment and assessment procedures, and the detailed statistical analyses, are provided in the original report by Rachman, Hodgson, and Marks (1971). The major findings arising out of the two central questions are illustrated in Figures 22.2 and 22.3. On all the important comparisons, both forms of behavioral treatment were more efficacious than the control treatment. With the exception of the patients' reports on their own anxiety, the changes observed after flooding or modeling treatment could not be distinguished from one another. In statistical terms, they were equally effective. As may be seen from the figures, however, the improvement observed after participant modeling was slightly larger. It was, of course, in the nature of the experimental design that all patients received the relaxation control treatment

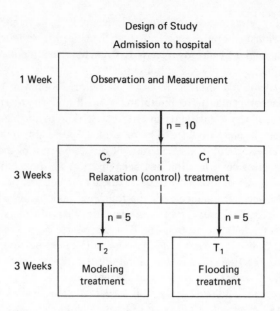

Design of Study

Admission to hospital

1 Week	Observation and Measurement

n = 10

3 Weeks	C_2 C_1 Relaxation (control) treatment

n = 5   n = 5

3 Weeks	T_2 Modeling treatment	T_1 Flooding treatment

FIGURE 22.1.   Experimental design of the first treatment experiment.

first. As earlier research (e.g., Boulougouris et al., 1971) consistently shows that in clinical trials of this character the first treatment is usually followed by larger changes than subsequent ones, it is improbable that the treatment effect was a result of a delayed order effect.

In a vain attempt to identify prognostic factors, we correlated 21 pretreatment variables with 5 outcome criteria, but no pointers emerged. We were, however, left with some clear clinical impressions. Some patients failed to improve despite high motivation and adequate cooperation, while others benefited from the treatment despite poor motivation and cooperation. Two patients who showed substantial improvement in the hospital setting but much less satisfactory improvement at home drew attention to the importance of including some domiciliary treatment.

During the follow-up period, 5 patients required a mean of 5 extra treatment sessions. Three required no further treatment upon completion of the experimental trial period, but 2 received more than 20 additional sessions in the hospital and at home. At the first follow-up checkpoint, 3 months after completion of the experimental treatment period, the improvements remained comparatively steady. The longer-term fate of these patients is described later.

The results of this study justified further research. Although disappointed by our 2 clear-cut failures out of 10, we were encouraged by the extent and speed of the improvements observed in the majority of our patients.

The absence of any demonstrable difference between the effects of flooding and those of participant modeling presented interesting questions. An

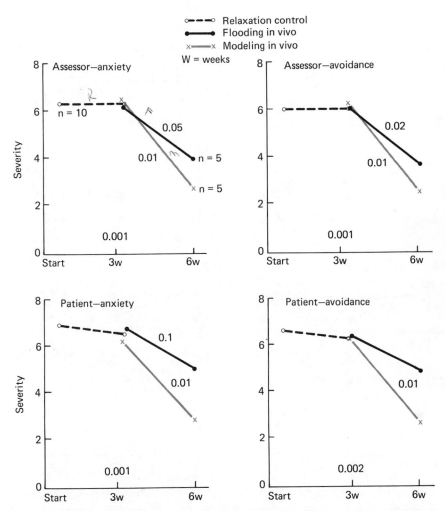

FIGURE 22.2. Change in assessor and patient ratings of obsessional anxiety and avoidance.

obvious possibility was that both methods were acting through a common factor, one that might also be present in Meyer's (1966) technique. In all three methods the patients are exposed, in the therapist's presence, to real-life situations that evoke discomfort and/or anxiety and are then discouraged or actively prevented from undoing the consequences of this exposure. Our view at the time was that these common features suggest that the improvement might be occurring at least partly through habituation to the discomfort-producing stimulation. The progress of this idea is taken up in Chapter 24 and again in Chapter 25.

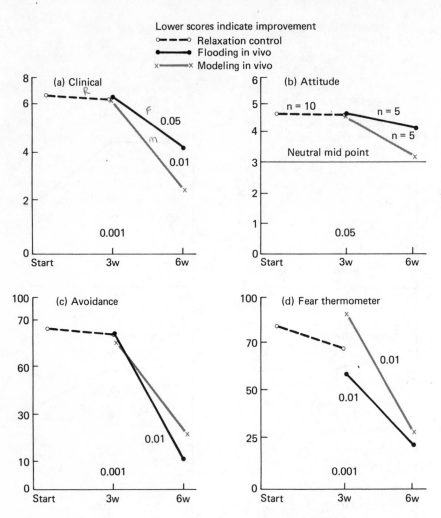

Lower scores indicate improvement
- o----o Relaxation control
- •——• Flooding in vivo
- x——x Modeling in vivo

FIGURE 22.3. Summary of changes in clinical ratings, attitudes, avoidance, and fear.

THE SECOND CLINICAL STUDY

Although our first study showed that flooding and participant modeling did not differ in their therapeutic effects, both of them were significantly more effective than the relaxation control treatment. Naturally, we then considered the possibility that flooding and participant modeling *together* might achieve more than either of them separately, in terms of both the speed and the magnitude of their therapeutic effects. So the major aim of our second study was to determine whether the combined effects of the two behavioral methods might be greater than the effects of each applied separately. At the same time, of course, we planned to gather further information about the general effectiveness of behavioral-modification methods in overcoming obsessional-compulsive disorders.

For this second study we selected 5 more chronic obsessional-compulsive patients drawn from the same general pool as the original group. The mean age of this second group was 32, and the mean duration of their problem was 8 years. Four of the 5 had received psychiatric treatment, and 1 had been considered a candidate for leucotomy.

The detailed results and computations are provided in the original paper (Hodgson et al., 1972). For present purposes the figures summarizing the changes provide the major points of interest. Figures 22.4 and 22.5 show the results obtained from the first 15 patients (i.e., the original 10 plus the 5 who received the combined modeling/flooding treatment).

FIGURE 22.4.   Changes in measures of obsessional problems.

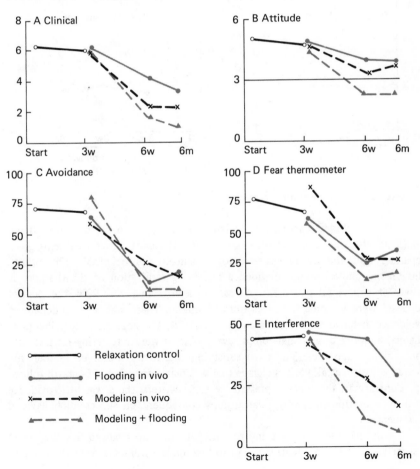

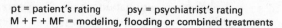

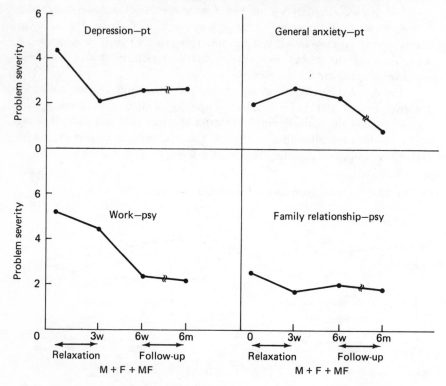

FIGURE 22.5.   Course of other problems.

The combined participant modeling/flooding treatment produced therapeutic results that were slightly better than those of either treatment given
separately, but the differences were not statistically significant. More important,
this second clinical study provided a reassuring replication of the therapeutic
power of behavioral treatment. As can be seen from Figure 22.4, the changes
achieved were in some instances quite dramatic. There was a steep decline in
avoidance behavior and associated anxiety/fear. Attitudes showed a favorable
change, and the obsessional-compulsive problems were interfering far less with
the patients' activities. The most satisfying change was observed in their improved adjustment at work, a change that was maintained at the 6-month follow-
up. Contrary to the fears expressed by some writers, there was little evidence
of a deterioration in family relationships consequent on successful behavioral
treatment.

Although there was a trend for the patients who received flooding to do
less well at the end of treatment and follow-up, the numbers were too small to

carry out appropriate statistical tests. For the first 15 patients, the failure rate was 1 out of 3. Once again, our search for prognostic factors, using the method employed in the first study, was unsuccessful.

THE THIRD STUDY

In order to confirm the main effects, we carried out a replication of study 2 on 5 additional chronic obsessional-compulsive patients drawn from the same clinical population by the same methods of selection. These 5 patients were all treated by the participant modeling/flooding treatment, and there was of course no random allocation to treatment group. Happily, the results achieved with these 5 patients were consistent with those obtained in the first two studies. The full details of this study, including detailed statistical analyses, can be found in Rachman, Marks, and Hodgson (1973).

Of the 20 chronic patients treated in these first 3 studies, 13 responded very well to treatment, 1 moderately well, and 6 only slightly or not at all. The 15 patients who received 3 weeks of relaxation control treatment did not change at all on the measures of obsessional-compulsive disorder, although they did experience some improvement in depression and anxiety. The results for all 20 patients are conveniently summarized in Figure 22.6, where it can be seen that, in contrast to the clinical value of the relaxation control treatment, the behavioral treatments produced rapid and steep improvements. These changes were evident in clinical ratings, behavioral-avoidance tests, discomfort/fear ratings, attitudes, and social activities.

At that stage of the research, we were sufficiently confident to conclude that behavioral treatments are capable of reducing obsessional-compulsive complaints and behavior. The methods were clearly superior to relaxation control. Consistent improvement was obtained across measures (see Figure 22.6). The major changes occurred during the first 3 (experimental) weeks of treatment, and this improvement was maintained up to the 6-month follow-up period—although it must be remembered that additional treatment was provided as required after completion of the experimental phase. The patients and their relatives confirmed that the changes shown in the rating scales and other tests reflected a genuine decrease in obsessional-compulsive rituals, avoidance, and discomfort.

Six patients failed to benefit to any significant degree from the treatment provided. Five of these patients were unable to comply with the instructions to desist from engaging in rituals between sessions; it is just possible that some of these patients might have benefited from continuous supervision during treatment, along the lines advocated by Meyer's group. The sixth patient cooperated fully yet failed, for reasons which are not clear.

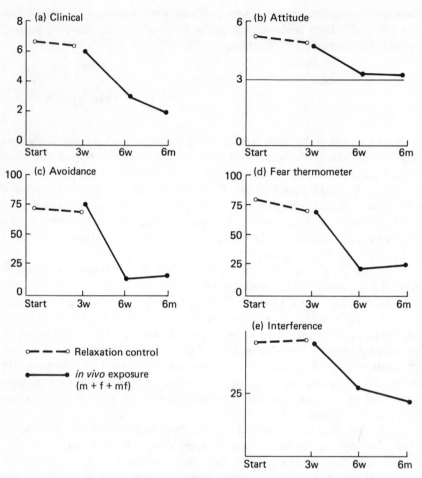

FIGURE 22.6. Changes on five measures as a result of relaxation (N=15) or modelling/ flooding treatment, all groups combined (N=20).

A second aim of these three studies was to explore the relative effectiveness of participant modeling and flooding. Few of the differences between the behavioral-treatment variations reached statistical significance. There were suggestions, however, that flooding produced more anxiety and slightly less improvement than participant modeling. Our clinical impression is that participant modeling is more easily accepted by patients. However, at this stage we had little reason to suppose that participant modeling would produce a superior outcome. Some of our patients said that they benefited from the modeling sessions, whereas others insisted that the sessions did not help. In addition to our impression that participant modeling is more acceptable to patients, we are firmly of the opinion that, at the very least, it facilitates exposure to the distressing stimuli. It also provides a simple, rapid, and efficient means of conveying to patients some of the more satisfactory alternative ways of cleaning themselves, ensuring the safety of their families and themselves, and so forth.

As we have pointed out, despite 3 attempts no useful prognostic indexes were detected. Our view is, however, that the most difficult patients in this group were those who complained of repetitive, *pervasive* checking rituals, often involving more than 100 checks per say. The patients with the best prognosis, based on our clinical impression, appear to be those with contamination fears and cleaning rituals that are focused on a restricted number of stimulus situations. To put it another way, patients whose disorders might be classified, in our terms, as "phobic-compulsive" respond best to this kind of treatment. Another impression that we gained from these 3 studies is that patients whose obsessional-compulsive problems have permeated almost all aspects of their lives are difficult to help.

CONDITION AT THE 2-YEAR FOLLOW-UP

All of the patients were reassessed 2 years after completion of the treatment; unfortunately, we could interview only 11 of the 20 (Marks, Hodgson and Rachman, 1975). For the 9 who were living outside London or were inaccessible for other reasons, only the self-rating and attitude scales were completed. In order to ensure that the patients who were interviewed did not constitute a significantly different subgroup, a retrospective cohort analysis was carried out. The results of this analysis (see Figure 22.7) show that the two groups were not significantly different. A pictorial summary of the 2-year results is provided in Figure 22.8.

The most striking feature of the results is how little change occurred after completion of the experimental treatment period. It turned out that the improvements achieved during the 3-week experimental treatment period were a good predictor of outcome at the 6- and 24-month follow-up points. The final figures for the 20 patients, grouped into the 3 categories used in the earlier parts of the study, were as follows: At the 2-year follow-up, 14 of the patients were classified as much improved, 1 as improved, and 5 as unchanged. One of the patients who had slipped back at 6 months, later made renewed progress and at the 2-year follow-up was classified as improved again. Although the actual experimental treatment period comprised 15 sessions, we did of course provide additional treatment when necessary. For the group as a whole, the mean number of experimental plus follow-up treatment sessions was 23. No patients dropped out during the trial (other than the one who discharged herself within 12 hours of entering the hospital), but one refused further domiciliary treatment after discharge.

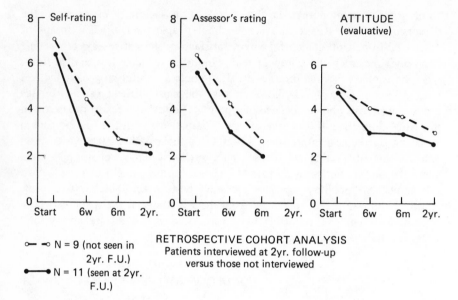

○─ ─○ N = 9 (not seen in
          2yr. F.U.)

●───● N = 11 (seen at 2yr.
          F.U.)

RETROSPECTIVE COHORT ANALYSIS
Patients interviewed at 2yr. follow-up
versus those not interviewed

FIGURE 22.7.   Changes in ratings of obsessional complaints for patients seen and those not interviewed at 2-year follow-up.

The original prognostic indexes were once again correlated with outcome data, this time at the 2-year follow-up. No meaningful pattern emerged. After 3 weeks of the experimental treatment, the concordance among clinical ratings, assessor ratings, and attitude measures was satisfactorily high. The behavioral-avoidance test results, however, correlated weakly with the clinical ratings. At the 6-month follow-up checkpoint, however, the concordance between avoidance test behavior and other measures had increased to a more significant level (see Hodgson and Rachman, 1974, prediction 4). The correlation matrix is provided in Marks, Hodgson, and Rachman (1975).

Bearing in mind the cautions necessary because of the acknowledged shortcomings of these studies, some tentative conclusions are in order. (The shortcomings include smallness of sample size, nonrandom allocation to participant modeling/flooding treatment for the last 10 patients, unrefined outcome measures, doubts about the credibility of the relaxation control treatment, and so on.) The behavioral treatments achieved wide-ranging and significant improvements in the majority of these chronic and moderately to very severe obsessional-compulsive patients. The maximum changes were achieved in a comparatively short time with a modest amount of therapist time. The treatment program had a high rate of acceptability and was well tolerated by the great majority of patients. There was a reasonable amount of concordance between outcome measures, with subjective and behavioral measures moving in the same direction (i.e., toward substantial improvement).

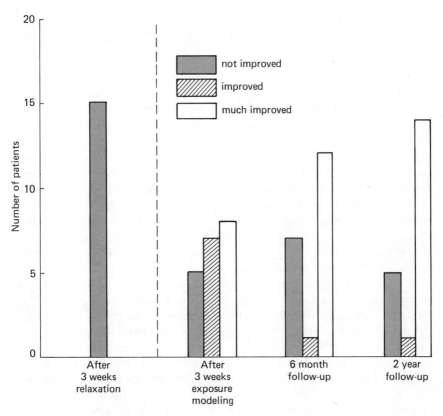

FIGURE 22.8.   Two-year follow-up. Number of patients improved on pooled self-ratings of obsessive anxiety and avoidance.

The clinical improvements were accompanied by a shift toward improvement in other aspects of the patients' lives. There was no case in which apparently successful treatment was followed by the appearance of either a substitute problem or a new disorder. The therapeutic changes were achieved without attempting to reshape or restructure the personalities of our patients— a direct attack on the obsessional-compulsive disorder characterizes the behavioral treatments used. The improvements observed at the end of the experimental treatment period were reassuringly stable, and at the time of the 2-year follow-up the majority of the patients were substantially better off than before undertaking the treatment. The major reason for our failures was the patients' inability to refrain from carrying out the rituals between treatment sessions and after sessions. There were some additional treatment failures outside of these treatment trials, in which the patient found the exposure to the contaminating or disturbing situation too distressing to tolerate. Luckily, the large majority of patients are able to tolerate this demanding form of treatment, particularly if suitable therapeutic support is provided.

We next turned our attention to an examination of the therapeutic properties of modeling. In particular, we were interested to learn whether the observed therapeutic effects were wholly or largely attributable to the patients' active participation in the contaminating experiences. We therefore designed an experiment to determine the relative contributions to therapeutic outcome made by the passive (symbolic) modeling aspects of treatment and the more active (participant) modeling aspects. Although we retained a practical interest in the contribution made by modeling, not least because it seemed to make treatment more acceptable for some patients, our primary interest was directed toward the theoretical questions stated earlier. Bandura (1969, 1977) attributes several important effects to therapeutic modeling. These include, among others, vicarious extinction of fear responses, transmission of useful information, and acquisition of adaptive new behavior.

It is easy to make a case for the operation of all three of these processes in our treatment program. Our earlier results had yielded evidence suggesting that after participant modeling treatment (coupled with response prevention), patients reported a reduction of fear and/or discomfort. Furthermore, our treatment program deliberately included operations designed to facilitate the acquisition of adaptive new behavior. For example, we included demonstrations of simple but effective methods of washing. (We quickly got used to the fact that large numbers of our patients seemed to have lost all idea of "normal" cleaning or checking behavior, whether connected with self-care, securing the house, or what have you). As for the transmission of useful information, we included as much of this as we thought appropriate in the commentaries that accompanied our therapeutic modeling displays. No doubt, a great deal of information was also transmitted inadvertently. Certainly, many of the habits and attitudes of our patients were altered in a way that was consistent with the information provided by the modeling therapists. To take one example, a few of the patients who were excessively frightened of being contaminated expressed surprise that after repeatedly touching the source of contamination the therapists did not experience any adverse consequences.

Noting the skepticism shown by clinicians at the time, we pointed out that "although these theoretical advantages often are conceded by psychotherapists, we have found that they tend to be skeptical about the possibility of altering the notoriously resistant behavior of obsessional-compulsive patients by such apparently simple and direct means. The willingness of therapists to admit the therapeutic power of passive modeling often seems to stop at mildly phobic student volunteers" (Röper, Rachman, and Marks, 1975, p. 272).

The general design and conduct of this experiment followed the same lines as the earlier studies. The only essential difference was that in this clinical trial all 10 patients received participant modeling during the second phase of the experiment. Five of the 10 patients started with 3 weeks of relaxation control treatment, while the other 5 had an initial period of 3 weeks comprising 15 daily sessions of passive modeling treatment. The patients, all moderately to severely disturbed obsessional-compulsives, were drawn from the same sources as the people who participated in the earlier trials.

The detailed results and analyses are given in Röper, Rachman, and Marks (1975), but the major findings are shown most easily in illustrated form. Figure 22.9 shows the ratings of fear and avoidance made by the patients and by the independent assessor on each of the four occasions. It can be seen that the

FIGURE 22.9.   Ratings of fear and avoidance made by the patients (self) and by independent, blind assessor (Psychological rating) on four occasions—before treatment, after treatment, and at the 6-month follow-up. The results for the two experiment groups are shown separately.

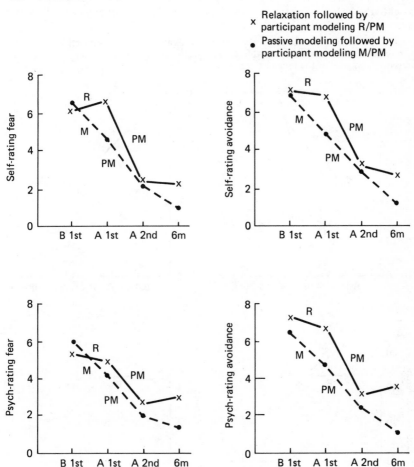

passive modeling treatment produced a moderate decline in fear and avoidance, certainly greater than that observed by the relaxation control treatment. However, the reductions in fear and avoidance observed after completion of the *participant modeling* treatment were considerably larger. It is also of interest that the reductions in fear and avoidance observed at the end of the experimental treatment periods were still present at the six-month follow-up checkpoint.

In Figure 22.10 we reproduce the results of the behavioral-avoidance tests and the subjective discomfort scores reported during the conduct of these tests. In addition, the results from the attitude scales and the Leyton Inventory interference score are given for each of the four test occasions. Once more the passive modeling treatment produced an outcome significantly superior to that observed after relaxation control; the five patients who started with passive modeling treatment showed an increase of nearly 50 percent in the number of behavioral-avoidance test tasks that they were able to complete after treatment. As with the other results, the participant modeling treatment yielded an even

FIGURE 22.10.   The results oт the behavioral avoidance tests, subjective fear scores (thermometer), attitude scales, and Cooper Test scores of interference shown for each of the two groups, on each of the four test occasions.

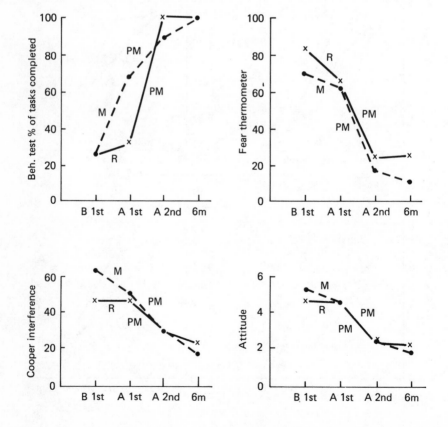

more striking improvement. On the so-called fear thermometer, subjective estimates of discomfort reported during the conduct of the behavioral tests in both the relaxation control and the passive modeling treatment were followed by a modest improvement. The reductions observed after participant modeling were markedly larger and statistically significant. The changes in attitude and in interference scores observed in the five patients who had passive modeling did not differ significantly from the scores returned by the patients who had relaxation control treatment instead. However, when these two groups of patients were switched into participant modeling during the second three-week phase of treatment, significant reductions in interference and unfavorable attitudes were observed. All of the changes described here were stable (i.e., still present at the six-month follow-up checkpoint).

For purposes of simple comparison, a group of five summary charts comparing the results from this modeling study with the results obtained in the earlier studies of the series are given (see Figure 22.11). The consistency of the results is clear. To some extent the results from the modeling experiment can be regarded as a satisfactory replication of the earlier findings, in that they confirm our conclusion that behavioral treatments are capable of producing significant and lasting clinical improvements within a short time.

Participant modeling is a reasonably powerful and effective method of treatment for the majority of patients—it being remembered that the people who participated in this treatment trial were handicapped by their obsessions and compulsions to a degree that required a period of in-patient treatment. Some of them were severely incapacitated, and the majority had been handicapped for several years before entering the treatment program. Before we go on to discuss the theoretical significance of these findings, it should be reiterated that all patients were given instructions to refrain from carrying out their rituals (response prevention) and that some of them required additional treatment after the experimental period had been completed.

Turning to the interpretation of the results, the evidence bears out Bandura's (1969) view that passive modeling is capable of reducing both fear and avoidance. It must be said, however, that although passive modeling is capable of producing some therapeutic changes, the effects of participant modeling are considerably stronger. Possible reasons for the augmented power of participant modeling are discussed by Rosenthal and Bandura (1978), Bandura (1977), and Rachman (1976d). It should be noted that this study could not, and indeed was not intended to, separate the effects of modeling from those of pure exposure. Both forms of modeling, passive and participant, necessarily involve exposure to the disturbing stimulus situations. In the passive form the patient observes, while in the participant form the patient observes and engages in the activity. It is very likely that engaged exposure will turn out to be considerably more effective than passive exposure, but this difference alone may not be sufficient to account for all the differences between passive and participant forms of therapeutic modeling.

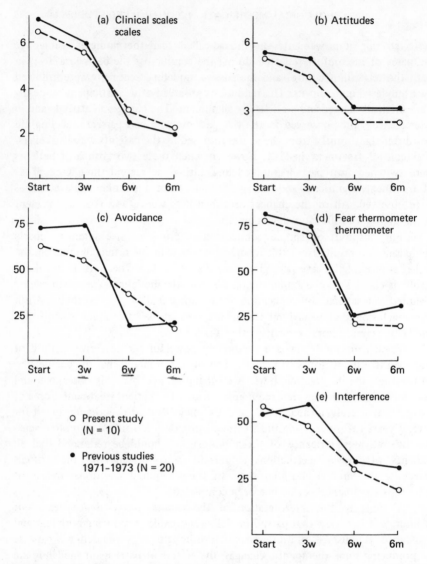

FIGURE 22.11. Summary charts of the main results obtained from all ten patients (i.e., the two experimental groups combined). These results from the present study are compared with those obtained in the earlier studies in this series; the consistency of the results is clear.

To summarize, then, our research indicates that behavioral treatment (flooding and/or modeling), coupled with instructions to refrain from carrying out compulsive rituals, is capable of bringing about significant therapeutic improvements of a wide-ranging kind in a short period. These improvements are reassuringly stable. Therapeutic improvements observed after these treatments are generally followed by moderate all-around improvements, and we have little evidence of the emergence of new problems (e.g., symptom substitution).

Leaving aside those who refuse treatment, we have encountered two main reasons for failure. The first and most common, it seems, is inability or unwillingness on the part of the patient to suspend or delay carrying out his or her rituals. So, for example, one of our outright failures was a man who carried out intense repetitive checks to ensure that there were no spots of excrement on his clothing or other possessions. The rituals, including multiple visual checks, were carried out at such a rate, and were so pervasive, that it was impossible to record their frequency. During the course of treatment, the patient was unable and/or unwilling to refrain from carrying out the checks. Another failure occurred with a patient who curcumvented the response prevention instructions by adopting a magical routine in place of her ordinary rituals. This young woman had intense fears of sexual contamination that she attempted to control by carrying out energetic cleaning rituals. She had a strong emotional reaction during the modeling-exposure sessions and reported great difficulty in suspending her cleaning rituals after sessions. When she was prevailed upon to cease decontaminating herself after the treatment sessions, she resorted to neutralizing the effects of the contamination by wiping them away with a handkerchief that she imbued with magical properties. For a few days it was thought that she was at last adhering to the response prevention part of the treatment, in that she was no longer carrying out excessive cleaning rituals, but we then learned that she was achieving the same end with her magical handkerchief. At the termination of the treatment period, neither her fears nor her rituals had been reduced.

The second type of failure arises from inability to tolerate the distress of the exposure treatment sessions and from the associated requirement that the patient refrain from neutralizing matters by executing the appropriate rituals after treatment. Some patients are willing to tolerate the distress during the treatment session only on condition that they be allowed to neutralize the contamination after each session. Patients who are unable to tolerate the exposure sessions generally deal with therapeutic demands by slowing down the exposure sequence to a snail's pace. At the end of three weeks of daily treatment they may have progressed no further than the ability to touch two or three contaminated items with the tip of one finger. Such insistence on extremely slow progress up the contamination hierarchy can sabotage the treatment program—in a sense the patient is operating a *treatment prevention* program in opposition to our response prevention program. Characteristically, the patients who find it impossible to tolerate the stress of exposure sessions will participate only to the minimal extent that they discern to be necessary in order to ensure that treatment is not abandoned.

SYNCHRONY AND DESYNCHRONY

We now turn to an analysis of our clinical data, using a three-systems analysis. As will be seen, the data do not easily lend themselves to such an analysis: The four studies were started in 1969, before we appreciated the advantages of this kind of analysis, and were not planned to fit into this framework.

We begin the analysis by restating our view that *treatments should produce results that reflect their main thrust*. Methods that concentrate on changing behavior directly should produce the greatest change in the behavioral components of the disorder concerned. Methods that involve mainly cognitive manipulation should produce the greatest change in cognitive components, and methods that emphasize psychophysiological change should produce the greatest change in that component. Accordingly, we have constructed a summary table (Table 22.1) in which the results of our clinical trials are restated in terms of the changes induced in the three components of obsessional-compulsive disorders. For the reasons given, it is an impressionistic summary in which we have attempted to compose a pattern out of misty fragments. The pattern is, we feel, consistent with expectations.

The data from our clinical trials were not collected or analyzed with Hodgson and Rachman's (1974) desynchrony hypotheses in mind, so we can provide little new information. In particular, we are not in a position to test the prediction that different and specifiable concordance patterns are produced by different types of treatment, and we do not have the data to enable us to test the prediction that patients with low concordance are less likely to show therapeutic change, either with desensitization or with the methods used in our studies. Most of the usable data are provided by Marks, Hodgson and Rachman (1975), Table 2. The main point of interest was the increasing concordance that emerged between the measures taken at the end of the 3-week experimental treatment and the measures taken at the end of the 6-month follow-up period. The data were consistent with Hodgson and Rachman's (1974) hypothesis 4. For example, the relationship between the patient's self-rating of obsessional anxiety and the obsessional-symptom score from the Leyton Inventory increased from 0.38 at 3 weeks and to 0.69 ($p = 0.05$) at the follow-up. Similarly, the Leyton trait and resistance scores become significantly correlated after the follow-up period. The changing relationship between the behavioral changes observed at the end of treatment and at follow-up, and the other measures of outcome, was especially interesting. For example, the correlation between behavioral change and attitude change increased from 0.24 (nonsignificant) to 0.44 ($p = > 0.05$) between the end of treatment and the 6-month follow-up checkpoint. The correlation between behavioral change and the Leyton obsessional symptom score increases from 0.16 (nonsignificant) at the end of treatment to 0.52 (significant) at follow-up. Between the end of treatment and the end of the follow-up period, the various clinical ratings showed a uniform change in the direction of closer correlations with the psychometric change scores—only 1 out of the 6 correlations was significantly positive at the end of treatment, but by the end of the follow-up period all 6 correlations were significantly positive. All of this points to increasing concordance between measures during the follow-up period. (It should be remembered, however, that the follow-up period is not "pure," in that some of the patients received addi-

TABLE 22.1: THERAPEUTIC RESULTS

TREATMENT TYPE	EMPHASIS	Outcome			
		BEHAVIORAL	OTHER ANXIETY/DISCOMFORT	COGNITIVE	PSYCHOPHYSIOLOGY
Flooding	direct behavioral change	+++	++	+	?
Passive modeling	cognitive changes	++	++	+	?
Participant modeling	cognitive and behavioral changes	+++	+++	++	?
Relaxation control	nonspecific cognitive and psychophysiological changes	0	+	0	+?

Note: Large changes are indicated by ++++, slight changes by ++, minimal change by +, and no change by 0. The patterns of change are consistent with the emphasis of each treatment type (e.g., flooding concentrates on producing direct changes in behavior and succeeds in this aim).

tional treatment.) From this pattern of changes, we infer that the treatment produced a good deal of desynchronous change. It is to be hoped that in future studies a methodical search for desynchronous changes will be incorporated into the experimental design.

THE MEDICAL RESEARCH COUNCIL TRIAL

A large-scale trial designed to replicate and extend these findings, and to assess the supplementary value of clomipramine, is now in the second-year follow-up stage; the findings obtained by the end of the 6-week hospital treatment period will be published shortly. Forty moderately to severely obsessional patients participated in this ambitious project, and the results of the behavioral treatment are consistent with our earlier findings. Large and significant group effects were achieved on the main measures of the obsessional behavior. Patients who took clomipramine showed highly significant improvements on all depression and mood measures, unlike those who took placebos. Somewhat surprisingly, there was little evidence of an interaction between clomipramine and behavioral treatment, and we found negligible support for the claim that the drug has a primary effect on obsessional problems. Improvements that appear to be secondary to the antidepressant effects of clomipramine were, however, clearly evident. The results of the trial provide useful support for our argument in support of greater specificity of outcome measures: The effects of the antidepressant drug were picked up by the measures of mood, and the effects of behavioral treatment were most evident in the behavioral tests (Rachman et al., 1979).

Chapter 23

Psychological Modification: Independent Studies

As always, the evaluation of a comparatively new method of treatment rests mainly on independent verification. Before embarking on a comparative analysis of the findings reported from different parts of the world, we can anticipate by observing that the overall pattern is encouraging despite 1½ exceptions. As only 7 of the 16 reports deal with studies that incorporated at least a modicum of experimental control, a division into controlled trials and noncontrolled clinical series would be unwieldy. Naturally, one places a different interpretation on these two types of studies, but some of the noncontrolled series contain important information.

In 1974 Meyer and his colleagues presented the results obtained with their method of treatment (sometimes called apotrepic therapy) in assisting 15 moderately to severely ill obsessional-compulsive patients (Meyer, Levy, and Schnurer, 1974). The patients were treated sequentially, and few experimental controls (e.g., randomization, control treatments, etc.) were imposed. Although full clinical assessments were carried out prior to and after treatment, insufficient quantified data were made available; at the time they wrote their report, they had too few follow-up data to warrant formal conclusions. Notwithstanding these shortcomings, this report is of considerable importance because of Meyer's valuable contribution to the development of treatments for obsessional-compulsive and other neurotic disorders, and because of the apparently excellent clinical results achieved. As always, the clinical material reported by Meyer and his co-workers is rich in interest. From the descriptions given there can be little doubt that the 15 patients were moderately to severely disturbed (e.g., the mean duration of symptoms was no less than 15.6 years).

The treatment procedures involved continual supervision during the patients' waking hours in order to ensure that all rituals were prevented. When this aim had been accomplished, emphasis shifted to the exposure procedure. The patient was systematically exposed to all the situations that evoked the urge to ritualize (some exposure training was, however, given during the period of intensive supervision). Participant modeling was also employed. "The therapist would frequently demonstrate the appropriate behavior in the stressful situation and then encourage the patient to imitate his behavior" (Meyer, Levy, and Schnurer, 1974, p. 247). When the patient was able to tolerate these provoking situations and refrain from resuming his or her ritualistic activities, the therapist gradually faded from the situation. Whenever necessary, the patient was given additional domiciliary treatment to ensure a satisfactory transition to the natural environment.

Meyer and his colleagues summarize their results in this way: "With the exception of case 9, every patient showed a marked diminution in compulsive behavior, sometimes amounting to a total cessation of the rituals ... It will be seen that at the end of treatment, out of 15 cases in the main group, 10 were either much improved or totally asymptomatic" (p. 251). The significance of this extraordinarily good therapeutic outcome will not be lost on anyone who has tried to help obsessional-compulsive patients overcome their frequently intractable problems. Although comprehensive follow-up information was not available to Meyer when the report was prepared, he has since informed us by personal communication that most of these patients have maintained their improvements.

In their noncontrolled clinical study, Wonnenberger and his associates (1975) also achieved excellent if narrow therapeutic results, with inadequate generalization. Using a method of treatment that bears a close resemblance to the techniques we have used (i.e., modeling-exposure and response prevention), they obtained significant clinical improvement in 6 of their 7 obsessional-compulsive patients. "Six patients showed significant reductions in anxiety and obsessional-compulsive avoidance behavior. Improvements were still present at follow-up 8 weeks later and generalized to the daily life situation of 5 patients, but only to a limited extent. Striking was the patient's motivation and low anxiety level during treatment. As a further result, the social behavior of 5 patients was positively influenced. An increase of depressive mood was not observed" (p. 135). In their interesting experimental analysis of the role of response prevention, Mills, Agras, Barlow, and Mills (1973) reported that each of their 5 cases showed "a dramatic reduction in the rate of ritualistic behavior after a period of response prevention" (p. 524). In the controlled comparison between flooding and thought-stopping treatments carried out by Hackmann and McLean (1975), even a comparatively small amount of treatment (4 + 4 sessions) was sufficient to produce a reasonable amount of clinical improvement—"a worthwhile clinical finding was that a fair amount of improvement occurred after only 8 outpatient sessions" (p. 263). In their controlled experimental trial, regrettably restricted by the small number of patients in each comparison group, Boersma and his colleagues (1976) reasonably concluded that "responsive prevention as carried out in this study, is a very effective method of treatment for compulsions . . . The improvement of the clients was shown by the measurement *in vivo*, the anxiety and avoidance scales, and by all the scales of the Leyton Obsessional Inventory. In addition, it was shown that at the end of treatment the client had become less depressed" (p. 22). The extent of the improvement can be gauged from the fact that "the main compulsion, as measured *in vivo*, improved at the post-test an average of 77.8 percent, and the other compulsions an average of 75.9 percent" (p. 22). In the clinical trial reported by Rabavilas, Boulougouris, and Stefanis (1976), significant clinical improvements were obtained in a group of 12 obsessional-compulsive patients. These improvements were obtained on all of the main clinical measures of obsessional disorder, in anxiety, and in avoidance behavior. At the conclusion of the comparatively brief experimental treatment period, "6 cases were improved . . . and they remain well . . . at 6 months' follow-up . . . 4 patients required further treatment with a mean of 9 sessions . . . They showed a moderate improvement by the end of additional treatment. Finally, 2 patients did not show any improvement" (p. 354).

The exposure and response prevention procedure is now being widely investigated and adopted; the most recent research reports come from Emmelkamp and Van Kraanen (1977) and Foa and Goldstein (1978). In the first of these reports, the results obtained with 14 obsessional-compulsive patients who underwent gradual exposure *in vivo* are given in detail. All patients had 10 sessions of treatment; half of them had exposure controlled by a therapist, while the other 7 controlled their own exposure experiences. Both versions of the treatment resulted in a significant improvement on all of the relevant mreasures. The magnitude of the changes can be seen from the fact that on the behavioral test the improvement in the main compulsion (both groups combined) was no less than 74 percent. On the other compulsions the average improvement was 77 percent. The stability of these improvements was confirmed at the 3-month follow-up checkpoint. As before, although the therapeutic response of the groups was extremely encouraging, a small minority of patients failed to improve. Two patients "whose compulsive rituals were frequently occasioned by obsessive ruminations" showed little improvement.

Important supporting evidence of the beneficial effects of exposure and response prevention was recently reported by Foa and Goldstein (1978), who treated 21 patients with excellent results—in certain respects superior to ours. In the main, their findings are remarkably similar not only to our own but also to most other published reports. The patients were exposed for extended periods to discomfort-evoking stimuli and were prevented from carrying out any discomfort-reducing rituals. Inventories and evaluation scales were completed by an independent assessor and by the patient on the following occasions: before contact with the therapist, after two weeks of contact with the therapist but with no treatment, after two weeks of therapy, and at repeated follow-ups. They obtained no significant changes in the two 2-week periods prior to commencing active treatment. However, significant improvements were evident at the end of the 2-week treatment period. In the majority of cases, these therapeutic gains were maintained and even increased during the follow-up period. The therapeutic improvements spread beyond the target symptoms to include occupational adjustment, social life, sexual adjustment, and family relations. The most striking feature of Foa and Goldstein's results is that "two-thirds of the patients became asymptomatic after treatment," a result that exceeds our own and is close to that of Meyer and his colleagues.

It is, of course, true that no control group was employed in the Foa-Goldstein series. The findings are nevertheless impressive. The changes were large, stable, and generalized. Moreover, the major changes took place within the remarkably short space of two weeks of intensive treatment. The possible contribution of nonspecific factors cannot be excluded, but the fact that no changes were achieved in the pretreatment period, with or without therapeutic contact, rules out at least some of the commonly encountered nonspecific therapeutic factors. A success rate in which two-thirds of the patients become asymptomatic within two weeks of intensive treatment conclusively rules out the possibility that Foa and Goldstein's results can be attributed to spontaneous remission. As we have already seen, the spontaneous-remission rate for this disorder, gauged over a two-year period, is likely to be in the region of roughly 40-50 percent. However, applying strict standards, this report has to be regarded as supportive but not conclusive.

A similarly impressive therapeutic outcome using several treatment procedures, mainly exposure and response prevention, was achieved under different conditions by trainee nurse-therapists working under the direction of psychologists and psychiatrists. Marks, Hallam, Connolly, and Philpott (1976) supervised the treatment of 34 obsessional-compulsive patients who were drawn from the same general population as our own patients and had similarly chronic disorders (mean duration 10 years). "Treatment was adapted to the needs of individual patients and families. The broad spectrum approach again involved the central principle of exposure *in vivo* to cues eliciting avoidance, checking or other rituals. Patients also had self-imposed response prevention, i.e., they were asked to refrain from engaging in rituals after such exposure. Therapists modeled exposure to stimuli which evoked rituals. Thought-stopping, self-regulation and social skills training were used when necessary" (p. 39). It is, of course, evident that this report takes us no further in isolating the factors responsible for therapeutic change, nor does it provide conclusive, controlled evidence about the effectiveness of the procedures. Nevertheless, as in the previous study, the results achieved in combating a chronic serious disorder were so large and impressive that they cannot be disregarded. On the contrary, they provide encouragement of a different sort. On the basis of these findings, it seems safe to conclude that the *techniques* used to modify the problems of people with obsessional-compulsive disorders are robust and can be transmitted and acquired with comparative ease.

The mean treatment time was 24 hours for out-patients and 34 hours for in-patients. The useful degree of improvement achieved during the treatment phase was evident on all major measures. So, for example, the total amount of obsessional behavior (as assessed on a standardized checklist) declined from 70 percent to a mere 20 percent at the end of treatment; the discomfort experienced during rituals declined from the score of 6 (on an 8-point scale) to less than 2; a rating of generalized disability showed a decline from 6 (again on an 8-point scale) to 3.5. The authors' own conclusions need no qualification: "The results are impressive as the obsessive-compulsive patients as a group were severely incapacitated. Lack of standardized measures precluded formal comparison with obsessives treated by other professionals. However, the results are of the same order as in obsessives treated by psychologists and psychiatrists" (p. 50).

The fine results turned in by the antipodean pair of Catts and McConaghy (1975) encourage the belief that the therapeutic powers of behavior therapy are not confined to the Northern Hemisphere. Two of their six patients showed substantial reductions in ritualistic behavior at discharge, and these changes were maintained at follow-up. The remaining four patients were improved at discharge and made further important advances during the follow-up period. The same broad pattern of improvement was noted in subjective-anxiety assessments and in the patients' social adjustment. In only one patient was there a lag in achieving improved social adjustment and reduced subjective anxiety, but even this patient was found to be substantially improved at the time of the follow-up assessment. As the authors correctly conclude, their results are consistent with the claims of other workers that "chronic compulsive behavior can rapidly respond to relatively brief periods of ritual prevention with supervision" (p. 40). They go on to comment that "the rapidity with which a marked reduction in symptoms occurred, once ritual prevention was initiated, was considered impressive evidence of its efficacy." They do not skirt the difficulties involved in providing the treatment, and comment that although ritual prevention and exposure "appeared essential components of the treatment," many of the patients suffered "considerable personality difficulties"; these were handled with "orthodox techniques including marital, individual and assertive therapy both as in- and out-patients" (p. 41). Because of the mixture of techniques and the absence of appropriate controls, this evidence cannot be taken as confirming the claims made for the efficacy of behavioral treatment; but it too is encouraging.

In a study involving prodigious efforts, Sookman and Solyom (1977) provided each of 33 chronic patients with 50 sessions of various forms of treatment. The overall results were less satisfactory than those reported with exposure plus response prevention, and some of the findings are puzzling. The main aim of these authors was to compare the efficacy of 4 types of behavioral treatment: flooding, aversion relief, thought stopping, and thought stopping combined with desensitization. The flooding and thought-stopping methods were most effective, and aversion relief was ineffective. It is curious that thought-stopping alone was found to be significantly more effective than thought stopping with desensitization. On the face of it, it appears that desensitization impeded the effects of the other method. If so, it is a rare and inexplicable result.

Another puzzling finding was that, contrary to expectations, thought stopping was most effective in reducing overt *rituals*—even though it is directed at the obsession, not the ritual. To add to the confusion, flooding (a method directed mainly at rituals) was most effective in reducing ruminations. Moreover, the negative results of aversion relief conflict with Solyom and his associates' (1971) earlier findings.

We can offer no specific explanation for the unusual aspects of these findings, but they may well have been influenced by pervasive nonspecific therapeutic factors (Rachman, 1971) and confused by pretreatment group differences. As Bandura (1969) has argued, nonspecific factors play a large part in inducing changes in disorders of moderate intensity and only a small part in changing severe disorders. The Sookman and Solyom (1977) sample was, like the Hackmann and McClean (1975) group, seemingly less disturbed than the patients treated by Rabavilas and his colleagues (1976), those treated by Meyer and his colleagues (1974), or those in our own treatment trials. The Leyton scores of the Sookman patients and of the Hackmann patients were well below those reported in the other trials, and the fact that they were all out-patients may be important. In our own research patients were excluded from the major treatment trials *unless* their problems were sufficiently severe to merit admission to a hospital. The difficulties encountered in treating some of these patients on an out-patient basis may also have contributed to the confusing outcome of the Sookman study. The major point to bear in mind, however, is that Sookman and Solyom did not use the best-established method—exposure and response prevention.

After studying Meyer's methods in London, Heyse (1975) returned to Munich and treated 24 in-patients, but with less success than his mentor. Seven remained unchanged; 7 improved slightly; and 17 showed moderate improvements. The comparison between modeling and response prevention methods yielded no differences. This report is the least encouraging so far and cannot be ignored, especially as the reasons for the 7 failures are not known. It should be borne in mind, however, that the results are nevertheless superior to those claimed by rival techniques. Yet it does recommend a sense of caution, and it leaves unanswered the question of why Meyer's method, on this occasion, lost some of its effectiveness in transport.

The trend of the noncontrolled and controlled series is extremely encouraging. Although we can make some general suggestions to account for the few published exceptions to this trend, it is, as always, difficult to explain negative results. The exceptions are a controlled trial on the effects of thought stopping, in which a poor clinical result was achieved (Stern, Lipsedge, and Marks, 1973); a small series reported by Ramsay and Sikkel (1971), who obtained mixed results; and the report by Heyse (1975).

To begin with, one needs to know whether the samples of patients who participated in these studies are comparable. These accounts leave little doubt about the comparability of the samples; with the exception of a series of fifteen patients treated by the unusual method of aversion relief (Solyom et al., 1971), the content of the disorders is similar. Most of the patients complained of classical obsessional-compulsive difficulties such as compulsive cleaning and checking rituals. Solyom's group was more heterogeneous than the others and contained an unusually large percentage of doubters and ruminators. In addition, the diagnosis of at least 2 of the patients was uncertain: "Both patients diagnosed as doubtful schizophrenics showed improvement" (p. 104).

In terms of the mean duration of illness, the samples fell within the range of 8 to 15 years (Meyer, 15 years; Rachman, 10; Rabavilas, 8; Boersma, 15)— leaving no doubt about the chronicity of the disorders. On this index of chronicity, and some others, it appears that the patients treated in Hackmann and McLean's (1975) Oxford trial were relatively mild cases (mean duration: 3.7 years).

The assessor's ratings of severity of the obsessional disorder in our own studies (Marks et al., 1975; Röper et al., 1975) were near the top of the 0-8 scale; in the Rabavilas study they were near the top of the 0-5 scale. They were somewhat lower in the Dutch study by Boersma (5.7 on the 0-8 scale) and markedly lower in the Oxford study (2.8 on a 0-6 scale). The self-ratings of severity of the obsessional disorder were high in our own patients (7 on the 0-8 scale) and in Rabavilas' patients (4.5 on a 0-5 scale), moderate in Boersma's (5.6 on a 0-8 scale), and moderately high in Hackmann's (4.0 on a 0-6 scale). The clinical ratings of obsessional-compulsive avoidance patterns were high in our own patients (nearly 7 on a 0-8 scale) and in the Dutch patients (over 7 on a 0-8 scale). By contrast, the avoidance behavior of the Oxford patients was rated by the assessor at only 2.6 on a 0-6 scale, and at 3.8 on the self-rating scale. Marked avoidance was elicited in our behavioral tests, but as this assessment has not featured in other research, no comparisons are possible. The scores obtained on the Leyton Inventory are comparable across groups. For example, our patients started with interference scores of just over 50 (Röper et al., 1975), Hackmann's with 46, and Boersma's with 50.

With the exception of the Canadian patients treated by Solyom and his colleagues, the content of the obsessional-compulsive disorders was comparable across these samples. The patients described in these reports were drawn from a population of *chronic* obsessional-compulsive neurotics, with the exception of the Oxford patients, whose problems were of shorter duration. Across samples, the disorders appear to have been severe as well as chronic. Again with the exception of the Oxford patients, most of the people who participated in these studies were, on average, near the top of the severity scale in terms of both their reported distress and the associated avoidance behavior. Where available, the Leyton scores consistently show elevated profiles. So, with the exceptions noted, the therapeutic findings were obtained from comparable populations of patients with severe and chronic obsessional-compulsive disorders.

THE CHANGES

With this information comparisons can be made between the extent and type of therapeutic changes reported in the various studies. For purposes of illustration, we constructed some simple schematic figures that summarize the major changes in obsessional-compulsive problems reported in the six controlled studies (see Figure 23.1). As the rating scales used in the various studies are not identical, we have sacrificed accuracy in order to reduce them to a common scale. In order to avoid conveying a misleading impression by virtue of this transformation, the scores are plotted as *trends* on an adjectival rather than a digital scale.

The most striking feature of these results is their consistency. In all of the control study reports, the average improvement in problem behavior was steep and swift, commonly dropping from severe to slight or mild. These trends are in conformity with most of the noncontrolled clinical series mentioned earlier. Among the control studies, that reported by Hackmann and McLean (1975) is the only one containing a noteworthy difference. As already mentioned, the patients in this study appear to have been less severely disturbed, and this is reflected in their scores at the pretreatment assessment points (on the obsessional scale, the general clinical scales, and the Leyton Intereference Scale). It is interesting that, nevertheless, their scores at the completion of the two (cross-over) treatments are similar to those of the other groups (i.e., at the posttreatment assessment point the Oxford patients returned scores that were similar to those achieved by patients in the Greek, Dutch, and London studies). Although all the indications are that once changes of this character have been obtained by behavioral treatment they are relatively enduring, it is a pity that only three of

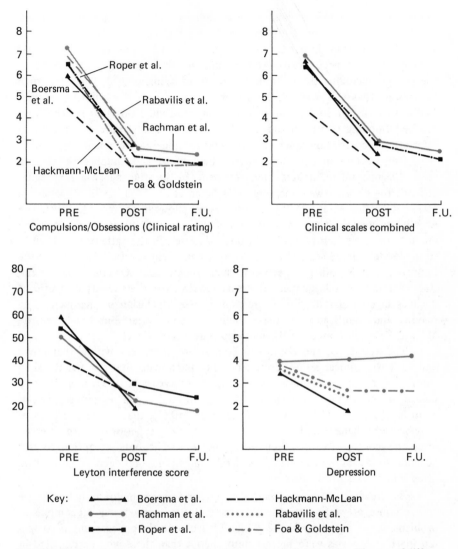

the control studies contain information about the state of the patients at the end of the follow-up period. One reason for this weakness, to be discussed in detail later, is that some research workers have used crossover designs that automatically preclude the collection of follow-up information.

Although its significance is not entirely clear, the scores obtained on the

Leyton Interference Scale show a large reduction at the conclusion of treatment. In all cases the reduction was from a very high score of ±50 to a moderate score of ±20 (except in the Oxford study, in which the pretreatment level was notably lower to begin with). At the conclusion of treatment, however, all of the groups, including the Oxford one, returned scores of ±20. There are some indications that this score declines even further during the follow-up period. In the first of our studies, we picked up a trend indicating that patients who received flooding treatment did not show as large and significant a decline in interference scores as those who had participant modeling treatment.

On the Leyton Symptom Score, the Oxford and Dutch patients both showed significant reductions after treatment. In the studies in which attitudes towards the disorder were measured (Rachman et al., 1971, 1973; Röper et al., 1975; Rabavilas et al., 1976), the scores all show an appreciable shift from negative to neutral. The clinical ratings of the course of the patients' depression are not consistent across studies. In our own research the patients were slightly to moderately depressed prior to treatment and changed very little, despite the improvements in other aspects of their functioning. On the other hand, Rabavilas and his colleagues and Boersma and his co-workers reported significant declines in clinical ratings of depression by the conclusion of treatment. The reasons and significance of these findings are not clear, but the large-scale Medical Research Council study may help clarify this subject.

The results of the controlled studies are consistent within themselves and with the clinical series described earlier in showing that significant reductions in obsessional-compulsive problems are observed after the completion of a course of behavioral treatment. In the control studies that employed placebo controls (Rachman et al., 1973; Röper et al., 1975), the therapeutic changes observed after behavioral treatment were significantly superior to those observed after the control treatment on most measures. The only exception to this generalization was our finding that general depression scores declined after relaxation (placebo) control treatment.

As already mentioned, a partial exception to the conclusion that exposure and response prevention treatment successfully reduces obsessional-compulsive problems is the report by Heyse. While it is true that the patients who participated in Heyse's series were more heterogeneous than those who participated in the other studies, it does not follow that this difference in sample selection accounts for the higher rate of failures (30%) reported by Heyse. The other possibility, not incompatible with the first, is that the treatment techniques that Heyse employed were different in some important respects. Short of having full audio-visual recordings of the treatment sessions or having observers present during the sessions, there is no way of ensuring comparability of treatment techniques. In the circumstances, the best course is to rely mainly on the results obtained in controlled experimental studies.

Some attention has been directed toward teasing out the comparative strengths of variations in behavioral treatment. In the controlled studies comparisons have been made between flooding and participant modeling, between passive modeling and participant modeling, between imaginal and actual presentations of stimuli, between short- and long-duration exposures, between flooding and gradual treatment, and between flooding and thought stopping. These questions are asked for two reasons. In the first place, there is a desire to increase therapeutic efficacy; in the second place, one needs to investigate the mechanisms responsible for change.

The most striking outcome of these comparison studies is that so few significant differences have emerged. Flooding treatment has been compared with relaxation control (Rachman et al., 1971), with participant modeling (Rachman et al., 1971; Rachman et al., 1973), with gradual *in vivo* exposure (Boersma et al., 1976), with thought stopping (Hackmann and McLean, 1975), and with aversion relief (Sookman and Solyom, 1977). Within the flooding paradigm, Rabavilas and his co-workers(1977) have compared long and short exposures and imaginal with *in vivo* exposures.

The results are as follows: Flooding is more effective than relaxation control treatment or aversion relief, equally effective as participant modeling, and probably superior to thought stopping. It is possible, however, that flooding treatment evokes more anxiety than modeling (Rachman et al., 1971; Boersma et al., 1976), and that it is less effective in reducing the interfering quality of the obsessional disorder (Rachman et al., 1971). Although we are not yet in a position to confirm these impressions, our clinical experience leads us to expect that flooding treatment will produce more dropouts in treatment and that it will be among the least readily accepted of the available alternatives. In regard to flooding treatment variables, Rabavilas and his colleagues suggested that long practice sessions *in vivo* may produce superior results. They also suggested that short and long sessions in fantasy do not differ significantly, and that long fantasy sessions may potentiate the effects of *in vivo* practice sessions.

Participant modeling treatment has been compared with relaxation control treatment (Rachman et al., 1971, 1973), with plain exposure (Boersma et al., 1976), with flooding (Rachman et al., 1971), and with passive modeling (Röper et al., 1975). The results are as follows: Participant modeling produces therapeutic results superior to those of relaxation control treatment, wider and larger therapeutic changes than passive modeling, and changes broadly equivalent to those obtained with flooding treatment.

The results obtained with thought stopping are contradictory. In their controlled trial Stern, Lipsedge, and Marks (1973) were unable to produce significant improvements with a tape-recorded thought-stopping procedure in a group of 11 chronic obsessional-compulsive patients. They qualified this disappointing result by saying that it might reflect the inadequacy of administering the thought-stopping procedure by tape recording, and also that their ratings were "crude, arbitrary and incomplete in some cases" (p. 661). Their qualifications may be justified when one considers the superior results reported by Hackmann and McLean in Oxford, and by Sookman and Solyom (1977). Although Hackmann's patients appear to have been significantly less severely handicapped than those participating in the other studies reported, small but statistically significant improvements were obtained on a range of measures. These improvements were comparable in extent to those that they achieved with *in vivo* flooding. In our view, however, their results should not be used as a basis for prematurely concluding that thought stopping is an effective treatment technique at least equivalent to flooding. In addition to the fact that their patients' problems were comparatively mild, they provided a mere 4 flooding sessions for each patient. Judging from our own experience, such a small amount of exposure treatment is unlikely to achieve substantial gains. Nevertheless, their results, supported by those of Sookman and Solyom (who gave 50 sessions as opposed to Hackmann's 4), encourage the hope that thought stopping might yet be developed into a useful therapeutic procedure.

RESPONSE PREVENTION

The broadly comparable effects achieved with different forms of behavioral treatment raises the possibility that there is some element or elements common to all of them and that it is this common element that is primarily responsible for inducing the therapeutic changes. This possibility is not new in behavior therapy. Similar trends and problems occurred in the research into the therapeutic modification of phobias (see Rachman, 1974a, 1977b; Marks, 1975). In the behavioral treatment of obsessional-compulsive disorders, there are two prominent candidates for nomination as the crucial common element: response prevention and exposure. In our research all patients received exposure, and we instructed them to refrain from carrying out their compulsive rituals once the treatment program had commenced. Response prevention instructions were an essential element in the treatment. In this we were following the lead given by Dr. Meyer at the Middlesex Hospital, supported by the animal research described by Baum (1970). In the other control studies and clinical series as well, it would appear that response prevention instructions were given explicitly or implicitly.

In Meyer's treatment technique response prevention is the cardinal feature. Explicit response prevention instructions were provided in the clinical series reported by Foa and Goldstein (1978), by Wonnenberger and his associates (1975), by Heyse (1975), and by Boersma and his colleagues (1976). Generally, this is the procedure adopted. The patients are dissuaded from performing compulsive rituals during sessions and encouraged to relinquish all avoidance behavior and rituals outside the therapy sessions. To quote Rabavilas and his colleagues (1977), the therapist "did not allow the patient to adopt avoidance behavior after having touched the contaminated object" (p. 351). Similarly, Hackmann and McLean's patients "were encouraged to believe that by giving in to fears they reinforced them, and by fighting to overcome them, the symptoms are weakened. Thus, in both treatments, one attempts to mobilize the patient's motivation to fight actively against the symptoms between treatment sessions, entering situations he would prefer to avoid, and attempting to curtail rituals and ruminations" (p. 267).

Mills, Agras, Barlow, and Mills (1973) investigated the role of response prevention in a series of 5 connected single-case studies. The first 4 patients were engaging in excessive and compulsive hand-washing rituals, while the fifth carried out complex rituals before retiring to bed and again upon rising in the morning. In the first 4 cases, the patients were required to record the frequency of their daily hand washing and of compulsive urges to carry out the rituals. In each instance a baseline observation period, generally lasting 7 to 10 days, was completed before introducing the response prevention instructions.

The baseline recordings, taken over a period of 1 week, consisted of the number of compulsive urges and ritualistic cleaning acts carried out under conditions in which contaminated objects were presented to the patient at hourly intervals for 10 hours. During the response prevention period, the taps were removed, thereby preventing the patient from washing. The interest of this study centers on the question of whether or not patients who undergo a period in which the rituals are physically prevented will show a reduction in the frequency of the compulsive rituals when the taps are replaced and it becomes physically possible once again to carry out the compulsive washing acts. From the nature of the instructions given to the patients at various stages of the case studies, it seems possible that the patients may well have interpreted the post-response prevention period as a continuation of the treatment, requiring them to continue their attempts to refrain from carrying out the rituals. Whatever their understanding of the implicit instructions inherent in the situation, the fact is that, after undergoing a period during which the ritualistic responses were physically prevented, all four of the patients showed a substantial reduction in the frequency of their compulsive cleaning activities. In two of the four cases, the reduced frequencies were not accompanied by a comparable decline in compulsive urges. Although the results are not entirely consistent, they suggest that the response prevention instructions produced a decline in the frequency of the compulsive behavior. It was inevitable that when given the response prevention instructions, patients reduced the frequency of these acts during the period covered by the instruction. What is of great interest is the fact that when baseline conditions were reintroduced (i.e., the response prevention instruction was withdrawn), the compulsive hand washing *did not* return to the original level. In other words, after carrying out the response prevention instructions for a prescribed period, the patients displayed an enduring reduction in the frequency of the compulsive acts—a reduction that outlasted the instruction period itself. It is not clear from the report whether the patients felt obliged to persist in their attempts at response prevention even when the explicit instruction was withdrawn. It should be remembered that the case investigations lasted, on average, four to seven weeks. The possibility that their patients did interpret the situation thus is strengthened by the fact that when Mills instituted "experimental probes" the frequency of compulsive hand washing did not return to the original baseline level.

The effect of the response prevention instructions on the *frequency* of compulsive urges is of particular interest. In the first patient, the successful institution of a response prevention period was not followed by a decline in the frequency of compulsive urges. However, with a return to baseline conditions, during which the compulsive hand washing showed a slight resurgence, the compulsive urges showed a smooth and marked decline to a point approaching 0. In the second patient, response prevention instructions were introduced on two separate occasions, and in both instances the reduction in compulsive hand washing was accompanied by an *increase* in the frequency of compulsive urges. In the third patient, the compulsive urges continued at a rate of between 25 and 35 per day throughout all the experimental manipulations, including response prevention and baseline recordings. The treatment manipulations had no effect on the frequency of the compulsive urges. Most interestingly, the compulsive urges did not appear to change even when the compulsive hand washing was stopped during the response prevention period. There was, however, a slight indication of a temporary increase in the frequency of urges as soon as the response prevention period commenced. A similar relationship between the institution of response prevention and a temporary increase of compulsive urges was observed in the next patient. In this fourth case, however, the compulsive urges declined slightly during the response prevention period, continued to do so during the succeeding placebo period, and finally disappeared during the placebo and baseline periods at the end of the experimental period of 47 days.

Some of the effects of the response prevention instructions were nonspecific. For example, in the fifth patient even the untreated rituals (i.e., those that had not been included in the response prevention) declined in frequency. Although response prevention instructions had inconsistent effects on urges, this study raised the possibility that the introduction of an instruction to refrain from carrying out the compulsive behavior may produce an increase, perhaps temporary, in the frequency of compulsive urges. This possibility received little support from our experimental study of the decay of compulsive urges, but the conditions in the two studies were rather different.

In interpreting the significance of the results reported by Mills and his associates (1973) it should be noted that the experimental manipulations necessarily included repeated exposure to the contaminating objects. Hence, it is impossible to reach firm conclusions about the specific, unique contribution of response prevention. It is, however, clear that exposure followed by a period of response prevention leads to a (comparatively) lasting reduction in the frequency of compulsive activity. There is also some evidence that response prevention instructions, without physically preventing the execution of the rituals, are sufficient to produce reductions in the frequency of rituals (Mills et al., 1973, case 2, p. 525). However, the authors point out that "there is an even greater effect when the [response prevention] instructions are issued during and after a period of [physical] response prevention" (p. 526)—a finding consistent with Meyer's treatment method.

Information about the effects of response prevention *instructions* was collected in our own treatment studies. So, for example, we found that providing response prevention instructions during a relaxation control treatment period of 3 weeks had little effect on the main indexes of obsessional-compulsive behavior (e.g., Rachman et al., 1971). In our experiment on the effects of passive and participant modeling (Röper et al., 1975), we found that conveying the response prevention instructions in association with 15 daily sessions of passive modeling treatment produced significant therapeutic improvements, but these were dwarfed by the magnitude of the improvements that followed parti-cipant modeling treatment combined with response prevention instructions. These results serve to emphasize the important contribution made by *in vivo* exposure practice, particularly when combined with response prevention instruc-tions.

With regard to the specific and unique contribution made by the exposure experiences, Mills and his associates obtained a small amount of interesting information on this question. It will be remembered that during the initial baseline period of study their patients were methodically exposed to contaminating objects and permitted to carry out ritualistic washing if they wished. That is, they were subjected to exposure without instructions to refrain from carrying out the compulsive responses. In all 4 cases, described in their report, this exposure was *not* followed by a reduction in the frequency of com-pulsive behavior; indeed, in three of the four cases this kind of methodical exposure, carried out in the absence of instructions to prevent the compulsive response, led to increases in the frequency of compulsive hand washing. To quote the author, "The effect of exposure alone, prior to response prevention was an increase rather than a decrease in the rate of hand washing" (p. 527). This comment on the results obtained from patient 3 applies equally well to patients 2 and 4. Of course, it can be argued that this form of methodical, repeated, but brief exposure is unlikely to bring about a reduction in obsessional-compulsive behavior precisely because it is insufficient—insufficient in terms of both the frequency and the duration of the exposures. (Our clinical experience with these methods suggests that 7 brief exposures to each of 10 discrete contaminating stimuli cannot be expected to produce significant therapeutic changes.) Rabavilas and his colleagues (1976) produced some evidence to support this contention, and external evidence drawn from the research on the treatment of phobic disorders is consistent with this point of view (Marks, 1975). Nevertheless, any statements about the therapeutic value of exposure experiences must be qualified by reference to the frequency and duration of the exposure experiences, and by reference to the inclusion or exclusion of response prevention. At this stage of knowledge, we can go no further than to say that exposure and response prevention are jointly capable of producing large and reliable improvements.

There is a pressing need for clarification of the separate and combined therapeutic contributions of exposure and of response prevention. In his potentially interesting clinical investigation, Lipsedge (1974) set out to investigate these questions. He intended to delineate the separate contributions of response prevention and of exposure by carrying out a crossover clinical study on 12 compulsive patients. Lipsedge planned to use 4 treatment conditions: response prevention, continuation of ritualistic cleaning, no treatment, and what he called "undoing the undoing." The questions were well chosen, the experimental manipulations potentially fruitful, but the choice of a crossover design was unfortunate. In the event, it proved impossible to adhere to the crossover pattern; the first two patients were virtually symptom free after only one treatment session, and the third patient was substantially improved. Hence, there was no point in switching them into the second of the prearranged treatment conditions. This meant breaking the planned random allocation of the next three patients. As luck would have it, all three of these patients did badly, and Lipsedge decided to return to the original crossover design, including a return to "random" allocation. By this time, of course, the study could no longer be salvaged and it was, as Lipsedge says, "an incomplete block design which failed to balance" (p. 22). The result cannot be interpreted in any formal sense, but there was a suggestion that, on a measure of compulsive activity, mere exposure was sufficient to bring about a slight improvement, although not as substantial as that obtained by the response prevention condition. On the subjective-anxiety scale, response prevention was seemingly more effective than mere exposure.

The unfortunate fate of this experiment highlights the shortcomings of the crossover type of experimental design, which has been used in several therapeutic studies of obsessional-compulsive neuroses. In circumscribed circumstances crossover designs can be useful. However, for the development and evaluation of therapeutic methods the drawbacks exceed the advantages. At best, a crossover design can provide information about acute effects. As Hackmann and McLean (1975) acknowledged in their study, the experimental design precluded the possibility of follow-up results—"Only follow-up results (precluded by the present design) could explore" the possibility that longer courses of treatment might combat the tendency to relapse (p. 266). Crossover designs are subject to strong order effects, with the first treatment generally producing the greatest amount of change (e.g., Rabavilas et al., 1976). Aside from the distorting consequences of these order effects, they introduce inequalities in baseline measurements. Indeed, if the first treatment under examination has any effects at all, this is bound to depress the pretreatment baseline of the second treatment to be examined. These two consequences of using a crossover design, and the probably confounding effects of giving patients interrelated sequential treatment instructions and procedures, virtually ensure that any differences produced by variations in treatment technique will be wiped out. The use of a crossover design increases the likelihood of differential effects becoming blurred, and it precludes an evaluation of the long-term effects of any treatment intervention.

Once the precise contributions of these two components of treatment, exposure and prevention, have been determined by empirical investigations, attention is bound to turn to questions about the mechanisms involved. There is good reason to suppose that after patients have undergone a period of response prevention, in which they literally are unable to carry out their rituals, they will carry out fewer rituals when they are once again free to do so. It seems that undergoing a period during which the compulsive rituals are blocked produces some change in the probability of future compulsive acts (and also some changes in subjective reactivity). One strong possibility is that during the response prevention period patients acquire new ways of responding, and some of these compete with or replace their more stereotyped compulsive behavior patterns. At a prognostic level, one might follow Bandura (1977) in exploring the possibility that undergoing the experience of a response prevention period alters people's perceptions of their own efficacy. The effects of exposure, viewed primarily as a procedure involving manipulation at the stimulus end of the sequence, seem to us to be best encompassed in habituation theory (to be discussed later).

It has been observed by Broadhurst (1976) that the thought-stopping technique has no adequate rationale. Clinically, this method has been used primarily in the treatment of obsessional ruminations, and the control trial by Stern, Lipsedge, and Marks (1973) was unsuccessful. The indifferent success achieved with this technique, coupled with its uncertain pedigree, gave rise to scepticism about its value. In this light the moderately good results achieved by Hackmann and McLean (1975) in only four thought-stopping treatment sessions, admittedly with a comparatively mildly disturbed group of patients, is perhaps surprising. Taken in conjunction with the recent optimistic report from Sookman and Solyom (1977), however, the thought-stopping method remains a serious, if unreliable, contender. Regrettably, the Sookman results are difficult to interpret because of pretreatment group differences and some internal inconsistencies.

The claims made by Solyom and his colleagues (1971) on behalf of the therapeutic value of aversion relief cannot be accepted until additional and independent confirmation is obtained; in Solyom's 1977 report with Sookman, aversion relief was seen to be ineffective. (The conflicting results reported by Solyom in 1971 and 1976 are confusing and underline the need for independent confirmation.) If this method has something particular to contribute, it may be in helping to modify what Solyom and his associates (1971) describe as "horrific temptations," or what seem to fit our definition of obsessional *impulses*. Aversion relief treatment was "much less effective in affecting change in rituals and obsessive ruminations" (p. 104).

A discouraging feature of Solyom and his colleagues' (1971) aversion relief study was the considerable amount of treatment apparently required in order to achieve therapeutic changes. If no improvement was noted after 20 to 40 sessions, treatment was terminated—although it should be pointed out that this figure is apparently contradicted by the statement that the mean number of treatment sessions was 40.5, with a range of 7 to 98 (see p. 104). The admirable perseverance of Solyom and his colleagues is borne out in his most recent study, each patient having received 50 treatment sessions (Sookman and Solyom, 1977).

By contrast, the amount of treatment provided in almost all other reports hovers around the figure of 15 sessions, with a range of only 4 in the Oxford study to 50 or more in the reports by Solyom. In our own work 15 treatment sessions was the minimum provided, and depending on the vagaries of random allocation, a patient might receive 2 blocks of 15 sessions. Rabavilas and his co-workers provided 8 treatment sessions, Boersma and his associates 15 sessions, Meyer and his associates anything ranging from 2 to 3 weeks up to as much as 6 months, depending on the requirements of the particular patient.

WHICH METHOD?

As matters stand, which behavioral method is to be preferred? The management of primary obsessional slowness, and of obsessions, is discussed at length in Chapters 15 and 19. Here we need only describe it briefly in order to set the context for the behavioral approach to the most common of the obsessional disorders.

Bearing in mind that the incidence of primary obsessional slowness, and of unaccompanied obsessions, is low and that we are not in possession of information adduced from controlled trials, the following guidelines are offered in the hope that they may be of some value to practicing therapists. Patients complaining of primary obsessional slowness appear to respond well to a program based on modeling and target-setting therapeutic instructions. Once an appropriate treatment program incorporating a ladder of targets has been constructed, the therapist provides some modeling for the patient. Thereafter, the patient's progress is monitored in a way that enables both therapist and patient to overcome obstacles as they arise. These treatment programs often require a good deal of domiciliary practice. In cases of obsessions uncomplicated by overt compulsive activities, it seems that the best approach available at present is habituation treatment and/or evocation of the thoughts to instruction, coupled with "response prevention" of any subsequent neutralizing activities. The possibilities of cognitive restructuring and of thought stopping are considered in Chapter 19.

Turning to the more common obsessional disorders, those characterized by repetitive compulsive activities (including those in which obsessions feature in a subsidiary role), the best combination we have at present comprises the two elements of exposure and response prevention. For some people the procedure benefits from the use of participant modeling procedures, and it is our impression that when this variant is used in a gradual manner, it is not only effective but also more easily accepted by patients.

It is also advisable to carry out as much of the treatment on a domiciliary basis as is possible and appropriate.

The combination of exposure and response prevention is a powerful and reliable method for achieving success. In the nature of response prevention, it seems to us to be improbable that the institution of this regime will by itself achieve much success. Unless the person is being exposed to the provoking stimulation, prevention of compulsive responses is likely to be empty. There has to be a response to prevent.

Consider a compulsive hand washer who is asked to refrain from washing her hands. If during this time she is shielded from coming into contact with the provoking contamination, abstinence from hand washing is largely meaningless. There is little or no need, no urge, to wash away the contamination. Response prevention in a "sterile" room will have little impact. Now, if the same person is asked to refrain from hand washing even after touching the contaminants, we have an entirely different set of conditions. An attempt is being made to break the abnormal connection between the stimulating event and the compulsive act.

In sum, the response prevention procedure makes sense when it is applied under the conditions that lead to the compulsive activities (or avoidance behavior in the case of fears). If it is instituted in a "vacuum," response prevention is likely to be of little value.

If response prevention is unlikely to be therapeutically effective except in combination with exposure, can the same be said of exposure? How important is the therapeutic contribution of pure exposure? Although exposure treatment alone may be therapeutically sufficient in some instances, failure to institute response prevention procedures can undermine the otherwise beneficial effects of exposure (e.g., Mills et al., 1973). If our prototypical hand washer cleans off the effects of the contaminating treatment exposures, she is unlikely to make satisfactory progress. However, in cases in which there is a strong phobic element repeated exposures can be expected to achieve a good deal, regardless of the role of response prevention. In checking compulsions, failure to institute response prevention is likely to end in therapeutic failure.

At one level the questions are simple and so, therefore, are the requirements of the pertinent experiment. The familiar dismantling tactic (e.g., Davison, 1968; Rachman, 1965) can be adopted. The three experimental conditions would be response prevention alone versus exposure alone versus exposure plus response prevention. However, it is likely that these procedures will have slightly different effects on compulsive cleaning and compulsive checking rituals. Consequently, care should be taken to construct homogeneous groups of subjects. As it is also likely that the three procedural variants will produce slightly different patterns and speeds of change in the three systems, assessment of all the components (subjective, behavioral, and psychophysiological) is advisable.

Although we have given them less attention than modeling plus exposure and response prevention, the therapeutic possibilities of desensitization, aversion relief, and thought stopping should not be ignored. In instances in which the major combination of methods fails or is impractical, unacceptable, or inappropriate, the use of these alternatives should be considered. As far as is currently known, however, these three covert procedures, like others of their type, are less powerful than the *in vivo* procedures.

Solyom and his colleagues' (1971) favorable report on the value of aversion relief needs confirmation. As it rests on an unfirm theoretical foundation and is slightly unpleasant, one would need persuasive evidence of a plausible rationale to recommend its use on a routine basis. Although thought stopping has its advocates, the evidence is inconsistent (see Stern et al., 1973, vs. Hackmann and McLean, 1975). Moreover, as Broadhurst (1976) has pointed out, it has no adequate theoretical rationale (but see Chapter 19 for some possibilities). As with aversion relief therapy, it is difficult to recommend the routine use of this type of treatment at present. Systematic desensitization has been used with some success in a number of single-case studies, but too often it appears to be a laborious way of tackling the problem. It is by no means clear why systematic desensitization apparently is less effective against obsessional-compulsive disorders than against phobic disorders, but one distinct possibility is that this imaginal form of presentation omits a crucial ingredient in overcoming compulsive disorders—response prevention. Using a three-systems analysis, it could be predicted that even if a course of systematic desensitization were successful in reducing any fear elements in the patient's disorder, the strong behavioral component (i.e., the compulsive rituals) might continue unaffected. The supplementary use of desensitization to reduce accompanying social or other fears is recommended.

In our clinical series the gross failure rate has been running at between 20 and 28 percent. Meyer, Levy, and Schnurer (1974) and Foa and Goldstein (1978) have had fewer failures in their series. Assuming that the superiority of Meyer's method is confirmed in controlled studies, we suspect that the *strictness* of the response prevention component—rather than the order of the treatment sequence or the insistence on close supervision as such—will prove to be the critical factor. Foa and Goldstein used strict instructions, but in other respects their method resembles ours more than Meyer's. Unfortunately, the strict Meyerian procedure, despite offering the hope of wider effectiveness, requires far more time and effort and a specialized ward organization. Perhaps it should be reserved for the most difficult problems. It certainly offers further hope for some of our failures—not for those who fail to improve because the demands of the treatment program produce excessive anxiety or distress but, rather, for those who fail to comply with the second stage of the treatment (i.e., the response prevention stage). These patients find that they are unable to refrain from carrying out the neutralizing rituals after the exposure sessions or even, in some cases, *during* the exposure sessions. Most of these failures occurred among patients who were carrying out compulsive checking rituals. Perhaps because of their greater pervasiveness and/or greater frequency, patients seem to have more difficulty in blocking checking rituals than in blocking cleaning rituals.

An extremely important strategy for these failures (and others) is to improve the patients' adherence to the exposure part of the treatment by giving them pharmacological help. If their feelings of discomfort, depression, or anxiety are damped by the use of appropriate drugs, they may be able to tolerate the treatment sessions more easily. A third possibility is that of increasing the patient's motivation for change, presumably through the use of a more intensive therapeutic preparation for the exposure sessions. Another possibility is to use a more gradual and graduated approach, thereby reducing the therapeutic demands made on the patient. A fifth possibility is to rely more heavily on the modeling aspects of the treatment program. Many of these possibilities are compatible and, when used in combination, may help overcome failures of the first kind.

For failures of the second kind, those that arise from a continuation of the neutralizing compulsive activities, Meyer's method offers the most hope. Here the greatest emphasis is placed on blocking the compulsive rituals. Therapists who start off with our method and encounter failure may find some advantage in switching to Meyer's method. It requires ward and nursing resources and the patient's willingness to undergo a possibly prolonged period of total response prevention, under constant supervision, for as long as it takes to bring about elimination of or substantial reduction in the ritualistic behavior. This blanketᶠing approach, with its greater call on therapeutic resources and the increased demands made on the patient, is, in our opinion, best reserved for instances in which the more direct and less demanding treatment program, which we use routinely, proves to be insufficient.

Before leaving the question of treatment failures, two recent observations made by Foa (1979) must be mentioned because of their potential importance. In the course of completing the clinical series referred to earlier, she noted that severely depressed patients showed little or no habituation. If confirmed, this finding may be of considerable practical significance. In addition, it is in keeping with Lader and Wing's (1969) report of the poor GSR habituation to auditory tones shown by agitated depressives; retarded depressives showed so little electrodermal activity that it was impossible to calculate a habituation rate. Does severe depression prevent the occurrence of emotional processing? And if it does, how and why does such habituation take place?

Secondly, Foa perceptively noted a peculiar habituation pattern among her obsessional patients with overvalued ideas (these patients, like the severely retarded cases, had a poor outcome). Although they showed signs of habituating to the provoking stimuli during treatment sessions, no lasting decrements occurred. At the start of the next session, their responses were as high as ever. Solution of these problems of habituation (and here we may add poor habituation among overanxious patients as well) may lead to an understanding of the causes of treatment failures.

Before returning to our recommendations regarding the methods and questions that might usefully be incorporated in future research on the treatment of obsessional-compulsive disorders, it is advisable to reexamine and partly reinterpret the clinical series reported before the developments that have been described in this chapter took place.

A REVIEW OF REVIEWS

As the work that preceded these recent developments has been the subject of several thorough reviews, no useful purpose would be served by treading this old territory. Instead, we have provided references to this early work and then proceeded to review the reviews in the light of recent findings. The reviews are provided by Yates (1970), Meyer, Levy, and Schnurer (1974), Eysenck and Rachman (1965), Mather (1970), and Wolpe (1958, 1973), among others. Some valuable case reports have been collected in books by Eysenck (1959, 1976), and we particularly recommend those by Meyer (1966), Walton and Mather (1963), Mills and his colleagues (1973), Taylor (1963), Wolpe (1963), and Worsley (1968). It should be remembered that there are several other methods that, while not classified as *behavior therapy*, bear some resemblance to those methods. Cognitive behavior therapy (e.g., Beck, 1976) and the individual therapy developed by Leonhard (see Röper, 1976) are among the most interesting of these relations.

Meyer and his associates (1974) correctly pointed out that, at the time of their writing, "the use of behavior therapy in the treatment of obsessional neuroses concerned single patients and there was only one control study available at that time." They detected two main strategies, "the first based on the theory of anxiety reduction and the principle of counter-conditioning ... The second strategy is to eliminate the habit which constitutes the obsessional-compulsive behavior" (Meyer et al., 1974, p. 234). Clear instances of the first strategy are provided in the case histories described by Wolpe (1963) and by Eysenck and Rachman (1965, p. 136). One of the best examples of the second strategy is Taylor's interesting treatment of a compulsive hair plucker, in which the treatment dealt directly with the woman's habit of pulling out her hair. No attempt was made to deal with the putative underlying emotional or subjective causes of the behavior. As is obvious, these two strategies reflect the contemporary view that obsessional-compulsive disorders are mainly of two types. This division is in keeping with Wolpe's classification of obsessional-compulsive disorders into anxiety-elevating and anxiety-reducing types. Eysenck and Rachman (1965) wrote that an "important consideration which arises in the treatment of every patient is whether to concentrate on the motor manifestations of the compulsive behavior or whether one should deal first and directly with the autonomic aspects of the neurotic behavior. This problem arises in the treatment of compulsive behavior and also in other disturbed motor reactions such as tics and cramps" (p. 138).

As can be seen from this quotation, it was assumed that anxiety-reducing obsessions and compulsions are best treated by methods, such as systematic desensitization, that are directed at reducing anxiety. In the anxiety-elevating compulsions, implicitly assumed to consist largely of habitual motor acts, the treatment was directed at modifying the compulsive behavior directly. Nowadays a three-systems analysis could lead one to much the same conclusion, but for slightly different reasons. If obsessional-compulsive disorders are regarded as comprising the three major components of subjective distress, psychophysiological disturbance, and behavior disorder, then it follows that the therapist might have to concentrate his or her efforts on one or another of these components, depending on the nature of the problem presented. Contemporary theorizing is consistent with these earlier views but, we hope, of wider explanatory value and, hence, with wider practical implications. There is a difficulty, however. On the whole, attempts to treat obsessional-compulsive disorders by techniques that rely wholly or largely on the presentation of imaginal material have been unsuccessful. Although there are some single-case exceptions, such as the success reported by Wolpe (1963) and a brief note by Hain, Butcher, and Stevenson (1966, p. 297), the most encouraging results have been obtained by techniques that rely largely on *in vivo* behavioral treatment. The drift of this evidence, indicating a general superiority of behavioral over cognitive methods, can raise doubts about the predictions that flow from a three-systems analysis. Our view is that this superiority is consistent with such an analysis; most of our therapeutic success and attendant knowledge relate to obsessional disorders in which the behavioral component (overt compulsions) is most prominent. With the shift of emphasis to the less common, but puzzling, obsessions, the superiority of cognitive methods may well emerge. *To come Fourth*

In disorders characterized by compulsive behavior, the presentation of an imaginal contaminant rarely leaves the subject feeling *literally* contaminated. From the point of view of the patient, it is hard to see how coming into contact with dirt or disease in the imagination can be experienced as a distressing or frightening event. Insofar as the fear expressed by disease-phobic compulsive patients reflects a fear of contracting or transmitting a disease, contact with an imaginary contaminant is inappropriate or insufficient. This observation should not be overinterpreted—their fears are rarely so simple and direct. As we have pointed out elsewhere, it is possible to hold apparently contradictory beliefs about the effects of such contaminating experiences. On the one hand, the person expresses a genuine fear of the disease; at the same time, if pressed, he or she will agree that the fear has no rational basis.

Historically, the medley of mainly imaginal methods tested on obsessional-compulsive patients during the 1960s gave way to *in vivo* modeling, exposure, and response prevention techniques in the 1970s. In their 1965 review Eysenck and Rachman had scanty clinical evidence on which to base their conclusions. Relying on the challenging laboratory research of Maier (1949) and Maier and Ellen (1951), they concluded that Maier's guidance method, which had been successful in overcoming compulsive behavior in animals, "offers another potentially useful technique if it can be successfully translated into the clinic" (p. 138). Speculating, they said that

> presumably any such attempt would, like Maier's guidance technique, be carried out in two stages. In the first, the patient would be prevented from carrying out his compulsive and obsessional behavior by physical or other coercion and his behavior would be redirected in a more appropriate manner. After this restraint and redirection had been carried out on a number of occasions, the patient would then be re-trained in order to ensure the adoption of a more adaptive and satisfactory alternative form of behavior. [p. 131]

This hope was not expressed in a sufficiently optimistic manner ["This formulation is rather vague and crude and it is to be hoped that a carefully planned . . . investigation . . . will at some stage be undertaken" (p. 132)], but the very next year Meyer (1966) reported the two case histories that helped prepare for the introduction of response prevention techniques.

In their 1974 review of the published clinical reports, Meyer, Levy, and Schnurer (1974) collated the findings of, among others, Wolpe, Lazarus, Marks and Gelder, and Cooper. They covered sixty-two patients treated by a variety of methods "based on learning principles" (p. 243) and drew these conclusions:

> Lumping all cases together, a very rough assessment of efficiency indicates that about 55 percent of the patients were judged as improved . . . In one report, where the possible therapist bias was reduced by using independent raters, the figure drops to 30 percent. One should bear in mind that the criteria of improvement are not comparable from report to report. Assessment of changes in target behavior is often anecdotal, and there is a total lack of no-treatment controls and, in general, inadequate follow-up. The sample of patients can hardly be regarded as homogeneous, and important differences such as duration, severity, type of disorder, presence of other ailments are evident. [p. 243]

This somewhat gloomy epitaph seems to us to summarize the conclusion of the first phase of this work. The altogether happier present outlook is a measure of the extent of recent advances. Discouraging reports, insofar as they referred to the treatment of obsessional-compulsive disorders, were accompanied by case studies and conference reports that were similarly pessimistic. It became evident that even among the few obsessional patients who responded well to the conventional behavioral treatments available at the time, the therapeutic task usually was unenviably arduous and lengthy. In some of the reported cases, more than 100 treatment sessions were required to achieve worthwhile results, and even when therapeutic efforts of this enormity were carried out, success was far from assured.

Why was progress so slow? Unfortunately, we cannot yet go beyond a restatement of the actual changes in procedure that were introduced. It seems to us that the changes of major importance were the introduction of *in vivo* exposure, modeling, and response prevention. There is no doubt that when we gain an improved understanding of the role of response prevention and of *in vivo* exposure, the events of the 1960s will be reinterpreted. Historians with a preference for simple outcomes will welcome evidence that response prevention is the major contributor to therapeutic change, for in this way most of the early therapeutic failures can be attributed to the omission of this element of treatment. If it turns out that *in vivo* exposure is the most effective ingredient, we will need to know why the mode of stimulus presentation should be so vital and, if so, how and why obsessions and compulsions differ from phobias in this respect. For what it is worth, our historical judgment leads us to predict that response prevention will prove to be the more important of the two identifiable treatment elements in treating checkers but that exposure will be seen to be more important in treating cleaners.

As they are a prominent part of this history, it is as well to examine the value of accumulating single-case studies and case reports. Did they help? The answer must be affirmative.

While the early case material is of some interest, particularly for the historically minded who enjoy tracing the pathway of an idea, the incompleteness of the information is a continuing source of irritation. Case reports have many merits, but conclusiveness is not one of them. It is impossible to reach conclusions because of the lack of comparability between reports and because of doubts about the validity of the therapeutic claims. In some of the clinical successes, response prevention was used—as it was in some of the failures. Similarly, *in vivo* presentations were used in both successful and unsuccessful cases.

In his important case studies, Meyer (1966) reported success and also attempted a new rationale. He attributed the successful treatment of his two severe, chronic obsessional-compulsive patients to the modification of their expectations of disaster. "Learning theories take into account the mediation of responses by goal expectancies developed from previously reinforcing situations. When these exceptions are not fulfilled, new expectancies may evolve which, in turn, may mediate new behavior. Thus, if the obsessional is persuaded or forced to remain in feared situations and prevented from carrying out the rituals, he may discover that the feared consequences no longer take place. Such modifications of expectations should result in the cessation of ritualistic behavior" (p. 275).

Meyer and his colleagues have changed the basis of their theoretical rationale. In their latest contribution the emphasis is placed on a descriptive analysis of the treatment components that are believed to be necessary, and response prevention carries off the blue ribbon (Meyer, Levy, and Schnurer, 1974). They conclude: "Our view is that it does not matter how the patient is exposed to the disturbing situations provided he or she is prevented from carrying out any rituals" (p. 258). Therapeutic outcome is said to be determined by the thoroughness of the response prevention program. Unfortunately, this latest contribution does not contain any development of Meyer's original and stimulating rationale based on expectancy theory.

Most obsessional-compulsive people recognize the irrational aspect of their actions and the accompanying rationale. Most people troubled by obsessions and compulsions do not expect "dreaded consequences" to occur; at least they do not *rationally* expect them to occur. However, they do "expect," correctly in most cases, that if they fail to avoid or escape from a noxious situation they will experience anxiety/discomfort.

Compulsive cleaners more readily agree that their ritualistic activities are irrational but nevertheless comforting. Compulsive checkers, however, tend to argue that although their compulsive activities are excessive, they do have a rational basis. For example, "It is rational to check the gas taps more than once, but my problem is that I check too frequently." They express the wish to reduce the probability of an unwanted event even at the cost of excessive caution. In balancing the risks against the costs, far greater weight is attached to the possible cost than to the probability of the unwanted consequence's occurring. In their determination to avoid the slightest possibility of the unwanted outcome, they are prepared to go to great lengths to reduce the probability of the occurrence—even to the extent of compulsively and repeatedly checking the situation. In these patients it is hard to see that changing their expectations, in the simple sense, will be therapeutically helpful. Before treatment begins, the patient's subjective estimate of the probability of the unwanted event's occurring is already extremely low. Attempting to change his or her expectations means that we have to lower an already low probability. Even if this attempt is successful, it seems intuitively unlikely to produce a significant reduction in the compulsive activities. We think it unlikely that attempts to modify the patient's expectations of the probability of the unwanted outcome, in the simple sense that we have elaborated here, will be therapeutically useful.

In cases of compulsive cleaning, there is little in the way of rational expectation to be changed. Before treatment begins, many patients agree that the probability of the unwanted event's occurring is extraordinarily low or nonexistent. Hence, attempts to change their rational expectation of the unwanted event's occurring are likely to be fruitless.

If the notion of modifying the expectations of obsessional-compulsive patients is to succeed, it must surely refer to some concept such as the expectation of psychological discomfort and not simply, or even mostly, to a rational expectation of the outcome of ritualistic acts or of their omission. If treatment is construed as an attempt to modify expectations of emotional discomfort, then we can make some headway. So response prevention can be seen as a method for exposing the person's expectations of anxiety/discomfort to repeated and prolonged disconfirmations (see, e.g., Seligman and Johnston, 1973). And as we have demonstrated in a small way so far, given the opportunity, compulsive urges and discomforts do decline spontaneously. Even if we block the execution of the compulsive acts, the person *will* lose his or her anxiety/discomfort, albeit more slowly than if he or she completed the ritualistic act. This is a disconfirmatory experience. If it is repeated, the person's expectation of prolonged and intolerable anxiety/discomfort will be weakened. As Meyer and his co-workers (1974) say, "New expectancies may evolve which, in turn, may mediate new behavior" (p. 275). A prospective analysis of the changes in expectation that occur during successful therapy would be most helpful—provided that "expectation" is not defined too narrowly and/or as a rational expectation of outcome. Bandura's (1977) unifying theory, which rests on the concept of expectations of personal efficacy, is in the same tradition as Meyer's.

Most of the independent reports on the therapeutic effects of exposure and response prevention are encouragingly consistent with our own findings. Some relatively minor exceptions have been reported and possible explanations for them considered. Either of the two treatment elements may be at least partially effective, but their combined effects are large and consistent. Of the other behavioral methods explored so far, thought stopping is promising, but some of the evidence is contradictory and firm conclusions must await further research.

Chapter 24

Psychological Modification: Theoretical Analyses

In an attempt to integrate the information on various methods of inducing psychological change, Bandura (1977) put forward the idea that all these procedures "whatever their form, alter the level and strength of self-efficacy" (p. 191). He hypothesizes that "expectations of personal efficacy determine whether coping behavior will be initiated, how much effort will be expended, and how long it will be sustained in the face of obstacles and aversive experiences" (p. 191). With behavioral methods of treatment in the forefront of his considerations, he argues that "persistence in activities that are subjectively threatening but in fact relatively safe produces, through experiences of mastery, further enhancement of self-efficacy and corresponding reductions in defensive behavior. In the proposed model, expectations of personal efficacy are derived from four principal sources of information. These include performance accomplishment, vicarious experience, verbal persuasion, and physiological states" (p. 191). Insofar as these "sources of information" are open to modification, separately or jointly, there is some resemblance here to the three-systems analysis. It differs from Lang's (1970) model, however, in placing primary emphasis on "expectations of personal efficacy."

Before considering the relevance of Bandura'a new model for the treatment of obsessional and compulsive disorders, it should be pointed out that it is by no means sure that placing the primary, indeed the sole, emphasis on cognitive changes is justifiable, and the application of a three-systems analysis is capable of integrating much of the available information. It is not entirely clear how Bandura's new model can encompass the role of motivational factors of the kind demonstrated in his earlier research [e.g., the experimental demonstration that when fearful adults are exposed to coping child models, a motivational boost is produced (Bandura et al., 1973)]. Do these factors work indirectly by facilitating performance accomplishments?

Applied to the modification of obsessions and compulsions, Bandura's theory leads one to predict that any method capable of inducing improvements in expectations of personal efficacy should succeed. As a corollary, methods of change that are not successful in inducing improvements in perceived efficacy will be unsuccessful. As the expectations of personal competence are derived from four sources of information, it follows that treatment methods that are successful in modifying any of these four sources should make a therapeutic contribution. Hence, any method that improves an obsessional patient's performance accomplishment in respect to his problem should make a therapeutic contribution. Along similar lines, if a person with obsessional-compulsive problems has vicarious experiences that increase his or her expectations of personal efficacy, this should enable him or her to make therapeutic progress. The theory allows for the contributory effects of verbal persuasion, but these are assessed in terms of their capacity for producing improvements in perceived self-efficacy. (It would of course be predicted that persuasive methods deliberately directed toward improving the person's sense of personal competence should be *most* successful.) The fourth major contributor to a sense of personal efficacy is the person's perception of his or her physiological reactivity in the appropriate situations. As before, any alteration in physiological state that contributes to an increase in perceived personal efficacy should make therapeutic progress more likely.

It is obvious how readily Bandura's theory can be turned to practical advantage and, more important at this stage of its development, to the generation of specific and testable hypotheses about the mechanisms of therapeutic change. Applying the ideas directly to the modification of obsessions and compulsions, it can be said that any procedure that induces an improvement in a person's expectation that he or she is capable of mastering the obsessional or compulsive problem should be therapeutically valuable. Broken down into the four principal sources of contribution to this sense of personal efficacy, any procedure that improves the obsessional-compulsive patient's ability to deal with or overcome the unwanted behavior (e.g., to block the compulsions) should be therapeutically beneficial. Along the same lines, vicarious experiences that improve one's perceived personal efficacy (e.g., exposure to a coping model engaging in a sufficient cleaning process) should make a useful contribution. Direct manipulation of physiological states is likely to be of value in helping obsessional-compulsive patients whose ritualistic activities are closely connected to excessive fear. To revert once more to our classical example, a person who has an excessive fear of contamination is likely to feel more confident of dealing with the necessary approach tasks if he or she gradually begins to experience a reduction in aversive physiological reactions when presented with the contaminating stimuli. By contrast, a patient whose major problems are repetitive checking rituals (with little associated fear) is unlikely to gain in confidence from attempts to change his or her physiological reactions. Then again, a person whose major problem is unwanted and intrusive thoughts is unlikely to change his or her expectations of personal efficacy after observing a coping model carry out some other task or by experiencing a reduction in his or her physiological reactions. Here the most direct route would appear to be verbal persuasion, presumably directed toward raising the patient's expectations of controlling or dismissing the unwanted thoughts.

There is little to be gained at present by extending this theoretical analysis of the putative effects of various treatment tactics, except to point out again that there are points of overlap between parts of Bandura's analysis and a three-systems approach. One advantage of the three-systems approach is that it prescribes a behavioral analysis of the problem, and this should automatically lead to a plan for modification. The modification program is in large part determined by the existing pattern of the disorder; attempts at modification are directed specifically at the components that show signs of disturbance. There seems to us to be little reason why this part of the three-systems approach should not be combined with Bandura's analysis. So, for example, if upon examination it turns out that the person's expectation of personal efficacy is being maintained at an unreasonably low level because of adverse physiological reactivity, this finding dictates the tactics to be adopted. To take another example, if the person feels that he or she cannot overcome intrusive obsessions because he or she lacks the coping skill, one is likely to select a tactic designed to improve coping performance and then give the patient an opportunity to experience the improvement.

Bandura's theory promises to provide a useful way of integrating a good deal of therapeutic information, and also provides a much needed rationale for predictive studies. However, there are some pieces of evidence that introduce doubts about the comprehensiveness of the theory, even if it succeeds in part. First, there are military examples in which reported self-confidence did not correlate with fear experienced in combat. Although confidence and courage generally showed a close correspondence, some soldiers with little confidence experienced only slight fear, while others with considerable confidence experienced high levels of fear (Rachman, 1978). Perhaps high demands distort the correlation. Second, in clinical practice one encounters some patients who perform fearlessly despite repeated expressions of low personal efficacy. Detailed analyses of the theory, plus Bandura's response, are given in a monograph devoted exclusively to the theory (Rachman, 1978c).

At a conceptual level there are arguments for supporting a three-components model of fear, and the application of this alternative leads to a different emphasis. It follows from a three-systems analysis that psychological changes can be produced by modifying one, two, or all three components. Naturally, modification of one component—say, the psychophysiological one—is likely to affect the remaining two components. Hence, directly changing a person's avoidance behavior may well produce a change in perceived personal efficacy. Similarly, directly reducing his psychophysiological responses to fear-provoking situations is likely to affect his or her perceived personal efficacy. Although there is good reason to expect that improvements in perceived personal efficacy are particularly helpful, there is no reason to suppose that all therapeutic changes are mediated by such improvements. This self-appraisal can be a producer of change or a result of change.

A THREE-SYSTEMS ANALYSIS

An analysis of the bases of change in the cognitive component of obsessional-compulsive disorders, especially the relatively pure obsessions, is given in Chapters 18 and 19. The present discussion deals mainly with explanations of the reduction of anxiety/discomfort that occurs after exposure and response prevention treatment. (As argued earlier, the subjective discomfort experienced by people who have these problems is not always characterized by fear—nevertheless, for purposes of this exposition this qualification will not be repeated throughout.) It will be assumed that the behavioral component can be reduced by direct training, especially if the subjective discomfort, cognitive abnormalities, and psychophysiological disturbances are first modified. In the absence of such preparatory changes, the behavioral component is likely to be more resistant to change; however, when behavioral shifts are accomplished even without such preparation (as in flooding treatment), the subjective and psychophysiological components are themselves modified in turn by this change in behavior. The changes *follow* the shift in behavior. In line with our three-systems analysis, obsessional-compulsive disorders are regarded as a net of three loosely coupled components. The components are not always of equal weight, and the relations between them vary from case to case. In instances in which the behavioral component is paramount and there is little accompanying subjective or psychophysiological disturbance, direct training and the introduction of appropriate reinforcement contingencies should be sufficient to accomplish a satisfactory clinical result.

In response prevention the formerly reinforced patterns of avoidance behavior are deliberately blocked. It is assumed that during this period of suspension alternate ways of achieving the desired consequences are given an opportunity to emerge. In its application to obsessional-compulsive disorders, response prevention probably works through three complementary processes. In the first place, repeated exposures to the discomfort-producing stimuli should lead to a gradual reduction in reactivity, and hence the need to carry out compulsive acts that reduce discomfort is undermined. Secondly, during the response prevention period the person acquires new and more appropriate ways of overcoming his or her discomfort (while at the same time learning that there is a strong tendency for the discomfort to decay spontaneously). Thirdly, the patient learns new response-outcome expectancies.

The reductions in anxiety/discomfort are less easily accounted for. The processes appear to be similar to those involved in the reduction of fear achieved by comparable methods for dealing with phobias, and they are as challenging to explain. The present attempt to explain the occurrence of therapeutic changes in obsessional disorders follows closely on earlier attempts to account for the fear reduction process in general (see, e.g., Rachman, 1978d). The development of three distinct and distinctly successful methods of reducing fear—desensitization, flooding, and modeling—raised the desirability of constructing a unifying theory to account for all three techniques. Earlier failures to achieve unification resigned many people to the need for less parsimonious multiple explanations.

The original contenders were the theory of reciprocal inhibition proposed by Wolpe (1958), extinction, and habituation. The arguments for and against reciprocal inhibition have been assessed elsewhere and, in the absence of any new information, cannot be advanced (see Rachman, 1974a). It is sufficient to say here that the theory can cope with much information and, not surprisingly, is particularly useful in construing fear reduction by desensitization, especially when the emphasis is shifted from muscular to mental relaxation (Rachman, 1968). However, the theory does not account for, and could not have predicted, the effects of flooding. As we have seen, desensitization proved to be of limited value in dealing with obsessional disorders. The possibility remains that reciprocal-inhibition theory might have something to contribute to our understanding of the treatment of exposure combined with response prevention. It has to be admitted, however, that while it is possible to make a reasonable attempt at providing a *post hoc* account of the effects of exposure, the absence of explicit attempts to provide an incompatible response presents a difficulty. Presumably, the reciprocal-inhibition theory will have to be extended in order to incorporate the contribution made by response prevention.

Assessment of the other two explanations, habituation and extinction, is hampered by the lack of clarity about whether the two processes can be distinguished from each other. Both are decremental processes, and the repeated presentation of the fearful or discomforting stimulus is the central operation in both. They also have some common parametric properties. These similarities and differences are considered elsewhere (Rachman, 1978d), and for our purposes the distinction of importance centers on the role of reinforcement. In theory, we can separate habituation and extinction by manipulating the occurrence of reinforcement (inserting or removing the pertinent reinforcer should have a significant effect on extinction but little or no effect on habituation). Experimentally, the two processes can be separated by comparing the decrements in fear responses observed after the repeated presentation of the fearful stimuli, with and then without the presentation of the "negative" reinforcement. For example, a dirt-phobic obsessional-compulsive patient could be presented with a specimen of dirt on numerous occasions. On the one hand, this could be followed by an aversive stimulus (and hence should *not* lead to extinction), while in the other case the dirt specimen would not be followed by any other stimulus (and hence should lead to extinction). However, if the fear reduction processes resemble habituation rather than extinction, then our prediction would be different. In both cases fear should be reduced. In a fear reduction technique based on habituation, the *consequences* of presenting the fearful stimulus should be comparatively unimportant unless the intensity of the stimulus is increased to extraordinarily high levels or an unusually intense aversive stimulus is used in the testing process.

A stumbling block for a habituation explanation of fear reduction is the therapeutic value of flooding—can we habituate to a high-intensity stimulus and/or prolonged stimulation? It has always been assumed that the answer must be negative, and the proponents of the habituation hypothesis, Lader and Wing (1966), specifically argued that habituation proceeds best when the stimuli are attenuated and the subject is at a low level of arousal. However, we now know that flooding treatment can be effective when the stimuli are not attenuated and even when the subject is highly aroused. In an experiment reported by Klorman (1974), habituation to intense stimuli was demonstrated successfully. Klorman's fearful subjects showed comparable patterns of rapid habituation to highly and mildly fear-provoking filmed material. A compatible finding was also obtained by Grey, Sartory and Rachman (1979). This reopens the door to an explanation based on habituation. Perhaps we were simply misled by the claim, quite likely to be correct in a range of circumstances, that habituation proceeds best with attenuated stimuli and at a low arousal level. However, we had—and have—no grounds for excluding the occurrence of habituation to intense stimuli (even under conditions of high arousal). In our own research on the treatment of obsessional patients, we accumulated evidence showing that something at least akin to habituation can and does occur even during and after exposure to intensely provoking stimulation.

Foa and Chambless (1978) recorded the subjective anxiety reported by 11 obsessional and 6 phobic patients during and between (fantasy) flooding sessions. Even allowing for some variation between the 3 compulsive checkers and the other patients, the regular declining course followed by the anxiety reports is compatible with a habituation model.

Klorman's (1974) experiment revives interest in the habituation hypothesis, but Klorman also made an unsuccessful attempt to confirm Lader and Wing's finding of a correlation between habituation of the GSR to auditory stimulation and fear reduction. Although this and similar failures (e.g., Gillan and Rachman, 1974) to confirm a correlation between auditory habituation and fear reduction are not fatal, it is as well to recall the importance placed on this finding in the original theorizing by Lader and Wing.

The absence of a consistent correlation may mean that there is no general attribute of proneness to habituation, and/or it may reflect a difference of habituation that takes place within and between sessions. All in all, the habituation hypothesis is worth reviving. Analysis of the role of extinction is bedeviled by uncertainty about the nature of reinforcement. Until one can identify the reinforcement, it is impossible to assess its role in maintaining the behavior.

Following a three-systems analysis leads one to postulate that the three components of obsessional-compulsive disorders may be differentially susceptible to the decremental processes of habituation and extinction (see also Rachman, 1978d). The psychophysiological component is particularly susceptible to habituation, and the avoidance behavior particularly susceptible to extinction. The subjective component seems open to both processes, habituation and extinction, but supporters of the extinction hypothesis might encounter difficulty in identifying the relevant reinforcement.

If we allow the possibility that at least two decremental processes are involved, and that these processes are not always synchronous, is there any way of disentangling the two? As proposed earlier, habituation and extinction can be teased apart by controlling the role of reinforcement. Habituation should proceed irrespective of the exclusion of reinforcement. Hence, if the psychophysiological component is subject mainly to habituation, it should decrease with repeated stimulation, regardless of the provision or exclusion of reinforcement. The behavioral-avoidance component should be more responsive to changes in reinforcement contingencies. If they are rearranged so that the avoidance behavior is followed by nonreinforcement and approach behavior is followed by positive reinforcement, then the avoidance behavior should decline in strength. There are few indications of whether subjective anxiety/discomfort is likely to be more susceptible to extinction or to habituation.

We can now return to the opening question. Do we need multiple explanations for fear reduction and, following from that, for the reduction of obsessional-compulsive disorders, or can we manage with a single theory? The answer seems to be that a single explanation is unlikely to be sufficient—but this conclusion is now offered for different, new reasons. Formerly it was argued that no single theory could account for the three main fear reduction methods (Rachman, 1974a). It is now suggested that although similar explanations can be applied to all three methods, it is unlikely that a single explanation will account for changes in all three of the components of fear or of obsessional disorders—even within a single method. The need for multiple explanations arises not from variations in the treatment methods but from the nature of the disorder itself—now conceived of as a set of loosely coupled components capable of changing desynchronously. It is suspected that they are differentially susceptible to habituation and extinction.

Our treatment method combining exposure and response prevention, whether preceded by explicit modeling or not, succeeds by modifying all three components of obsessional disorders. The therapeutic information is transmitted implicitly (or, when modeling is added, explicitly) and helps modify the abnormal cognitive aspects of the person's problems. The repeated exposures to the fearful or discomforting stimuli lead to psychophysiological and subjective habituation, and the response prevention periods help extinguish the avoidance behavior. New and more appropriate forms of approach behavior are encouraged.

It can, however, be objected that habituation and extinction are indistinguishable and that, hence, these arguments are untenable. Certainly, the dismantling process is complicated if one adopts a different view of extinction (e.g., Seligman and Johnston, 1973).

FAILURES: A LEAK IN THE SYSTEM

An adequate theory needs to account for (and predict) failures no less than successes. We have drawn attention to two types of failure, and it is instructive to see how the various explanations cope with them. All theories are able to deal easily with first type of failure: The person is unable to carry out the core of the program because of excessive discomfort. In effect, the treatment is not tested. However, the second type of failure, based we believe on inability to refrain from carrying out the relevant compulsion during response prevention periods, does pose problems. We accept, subject to controlled confirmation, that the programs of Meyer and his colleagues (1974) and Foa and Goldstein (1978) achieve superior clinical results. The most obvious differences between their methods and ours is the emphasis placed on *strict* response prevention. Presumably, the use of a strict system increases the applicability of the method— there is as yet no reason to suppose that the *degree* of improvement obtained in successful cases is influenced by the strict application of response prevention. If the assumptions are justified, we need to ask why strict response prevention reaches more people. Or, to put it another way, why does a leak in the system limit its applicability?

Meyer and Foa assume that if a patient engages in "illicit" responses the program is weakened. But *why* should this be assumed? According to an anxiety/ discomfort reduction hypothesis, one might say that illicit responses (rituals) lead to a restoration of comfort and, hence, are strengthened. A response competition theory, compatible with the first hypothesis, might be used to point out that reinforcements of the illicit compulsion interfere with the acquisition of more adaptive behavior. Both of these possibilities can be incorporated into a three-systems analysis, and moreover, the *successes* that are accomplished, even with a leaking system, raise no problems. In disorders in which the (compulsive) behavioral component is paramount, strict response prevention is especially helpful. However, in disorders in which the psychophysiological component is paramount, controlled, repetitive stimulus exposures may be a critical treatment tactic. *Strict* response prevention is not essential—the same can be said of disorders in which the cognitive component is paramount. (Incidentally, advocates of strict response prevention need to account for the successes achieved within a leaky system.)

Presumably, a proponent of Bandura's self-efficacy theory would argue that strict response prevention helps because it ensures that the person's self-perception is protected. If we define illicit responses as failures, then strict response prevention serves to reduce the failure rate—and prepares the ground for mastery experiences. In most cases of compulsive behavior, the experience of successfully refraining would be regarded as a "performance accomplishment," an occurrence that increases perceived personal efficacy. However, strict response prevention—certainly as practiced by Meyer and by Foa—depends on intensive supervision by a therapist. This is scarcely likely to improve one's feelings of *personal* efficacy. Indeed, it could be argued that strict, *externally supervised* response prevention is bound to be a weak and unreliable method.

It will be recalled that according to Bandura (1977), expectations of personal efficacy are derived from four main sources—"personal accomplishment, vicarious experience, verbal persuasion, and physiological states." On these grounds our treatment program—which comes a little closer to providing these four sources of change than Meyer's—should produce superior results. When the two treatment methods are compared directly, Bandura's theory may tip the scales in our direction.

To sum up, strict response prevention is likely to prove especially helpful in changing disorders that are characterized mainly by a behavioral component. It may play a smaller part in changing disorders characterized mainly by a cognitive or a psychophysiological component. In these, a leak in the system may be less serious.

RESEARCH PROBLEMS

As with any clinical research, two broad types of problems can be investigated: those of a technological character and those of a scientific character. The technological questions refer to improvements in technique, reduction of the failure rate, the ascertainment of prognostic indexes, and so on. The scientific questions address problems related to the mechanisms that are responsible for therapeutic change. Plainly, a number of questions are both technological and scientific.

It would be worth while exploring the value of an explanation based on modifying the patient's expectations, and Bandura's theory provides a valuable starting point. Also, a good deal of progress can be achieved from the application of a three-systems analysis to the therapeutic process. Although there is scanty direct evidence on the subject, there seems little doubt that the treatment technique does produce desynchronous changes. An elaboration of these changes and a better understanding of them would be welcome.

On the methodological side, there is an urgent need for improved measures of outcome. We need to dispense with measures that have made little contribution so far and replace them with new ones, preferably ones with greater specificity. Part of the problem with the conventional techniques of assessment is precisely that they are so general and, therefore, inevitably imprecise. They oblige one to view the essential phenomena through a series of blurred lenses.

The new battery of assessment measures should be widened in scope to enable research workers to carry out analyses of the concordance, discordance, synchrony, and desynchrony of the three systems. None of the controlled trials or clinical series reported so far addressed questions of this character. Indeed, with the exception of the Athenian group, no one has yet included psychophysiological assessments of therapeutic change. There is even a tendency for some research workers to neglect behavioral assessments of the order, manner, and extent to which compulsions change during and after therapy. In general, the outcome research reflects the excessive reliance that has been placed on broad clinical ratings of outcome. While it is true that in some respects this emphasis is consistent with practical demands, the value of these ratings—even for practical purposes—has been exaggerated. It is widely agreed that the clinical ratings are crude estimates, and that they do not necessarily reflect true changes in clinical status. The story of psychotherapy research is replete with examples of therapists who based their claimed success rates of over 90 percent entirely on such generalized clinical ratings. Inevitably, when these claims were subjected to other tests in controlled examinations they dissolved (see Rachman and Wilson, 1979).

There is a continuing need to refine the nature and delivery of the treatment. One aim is for improvements of wider range, greater magnitude, and extended durability. It is also important to get to the bottom of the treatment failures with a view to anticipating and then preventing them. We have also to keep alert to the possibility that certain variations of treatment may be more suitable for particular kinds of problems and patients. With this aim in mind, plus the practical need to give advice to the patients and their relatives, the search for reliable prognostic indexes has to continue. Although the evidence accumulated so far is encouraging, we need repeated confirmations that the long-term effects of behavioral therapy are sufficiently stable. The supplementary value of drug treatment is of great importance, and investigations are under way.

AN ALTERNATE STRATEGY

Most of this discussion (and the ensuing proposals) is of course rooted in the conventional model of therapeutic research. As mentioned in the introduction to this chapter, there are grounds for uneasiness about the nature and direction of outcome research.

Conventional outcome studies have many merits and undoubtedly are a great improvement on the unsystematic accumulations of case reports that formerly provided the sole evidence on which to reach conclusions about therapeutic effects. The main features of these "conventional" outcome studies are the inclusion of control groups, random allocation to treatment, and the use of more than one type of pre- and posttreatment measurement (with an emphasis on clinical ratings and the employment of independent and blind assessors). These tactics all contribute to improving the reliability of the findings, but most of them contain implicit assumptions that should be identified and then examined critically.

The main thrust of our argument is that a revision of the three assumptions listed at the opening of this chapter (the illness model, the lump theory, and excessive generality) will enable research to progress more rapidly and fruitfully (see Rachman and Wilson, 1979, for a full discussion of outcome research).

On the measurement question, reliance on imprecise and degraded information that assumes a nonexistent degree of generality of behavior is bound to obscure the effects of any form of therapy and, hence, to preclude the conduct of exact evaluation research. Crude measuring instruments, based on a mistaken conception of the properties of the material to be measured, are a poor foundation for research. In passing, it is worth mentioning that the use of generalized measures in assessing the effects of therapy is more than a research problem; therapeutic decisions based on poor-grade information are against the interests of the patient.

The specific therapeutic contributions of behavior therapy, such as they are, are best evaluated by specific measures of change. The continued use of generalized measures will simply reproduce inconclusive results. It is inevitable that comparisons based on generalized measures (which always seem to lean slightly to the right of the midpoint of any scale) will tend to blur the differences between treatments—any treatments. If, on the other hand, one wishes to isolate the specific, differential effects of particular treatment tactics, then it is advisable to select closely specified, replicable measurement procedures. Behavioral tests, psychophysiological assessments of reactivity to specific stresses, and standardized data-based interviews of the client and an informed relative or friend will replace personality questionnaires, projective tests, generalized rating scales, degree of "constructive personality change," and percentages of cure/improvement/no-change categories (see Mischel, 1977).

The case for undertaking evaluative studies that follow the pattern of conventional outcome research is weak, and there are positive alternatives. By setting aside these assumptions concerning the medical model, the lump theory, and the generality of psychological problems, we can proceed to a new attack on the question of therapeutic effectiveness. The definition of the person's problems and the means of assessing them would become more properly psychological and more specific. Unsuitable delivery systems would have to be changed or replaced. The selection of closely specified measurements and the design of outcome experiments, based on a three-systems analysis, will enable us to study both process and outcome questions simultaneously and in a fruitful new manner.

The move toward greater specificity of our measurements is allied to the establishment of specifiable treatment goals. The effects of treatment can be stated in quantified degrees of success rather than in generalized reports of cure, relapse, or improvement.

A proposal of a different character arises from dissatisfaction with the trend toward the undirected accumulation of disparate facts. Where possible, outcome studies should collect evidence that bears on significant theoretical questions. So, for example, one should bear in mind whether the observed effects, be they positive or negative, can be accommodated by existing theory. Questions of this kind can be put in the narrow sense (e.g., "Does response prevention achieve the specified therapeutic goals, and if so, for the theoretical reasons given?"). Or they can be asked in the broader sense (e.g., "Is this behavior change method best conceived of as a means of increasing perceived personal efficacy?"). In the example already given, do the therapeutic results achieved by people with intense compulsions conflict with the medical model of obsessional neuroses and/or the emerging psychological model of obsessions?

Notwithstanding the valuable advances in our capacity to help people with severe obsessional-compulsive problems, there are obstacles ahead. Even if our alternate strategy fails to appeal, recognition of the dubious assumptions underlying current approaches is overdue.

SUMMARY

Bandura's integrative theory, according to which psychological change is governed by perceived personal efficacy, is cohesive and stimulating. After assessing its advantages we presented an alternate perspective based on the three-systems approach. If obsessional disorders are regarded as comprising three loosely coupled components, it follows that different therapeutic procedures are likely to affect each component differentially. It was argued that the psychophysiological component will respond most readily to habituation procedures, the compulsive behavior to direct behavioral procedures such as exposure plus response prevention, and the cognitive elements to cognitive and behavioral methods. Desynchronous changes were predicted, depending on the therapeutic procedure adopted.

It was also argued that conventional outcome research has been hampered by the acceptance of three dubious assumptions: that the medical model is appropriately applied to obsessional disorders, that these disorders fit into a "lump" model, and that generalized outcome measures are preferable. A series of positive alternatives to replace current tactics was presented.

SECTION D

Chapter 25

Theoretical Considerations

In this concluding chapter consideration is given to a number of topics of theoretical significance, excluding those, such as the persistence of compulsions, that have already been dealt with at length. The topics include the relations among phobias, obsessions and compulsions; the nonrandom distribution of obsessions and compulsions; learned helplessness; and the three-systems approach to obsessional disorders.

PHOBIAS, OBSESSIONS, AND COMPULSIONS

Throughout this book attention has been drawn to the close connection between obsessional-compulsive problems and excessive fears (phobias). It is possible to distinguish among different degrees of association; while the relationship between phobias and cleaning compulsions is particularly close, that between phobias and primary obsessional slowness is slender. In this section we will consider the consequences of the connection between phobias and compulsions for theories of the genesis and maintenance of obsessional-compulsive disorders. In order to facilitate the analysis, the cardinal points are summarized as follows:

1a. The psychophysiological responses to phobic and obsessional-compulsive stimuli appear to be similar—both involve an increase in autonomic responsiveness, particularly heart rate (but see 6a).

1b. These autonomic increments can be provoked by tangible or imaginal presentations of phobic or obsessional material.

1c. The presentation of stimulus material related to compulsive activities produces psychophysiological reactions similar to those observed after the presentation of stimulus material related to pure obsessions.

1d. After successful treatment autonomic responses to phobic and obsessional-compulsive material are diminished.

2a. The subjective responses to phobic and obsessional-compulsive material are similar—both involve an increment in discomfort.

2b. These increments in subjective discomfort can be provoked by the presentation of tangible or imaginal phobic or obsessional material.

2c. The presentation of material related to compulsive activities produces subjective reactions similar to those seen after the presentation of material related to pure obsessions.

2d. After successful treatment the subjective responses to phobic and obsessional material are diminished.

3a. Both phobic and obsessional-compulsive reactions are associated with extensive avoidance behavior.

3b. After successful treatment there is a marked diminution in the extent and intensity of avoidance behavior.

4a. There is clinical evidence of excessive fear among obsessional-compulsive patients (see Kringlen, 1965; Skoog, 1959; Videbech, 1975).

4b. Adult obsessional patients report an elevated incidence of childhood fears (e.g., Ingram, 1961; Lo, 1967; Videbech, 1975; Warren, 1960).

4c. There is an elevated incidence of anxiety neuroses among the relatives of obsessional patients (Rosenberg, 1967).

5. The majority of phobic and obsessional patients respond favorably to similar methods of behavior therapy.

6a. Compulsive cleaners are predicted to be more fearful than compulsive checkers or patients with primary obsessional slowness.

6b. More cleaners than checkers report a sudden onset of their difficulties.

6c. The female:male ratio is higher in compulsive cleaners (and also in phobics) than in compulsive checkers.

7. There are differences between phobic and obsessional stimuli; obsessions have a larger endogenous stimulus element (e.g., Ramsay, 1976) and phobias are to a greater extent precipitated by external stimulation.

8. Obsessions are more frequently associated with depression.

9. It is possible that phobic and obsessional reactions share a common resistance to habituation.

It is not suggested that cleaning compulsions are identical with phobias, merely that they are closely related. There are differences in content and possibly a temporal difference as well. In the main, phobic reactions are reactions to imminent threat while obsessional fears tend to relate to delayed threats.

Insofar as there is a close connection between phobias and obsessional-compulsive problems, one is justified in searching for similar determinants to account for the genesis of the two disorders. Unfortunately, the most prominent psychological theory proposed to account for the acquisition of excessive fears, conditioning theory, is wanting (see Rachman, 1977b, 1978d). While the conditioning theory of fear acquisition can account for the development of some fears, it lacks comprehensiveness and is also inadequate in some other respects. It follows that the conditioning theory cannot provide an adequate explanation for the genesis of obsessional-compulsive disorders.

The major arguments against acceptance of the theory include the facts that people fail to acquire fears in theoretically fear-evoking situations and that it is difficult to produce conditioned fear reactions in human subjects in the laboratory. Moreover, the theory rests on the untenable equipotentiality premise. Furthermore, fears can be acquired indirectly, contrary to the demands of the conditioning theory. In recognition of these shortcomings, it has been suggested that "fears can be acquired by three pathways: conditioning, vicarious exposures, and the transmission of information and instruction . . . Vicarious and informational transmission of fears can take place in the absence of direct contact with the fear stimuli" (Rachman, 1977b).

As cleaning compulsions and the associated fears of contamination tend to have a tangible onset suggestive of a conditioning process, such compulsions may well be generated by conditioning. On the other side, checking compulsions generally have a gradual onset, and this pattern seems to fit less comfortably with a conditioning explanation—it being remembered at the same time that fear is presumed to play a lesser role in checking compulsions than in cleaning compulsions. Presumably, vicarious and instructional processes are most prominent in promoting checking—although the available information on parental modeling of compulsive behavior is weak and discouraging. The direct transmission of specific patterns of obsessional-compulsive behavior, by modeling or by instruction, is unlikely to be a common occurrence. Rather, the evidence points toward the transmission of general dispositions and attitudes on which obsessions and compulsions can take root.

In our view there are four major determinants of obsessions and compulsions—specific learning exposures (including conditioning), social learning, a genetic contribution, and mood disturbances. The last two of these determinants play a part in all obsessional disorders, but social learning is likely to be especially prominent in checking disorders and specific exposures especially prominent in cleaning disorders.

For obsessional-compulsive problems in which fear plays a prominent part, however acquired, Mowrer's two-stage theory is still applicable, despite its shortcomings. It introduced the idea that fear can energize behavior and is not merely a nonconsequential reaction to stimuli associated with pain. This motivating quality of fear is the key idea of the theory, and Mowrer went on to add that the reduction of fear stamps in new behavior. It acts as a reinforcement. The last part of the theory is the proposition that behavior motivated by fear is of the avoidance type and that when it is successfully executed, it leads to a reduction of fear and, hence, to a strengthening of the avoidance behavior itself. As Mowrer stated, "Fear . . . motivates and reinforces behavior that tends to avoid or prevent the recurrence of the pain-producing (unconditioned) stimulus" (Mowrer, 1939, p. 554). In elaborations of these ideas, Mowrer shifted the emphasis from the cause of the fear to its secondary motivating properties, and argued that "fear in the case of both active and passive avoidance behavior is an essential intermediary 'cause' or 'variable'" (Mowrer, 1960, p. 49). Although Mowrer's view that "fear is a decisive causal factor in avoidance behavior" (p. 97) is almost certainly incorrect (see Rachman, 1976b), there is ample support for the idea that fear often plays an important part in generating and maintaining avoidance behavior.

In the case of cleaning compulsions and to a lesser extent checking compulsions, our own evidence is at least consistent with the views proposed by Mowrer, although there are exceptions, such as compulsive cleaners with little fear. If we agree to go beyond the concept of fear to include the broader concept of subjective discomfort, our research shows that exposure to the pertinent contaminating or otherwise disturbing stimulus reliably produces an increase in subjective discomfort. Moreover, execution of the appropriate cleaning or other compulsive ritual is usually followed by a prompt reduction in subjective discomfort. It should be pointed out that the two-stage theory has limited relevance to the maintenance of compulsive behavior unless one goes beyond the insistence on the necessity for the person experiencing *fear*; many patients, particularly those displaying checking compulsions, deny that their discomfort resembles fear. Once we concede this point and proceed from the proposition that exposure to the provoking situation produces subjective discomfort, then the modified two-stage theory retains some value. It follows these lines.

Exposure to a fear-provoking or otherwise disturbing situation produces subjective discomfort. This gives rise to escape or avoidance behavior, and tactics that are repeatedly successful in reducing the subjective discomfort are strengthened. This explanation can accommodate a good deal of information, but it is not without problems. In the first place, there is a significant minority of exceptions in which the checking compulsions persist despite the absence of any reductions in subjective discomfort or fear. In addition, we have mentioned on several occasions the necessity for incorporating the longer-term human motives. Human behavior is not maintained merely by its immediate consequences. People who compulsively check the security of their home are doing so in anticipation of future events, just as some people who carry out compulsive cleaning rituals are hoping to avoid the development of disease or discomfort months or years in the future. Furthermore, allowance must be made for the fact that a certain percentage of compulsive rituals have a significant symbolic content. Our young patient who washed his hands in order to prevent harm from coming to his parents, some 5,000 miles away, was carrying out a symbolic act that achieved a reduction in subjective discomfort, albeit imperfectly.

If the reduction of subjective discomfort plays a major role in ensuring the persistence of compulsive activities in most cases, it follows that a reversal of this effect should lead to an extinction of the ritualistic behavior. Similarly, the substitution of a more effective method for reducing subjective discomfort should see a weakening of the ritualistic behavior. Direct tests of these deductions from the theory have yet to be carried out, but the therapeutic evidence collected so far is not inconsistent with these deductions.

On the question of why cleaning compulsions are, relatively speaking, common, it would seem that we are obliged to invoke Seligman's (1971) concept of prepared connections or some related concept of "selectivity." Fears of dirt and contamination occur far more widely and more commonly than would be the case if fears were determined on a random basis. Even if Seligman's theory cannot be supported, we see no acceptable alternative to some version of a prepared connection, as the equipotentiality premise is unlikely to be sustained.

Before leaving the problem of why obsessions and compulsions persist despite their many unwanted effects, it is necessary to draw attention for the last time to the paradoxical persistence of thoughts and actions that consistently produce predominantly aversive consequences. In addition to the obvious examples of unwanted and unacceptable obsessional ideas and images, we have also to contend with what Wolpe (1958) described as the "anxiety-elevating" compulsions. A likely explanation for the persistence of these aversive acts is that they are tolerated in the short run, despite their aversive consequences, in order to achieve some longer-term satisfaction or relief. In addition, and not necessarily incompatible with this first possibility, obsessions and some compulsions might persist as a result of a sensitizing process. In his expanded and revised theory of neurosis, Eysenck (1976) placed considerable emphasis on the incubation of anxiety. He points out that we now have sufficient laboratory examples in which the presentation of a conditioned stimulus can be followed by an enhancement of the conditioned response rather than by extinction. He argues that conditioned stimuli that do not produce drives are indeed subject to the classical law of extinction while conditioned stimuli that do produce drives follow the law of enhancement (incubation). For obvious reasons the experimental analysis of incubation effects in human subjects is rarely undertaken. In the circumstances it might be best to carry out analyses of what appear to be processes of incubation in obsessional patients, particularly those who suffer from pure obsessions. At a descriptive level many of these obsessions appear to undergo *natural enhancement* (i.e., to undergo internal sensitization). The development of the incubation argument in respect of obsessional-compulsive disorders will be followed with considerable interest.

Thus far we have approached the nature and genesis of the disorder in an overly simple fashion, following the "lump" theory. A comprehensive account of the factors promoting the disorders may demand a three-systems analysis.

It seems to us improbable that the content of obsessions and compulsions is wholly undetermined—a matter of chance. The incidence of certain types of obsession and compulsion is so high as to rule out the possibility of random variation. Within this relatively uncommon class of disorders, fears of contamination and dirt associated with compulsive hand washing (for example) are encountered so frequently that any theory that rests on the premise that the content of the obsession or compulsion is a matter of relative indifference is bound to falter.

The belief that "what an organism learns about is a matter of relative indifference" (Seligman and Hager, 1972), otherwise known as the equipotentiality premise, was effectively criticized by Seligman (1970), who went on to apply the same criticisms to theories about the genesis of phobias (Seligman, 1971). It is necessary to allow for some form of selectivity in the representation of phobic stimuli. Fears are not randomly distributed; for example, fear of snakes is extremely common and fear of lambs uncommon (Rachman, 1974). Insofar as there is a connection between fear and certain types of compulsive behavior, especially cleaning rituals, any theory of compulsive behavior must take into account the nonrandom distribution of fears. Indeed, even if no such connection is claimed, the need to explain the nonrandom distribution of the content of obsessional disorders remains.

We now turn to an examination of two related questions and the value of one attempted solution. The two problems that need to be addressed are the nonrandom distribution of the content of obsessions and compulsions and the consequences of a revised theory of fear (Seligman, 1971; Rachman, 1977b) for our hypothesis regarding the relation between fears and compulsions. Any explanation of obsessions and compulsions that attaches importance to the role of learning, and very few do not (e.g., Schilder, 1938), needs to take into account the failure of the equipotentiality premise. Until recently most psychological theories contained an implicit assumption that the premise was sound. "In classical conditioning the choice of conditioned stimulus, unconditioned stimulus, and response matters little; that is, all conditioned stimuli and unconditioned stimuli can be associated more or less equally well, and general laws exist which describe the acquisition, extinction, inhibition, delay of reinforcement, and spontaneous recovery of all conditioned and unconditioned stimuli" (Seligman and Hager, p. 2). After presenting contrary evidence and critical arguments, Seligman (1971) developed the concept of preparedness and applied this alternate idea to an analysis of phobias. A learned association that is readily acquired is defined as *prepared*, and one that is acquired with considerable difficulty is *unprepared*. "If the organism makes the response consistently after only a few pairings, it is somewhat prepared. If the response appears only after many pairings, the organism is unprepared" (Seligman, 1970, p. 408). Seligman went on to postulate that "phobias are highly prepared to be learned by humans and, like other highly prepared relationships they are selective and resistant to extinction, and probably are non-cognitive" (1972, p. 455). He also suggested that most phobias are of biological significance and argued that "the great majority of phobias are about objects of natural importance to the survival of the species. It does not deny that other phobias are possible, it only claims that they should be less frequent, since they are less prepared." Human phobias are "largely restricted to objects that have threatened survival, potential predators, unfamiliar places, and the dark" (Seligman and Hager, 1972, p. 465). Prepared associations, including prepared phobias, should extinguish slowly. Unprepared connections, on the other hand, should be subject to easy extinction. In summary, then, phobias are examples of prepared learning and, as such, are biologically significant, common, and readily acquired. They should show the empirical properties of resistance to extinction and broad generalization. Some valuable supporting evidence has already been produced in a series of fascinating experiments conducted mainly at Uppsala University (see Ohman, Fredrikson, and Hugdahl, 1978).

Seligman's criticisms of the equipotentiality premise are convincing and directly applicable to earlier views about the acquisition of obsessional-compulsive problems. Although the constructive part of the theory, centered on the concept of preparedness, is persuasive, some difficulties have already emerged (see Rachman and Seligman, 1976; Rachman, 1978b). Before we turn to an examination of the status of the concept, extrapolation to obsessional and compulsive phenomena is necessary. Like phobias, the content of most obsessions and compulsions should be of biological significance, show a nonrandom distribution, and be acquired relatively easily (to use one of Seligman's terms, they should be acquired even with degraded input). Insofar as they are prepared, obsessions and compulsions should show considerable resistance to extinction and broad generalization.

There are at least five difficulties with the concept of prepared phobias and, by extension, the concept of prepared obsessions and compulsions (Rachman, 1978b). First, Rachman and Seligman (1976) described two clinical cases that ran contrary to prediction. Second, de Silva, Rachman, and Seligman (1977) found that although the content of the phobias and obsessions of over 150 psychiatric patients fell within the descriptive terms of the concept of preparedness, the clinical predictions that flow from the theory were not supported. Third, some anthropological evidence (to be discussed later) is not consistent with the emphasis on the biological significance of prepared associations. Fourth, a definition that rests on ease of acquisition excludes many common, significant fears (such as social fears, agoraphobias, etc.) that arise gradually. Fifth, the concept does not attach sufficient importance to the match between the "prepared" stimulus and the aversive event(s).

UNPREPARED FEARS

One of the obsessional patients described by Rachman and Seligman (1976), who had an unprepared phobia, was admitted to the hospital with a chronic and severe disorder in which the main features were compulsive rituals that arose out of her powerful fear of chocolate. She complained of and demonstrated extreme fear when confronted with chocolate or any object or place associated with chocolate.

According to the patient and the independent account given by her husband, her psychiatric complaints had begun shortly after the death of her mother, to whom she was inordinately attached. After the death she was depressed for a prolonged period and also became aware of a strong aversion toward, and probably a fear of, cemeteries and funeral parlors. She first became aware of a slight distaste for chocolate several months after the death of her mother, but it was nearly four years after this event that it became clear to her and her husband that she was actively avoiding chocolate and indeed had become extremely frightened of it. Prior to her mother's death, she had eaten chocolate with enjoyment; but this pleasure seemingly waned gradually in the period after her mother's death.

For purposes of the present discussion, the most relevant characteristics of this patient's chocolate phobia were its rarity, its gradual onset, the intensity of the fear and the associated compulsions and avoidance behavior, the widespread generalization from chocolate to a large variety of brown objects, and its resistance to modification. The rarity, gradual acquisition, and biological significance of the fear warranted the description of *unprepared* phobia. Contrary to prediction, however, it proved extremely resistant to modification. Even an intensive course of behavioral treatment was able to produce comparatively slight improvements. Her avoidance behavior and compulsions were enduring, extensive, and pronounced.

Rachman and Seligman were cautious in drawing conclusions on the basis of this and one other unprepared phobia, and mentioned two reservations. In the first place, the chocolate-phobic patient was comparatively inarticulate and provided a spotty history of the development of her phobic compulsions. Secondly, the therapist was able to construct or reconstruct a possible relationship between her fear of chocolate and an earlier but persistent and strong fear of scenes connected with death. It is possible that the fear of chocolate had as its origin a strong emotional reaction to the death of her mother, at which time she had been obliged to observe the coffin containing the body. The patient

believed that the coffin was dark brown in color and that it may have contributed to the association that she had formed between death and chocolate. Even
more telling, she felt sure that at the time of her mother's death she noticed a
bar of chocolate on the table on which the coffin rested. The symbolic connection between death, the color brown, and chocolate might be based on too
fanciful an interpretation, but there was confirmatory evidence of her fear of
death scenes. During a behavioral-avoidance test, the patient displayed inability
to approach funeral parlors, and considerable fear was aroused during the
attempt.

In their discussion of this patient and the second patient described by
them, Rachman and Seligman introduced the possibility that "symbolic transformation might well be a hallmark of unprepared phobias" (1976, p. 337).
Whether symbolic transformations are indeed a hallmark of prepared phobias
and/or obsessions, they were equally prominent in another case of an
unprepared obsession, encountered the following year.

The patient, a middle-aged woman, complained of an obsession related to
colors and heat. It apparently developed gradually (again, no easy acquisition)
during the terminal illness of her husband, but in her early adulthood she had
experienced a breakdown characterized by anxiety and obsessional thoughts.
In her own words, "The main problem is colors. I cannot look at any of the
colors that are in the fire, red, orange or pink."

The colors blue, green, brown, white, and gray were neutral, and the
patient used them to "neutralize" the effects of the fiery colors. "If I happen to
see a fire color, I've got to immediately look at some other color to cancel it out.
I've got to look at a tree or flowers out in the grounds, something brown or
white, to neutralize it." For a considerable time she had walked around with a
small piece of green carpet material that she used to neutralize the effects of
orange. Although at the time of her admission to the hospital her neutralizing
activities were predominantly visual, the reappearance of earlier neutralizing
statements was sometimes reported.

During the course of the investigation, it turned out that the patient had
an association between fiery colors and heat. Any stimuli associated with the
fiery colors or the sensation of heat were capable of inducing what she described
as "traumatic feelings." The most common provocation was visual stimuli,
followed by tactile stimulation.

She described the traumatic feeling evoked by colored or hot stimuli in
this way:

> It starts in my mind, and when I look at the color I start to tremble, and I
> go hot all over just as though I'm on fire. I cannot stand up, I've got to sit
> down or else I'll fall. I feel sick and all I can say is that it's a traumatic
> feeling, that's the only word I can think of to describe it. And if it's the
> last color I look at before I get into bed, I just won't sleep all night.

I try to fight it, and get into bed and tell myself that it's ridiculous. I know it can't hurt me physically, although it does harm me mentally. I lie there and this hot feeling comes over me and I start to tremble. If that happens I have to get up, put all my clothes on again and start once more as though I am getting into bed. Sometimes I have had to do this four or five times before finally getting to sleep. The same thing happens to me when I get up in the morning, or when I go to the toilet.

Hot is another difficult thing. Anything that's hot. The radiators, water— I cannot wash in hot water and this is why I avoid having a bath. Sometimes, if I am very brave, I can run a little hot water in before I get into the bath. Usually I have to bathe in cold water.

The colors and heat are connected. And it's not just hot things and red things that cause problems, but also the things that I associate with them.

I think it all began some years ago when I had a sort of nervous breakdown. At the onset I went very hot; it seemed to happen overnight somehow. I was in bed and woke up feeling very hot. It was connected with an obsession that I had about my ailing mother at that time. I feared for her safety and when I got a horrible thought that she might have an accident or a serious illness, this horrible hot feeling came over me. At the time I managed to get over it and for many years, had no difficulties. After my husband died, I lived alone for some time and was all right.

It's hard to say exactly when the obsession started. It was gradual. My obsession about colors must have been coming on for a couple of years very, very gradually. I only noticed it fully during the past twelve years when it has got worse and worse. I can't look at certain colors, can't bathe, can't do any cooking, have to repeat many activities over and over again.

As in the earlier case, the content of this obsession was unprepared. The fear of and excessive concern with colors is extremely unusual, lacks any biological significance (except perhaps by virtue of its association with fire), and was acquired gradually. Despite having the defining characteristics of an unprepared fear, it showed the empirical qualities of a prepared phobia (i.e., was extremely resistant to modification and generalized broadly). As in the earlier case, there were undeniable signs of symbolic transformation, but their nature and significance were never made clear.

Despite the discouragement of these contrary cases, we undertook an extensive retrospective analysis of 69 phobic and 82 obsessional patients (de Silva, Rachman, & Seligman, 1977). After constructing scales for rating the preparedness of the content of the disorder, independent ratings were made of each of the patients. Although the rating system for the content of the disorder proved to be successful, a similar scheme for rating the purpose of the abnormal behavior failed and was therefore discarded. The preparedness of the content of the obsessions and phobias was determined by the extent to which the object or situation was judged to be dangerous to pretechnological man. So objects or situations judged to be "probably dangerous to pretechnological man under not uncommon circumstances" were given the highest rating, whereas those judged "very unlikely to have ever been dangerous" were given the lowest rating. Predators, blood, and thunderstorms received high ratings, while flowers, safe appliances, and so forth received low ratings.

The main result was that in the majority of cases the phobias and obsessions were rated as prepared. Although the numbers are small, more unprepared obsessional cases than phobic cases emerged from the ratings. The majority of obsessions were prepared, but there was a notable number of unprepared cases—13 out of 82 patients had ratings of less than 5 (e.g., fear of splintered glass, fear of "fatal" numbers, etc.). To our considerable disappointment, however, there was no relationship between the prepared content of the obsession and therapeutic outcome. Neither was there any relationship between preparedness and mode of onset or severity of the disorder or degree of generalization. In sum, even though the large majority of obsessional cases were rated as prepared, they did not show the empirical properties predicted by Seligman's theory.

These findings were interpreted as weakening "the clinical usefulness of the concept of preparedness" (p. 75). The authors went on to argue that on a narrow construction of the hypothesis the results were not disconfirmatory. In fact, the data tended to confirm the very high incidence of prepared phobias and prepared obsessions. If the hypothesis is construed broadly as saying that, among the disorders that are seen at clinics, prepared obsessions and phobias will be more resistant to extinction, it is disconfirmed. (The advantages of changing the emphasis of the definition from "ease of acquisition" to "resistance to extinction" or "phobic content" are considered in Rachman, 1978b.)

The hypothesis can be salvaged. Since we were dealing with the most intense tail end of the distribution of human fears and obsessions—phobias and obsessional disorders—it is possible that the predicted empirical properties were masked by the generally high intensity of the fears and obsessions. As with obsessions, "A more representative sample of the whole range of human fears, in which clinical phobias would be a small minority, might well reveal that more prepared fears are more resistant to treatment" (p. 75). Within a clinical sample, however, we observed slight but dramatic evidence of the difficulties that can arise in the treatment of unprepared obsessions or phobias.

Our failure to find support for the clinical predictions that flow from the theory of preparedness lessens our confidence in the usefulness of the theory but does not disconfirm the theory itself. It is entirely possible for the essentials of the theory to be in order, even if the clinical implications drawn from it are found to be incorrect. So for example, the argument that the distribution of human fears is non-random and therefore indicative of evolutionary pressure on learning to be afraid of specific objects or situations . . . is not weakened. And it is this non-randomness that forms the core of the preparedness concept. It may well be that the clinical predictions fail precisely because they are clinical—in dealing with a restricted sample, relatively homogeneous in intensity, one may inadvertently have masked the differences between prepared and unprepared phobias . . . Nevertheless . . . the concept of preparedness is not useful in predicting the outcome of therapy for phobic and obsessional disorders. [de Silva, Rachman, and Seligman, 1977]

Even though our research into the clinical implications of the preparedness concept regrettably produced little enlightenment beyond demonstrating that a large percentage of obsessions and phobias can be described as prepared according to the definition set forth in the theory, it drew attention once more to the symbolic quality of some obsessions and compulsions. In the two cases of unprepared obsessions described earlier, there was good reason to suppose that the obsession—chocolate or fiery colors—had taken on some symbolic meaning. To these two examples we can add the observation that many compulsive rituals appear to be carried out in a symbolic manner or for symbolic reasons. It is quite characteristic to find that a patient who engages in excessive, compulsive handwashing rituals turns out to be peculiarly indifferent to bodily dirt. In one of the most severe cases we have encountered, the patient washed her hands up to 100 times each day in a mixture of hot water and antiseptic, but appeared to be relatively unconcerned about the dirt and contamination that had accumulated on the rest of her body. She rarely bathed and seemed to have little desire to do so. In another case, referred to earlier, a young man who was troubled by unacceptable, intrusive thoughts about harm coming to his close relatives succeeded in neutralizing the thought, and thereby protecting his relations, by repeatedly washing his hands. He was of course aware that the ritualistic cleaning had no influence on their lives, and he recognized the symbolic quality of his protective rituals. The anthropological literature is replete with examples of cleaning rituals that fulfill symbolic rather than hygienic needs. For example, Hindus achieve spiritual cleanliness by rinsing themselves in thickly polluted rivers.

CULTURAL VARIATIONS

Indeed, it could be objected that the anthropological evidence on cleanliness indicates a wider cultural variation than a preparedness interpretation of compulsive cleaning would predict. Seligman's general argument, and the emphasis on the biological significance of preparedness in particular, may lead one to expect a higher degree of cultural and historical uniformity than is reported—such uniformity does, however, greatly exceed a random variation pattern. According to Kroeber (1948), "there is immense variation [in cultural attitudes toward bodily cleanliness] both between different nations and in the same nation at different times" (p. 600). Although the early Romans devoted a great deal of time and effort to bodily cleanliness, the early Christians "felt themselves increasingly in conflict not only with the established pagan religion but with many of its attitudes and trends," and baths were part of this unacceptable culture. They were considered to be excessively indulgent and "before long overcleanliness, and then what we would consider minimum cleanliness, came to be considered one of the roads to ruin" (p. 600). For many devoted ascetics there is a conflict between spiritual cleanliness and bodily cleanliness. According to Kroeber, "for over two centuries, cultivated Europe . . . washed little and looked on bathing as rarely needed and as likely to be dangerous to health" (p. 601).

Not only are there historical variations in attitudes toward bodily cleanliness; variations are also evident within the same society (e.g., India). Kroeber also draws attention to cross-cultural differences. "The cleanliness of the Japanese is proverbial and almost obsessive . . . The contrast is marked with China, where seamy sides are common" (p. 602). Lastly, as already mentioned, people can engage in seemingly contradictory behavior—obtaining spiritual purification in polluted waters. Kroeber concluded, correctly, that we simply do not know whether or not impulses toward cleanliness and neatness "are congenital in individual human beings" (p. 602).

The fact that washing is not universally and consistently encouraged in all cultures weakens the notion of a prepared response to dirt and contamination but does not destroy it. As in prepared fears, the lurking tendency has yet to be ignited by an appropriate aversive event (Rachman, 1978b). Even in "dirty" cultures, some compulsive cleaners will be found struggling against contamination.

If the problem is approached by examining the observable cleaning behavior that occurs within and between cultures, care must be taken not to confuse hygienic and symbolic intentions. Many cleaning activities have obvious and important symbolic significance (see Kroeber, 1948, for examples). Although there are some fascinating similarities between the symbolic significance of personal rituals and that of religious rituals, the differences between these two kinds of activities should not be overlooked. The general similarities between compulsive rituals and religious or social rituals are that they are repetitive, stereotyped, and often produce short-term relief of discomfort. From our point of view, however, the differences between compulsive rituals and socioreligious rituals are probably of greater importance. Unlike social rituals, compulsive rituals are seldom imitative, always personal, and generally aimed at preventing unwanted outcomes rather than at achieving a desired event (see Malinowski, 1954, and Chappel and Coon, 1953).

The present position can be summed up as follows: The content of obsessions and compulsions is not random; certain types of obsessions and compulsions appear to be acquired more widely and more readily than other types. The defining characteristics proposed by Seligman (1971) for identifying prepared phobias (and, by extension, obsessions as well) can be operated successfully, but his scheme has weaknesses and may have to be revised. The large majority of phobias and obsessions evident in a clinical population do, however, fall within the *clinical definition* of preparedness derived from Seligman's theory. In this, as in other respects, there is an affinity between phobias and obsessions. If we rely on the original definition of preparedness based on ease of acquisition, many obsessions and fears would be excluded.

Contrary to the predictions drawn from the theory, the degrees of preparedness of obsessions and phobias do not necessarily correlate with resistance to modification, broad generalization, and so on. Unprepared obsessions occur and may well prove to be particularly difficult to modify. Symbolic transformations may play an important part in unprepared obsessions.

Even though the content of obsessional-compulsive disorders is evidently nonrandom, the intracultural, cross-cultural and historical variations in attitudes toward bodily cleanliness are not fully consistent with the view that the fear of dirt and/or contamination and the associated cleaning rituals are prepared and of evolutionary-biological significance. To this extent, there is no easy match between the clinical ratings, which firmly place this type of fear and ritual in the prepared category, and the anthropological evidence, which is marked by variations both within cultures (i.e., historical) and across cultures. The resolution of this discrepancy is presumably to be found in the particular experiences of the people who develop obsessions and phobias—they have been exposed to an appropriate aversive event and a prepared stimulus. Nobody experiences a compelling urge to wash his or her hands after touching silk, but many people do have these urges after touching waste products. Although the overall incidence of obsessional disorders may well be larger in a "clean" culture, it is to be expected that even in "dirty" cultures a small minority of people will be fearful of contamination and hence practice compulsive cleaning.

A PSYCHOLOGICAL ANALYSIS
OF DEPRESSION AND OBSESSIONS

In addition to its intrinsic interest, the application of a psychological theory of depression to the analysis of obsessional-compulsive disorders illustrates the feasibility of approaching these problems as psychological rather than psychiatric phenomena.

✳Obsessional-compulsive phenomena and depression are so intertwined that no theory of obsessions can achieve comprehensiveness unless it succeeds in integrating the two phenomena. In the absence of an adequate psychological theory of depression, there can be no comprehensive theory of obsessions.

The most ambitious modern psychological theory of depression, composed by Seligman (1975), states that "this . . . is our theory of helplessness:

the expectation that an outcome is independent of responding (1) reduces the motivation to control the outcome; (2) interferes with learning that responding controls the outcome; and, if the outcome is traumatic, (3) produces fear for as long as the subject is uncertain of the controllability of the outcome, and then produces depression" (pp. 55-56).

The theory has been reformulated and elaborated (Abramson, Seligman, and Teasdale, 1978) in order to cope with some earlier weaknesses (e.g., its silence on the problem of lowered self-esteem and the absence of symmetry between failure and success helplessness), and in order to absorb the rapidly accumulating experimental evidence. Although the new, complex version is not without problems, it is coherent, successfully accounts for many disparate findings, introduces useful limiting conditions, and enriches our view of depression. Even at this early stage of its development, and bearing in mind that Seligman and his co-workers are not asserting that their account describes the sole path to depression, the theory is productive and enlightening (incidentally, one effect of their reformulation is to threaten the term *depression* with redundancy). As we now hope to show, applying the theory to obsessional phenomena and their interpretation expands our conception of these matters and leads to some novel predictions.

At the risk of oversimplifying, this is what the reformulated theory states. A sufficient condition for the induction of helplessness is that the individual expects that a highly preferred event is unlikely and that he or she has no response available to make it more likely. This revision takes into account the important contribution of individual preference and emphasizes the importance of perceived competence. Another important addition to the theory is the introduction of an attributional element. According to Abramson, Seligman, and Teasdale, the person's attribution of responsibility for his or her helplessness will determine the chronicity and generality of the consequent depression.

There are three attributional factors, each of them bipolar. The person can attribute his or her helplessness to internal or external forces, to global or specific inadequacies, and finally to stable or unstable factors. If helplessness is attributed to internal factors, this is likely to lead to lowered self-esteem. If failures are attributed to global factors, then general deficits will follow. If helplessness is attributed to stable factors, then the deficits are likely to be chronic.

The consequences of helplessness experiences are threefold: They result in emotional, cognitive, and motivational deficits. The intensity of these deficits is determined by the degree to which the uncontrollable outcome is desired or preferred. Similarly, if the uncontrollable outcome is highly aversive, then the ensuing deficits will likewise be intense.

The worst combination of factors occurs when a highly preferred event is unattainable because the person has no suitable response to make *and* attributes this failure to internal, global, and stable properties. In this set of circumstances, the person will experience intense, chronic, and general deficits—emotional, cognitive, and motivational—and a significant lowering of self-esteem.

One of the more interesting recent findings described by Abramson and her colleagues is that under certain conditions helplessness produces a rebound effect. Given the opportunity, people who have recently experienced feelings of helplessness will strive unusually hard to achieve control of the next situation in which the challenge of uncontrollability is presented. Anticipating some of our later arguments, it is not farfetched to regard many obsessional-compulsive activities as rebound phenomena. After exposure to highly preferred but uncontrollable situations that induce a sense of helplessness, the person might strive unduly tenaciously to achieve an extra degree of control in unrelated but more easily manageable situations (e.g., controlling the risk of damage from gas leakages, controlling the threat of infection through excessive cleaning, etc.).

Abramson, Seligman, and Teasdale make four general recommendations for overcoming feelings of helplessness. Patients can be encouraged to change their expectations regarding the outcomes of their actions, alter the valence of their preferred outcomes, change their conceptions of uncontrollability, or reduce or alter their unrealistic attributions. The translation of these recommendations into treatment techniques will be taken up presently.

Abramson and her associates also go on to make some stimulating observations about the nature and identification of people who are peculiarly vulnerable to a sense of helplessness. In part, this vulnerability is determined by the person's attributional style. It is suggested that people differ in the readiness and extent to which they attribute failures to internal, global, and stable attributes. Another important determinant of vulnerability is the person's history of aversive and/or uncontrollable but important experiences. Lastly, they raise the possibility that some people have a tendency to exaggerate the aversiveness (and/or the desirability) of various outcomes. In all, it is a rich theory.

VULNERABILITY

If we begin by examining the applicability of the concept of vulnerability to an analysis of obsessional-compulsive disorders, some tempting connections can be proposed. We can take as our first example the suggestion that people who exaggerate the aversiveness of outcomes are more vulnerable to experienced helplessness, and here our experiments on the obsessional thoughts of a non-psychiatric sample have produced some relevant information. The great majority of our subjects reported that they experienced unwanted thoughts, but their tolerance for these thoughts and their definition of unacceptability were different from those of the obsessional patients (Rachman and de Silva, 1978).

Compared with our nonpsychiatric subjects, obsessional patients certainly do exaggerate the aversiveness of their intrusive thoughts. A second, independent fragment of evidence that points in the same direction is contained in the research report by Liddell (1976). Liddell found that although her obsessional patients had recalled fewer aversive childhood experiences than their comparison controls, they rated them as being significantly more aversive. A third piece of evidence comes from clinical reports and our own experience with patients over the years. As a group, obsessional patients tend to have higher standards of personal conduct—in terms of the revised Seligman theory, they exaggerate the desirability of certain outcomes. This combination of tendencies toward exaggerating aversiveness and desirability is bound to lead to an increased probability in the occurrence of disappointments and, hence, of feelings of helplessness.

With regard to the second determinant of vulnerability, attributional style, the worst combination is that which combines internal, global, and stable attributions. If the tendency to use one or all of these attributions excessively does in fact characterize obsessional patients, then experimental and psychometric investigations should show that they are more intropunitive and/or more inclined to regard the locus of control as internal rather than external. They should also show evidence of a tendency to overgeneralize and to expect undue stability (especially in their own ability to control events).

With regard to the third determinant of vulnerability, a history of aversive and/or uncontrollable experiences, what little information we have runs contrary to a simplistic interpretation of this point. At present we have no reason to believe that obsessional patients have in fact experienced *more* aversive or uncontrollable events. On the other hand, there is clinical evidence to support the hypothesis that a significant number of obsessional patients come from homes in which parental control was excessive. When this parental overcontrol was exercised predominantly in the form of overprotection, we have reason to expect a phobic-compulsive type of disorder classically characterized by excessive cleaning (see Rachman, 1976d). On the other hand, when the parental overcontrol was exercised mainly in the form of undue criticism, then we predict that compulsive checking behavior is more likely to emerge.

OBSESSIONS, COMPULSIONS, AND HELPLESSNESS

The definition of learned helplessness is more relevant to the phenomenology of *obsessions* than to that of compulsions. It connects occasionally with what we know of compulsive checking and bears only a slight resemblance to the phenomenology of compulsive cleaning. If this estimation of the match between learned helplessness and the three main obsessional-compulsive categories is appropriate, it should follow that the importance of learned helplessness, and hence the importance of depression, should vary across these categories. Depression should be most prominent in obsessions, moderately in evidence in compulsive checking, and least evident in compulsive cleaning. This first rough match between learned helplessness and obsessional-compulsive problems must, however, be qualified by reference to the critical role of attribution.

In our experience patients suffering mainly from obsessional difficulties characteristically attribute their inability to overcome the problem to their own shortcomings. They make an internal attribution. The prediction that follows from this reasoning is that purely obsessional patients should give evidence of lower self-esteem than compulsive cleaners or checkers. Again on the basis of our clinical experience, obsessional patients tend to make limited rather than global attributions, and it should follow that their deficits need not be excessively generalized. The prediction would be that most of these patients can continue to function despite their lowered self-esteem and emotional deficits. There seems little reason to suppose that the attributions will result in widesepread cognitive or motivational deficits. As for the third attributional factor, stable/unstable, we have no grounds for making any predictions.

Similarly, we have little clinical or other grounds for concluding that compulsive checkers have a tendency to make attributions about their insufficiencies in any consistent style. In the absence of information about their attributional style, it is impossible to make predictions about the range or intensity of their deficits.

As compulsive cleaners seldom fail—in the narrow sense of removing the disease or dirt contamination—there is little reason to suppose, on these grounds alone, that they should be particularly prone to feelings of helplessness. Clinically, we have observed that they often attribute whatever insufficiency of cleaning they encounter to the carelessness of others rather than to their own inefficiency. In this respect they are more prone to make external attributions than other obsessional-compulsive patients; if this is correct, it should follow that their self-esteem is less damaged than that of obsessional or compulsive checking patients. In addition to attributing inadequate control to the carelessness of other people (e.g., by spreading contamination, etc.), these compulsive cleaning patients, like the compulsive checkers, often attribute their own inadequacies to excessive fatigue. In Seligman's classificatory system, this would be termed an internal, global, but *unstable* attribution. In the revised theory unstable attributions should lead to temporary deficits—a prediction that, like most of those already discussed, can be tested without difficulty. The events most likely to induce helplessness are social—our relations with other people are of primary value and are difficult to arrange at will.

As mentioned earlier, Seligman and his co-workers made four recommendations that they hope will prove to be effective in reducing helplessness and its consequences. Insofar as they apply to the modification of obsessional-compulsive problems, it seems to us that the recommendation regarding improved competence, or power to control events, is likely to prove most effective and, hence, most important. To a considerable extent the behavioral treatments described earlier can be construed in these terms. The purpose of the behavioral retraining is to increase the patient's capacity for control and, at the same time, or consequent to the achievement of such control, alter his or her perceived personal efficacy. In modeling and flooding treatments, the patient is shown how to acquire control over the provoking stimuli and also over his or her own adverse and unwanted reactions to such stimuli. So far the notion of controllability has been applied little, and unsystematically at that, to the treatment of obsessions. Nevertheless, the possibilities are numerous and promising.

Two of the remaining recommendations put forward by Seligman and his co-workers—changing the valence of the preferred outcomes and altering unrealistic attributions—are therapeutic aims that seem best suited to cognitive therapy of the type described by Beck (1976) and others, rational therapy as described by Ellis and Grieger (1978), and so on. Their fourth recommendation, changing outcome expectancies, would probably result from successful modification along the lines already described (i.e., a combination of behavioral and cognitive therapy).

LEARNED HELPLESSNESS
AND PERCEIVED COMPETENCE

Although Seligman and his co-workers are interested primarily in explaining a psychological (deficit) state and Bandura's (1977) theory is an attempt to account for psychological changes, there are some points of similarity between their views. Both can be described as expectancy theories, and both center on the person's sense of control or mastery. From one point of view, Bandura and Seligman are dealing with opposite poles of the same continuum—with a sense of competence at one end and a sense of futility at the other.

As the learned-helplessness theory is an attempt to account for depression, it is of more immediate relevance to an analysis of obsessions and compulsions. Taken in a narrow sense, however, it can be said that the Seligman theory traces the consequences of an absence or loss of mastery of important outcomes while the Bandura theory deals with the acquisition of mastery over important aversive outcomes. (For the sake of simplicity, we are considering Bandura's views on therapeutic change apart from his wider social-learning theory.) Seligman and his co-workers explain the consequences of a sense of inadequate control and attach special importance to the person's attribution of the reasons for failure. They then proceed to deduce implications for treatment. With some tailoring, most of their recommendations, dealing as they do with the value of modifying the person's expectations of outcome, can be accommodated within Bandura's proposals. No doubt both theorists would agree that the modification of excessive physiological reactivity, the acquisition of increased competence, and improvement in cognitive appraisal are all therapeutically efficacious. But they part company when Seligman attaches importance to multiple attributional changes and Bandura argues for the central importance of perceived personal efficacy. It is too early to say whether these differences will prove to be critical or peripheral. In our opinion their common emphasis on the importance of the person's expectations of coping or failing is, for the present at least, the point of greatest interest. We also feel that both analyses would benefit from the inclusion of the perspective provided by a three-systems analysis.

THE REBOUND PHENOMENON

Abramson, Seligman, and Teasdale (1978) drew together some of the evidence on the positive consequences of experiencing helplessness and, in particular, on the phenomenon of facilitation or, to use their term, *compensatory rebound*. There are some indications that under specifiable conditions the reaction to a helplessness experience takes the form of increased determination to gain control over situations other than that in which the person experienced help-lessness. These compensatory attempts to reassert control once the person has left the uncontrollable situation are thought to be more likely to occur when the person makes an external attribution for his or her failure. It is too early to determine whether the compensatory-rebound phenomenon is relevant to the genesis and maintenance of compulsive behavior, but the possibility should be kept in mind. It is not unreasonable to suppose that people carry out repetitive compulsive acts (such as checking) in an attempt to assert control over a more manageable situation after having experienced helplessness in other, more important situations. So, for example, a socially inadequate and isolated person might well experience profound feelings of helplessness and then make com-pensatory attempts to assert control over potential inanimate dangers in his or her domestic situation. Highly preferred *social* outcomes might be unlikely and beyond control, but potentially aversive domestic accidents involving infections, stoves, taps, and so on are subject to control. This line of reasoning has obvious similarities to the notion of ritualistic behavior as displacement activity but differs in its most essential points from either the overload theory (Holland, 1974) or the hydraulic type of theory favored by Freudian theorists.

If we pursue the idea of obsessional-compulsive activities representing attempts to cope with stress, and specifically to reassert or achieve some control after an experience of helplessness, we might succeed in tracing a causal link between the onset of depression and the subsequent appearance of obsessions or compulsions. Although it is too early to place much weight on this possibility, the indications are that external attributions of failure are more likely to lead to compensatory-rebound behavior—hence, external attributions during a depressive episode are more likely to be followed by the appearance of compulsions. Although this reasoning may be applicable to the occurrence of compulsive behavior, it seems unlikely that obsessions can be construed as part of a compensatory rebound. This line of reasoning is unable to explain why, if the person is attempting to reassert control in a new situation, he or she should experience *unwanted, alien* thoughts and impulses. Far from helping the person attain a measure of control, these unwanted obsessions are themselves instances of uncontrollable and unwanted outcomes. It rather seems that obsessions are better regarded as reactions to stress and that failure to control or remove them may produce a sense of helplessness. Although the possibility of a link between experiences of helplessness and the subsequent genesis of compulsions (as a rebound phenomenon) seems plausible and can be supported by some slight evidence, Videbech's (1975) finding that *compulsions* appear to be relatively unaffected by the onset of depression—unlike obsessions, which were observed to show a substantial increase in incidence during depression—presents difficulties.

These possibilities led us to reconsider the nature of compulsive activities in the light of the learned-helplessness theory. Abramson and her colleagues (1978) illustrate their theory with a number of examples, and the following one is pertinent to the question of obsessions and compulsions. They state that depression occurs when people say to themselves, in relation to a particular outcome, that they really want to prevent some outcome but feel that there is nothing they can do to reduce the likelihood of its occurring. Regardless of whether they act or fail to act, the unwanted outcome is bound to occur. This description can be applied without additional tailoring to the subjective reports of patients who are troubled mainly by obsessions. It does not, however, match the accounts given by patients whose major problem is excessive compulsive activity. They are more inclined to say that an undesirable outcome is threatening unless and until some preventive action is taken—hence the need to check repeatedly or even to wash repeatedly. It would be uncharacteristic for a compulsive checker to say that the undesirable outcome is likely to occur regardless of whether he or she carries out the checking ritual or not—quite the contrary.

When these patients are pressed to defend their tactics, often but not always they will conclude by saying that their compulsive behavior is at rock bottom irrational. However, most patients feel that, at least part of the time, their compulsive activities are to some extent defensible. Translated into the terms of the learned-helplessness theory, this means that for at least part of the time they are expecting, or at least hoping, to attain an increased degree of control over a highly preferred or unwanted outcome. To this extent, then, they are not displaying the behavior that is said to characterize people experiencing learned helplessness.

Introduction of the concept of compensatory-rebound behavior complicates the picture, of course, and in our view it is not unreasonable to interpret at least some manifestations of compulsive behavior (especially compulsive checking) as attempts to reassert or achieve a measure of control in a new situation, subsequent to having experienced helplessness over a highly preferred outcome. Once again one thinks of the socially incompetent and helpless person resorting to compulsive checking or cleaning rituals within the contained environment of his or her own home.

HELPLESSNESS AND OBSESSIONS

Our attempt to marry the theory of learned helplessness and the clinical data on depression associated with obsessional-compulsive disorders proved interesting but not as productive as one might have hoped. Turning next to the fate of obsessions during depressive episodes, it will be recalled that three patterns have been distinguished: losers, gainers, and keepers. Using the learned-helplessness theory, it is possible to put a reasonable construction on two of these three sequences. In the case of gainers, it can be argued that exposure to uncontrollable situations produces learned helplessness, which then leads to emotional, cognitive, and motivational deficits. On the cognitive side, the person loses the ability to deal with troublesome thoughts (by normal dismissal procedures, etc.), and in any event the process of dismissal becomes more difficult because of the increased emotional sensitivity characteristic of the state of helplessness.

As far as keepers are concerned, it can be supposed that they go through the same chain of events as gainers but that in addition the whole process is compounded by the obsessions themselves. These unwanted ideas are essentially uncontrollable internal events and are themselves capable of producing helplessness. It is likely that with the onset of depression the person's capacity for dealing with and/or tolerating the obsessions diminishes (as suggested earlier, this can be checked by assessing the success of thought control during depression and again during remission). Why the keepers fail to show a worsening of obsessions, if they do fail to do so, is hard to explain. In the case of losers, no ready explanation can be derived from the theory. If we take the decline or disappearance of obsessions during a depressive episode as evidence of *improved* control of these unwanted thoughts, then we are obliged to resort, rather lamely, to the compensatory-rebound phenomenon. This lacks conviction, and as far as we are able to see, the learned-helplessness theory has no obvious application to the occurrence of losers. *frustrated avoids*

Another phenomenon that eludes the theory, the possible constancy of compulsions during and after depressive episodes, has already been mentioned. Neither does the theory help us in coming to grips with the negative correlation between depressive retardation and the occurrence of obsessions. All of these possibilities are illustrated in Table 25.1.

Success in gaining control over the duration and/or frequency of the obsessions should be followed by a decline in subjectively experienced feelings of learned helplessness and in the behavioral deficits attributable to learned helplessness. This is easily tested, but in doing so attempts should be made to ensure that the person has in fact improved his or her control over the obsessions. One would need evidence of a decline in the duration and/or frequency of the obsessions and of an improvement in the person's perceived control. Of course, it follows from our analysis of the relation between obsessions and helplessness (see Table 25.1) that success in achieving control over obsessions is most likely to result in reduced helplessness among *gainers*. This specific prediction is open to direct test.

DEPRESSION AND THOUGHT CONTROL

The loss of controlling power during depression was remarked by Dr. Johnson: "If fancy presents images not moral or religious, the mind drives them away when they give it pain," but "when melancholick notions take the form of duty, they lay hold on the faculties without opposition, because we are afraid to exclude or banish them" (quoted by Hunter and Macalpine, 1963, p. 418). Presumably, Abramson, Seligman, and Teasdale (1978) would agree with Johnson's general observation but not with his last phrase. During depression, they might say, the person loses the cognitive ability to exert control over thoughts and also experiences a diminution in the drive to do so. As for Johnson's observation that melancholic notions are harder to banish than other images, he would have been glad to learn that Teasdale and Rezin (1978) have provided experimental support for his view. Precisely why thought control declines during depression remains to be clarified. According to the Seligman

TABLE 25.1 THE FATE OF OBSESSIONS DURING DEPRESSIVE EPISODES, CONSTRUED IN TERMS OF SELIGMAN'S THEORY

Losers	Obsessions present →	Exposed to uncontrollable situations →	Learned helplessness →	Lack of effort to cope → Obsessions decline (Why?)
Gainers	No obsessions →	Exposed to uncontrollable situations →	Learned helplessness →	Cognitive deficits, loss of control of thoughts → Obsessions develop
Keepers	Obsessions present →	Exposed to uncontrollable situations →	Learned helplessness →	Persisting obsessional activities (failure to exert control) → Increase in learned helplessness
Nonobsessionals	No obsessions →	Exposed to uncontrollable situations →	Learned helplessness →	Cognitive deficits → No obsessions (Why?)

theory, it can be regarded as a manifestation of a more general cognitive deficit—and correctly so. But the time has arrived to probe more deeply into this question.

The prominence of indecisiveness in both obsessional disorders and depressive episodes also can be regarded as a manifestation of the *cognitive deficit* that results from exposure to situations that induce a sense of helplessness. We can go a little further and predict that there should be a relationship between the occurrence of indecisiveness and global, internal attributions of responsibility for failure. Stated positively, it can be predicted that global, internal attributions of failure to influence the probability of highly preferred outcomes will result in a significant increase in indecisiveness. By contrast, specific, external attributions should bear little relationship to the emergence of indecisiveness.

Relative to depressive patients, those who have obsessions as well as depression have a lower suicide rate. It is conceivable that one contributing factor to this difference is the experienced sense of helplessness. If it is attributed to internal, global, and stable factors, then presumably the person is at high risk. If, on the other hand, the person reacts to his or her feelings of helplessness by making attempts at compensatory-rebound activities—such as compulsive actions—this reflects and in turn contributes to shifting the attribution from global and stable to specific and unstable. After all, the depressed patient who succeeds in carrying out compulsive cleaning or checking activities receives intermittent confirmation of his or her ability to influence the probability that a highly preferred outcome will be achieved.

To conclude this exercise, it is apparent that the theory of learned helplessness has considerable explanatory potential, but at present its direct applications to clarifying the nature of obsessions and compulsions are limited. Nevertheless, we feel that some clarity has been achieved and that a number of specific predictions flow from the analysis.

A THREE-SYSTEMS APPROACH

As a three-systems analysis has already been applied in various parts of the present exposition and elsewhere in the discussion of fear (see Rachman and Hodgson, 1974; Hodgson and Rachman, 1974; Rachman, 1974a, 1978d), here we will consider only the broader consequences of the approach.

In addition to its value as a generator of new hypotheses, the three-systems approach enables us to dispense with the premise that obsessional-compulsive disorders have a unitary composition. To borrow a critical term applied to an earlier conception of *fear*, obsessional disorders are not to be regarded as a "lump" (see Lang, 1970; Rachman, 1974). There is good reason to suppose that obsessional difficulties, like fears, consist of at least three loosely coupled components—subjective, behavioral, and psychophysiological. Although this supposi-

Possible

tion is especially plausible with respect to obsessional disorders in which there is an important phobic element, there are advantages in applying a three-systems analysis to all forms of the disorder—cleaning and checking compulsions, obsessions, and primary slowness. Indeed, for some purposes such an analysis provides a useful framework for making comparisons among the various forms of the disorder. To facilitate matters a three-systems analysis will be applied in turn to each of the following aspects of obsessional-compulsive disorders: nature, modification, genesis, and maintenance.

Viewed from the point of view of a three-systems approach, the various forms of obsessional disorder take on different shades of emphasis. In all four major forms, there is an element of subjective discomfort, but people who suffer from obsessions or compulsive cleaning rituals complain of more subjective discomfort than people who display primary obsessional slowness. Psychophysiological disturbances are prominent in cleaning compulsions and obsessions and seemingly unimportant in cases of slowness. Consistent with our emphasis on the distinction between passive and active avoidance, the behavioral component of obsessional disorders has been subdivided into active and passive forms, with the results shown in Table 25.2.

The present analysis suggests a slightly different approach to the modification of obsessions and to the evaluation of the effects of such attempts at modification. The differing prominence of the components in the various forms of the disorder should lead to variations in emphasis in the various modification procedures currently available. In Chapter 19 the therapeutic consequences of applying a three-systems analysis to obsessions were argued in detail. In these cases, as in all other forms of the disorder, the modification procedure should be matched far more closely than under present conditions by the specific problems presented by the person. For example, in a disorder that is primarily obsessional the subjective component is of central importance and the modification procedure should deal with it directly. It follows, of course, that the effect of the intervention should be assessed first and foremost by reference to the subjective component. The fact that a modification procedure has little or no effect on the mild psychophysiological disturbance presented by an obsessional patient is of secondary importance. The central question is whether or not the modification procedure is capable of producing an improvement in the key component—in these cases it is inevitably the subjective component that is critical.

In contrast to cases of obsession, people who are incapacitated by primary obsessional slowness have a major disturbance of the behavioral component and only a lesser disturbance in subjective comfort or psychophysiological function. It is the disturbed behavioral component that requires direct modification, and as before. the effect of the intervention should be evaluated predominantly in terms of its success in changing the critical component—the disturbance of behavior.

The greater specificity inherent in this approach offers advantages over

TABLE 25.2 FOUR MAJOR TYPES OF OBSESSIONAL DISORDER IN TERMS OF A THREE-SYSTEMS ANALYSIS

COMPONENTS	SUBJECTIVE	PSYCHOPHYSIOLOGICAL	*Avoidance Behavior*	
			PASSIVE	ACTIVE
Cleaning compulsions	+++	++	+++	++
Checking compulsions	++	+	+	+++
Obsessional thoughts, etc.	+++	++	+	+
Primary obsessional slowness	+	0	0	++

χtraditional approaches to treatment and treatment evaluation. Instead of assessing the person's problems in generalized, blunt categories, such as ratings of clinical severity, or assessing the effect of the intervention by means of generalized ratings of clinical improvement, the *specific effects* produced by these procedures can be assessed separately for each target component. A three-systems approach provides an opportunity for replacing our blunt instruments and methods of evaluation with more precise, closely tailored instruments and methods.

A three-systems analysis of obsessional disorders has already produced some new ideas on which to base modification techniques, and also helps clarify the mode of operation of some of the established methods of modification. To take one example quoted by Rachman (1974a), a three-systems analysis of fear clarifies the clinical observation that the evocation of fear during flooding treatment is *not* necessary for success. While it may be facilitative in limited cases, the deliberate arousal of fear is not always necessary and should be avoided. In part, the mistaken belief that flooding treatment required the evocation of fear can be traced to the unstated premise that fear constitutes a lump. Recognition of the possibility that fear and avoidance may take independent courses led to a relaxed acceptance of the seemingly inexplicable observation that flooding treatment can succeed even in the absence of fear evocation.

An interesting subsidiary finding of the work on flooding concerned the relatively rapid recovery that patients make after experiencing some initial disturbance. It was noted that the increments in fear "tend to be well-tolerated, relatively brief, and to have no longer-term consequences" (Rachman and Hodgson, 1974, p. 315). In the experiment on the spontaneous decay of compulsive urges, the discomfort that obsessional patients experience after exposure to their provoking stimulus situation was seen to dissipate spontaneously. However, the time course seems to be slightly longer than that observed to occur among phobic patients.

Recognition of desynchrony between subjective discomfort and avoidance behavior enables therapists to provide realistic reassurance to patients in whom a cognitive lag occurs during a treatment program (Rachman, 1974a, 1978d). Sometimes during the conduct of a flooding session the patient readily acquires the ability to engage in previously avoided activities, but the change is accompanied by persistent feelings of subjective discomfort. If the desynchrony can be anticipated and understood, in a way that would not be possible if we were confined to the two-stage theory of fear and avoidance, then the therapist is in a position to explain to the patient that his or her newly restored approach behavior will cease to be accompanied by subjective discomfort. It has been pointed out that phobic patients who complain, particularly during flooding treatment, that they still feel frightened even though they have resumed traveling are not being pests, but are experiencing a "genuine and partly under-stood phenomenon" (Rachman, 1975). It is to be expected that during the follow-up period the subjective remnants of discomfort will wane with continued practice of the normal approach behavior.

The application of the three-systems analysis has led to renewed emphasis on the importance of behavioral-avoidance tests. In addition to its importance in research investigations, the routine therapeutic use of a behavioral-avoidance test as a pretreatment measure is to be recommended on two grounds: It provides some objective information about the nature and intensity of the person's avoidance behavior and subjective discomfort, and it sometimes reveals a considerable amount of desynchrony. If in the natural course of events the subjective discomfort has withered away and the person is left with a repetitive pattern of avoidance behavior (as in primary obsessional slowness), the conduct of a behavioral-avoidance test may reveal this otherwise unacknowledged or unrecognized change. Whereas a strict adherence to the two-stage theory of fear and avoidance might in the past have led one to conclude that obsessional patients who persistently carry out rituals despite the absence of any discomfort were malingering, freedom from undiscriminating use of the theory enables one

At present we have unclear notions about how obsessions and compulsions are generated; hence, a full analysis in terms of the three-component model would merely serve to heap new speculations on old ones. It can be said, how-ever, that an adequate theory of the genesis of these disorders should allow for the possibility that the components might be generated desynchronously. So, for example, it is likely that in the early stages of the development of, say, compulsive cleaning difficulties the subjective component is particularly pro-nounced. Stated negatively, a three-systems analysis leads us to expect that any theory offered to account for the genesis of obsessions and compulsions that rests on the premise that these disorders are unitary in composition is likely to run into difficulty.

On the question of the maintenance of obsessional-compulsive disorders, we have to face the possibility that a comprehensive explanation may require slightly different accounts to incorporate the persistence of each of the three components, which, although related, may well fluctuate and vary independently of each other. Once again stating it in the negative form, this means that an explanation that accounts for the persistence of, say, the subjective-discomfort component may throw little light on the persistence of avoidance behavior. Their relative independence—as, for example, in primary obsessional slowness—means that a single explanation is unlikely to succeed. However, as there is so little information on the relationship between these components to guide us, speculation would be premature. The main point is to recognize that ultimately we may need more than a single explanation to account for the persistence of all three components, just as we may need more than a single explanation to account for the *genesis* of all three components of obsessional-compulsive disorders.

The application of a three-systems analysis can provide a basis for a new and much-needed strategy for research into the effects of therapeutic interventions. The lump theory approach to outcome research has had the inevitable effect of blunting and distorting the very processes under investigation and has played a major part in producing the present impasse in outcome research (Rachman and Wilson, 1979) and the attendant pessimism. Low correlations between subjective reports and behavioral performance are regarded as unfortunate and as no more than a reflection of the low reliability of the measures. Hence, the tendency has been to exclude measures that failed to produce high correlations. Instead, preference has been given to measures that reduce the likelihood of diversity of effects. This desire for homogeneity usually results in the selection of broad, generalized rating schemes. It also leads to the use of the same or similar scales by the patient, the therapist, and the independent assessor. While this tactic produces reassuringly higher correlations between scores, there is some question about whether this kind of reliability is worth the effort.

The emphasis of the lump theory approach on homogeneity and generalized outcome measures has blurred the differences between treatments. One of the remarkable features of most of the recent comparative research on the effects of various forms of treatment for neurosis has been the failure to uncover major differences between the various forms of treatment (e.g., Sloane et al., 1975). In part, this reflects the operation of powerful and pervasive nonspecific effects that apparently are common to many forms of treatment (Rachman, 1971). It is likely, however, that the relative failure to find differences in treatment effects can be attributed in large part to the tactics dictated by a restrictive assumption about the nature of the disorders under study (i.e., by the assumption that the disorders are unitary in composition). Another reason for the failure is that, given the considerable amount of spontaneous improvement that occurs in neuroses, the room for demonstrating differential therapeutic changes over and above the spontaneous ones is limited (Rachman, 1971). Other weaknesses in conventional outcome research, such as the operation of the medical model and the assumption of an exaggerated generality of psychological problems, are discussed elsewhere (Rachman and Wilson, 1979).

There is good reason to suppose that the use of a three-systems approach to obsessional-compulsive disorders will not only provide a new strategic base but also prove fruitful in generating new notions about therapeutic change. It would provide the basis for a new type of design, one that incorporates measures of all three components. The interrelations among these components, and particularly their relative speeds of change, will become the new focus of interest. Once this proposal has been carried out, we will be in a position to study not only the effects of therapy in general but also the specific effects on each of the three components. There is good reason to expect that different treatment techniques will give rise to varying effects on each of the three components. Outcome research that makes allowance for the concepts of concordance and synchrony of change will enable us to carry out experimental analyses of the processes of therapeutic change as well as the overall outcome. By emphasizing the diversity of a person's reactions to therapy, and the temporal sequence of these changes, we are more likely to approach an understanding of the operative mechanisms. Such an emphasis will make it easier to identify the mode of action of different types of treatment (e.g., modeling versus desensitization). And in this way we can trace the strengths and weaknesses of each type of modification procedure.

In short, the selection of closely specified measurements and the design of outcome experiments based on a three-systems analysis will enable us to study both process and outcome questions simultaneously and in a fresh manner.

The Maudsley Obsessional-Compulsive Inventory (MOC)

**THE MAUDSLEY
OBSESSIONAL-COMPULSIVE INVENTORY (MOC)**

Instructions: Please answer each question by putting a circle around the "TRUE" or the "FALSE" following the question. There are no right or wrong answers, and no trick questions. Work quickly and do not think too long about the exact meaning of the question.

1. I avoid using public telephones because of possible contamination.	TRUE	FALSE
2. I frequently get nasty thoughts and have difficulty in getting rid of them.	TRUE	FALSE
3. I am more concerned than most people about honesty.	TRUE	FALSE
4. I am often late because I can't seem to get through everything on time.	TRUE	FALSE
5. I don't worry unduly about contamination if I touch an animal.	TRUE	FALSE
6. I frequently have to check things (e.g., gas or water taps, doors, etc.) several times.	TRUE	FALSE
7. I have a very strict conscience.	TRUE	FALSE
8. I find that almost every day I am upset by unpleasant thoughts that come into my mind against my will.	TRUE	FALSE
9. I do not worry unduly if I accidentally bump into somebody.	TRUE	FALSE
10. I usually have serious doubts about the simple everyday things I do.	TRUE	FALSE

11. Neither of my parents was very strict during my childhood.   TRUE   FALSE
12. I tend to get behind in my work because I repeat things over and over again.   TRUE   FALSE
13. I use only an average amount of soap.   TRUE   FALSE
14. Some numbers are extremely unlucky.   TRUE   FALSE
15. I do not check letters over and over again before mailing them.   TRUE   FALSE
16. I do not take a long time to dress in the morning.   TRUE   FALSE
17. I am not excessively concerned about cleanliness.   TRUE   FALSE
18. One of my major problems is that I pay too much attention to detail.   TRUE   FALSE
19. I can use well-kept toilets without any hesitation.   TRUE   FALSE
20. My major problem is repeated checking.   TRUE   FALSE
21. I am not unduly concerned about germs and diseases.   TRUE   FALSE
22. I do not tend to check things more than once.   TRUE   FALSE
23. I do not stick to a very strict routine when doing ordinary things.   TRUE   FALSE
24. My hands do not feel dirty after touching money.   TRUE   FALSE
25. I do not usually count when doing a routine task.   TRUE   FALSE
26. I take rather a long time to complete my washing in the morning.   TRUE   FALSE
27. I do not use a great deal of antiseptics.   TRUE   FALSE
28. I spend a lot of time every day checking things over and over again.   TRUE   FALSE
29. Hanging and folding my clothes at night does not take up a lot of time.   TRUE   FALSE
30. Even when I do something very carefully I often feel that it is not quite right.   TRUE   FALSE

Scoring Key for the Maudsley Obsessional-Compulsive Inventory

SCORING KEY FOR THE
MAUDSLEY OBSESSIONAL-COMPULSIVE INVENTORY

Instructions: Score 1 when a response matches that of this key and 0 when it does not; maximum scores for the five scales are, therefore, respectively 30, 9, 11, 7, 7. Factor 5 (i.e., ruminations) has not been scored, since only Q2 and Q8 loaded on it. A "TRUE" response to these two items is possibly a sign of ruminations. Only the checking, washing, and total obsessional scores have been validated; the "slowness-repetition" and doubting-conscientious" factors need replication and validation.

	Total Obsessional Score	Checking	Washing	Slowness-Repetition	Doubting-Conscientious
Q1	True	—	True	—	—
Q2	True	True	—	False	—
Q3	True	—	—	—	True
Q4	True	—	True	True	—
Q5	False	—	False	—	—
Q6	True	True	—	—	—
Q7	True	—	—	—	True
Q8	True	True	—	False	—
Q9	False	—	False	—	—
Q10	True	—	—	—	True

	Total Obsessional Score	Checking	Washing	Slowness-Repetition	Doubting-Conscientious
Q11	False	—	—	—	False
Q12	True	—	—	—	True
Q13	False	—	False	—	—
Q14	True	True	—	—	—
Q15	False	False	—	—	—
Q16	False	—	—	False	—
Q17	False	—	False	—	—
Q18	True	—	—	—	True
Q19	False	—	False	—	—
Q20	True	True	—	—	—
Q21	False	—	False	—	—
Q22	False	False	—	—	—
Q23	False	—	—	False	—
Q24	False	—	False	—	—
Q25	False	—	—	False	—
Q26	True	True	True	—	—
Q27	False	—	False	—	—
Q28	True	True	—	—	—
Q29	False	—	—	False	—
Q30	True	—	—	—	True

Bibliography

Abramson, L. Y., Seligman, M. E. P. and Teasdale, J. D. (1978) Learned helplessness in humans: Critique and reformulation. *J. of Abnormal Psychol.*, 87, 49-74.

Adams, P. (1972) Family characteristics of obsessive children. *American J. Psychiat.*, 128, 1414-17.

Akhtar, S., Wig., N.H., Verma, V. K., Pershod, D. and Verma, S. K. (1975) A phenomenological analysis of symptoms in obsessive-compulsive neuroses. *Brit. J. Psychiat.*, 127, 342-48.

Alexander, J. (1928) *Thought-Control in Everyday Life*. New York: Funk and Wagnall.

Bandura, A. (1969) *The Principles of Behavior Modification*. New York: Holt, Rinehart and Winston.

————. (1977) *Social Learning Theory*. Englewood Cliffs, N.J.: Prentice-Hall.

————. (1978) On paradigms and recycled ideologies. *Cognitive Ther. & Res.*, 2, 79-103.

Bandura, A., Adams, N. and Beyer, J. (1977) Cognitive processes mediating behavioral change. *J. Personality and Social Psychol.*, 35, 125-39.

Bandura, A. and Barab, P. (1973) Conditions governing disinhibitory effects through symbolic modeling. *J. of Abnormal Psychol.*, 82, 1-9.

Bandura, A., Blanchard, E. B. and Ritter, B. (1969) The relative efficacy of desensitization and modeling approaches for inducing behavioral, affective and attitudinal changes. *J. Personality and Social Psychol.*, 13, 173-99.

Bandura, A., Grusec, J. and Menlove, F. (1967) Vicarious extinction of avoidance behavior. *J. Personality and Social Psychol.*, 5, 449-55.

Bandura, A. and Rosenthal, T. (1966) Vicarious classical conditioning as a function of arousal level. *J. Personality and Social Psychol.*, 3, 54-62.

Barnes, C. A. (1952) A statistical study of the Freudian Theory of levels of psychosexual development. *Genetic Psychology Monographs*, 45, 105-75.

Barrett, W., Caldbeck-Meenan, J. and White, J. G. (1966) Questionnaire measures and psychiatrists' ratings of a personality dimension. *Brit. J. Psychiatry*, 112, 413-15.

Bartlett, F. (1958) *Thinking*. New York: Basic Books.

Barton, R. (1965) Diabetes insipidus and obsessional neurosis. *The Lancet*, 1, 133-35.

Bass, B. (1973) An unusual behavioral technique for treating obsessive ruminations. *Psychotherapy: Theory & Practice*, 10, 191-92.

Baum, M. (1970) Extinction of avoidance responding through response prevention (flooding). *Psychological Bulletin*, 74, 276.

Beaumont, G. (1973) Clomipramine (Anafranil) in the treatment of obsessive-compulsive disorders—A review of the work of Dr. G. A. Collins. *J. of International Medical Res.*, 1, 423-24.

Beck, A. (1976) *Cognitive Therapy and the Emotional Disorders*. New York: International Universities Press.

Beech, H. R. (1971) Ritualistic activity in obsessional patients. *J. of Psychosomatic Res.*, 15, 417-22.

Beech, H. R. (Ed.) (1974) *Obsessional States*. London: Methuen.

Beech, H. R. and Liddell, A. (1974) Decision-making, mood states and ritualistic behavior among obsessional patients. In *Obsessional States*, edited by H. R. Beech. London: Methuen.

Beech, H. R. and Perigault, J. (1974) Toward a theory of obsessional disorder. In *Obsessional States*, edited by H. R. Beech. London: Methuen.

Beloff, H. (1957) The Structure and Origin of the Anal Character. *Genetic Psychology Monographs*, 55, 141-72.

Berg, I., Butler, A. and Hall, G. (1976) The outcome of adolescent school phobia. *Brit. J. Psychiat.*, 128, 80-85.

Berman, L. (1974) Obsessive-compulsive neurosis in children. *J. of Nervous and Mental Disease*, 95, 26-39.

Bernstein, I., Callaghan, W. and Jaranson, J. (1975) Lobotomy in private practice. *Archives of General Psychiatry*, 32, 1041-47.

Black, A. (1974) The natural history of obsessional neurosis. In *Obsessional States*, edited by H. R. Beech. London: Methuen.

Block, J. (1975) Recognizing the coherence of personality. *Proceedings*, International Congress of Psychology, Stockholm.

Boersma, K., Den Hengst, S., Dekker, J. and Emmelkamp, P. (1976) Exposure and response prevention: A comparison with obsessive-compulsive patients. *Behav. Res. & Ther.*, 14, 19-24.

Boulougouris, J. (1976) Variables affecting behavior modification of obsessive patients by flooding. *Proceedings*, Conference of the European Association of Behavior Therapy, Spetsae, Greece, 1976.

Boulougouris, J. and Bassiakos, L. (1973) Prolonged flooding in cases with obsessive-compulsive neurosis. *Behav. Res. & Ther.*, 11, 227-31.

Boulougouris, J., Marset, P. and Marks, I. M. (1971) Superiority of flooding (implosion) to desensitization for reducing pathological fear. *Behav. Res. & Ther.*, 9, 7-16.

Boulougouris, J. C., Rabavilas, A. D. and Stefanis, C. (1977) Psychophysiological responses in obsessive-compulsive patients. *Behav. Res. & Ther.*, 15, 221-30.

Brickner, R., Rosner, A. and Munro, R. (1940) Physiological aspects of the obsessive state. *Psychosomatic Medicine*, 2, 369-83.

Bridges, P., Goktepe, E. and Maratos, J. (1973) A comparative review of patients with obsessional neurosis and with depression treated by psychosurgery. *Brit. J. Psychiatry*, 123, 663-74.

Broadbent, D. E. (1958) *Perception and Communication*. Oxford: Pergamon Press.

_____. (1971) *Decision and Stress*. London: Academic Press.

Broadhurst, A. (1976) It's never too late to learn. In *Case Studies in Behavior Therapy*, edited by H. J. Eysenck. London: Routledge and Kegan Paul.

Brooks, J. (1969) The Insecure Personality: A Factor Analytic Study. *Brit. J. of Medical Psychol.*, 42, 395-403.

Brown, F. (1942) Heredity in the psychoneuroses. *Proc. Royal Society Medicine*, 35, 785-90.

Bunyan, J. (1947) *An Anthology*, edited by A. Stanley. London: Eyre and Spottiswoode.

Burton, R. (1963) Generality of honesty reconsidered. *Psychol. Review*, 70, 481-99.

Capstick, N. (1973) The Graylingwell study. *J. of International Medical Res.*, 1, 392-96.

Capstick, N. (1975) Clomipramine in the treatment of true obsessional state—A report on four patients. *Psychosomatics* 16, (1), 21-25.

Candy, J., Balfour, H., Cawley, R., Hildebrand, H., Malan, D., Marks, I. and Wilson, J. (1972) A feasibility study for a controlled trial of psychotherapy. *Psychological Medicine*, 2, 345-62.

Carr, A. (1970) A psychophysiological study of ritual behaviors and decision processes in compulsive neurosis. Unpublished doctoral dissertation, University of Birmingham.

_____. (1974) Compulsive neurosis: A review of the literature. *Psychological Bulletin*, 81, 311-18.

Catts, S. and McConaghy, N. (1975) Ritual prevention in the treatment of obsessive-compulsive neurosis. *Australian and New Zealand J. of Psychiat.*, 9, 37-41.

Cawley, R. H. (1974) Psychotherapy and obsessional disorders. In *Obsessional States*, edited by H. R. Beech. London: Methuen.

Chapman, A. (1976) *A Textbook of Clinical Psychiatry*. Philadelphia: Lippincott.

Chapple, E. and Coon, C. (1953) *Principles of Anthropology*. New York: Holt.

Cheng, S., Tait, H. and Freeman, W. (1956) Transorbital lobotomy vs. electroconvulsive shock therapy in the treatment of mentally ill tuberculosis patients. *American J. Psychiat.*, 113, 32-56.

Comrey, A. L. (1965) Scales for measuring compulsion, hostility, neuroticism and shyness. *Psychological Reports,* 16, 697-700.

Cooper, J. E. and Kelleher, M. Y. (1973) The Leyton Obsessional Inventory: A principal components analysis on normal subjects. *Psychological Medicine,* 3, 204-8.

Cooper, J. (1970) The Leyton Obsessional Inventory. *Psychological Medicine,* 1, 48-64.

Cooper, J. and McNeil, J. (1968) A study of houseproud housewives and their interaction with their children. *J. of Child Psychol. and Psychiat.,* 9, 173-88.

Cowie, V. (1961) The incidence of neurosis in the children of psychotics. *Acta Psychiatrica Scandinavica,* 37, 37-71.

Dai, B. (1957) Obsessive-compulsive disorders in Chinese culture. *Social Problems,* 4, 313-21.

Davison, G. C. (1968) Systematic desensitization as a counterconditioning process. *J. of Abnorm. Psychol.,* 73, 91-99.

DeNike, T. (1968) Neurotic disorders. In *Foundations of Abnormal Psychology,* edited by P. London and D. Rosenhan. New York: Holt.

de Silva, P., Rachman, S. and Seligman, M. (1977) Prepared phobias and obsessions: Therapeutic outcome. *Behav. Res. & Ther.,* 15, 54-77.

Dollard, J. and Miller, N. (1950) *Personality and Psychotherapy.* New York: McGraw-Hill.

Ellis, A. and Grieger, R. (1978) *Handbook of Rational-Emotive Therapy.* New York: Springer.

Elsarrag, M. (1968) Psychiatry in Northern Sudan. *Brit. J. Psychiatry,* 114.

Emmelkamp, P. and Kwee, K. (1977) Obsessional ruminations: A comparison between thought-stopping and prolonged exposure in imagination. *Behav. Res. & Ther.,* 15, 441-44.

Emmelkamp, P. and Van Kraanen, J. (1977) Therapist-controlled exposure *in vivo* vs. self-controlled exposure *in vivo:* A comparison with obsessive-compulsive patients. *Behav. Res. & Ther.,* 15, 491-96.

Everitt, B., Gourlay, A. and Kendell, R. (1971) An attempt at validation of traditional psychiatric syndromes by cluster analysis. *Brit. J. Psychiatry,* 119, 399-412.

Eysenck, H. J. (1947) *Dimensions of Personality.* New York: Praeger.

_____. (1957) *The Dynamics of Anxiety and Hysteria.* London: Routledge and Kegan Paul.

_____. (1959) *Manual of the Maudsley Personality Inventory.* London: University of London Press.

_____. (1967) *The Biological Basis of Personality.* Springfield, Ill.: Charles C. Thomas.

_____. (1970) The classification of depressive illness. *Brit. J. Psychiatry,* 117, 241-50.

_____.(1976) *The Measurement of Personality.* England: MTP Press.

_____. (1976a) The learning theory model of neurosis—A new approach. *Behav. Res. & Ther.,* 14, 251-68.

_____.(1976b) *Sex and Personality.* London: Open Books.

_____.(1977) *You and Neurosis.* London: Temple Smith.

Eysenck, H. J. and Eysenck, S. B. G. (1964) *Manual of the Eysenck Personality Inventory.* London: University of London Press.

———. (1977) *Psychoticism as a Dimension of Personality.* London: Hodder & Stoughton.

Eysenck, H. J. and Rachman, S. (1965) *The Causes and Cures of Neurosis.* London: Routledge and Kegan Paul.

Eysenck, S. B. G. and Eysenck, H. J. (1968) The measurement of psychoticism: A study of factor stability and reliability. *Brit. J. Soc. Clin. Psychol.,* 7, 286-94.

Fernandez, R. & Lopez-Ibor, R. (1969) Mono-chlorimipramine in the treatment of psychiatric patients resistant to other therapies. *Act. Iso. Esp. Neurol.,* 26, 119-47.

Fernando, S. (1977) Hostility, personality and depression. *Brit. J. of Med. Psychol.,* 50, 243-49.

Finney, J. C. (1961) The MMPI as a measure of character structure as revealed by factor analysis. *J. of Consulting Psychol.,* 25, 327-36.

Fisher, S. and Greenberg, R. P. (1977) *The Scientific Credibility of Freud's Theories and Therapy.* New York: Harvester Press.

Foa, E. (1977) Lecture given at the Institute of Psychiatry, London.

———. (1978) Personal communication.

———. (1979) Failures in treating obsessive-compulsives. *Behav. Res. & Ther.,* 17, 169-176.

Foa, E. B. and Chambless, D. L. (1978) Habituation of subjective anxiety during flooding in imagery. *Behav. Res. & Ther.,* 16, 391-400.

Foa, E. B. and Goldstein, A. (1978) Continuous exposure and strict response prevention in the treatment of obsessive-compulsive neurosis. *Beh. Ther.,* 17, 169-176.

Forbes (1969) The validity of the 16PF in the discrimination of the hysteroid and obsessoid personality. *British J. Soc. Clin. Psychol.,* 8, 152-59.

Foulds, G. A. (1965) *Personality and Personal Illness.* London: Tavistock Publications.

Foulds, G. A. and Caine, T. M. (1958) Psychoneurotic symptom clusters, trait clusters and psychological tests. *J. Ment. Sci.,* 104, 722.

———. (1959) Symptom clusters and personality types among psychoneurotic men compared with women. *J. Ment. Sci.,* 105, 469.

Freud, S. (1908) Character and anal eroticism. Reprinted in *Complete Psychological Works,* vol. 9, edited by J. Strachey, London: Hogarth Press, 1959.

———.(1949 ed.) *Introductory Lectures.* London: Hogarth Press.

———. (1973 ed.) *The Complete Psychological Works of Sigmund Freud,* vols. 1-24, edited by J. Strachey. London: Hogarth Press.

Geer, J. (1966) Fear and autonomic arousal. *J. Abnorm. Psychol.,* 71, 253-55.

Gertz, H. O. (1966) Paradoxical intention in obsessives. *American J. Psychiatry,* 23, 548-53.

Gillan, P. and Rachman, S. (1974) An experimental investigation of desensitization in phobic patients. *Brit. J. Psychiatry,* 124, 392-401.

Gittelson, N. (1966a) The effect of obsessions on depressive psychosis. *Brit. J. Psychiatry,* 112, 253-59.

_____. (1966b) The fate of obsessions in depressive psychosis. *Brit. J. Psychiatry,* 112, 705-8.

_____. (1966c) Depressive psychosis in the obsessional neurotic. *Brit. J. Psychiatry,* 112, 883-87.

_____. (1966d) Phenomenology of obsessions in depression. *Brit. J. Psychiatry,* 112, 260-65.

Goktepe, E., Young, L. and Bridges, P. (1975) A further review of the results of stereotactic subcaudate tractotomy. *Brit. J. Psychiatry,* 126, 270-80.

Goodman, L. A. and Kruskal, W. H. (1963) Measures of association for cross-classification. *J. American Stat. Assoc.,* 58, 310-17.

Goodwin, D., Guze, S. and Robins, E. (1969) Follow-up studies in obsessional neurosis. *Archives of General Psychiatry,* 20, 182-87.

Gottheil, E. (1965) An empirical analysis of orality and anality. *Journal of Nervous and Mental Disease,* 141, 308-17.

Gottheil, E. and Stone, G. C. (1968) Factor analytical study of orality and anality. *J. of Nervous and Mental Disease,* 146, 1-17.

Gray, J. A. (1970) The psychophysiological basis of introversion-extraversion. *Behav. Res. & Ther.,* 8, 249-66.

_____. (1971) *The Psychology of Fear and Stress.* New York: McGraw-Hill.

Grey, S., Sartory, G. and Rachman, S. (1979) Synchronous and desynchronous changes during fear reduction. *Behav. Res. & Ther.,* 17, 137-48.

Grimshaw, L. (1964) Obsessional disorder and neurological illness. *J. of Neurology, Neurosurg., Psychiat.,* 27, 229-31.

Grygier, T. G. (1961) *The Dynamic Personality Inventory.* London: NFER.

Gurney, C., Roth, M., Garside, R., Kerr, T. and Schapira, K. (1972) Studies in the classification of affective disorders. *Brit. J. Psychiatry,* 121, 162-66.

Hackmann, A. and McClean, C. (1975) A comparison of flooding and thought-stopping treatment. *Behav. Res. & Ther.,* 13, 263-69.

Hain, J., Butcher, R. and Stevenson, I. (1966) Systematic desensitization theory: An analysis of results in 27 patients. *Brit. J. Psychiatry,* 112, 295-308.

Hamilton, M. (1960) A rating scale for depression. *J. of Neurology, Neurosurg., Psychiat.,* 23, 56-62.

Hare, E., Price, J. and Slater, E. (1971) Age distribution of schizophrenia and neurosis: Findings in a national sample. *Brit. J. Psychiatry.,* 119, 445-58.

_____. (1972) Fertility in obsessional neurosis. *Brit. J. Psychiatry,* 121, 197-205.

Hartshorne, H. and May, M. (1928) *Studies in the nature of character.* New York: Macmillan.

Hazari, A. (1957) An investigation of obsessive-compulsive character traits and symptoms in adult neurotics. Ph.D. Thesis, University of London Library.

Herrnstein, R. J. (1969) Method and theory in the study of avoidance. *Psychological Review,* 76, 49-69.

Hetherington, E. M. and Brackbill, Y. (1963) Etiology and covariation of obstinacy, orderliness and parsimony in young children. *Child Development,* 34, 919-43.

Heyse, H. (1975) Response prevention and modeling in the treatment of obsessive-compulsive neurosis. In *Progress in Behavior Therapy,* edited by J. Brengelmann. Berlin: Springer Verlag.

Hilgard, E. R. (1956) *Theories of Learning, 2nd ed.* Englewood Cliffs, N.J.: Prentice-Hall.

Hodgson, R. J. and Rachman, S. (1970) An experimental investigation of the implosion technique. *Behav. Res. & Ther.*, 8, 21-27.

_____. (1972) The effects of contamination and washing in obsessional patients. *Behav. Res. & Ther.*, 10, 111-17.

_____.(1974) 2. Desynchrony in measures of fear. *Behav. Res. & Ther.*, 12, 319-26.

_____. (1976) The modification of compulsive behavior. In *Case Studies in Behavior Therapy*, edited by H. J. Eysenck. London: Routledge and Kegan Paul.

_____. (1977) Obsessional compulsive complaints. *Behav. Res. & Ther.*, 15, 389-95.

_____. (1979) The Freudian theory of obsessions and compulsions (to be published).

Hodgson, R., Rachman, S. and Marks, I. (1972) The treatment of chronic obsessive compulsive neurosis. *Behav. Res. & Ther.*, 10, 181-89.

Hodgson, R. J., Rankin, H. and Stockwell, T. R. (1979) Introversion, obsessional personality and obsessional-compulsive complaints (submitted for publication).

Holland, H. C. (1974) Displacement activity as a form of abnormal behavior in animals. In *Obsessional States*, edited by H. R. Beech. London: Methuen.

Hornsveld, R., Kraaimaat, F. and Van Dam-Baggen, R. (1979) Anxiety/discomfort and handwashing in obsessive-compulsive and psychiatric control patients. *Behav. Res. & Ther.*, 17, 223-28.

Horowitz, M. (1975) Intrusive and repetitive thoughts after experimental stress. *Archives of General Psychiatry*, 32, 1457-63.

Horowitz, M and Becker, S. (1971) Cognitive response to stress and experimental demand. *J. of Abnormal Psychol.*, 78, 86-92.

Horowitz, M., Becker, S., Moskowitz, M. and Rashid, K. (1972) Intrusive thinking in psychiatric patients after stress. *Psychological Reports*, 31, 235-38.

Hunter, R. and MacAlpine, I.., eds. (1963) *Three Hundred Years of Psychiatry*. London: Oxford University Press.

Ingram, I. M. (1961) Obsessional illness in mental hospital patients. *J. of Mental Science*, 197, 382-402.

Ingram, I. and McAdam, W. (1960) The EEG, obsessional illness and obsessional personality. *J. of Mental Science*, 106, 686-91.

Inouye, E. (1965) Similar and dissimilar manifestations of obsessive-compulsive neurosis in monozygotic twins. *American J. Psychiat.*, 121, 1171-75.

James, William. *The Varieties of Religious Experience*, 1942 ed. London: Longmans.

Janet, P. (1901) *The Mental State of Hysterics.* New York and London: Putnam.

_____. (1903) *Les Obsessions et la Psychasthenie*, 2nd ed., (1908). Paris: Bailliere.

Jarvie, H. (1953) Episodic rate, theta rhythm and obsessions. *J. of Mental Science*, 99, 252-56.

Jaspers, K. (1963) *General Psychopathology.* Chicago: University of Chicago.

Judd, L. (1965) Obsessive-compulsive neurosis in children. *Archives of General Psychiatry*, 12, 136-43.

Katchadourian, H. and Racy, J. (1969) The diagnostic distribution of treated psychiatric illness in Lebanon. *Brit. J. Psychiatry*, 115, 1309-22.

Kayton, L. and Borge, C. (1967) Birth order and the obsessive-compulsive character. *Archives of General Psychiatry*, 17, 751-55.

Kendell, R. (1968) *The Classification of Depressive Illnesses*. London: Oxford University Press.

Kendell, R., Cooper, J., Gourlay, A. and Copeland, J. (1971) Diagnostic criteria of American and British psychiatrists. *Archives of General Psychiatry*, 25, 123-30.

Kendell, R. E. and Discipio, W. J. (1970) Obsessional symptoms and obsessional personality traits in patients with depressive illnesses. *Psychol. Med.*, 1, 65-72.

Kiloh, L. and Garside, R. (1963) The independence of neurotic depression and endogenous depression. *Brit. J. Psychiat.*, 109, 451-63.

Kiloh, L., Andrews, G., Neilson, M., and Bianchi, G. (1972) The relationship of endogenous and neurotic depression. *Brit. J. Psychiat.*, 121, 183-96.

Klerman, G. (1972) Clinical phenomenology of depression. In *Recent Advances in the Psychobiology of Depressive Illnesses*, edited by R. Williams. Washington, D.C.: NIMH, USGPO.

Kline, P. (1968) Obsessional traits, obsessional symptoms and anal erotism. *Brit. J. Med. Psychol.*, 41, 299-305.

_____.(1969) The anal character: A cross-cultural study in Ghana. *Brit J. Social and Clin. Psychol.*, 8, 201-10.

Klorman, R. (1974) Habituation of fear: Effects of intensity and stimulus order. *Psychophysiology*, 11, 15-26.

Knight, G. (1964) The orbital cortex as an objective in surgical treatment of mental illness. *Brit. J. Surgery*, 51, 114-24.

Koestler, A. (1960) *The Lotus and the Robot*. London: Hutchinson.

Kogan, N. and Wallach, M. (1967) *New Directions in Psychology 3*. New York: Holt, Rinehart and Winston.

Kolb, L. (1973) *Modern Clinical Psychiatry*, 8th ed. Philadelphia: Saunders.

Kringlen, E. (1965) Obsessional neurotics: A long-term follow-up. *Brit. J. Psychiat.*, 111, 709-22.

_____.(1970) Natural history of obsessional neurosis. *Seminars in Psychiat.*, 2, 403-19.

Kroeber, A. (1948) *Anthropology*. New York: Harcourt Brace Jovanovich.

Kumar, K. and Wilkinson, H. (1971) Thought stopping: A useful treatment in phobias of internal stimuli. *Brit. J. Psychiat.*, 119, 305-7.

Lader, M. (1975) *The Psychophysiology of Mental Illness*. London: Routledge and Kegan Paul.

Lader, M. and Wing, L. (1966) *Physiological Measures, Sedative Drugs and Morbid Anxiety*, Maudsley Monograph. London: Oxford University Press.

_____. (1969) Physiological measures in agitated and retarded depressed patients. *J. Psychiat. Research*, 7, 89-100.

Landon, H. (1970) *Beethoven*. London: Thames and Hudson.

Lang, P. J. (1968) Fear reduction and fear behavior: Problems in treating a construct. In *Research in Psychotherapy*, edited by J. M. Schlien. Washington, D.C.: American Psychological Association, 3, 90-103.

————.(1969) The mechanics of desensitization and the laboratory study of fear. In *Behavior Therapy: Appraisal and Status*, edited by C. Franks. New York: McGraw-Hill.

————.(1970) Stimulus control, response control, and the desensitization of fear. In *Learning Approaches to Therapeutic Behavior*, edited by D. J. Levis. Chicago: Aldine Press.

————.(1977) Imagery in therapy: An information processing analysis of fear. *Behav. Ther.*, 8, 862-86.

Lang, P. J., Melamed, B. G. and Hart, J. (1970) A psychophysiological analysis of fear modification using an automated desensitization procedure. *J. Abnormal Psychol.*, 72, 220-34.

Lazare, A., Klerman, G, and Armor, D. (1966) Oral, obsessive and hysterical personality patterns. *Arch. Gen. Psychiat.*, 14, 624-40.

————, (1970) Oral, obsessive and hysterical personality patterns: Replication of factor analysis in an independent sample. *J. Psychiat. Research*, 275-90.

Levitt, E. and Lubin, B. (1975) *Depression*. New York: Springer.

Levy, R. (1977) Personal communication.

Lewis, A. J. (1934) Melancholia: A clinical survey of depressive states. *J. of Mental Science*, 80, 1-42.

————.(1936) Problems of obsessional illness. *Proc. Royal Society Medicine*, 29, 325-36.

————. (1957) Obsessional illness. *Acta neuropsyquiat. argent.*, 3, 323-35.

————. (1965) A note on personality and obsessional illness. *Psychiatrica Neurologica, Basel*, 150, 299-305.

————.(1966) Obsessional disorder. In *Price's Textbook of the Practice of Medicine, 10th ed.*, edited by R. Scott. London: Oxford University Press.

————.(1967a) *Inquiries in Psychiatry*. London: Routledge and Kegan Paul.

————.(1976b) *The State of Psychiatry*. London: Routledge and Kegan Paul.

Liddell, A. (1976) An investigation of psychological mechanisms in obsessional patients. Unpublished doctoral dissertation, University of London.

Lipsedge, M. (1974) Therapeutic approaches to compulsive rituals. M. Phil. Thesis, London University.

Lishman, W. A. (1968) Brain damage in relation to psychiatric disability after head injury. *Brit. J. Psychiat.*, 114, 373-410.

Lo, W. (1967) A follow-up study of obsessional neurotics in Hong Kong Chinese. *Brit. J. Psychiat.*, 113, 823-32.

MacKinnon, D. W. (1944) The structure of personality. In *Personality and the Behavior Disorders*, vol. 1, edited by J. McV. Hunt. New York: Ronald Press.

Maier, N. R. F. (1949) *Frustration: The Study of Behavior Without a Goal*. New York: McGraw-Hill.

Maier, N. R. F. and Ellen, P. (1951) Can the anxiety-reduction theory explain abnormal fixations? *Psychological Review*, 58, 435-45.

Makhlouf-Norris, F., Jones, H. G. and Norris, H. (1970) Articulation of the conceptual structure in obsessional neurosis. *Brit. J. Soc. Clin. Psychol.,* 9, 264-74.

Malinowski, B. (1954) *Magic, Science and Religion.* Garden City, N.Y.: Doubleday.

Mandler, G. and Watson, D. (1966) Anxiety and the interruption of behavior. In *Anxiety and Behavior,* edited by C. Spielberger. New York: Academic Press.

Marks, I. (1969) *Fears and Phobias.* London: Heinemann Medical.

_____. (1975) Behavioral treatments of phobic and obsessive-compulsive disorders: A critical appraisal. In *Progress in Behavior Modification,* edited by M. Hersen, R. M. Eisler, and P. M. Miller. New York: Academic Press.

Marks, I. M., Crowe, M., Drewe, E. Young, T. and Dewhurst, W. G. (1969) Obsessional-compulsive neurosis in identical twins. *Brit. J. Psychiatry,* 115, 991-98.

Marks, I. M., Hallam, R., Connolly, J. and Philpott, R. (1976) *Nursing in Behavioral Psychotherapy.* London: Royal College of Nursing.

Marks, I. M., Hodgson, R. and Rachman, S. (1975) Treatment of chronic obsessive-compulsive neurosis by in vivo exposure. *Brit. J. Psychiatry,* 127, 349-64.

Marks, I. M. and Rachman, S. (1978) *Interim Report to the Medical Research Council.*

Martin, D. V. and Caine, T. M. (1963) Personality change in chronic neurotics in a therapeutic community. *Brit. J. Psychiatry,* 109, 267.

Masserman, J. H. (1943) *Behavior and Neuroses.* Chicago: University of Chicago Press.

Mather, M. (1970) Obsessions and compulsions. In *Symptoms of Psychopathology,* edited by C. Costello. New York: Wiley.

Mathews, A. M. (1971) Psychophysiological approaches to the investigation of desensitization. *Psychological Bulletin,* 76, 73-91.

Maudsley, H. (1895) *The Pathology of the Mind,* revised ed. London: Macmillan.

Melvin, D. (1955) An experimental and statistical study of two primary attitudes. Ph.D. thesis, University of London.

Metzner, R. (1963) Some experimental analogues of obsession. *Behav. Res. & Ther.,* 1, 231-36.

Meyer, V. (1966) Modification of expectations in cases with obsessional rituals. *Behav. Res. & Ther.,* 4, 273-80.

_____. (1978) Personal communication.

Meyer, V. and Chesser, E. (1970) *Behavior Therapy in Clinical Psychiatry.* Middlesex: Penguin Books.

Meyer, V., Levy, R. and Schnurer, A. (1974) The behavioral treatment of obsessive-compulsive disorder. In *Obsessional States,* edited by H. R. Beech. London: Methuen.

Mills, H., Agras, S., Barlow, D. and Mills, J. (1973) Compulsive rituals treated by response prevention. *Archives of General Psychiatry,* 28, 524-29.

Milner, A. (1966) A decision theory approach to obsessional behavior. Unpublished dissertation, University of London.

Milner, A., Beech, R. and Walker, V. (1971) Decision processes and obsessional behavior. *Brit. J. Social and Clin. Psychol.*, 10, 88-89.

Mischel, W. (1968) *Personality and Assessment.* New York: Wiley.

_____. (1972) *Introduction to Personality.* New York: Holt, Rinehart and Winston.

_____. (1973) Toward a cognitive social learning reconceptualization of personality. *Psychological Review*, 80, 252-83.

_____. (1977) On the future of personality measurement. *American Psychologist*, 32, 246-64.

Mitchell-Heggs, N., Kelly, D. and Richardson, A. (1976) A stereotactic limbic leucotomy—A follow-up at 16 months. *Brit. J. Psychiatry*, 128, 226-40.

Mowrer, O. H. (1939) A stimulus-response theory of anxiety. *Psychological Review*, 46, 553-65.

_____. (1950) *Learning Theory and Personality Dynamics.* New York: Ronald Press.

_____.(1960) *Learning Theory and Behavior.* New York: Wiley.

Neisser, U. (1967) *Cognitive Psychology.* Englewood Cliffs, N.J.: Prentice-Hall.

_____. (1976) *Cognition and Reality.* San Francisco: W. H. Freeman.

Nemiah, J. (1967) Obsessive compulsive neurosis. In *A Comprehensive Textbook of Psychiatry*, edited by A. M. Freedman and H. I. Kaplan. Baltimore: Williams and Wilkins.

Noreik, K. (1970) A follow-up examination of neuroses. *Acta Psychiatrica Scandinavica*, 46, 81-95.

Ohman, A., Fredrikson, M. and Hugdahl, K. (1978) Towards an experimental model of simple phobic reactions. *Behav. Analysis and Modification*, 2, 97-114.

Okasha, A., Kamel, M. and Hassan, A. (1968) Preliminary psychiatric observations in Egypt. *Brit. J. Psychiatry*, 114, 949-56.

Orme, J. E. (1965) The relationship of obsessional traits to general emotional instability. *Brit. J. Med. Psychol.*, 38, 269-70.

Pacella, L., Polatin, P. and Nagler. (1944) Clinical and EEG studies on obsessive-compulsive states. *American J. Psychiatry*, 100, 830-38.

Paul, G. (1966) *Insight vs. Desensitization in Psychotherapy.* Stanford, Calif.: Stanford University Press.

Paykel, E., Klerman, G. and Prusoff, B. (1976) Personality and symptom patterns in depression. *Brit. J. Psychiatry*, 129, 327-34.

Paykel, E. and Myers, J. (1969) Life events and depression. *Archives of General Psychiatry*, 21, 753-60.

Paykel, E., Prusoff, B. and Tanner, J. (1976) Temporal stability of symptom patterns in depression. *Brit. J. Psychiatry*, 128, 327-34.

Paykel, E. S., Prusoff, B. and Uhlenhuth, E. H. (1971) Scaling of life events. *Archives of General Psychiatry*, 25, 340-42.

Payne, R. (1960) Cognitive abnormalities. In *Handbook of Abnormal Psychology*, edited by H. J. Eysenck. London: Pitmans.

Philips, H. C. (1977) A psychological analysis of headache. In *Contributions to Medical Psychology*, edited by S. Rachman. Oxford: Pergamon Press.

Pollitt, J. (1957) Natural history of obsessional states. *Brit. Med. J.*, 1, 195-98.

_____. (1969) Obsessional states. *Brit. J. of Hospital Medicine,* 2, 1146-50.

Pylyshyn, Z. (1973) What the mind's eye tells the mind's brain. *Psychological Bulletin,* 80, 1-22.

Rabavilas, A. and Boulougouris, J. (1974) Physiological accompaniments of ruminations, flooding and thought-stopping in obsessive patients. *Behav. Res. & Ther.,* 12, 239-44.

Rabavilas, A., Boulougouris, J. and Stefanis, C. (1976) Duration of flooding sessions in treatment of obsessive patients, *Behav. Res. & Ther.,* 14, 349-56.

Rachman, S. (1965) Studies in desensitization—1: The separate effects of relaxation and desensitization. *Behav. Res. & Ther.,* 3, 245-51.

_____. (1968) *Phobias: Their Nature and Control.* Springfield, Ill.: Charles C. Thomas.

_____. (1969) Treatment by prolonged exposure to high intensity stimulation. *Behav. Res. & Ther.,* 7, 299-302.

_____. (1970) *Verhaltenstherapie bei Phobien,* translated by J. Bergold. Munich: Urban and Schwarzenburg.

_____. (1971) *The Effects of Psychotherapy.* Oxford: Pergamon Press.

_____. (1973) Some similarities and differences between obsessional ruminations and morbid preoccupations. *Canadian Psychiatric Association Journal,* 18, 71-74.

_____. (1974a) *The Meanings of Fear.* Middlesex: Penguin Books.

_____. (1974b) Primary obsessional slowness. *Behav. Res. & Ther.,* 11, 463-71.

_____. (1976a) The modification of obsessions: A new formulation. *Behav. Res. & Ther.,* 14, 437-43.

_____. (1976b) The passing of the two-stage theory of fear and avoidance. *Behav. Res. & Ther.,* 14, 125-31.

_____. (1976c) Observational learning and therapeutic modeling. In *Theoretical and Experimental Bases of the Behavior Therapies,* edited by P. Feldman and A. Broadhurst. New York: John Wiley & Sons.

_____. (1976d) Obsessional-compulsive checking. *Behav. Res. & Ther.,* 14, 269-77.

_____. (1977a) Obsessional ruminations. *Behav. Res. & Ther.,* 9, 229-35.

_____. (1977b) The conditioning theory of fear acquisition: A critical examination. *Behav. Res. & Ther.,* 15, 375-87.

_____. (1978a) An anatomy of obsessions. *Behavior Analysis and Modification,* 2, 253-78.

_____. (1978b) Biologically significant fears. *Behavior Analysis and Modification,* 2, 234-39.

_____. ed. (1978c) Perceived self-efficacy. *Adv. Behav. Res. Ther.,* 1, No. 4.

_____. (1978d) *Fear and Courage.* San Francisco: W. H. Freeman.

_____. (1979) Psychosurgical treatment of obsessional-compulsive disorders. In *The Psychosurgery Debate,* edited by E. Valenstein. San Francisco: W. H. Freeman.

Rachman, S., Cobb, J., MacDonald, B., Mawson, D., Sartory, G. and Stern, R. (1979) The behavioral treatment of obsessional-compulsive disorders, with and without domipramine. *Behav. Res. Ther.,* 17, in press.

Rachman, S. and de Silva, P. (1978) Abnormal and normal obsessions. *Behav. Res. & Ther.*, 16, 233-48.

Rachman, S., de Silva, P. and Röper, G. (1976) The spontaneous decay of compulsive urges. *Behav. Res. & Ther.*, 14, 445-53.

Rachman, S. and Hodgson, R. (1974) Synchrony and desynchrony in fear and avoidance. *Behav. Res. & Ther.*, 12, 311-18.

Rachman, S., Hodgson, R. and Marks, I. (1971) The treatment of chronic obsessional neurosis. *Behav. Res. & Ther.*, 9, 237-47.

Rachman, S., Hodgson, R. and Marzillier, J. (1970) The treatment of an obsessional-compulsive disorder by modeling. *Behav. Res. & Ther.*, 8, 385-92.

Rachman, S., Marks, I. and Hodgson, R. (1973) The treatment of chronic obsessive-compulsive neurosis by modeling and flooding in vivo. *Behav. Res. & Ther.*, 11, 463-71.

Rachman, S. and Philips, C. (1978) *Psychology and Medicine*. Middlesex: Penguin Books.

Rachman, S. and Seligman, M. E. P. (1976) Unprepared phobias: "Be Prepared." *Behav. Res. & Ther.*, 14, 333-38.

Rachman, S. and Wilson, G. T. (1979) *The Effects of Psychological Therapy*. Oxford: Pergamon Press.

Rack, P. (1973) Clomipramine in the treatment of obsessive states. *J. of International Medical Research*, 1, 397-99.

Ramsay, R. (1976) Behavioral approaches to obsessive-compulsive neurosis. In *The Treatment of Phobic and Obsessive-Compulsive Disorders*, edited by J. C. Boulougouris and A. D. Rabavilas. Oxford: Pergamon Press.

Ramsay, R. and Sikkel, R. (1971) Behavior therapy and obsessive neurosis. *Proceedings*, European Conference on Behavior Therapy, Munich, 1971.

Raskin, A., Schulterbrandt, J., Boothe, H., Reatig, N. and McKeon, J. (1971) Suggestions for selecting appropriate depression subgroups. In *Recent Advances in Psychology of Affective Illnesses*, edited by R. Williams. Washington, D.C.: NIMH, USGPO.

Ray, S. (1964) Obsessional states in New Delhi. *Brit. J. Psychiatry*, 110, 181-82.

Reed, G. F. (1968) Some formal qualities of obsessional thinking. *Psychiatric Clinics*, 1, 388-92.

————. (1969a) Obsessionality and self-appraisal questionnaires. *Brit. J. Psychiatry*, 115, 205-9.

————. (1969b) Under-inclusion: A characteristic of obsessional personality disorder: 1. *Brit. J. Psychiatry*, 115, 781-85.

————. (1969c) Under-inclusion. A characteristic of obsessional personality disorder: 2. *Brit. J. Psychiatry*, 115, 787-90.

————. (1976) Indecisiveness in obsessional-compulsive disorders. *Brit. J. Social & Clin. Psychol.*, 15, 443-45.

Rigby, B., Clarren, S. and Kelly, D. (1973) A psychological and physiological evaluation of the effects of intravenous clomipramine. *J. of International Medical Research*, 1, 308-12.

Robins, L. and Guze, C. (1972) Classification of affective disorders. In *Recent Advances in the Psychobiology of Depressive Illnesses*, edited by R. Williams. Washington, D.C.: USGPO.

Rockwell, L. F. and Simons, D. (1947) The EEG and personality organization in the obsessive-compulsive reactions. *Archives of Neurology and Psychiatry*, 57, 71-77.

Röper, G. (1976) Leonhard's "Individual Therapy" and its relation to behavior therapy. *Behav. Res. & Ther.*, 14, 233-44.

Röper, G., Rachman, S. and Hodgson, R. (1973) An experiment on obsessional checking. *Behav. Res. & Ther.*, 11, 271-77.

Röper, G. and Rachman, S. (1975) Obsessional-compulsive checking: Replication and development. *Behav. Res. & Ther.*, 14, 25-32.

Röper, G., Rachman, S. and Marks, I. (1975) Passive and participant modeling in exposure treatment of obsessive-compulsive neurotics. *Behav. Res. & Ther.*, 13, 271-79.

Rosen, I. (1957) The clinical significance of obsessions in schizophrenia. *Journal of Mental Science*, 103, 773-86.

Rosen, M. (1975) A dual model of obsessional neurosis. *Journal of Consulting and Clinical Psychology*, 43, 453-59.

Rosenberg, B. G. (1953) Compulsiveness as a determinant in selected cognitive-perceptual performances. *Journal of Personality*, 21, 406-16.

Rosenberg, C. (1967) Familial aspects of obsessional neurosis. *Brit. J. Psychiatry*, 113, 405-13.

Rosenberg, C. (1968) Complications of obsessional neurosis. *Brit. J. Psychiatry*, 114, 477-78.

Rosenthal, D. (1970) *Genetic Theory and Abnormal Behavior*. New York: McGraw-Hill.

Rosenthal, T. and Bandura, A. (1978) Psychological modeling: Theory and practice. In *Handbook of Psychotherapy and Behavior Change*. Eds. S. Garfield and A. Bergin. New York: John Wiley & Sons, Inc.

Rudin, E. (1953) Ein Beitrag zur Frage der Zwangskrankheit. *Archiv. für Psychiatrie Nervenkrankheiten*, 191, 14-54.

Rutter, M. (1966) *Children of Sick Parents*. London: Oxford University Press.

Rutter, M., Tizard, J. and Whitmore, S. (1970) *Education, Health and Behavior*. London: Logmans.

Sandler, J. and Hazari, A. (1960) The obsessional: On the psychological classification of obsessional character traits and symptoms. *Brit. J. Med. Psychol.*, 33, 113-22.

Sarason, I. G., Smith, R. E. and Diener, E. (1975) Personality research: Components of variance attributable to the person and the situation. *Journal of Personality and Social Psychology*, 32, 199-204.

Sargant, W. and Slater, E. (1950) Treatment of obsessional neurosis. *Proc. Royal Society of Medicine*. 43, 1007-9.

Schilder, P. (1938) The organic background of obsessions and compulsions. *American J. Psychiatry*, 94, 1937-1416.

Schuyler, D. (1974) *The Depression Spectrum*. New York: Aronson.

Schwartz, G. (1971) Cardiac responses to self-induced thoughts. *Psychophysiology*, 8, 462-67.

Sears, R. (1963) Dependency motivation. In *Nebraska Symposium on Motivation*, edited by M. Jones. Lincoln: University of Nebraska Press.

Seligman, M. E. P. (1970) On generality of the laws of learning. *Psychol. Review*, 77, 406-18.

_____.(1971) Phobias and preparedness. *Behav. Ther.*, 2, 307-20.

_____. (1975) *Helplessness.* San Francisco: W. H. Freeman.

Seligman, M. E. P. and Hager, J. L. (1972) *Biological Boundaries of Learning.* Englewood Cliffs, N.J.: Prentice-Hall.

Seligman, M. E. P. and Johnston, J. (1973) A cognitive theory of avoidance learning. In *Contemporary Approaches to Conditioning and Learning,* edited by J. McGuigan and B. Lumsden. New York: Wiley.

Shackleton, C. H. (1976) Personal communication.

_____. (1977) Satiation treatment for obsessional ruminations. M. Phil. dissertation, University of London.

Shields, J. (1973) Heredity and psychological abnormality. In *Handbook of Abnormal Psychology, 2nd ed.,* edited by H. J. Eysenck. London: Pitmans.

Skoog, G. (1959) The anancastic syndrome. *Acta Psychiatrica et Neurologica Scandinavica,* 34, suppl. 134.

Slade, P. (1974) Psychometric studies of obsessional illness and obsessional personality. In *Obsessional States,* edited by H. R. Beech. London: Methuen.

_____. (1976) An investigation of psychological factors involved in the predisposition to auditory hallucination. *Psychological Medicine,* 6, 123-32.

Slater, E. and Cowie, V. (1971) *The Genetics of Mental Disorders.* London: Oxford University Press.

Slater, P. (1945) Scores of different types of neurotics on tests of intelligence. *Brit. J. Psychol.,* 35, 40-42.

Sloane, B. et al. (1975) *Psychotherapy Versus Behavior Therapy.* Cambridge, Harvard University Press.

Solomon, R., Kamin, L. and Wynne, L. (1953) Traumatic avoidance learning: The outcomes of several extinction procedures with dogs. *J. of Abnormal and Social Psychology,* 48, 291-302.

Solyom, L., Garza-Perez, J., Ledwidge, B. L. and Solyom, C. (1972) Paradoxical intention in the treatment of obsessive thoughts: A pilot study. *Comprehensive Psychiatry,* 13, 291-97.

Solyom, L., Zamanzadeh, D., Ledwidge, B. and Kenny, F. (1971) Aversion relief treatment of obsessive neurosis. In *Advances in Behavior Therapy,* edited by R. Rubin et al. London: Academic Press.

Sookman, D. and Solyom, L. (1977) The effectiveness of four behavior therapies in the treatment of obsessive neurosis. In *The Treatment of Phobic and Obsessive-Compulsive Disorders,* edited by J. C. Boulougouris and A. D. Rabavilas. Oxford: Pergamon Press.

Snaith, R., McGuire, R. and Fox, K. (1971) Aspects of personality and depression. *Psychological Medicine,* 1, 239-46.

Stagner, R. and Moffit, J. (1956) A statistical study of Freud's theory of personality types. *J. of Clinical Psychology,* 12, 72-74.

Stampfl, T. G. (1967) Implosive therapy. In S. G. Armitage (ed.) *Behavior Modification Techniques in the Treatment of Emotional Disorders.* Battle Breek: V. A. Publication.

Steiner, J. (1972) A questionnaire study of risk-taking in psychiatric patients. *Brit. J. Med. Psychol.,* 45, 365-74.

Steiner, J., Jarvis, M. and Parrish, J. (1970) Risk-taking and arousal regulation. *Brit. J. Med. Psychol.,* 43, 333-48.

Stengel, E. (1945) A study on some clinical aspects of the relationships between obsessional neurosis and psychotic reaction types. *J. of Mental Science,* 91, 166-87.

Stern, R. S. (1970) Treatment of a case of obsessional neurosis using a thought-stopping technique. *Brit. J. Psychiatry,* 117, 441-42.

Stern, R. S. and Cobb, J. (1978) Phenomenology of obsessive-compulsive neurosis. *Brit. J. Psychiatry,* 132, 233-39.

Stern, R. S. Lipsedge, M. and Marks, I. (1973) Obsessive ruminations: A controlled trial of a thought-stopping technique. *Behav. Res. & Ther.,* 11, 659-62.

Sternberg, M. (1974) Physical treatments in obsessional disorders. In *Obsessional States,* edited by H. R. Beech. London: Methuen.

Stevens, B. (1969) *Marriage and Fertility of Women Suffering from Schizophrenia or Affective Disorders,* Maudsley Monograph no. 19. London: Oxford University Press.

Strachey, J., ed. (1973) *The Standard Edition of the Complete Psychological Works of Sigmund Freud,* vol. 10, 319-20. London: Hogarth Press.

Strom-Olsen, R. and Carlisle, S. (1971) Bi-frontal stereotactic trachotomy. *Brit. J. Psychiat.,* 118, 141-54.

Sykes, M. and Tredgold, R. (1964) Restricted orbital undercutting. *Brit. J. Psychiatry,* 110, 609-40.

Tan, E., Marks, I. and Marset, P. (1971) Bimedial leucotomy in obsessive-compulsive neurosis: A controlled serial inquiry. *Brit. J. Psychiatry,* 118, 155-64.

Tart, C. (1975) *States of Consciousness.* New York: Dutton.

Taylor, J. G. (1963) A behavioral interpretation of obsessive-compulsive neurosis. *Behav. Res. & Ther.,* 1, 237-44.

Teasdale, J. (1974) Learning models of obsessional-compulsive disorder. In *Obsessional States,* edited by H. R. Beech. London: Methuen.

Teasdale, J. and Bancroft, J. (1977) Manipulation of thought content as a determinant of mood and corrugator EMG activity in depressed patients. *J. Abnormal Psychol.,* 86, 235-41.

Teasdale, J. and Rezin, V. (1978) The effects of reducing frequency of negative thoughts on the mood of depressed patients. *Brit. J. Soc. & Clin. Psychol.,* 17, 65-74.

Templer, D. I. (1972) The Obsessive-Compulsive Neurosis: Review of research findings. *Comprehensive Psychiatry,* 13, 375-83.

Tienari, P. (1963) Psychiatric illnesses in identical twins. *Acta Psychiat. Scan.,* Supplement 171.

Treisman, A. (1969) Strategies and models of selective attention. *Psychological Review,* 76, 282-99.

Tseng, W. (1973) Psychopathologic study of obsessive-compulsive neurosis in Taiwan. *Comprehensive Psychiatry,* 14, 139-50.

Ullmann, L. and Krasner, L. (1975) *A psychological approach to abnormal behavior,* 2nd ed. Englewood Cliffs, N.J.: Prentice-Hall.

Vaughan, M. (1976) The relationship between obsessional personality, obsessions in depression and symptoms of depression. *Brit. J. Psychiatry,* 129, 36-39.

Videbech, T. (1975) The psychopathology of anancastic endogenous depression. *Acta Psychiatrica Scandinavica,* 52, 336-73.

Volans, P. J. (1976) Styles of decision-making and probability appraisal in selected obsessional and phobic patients. *Brit. J. Soc. and Clin. Psychol.,* 15, 305-17.

Walker, V. J. (1967) An investigation of ritualistic behavior in obsessional patients. Unpublished Ph.D. thesis, Institute of Psychiatry, University of London.

Walker, V. J. and Beech, H. R. (1969) Mood states and the ritualistic behavior of obsessional patients. *Brit. J. Psychiatry,* 115, 1261-68.

Wallace, R. and Benson, H. (1972) The physiology of meditation. *Scientific American,* 226, 84-91.

Walton, D. and Mather, M. D. (1963) The application of learning principles to the treatment of obsessive-compulsive states in the acute and chronic phases of illness. *Behav. Res. & Ther.,* 1, 163-74.

Walter, C. J. S. (1973) Clinical impressions on treatment of obsessional states with intravenous clomipramine. *J. Int. Medical Research,* 1, 5, 413-16.

Warren, W. (1960) Some relationships between the psychiatry of children and of adults. *J. of Mental Science,* 106, 815-26.

Waxman, D. (1975) An investigation into the use of anafranil in phobic and obsessional disorders. *Scottish Medical Journal,* 20, 61-66.

Wilner, A., Reich, T., Robins, I., Fishman, R. and van Doren, T. (1976) Obsessive-compulsive neurosis. *Comprehensive Psychiatry,* 17, 527-39.

Welner, N. and Horowitz, M. (1975) Intrusive and repetitive thoughts after a depressing experience. *Psychological Reports,* 37, 135-38.

Willett, R. A. (1960) The effects of surgical procedures on behavior. In H. J. Eysenck (ed.) *Handbook of Abnormal Psychology,* London: Pitman.

Wilson, G. T. (1977) Personal communication.

Wolpe, J. (1958) *Psychotherapy by Reciprocal Inhibition.* Stanford, Calif.: Stanford University Press.

_____. (1963) Behavior therapy in complex states. *Brit. J. Psychiatry,* 110, 28-34.

_____. (1973) *The Practice of Behavior Therapy,* 2nd ed. Oxford: Pergamon Press.

Woodruff, F., Murphy, G. and Herjanic, M. (1967) The natural history of affective disorders. *J. of Psychiat. Research,* 5, 255-63.

Woodruff, F. and Pitts, F. (1963) Monozygotic twins with obsessional illness. *American J. Psychiatry,* 120, 1075-80.

Wonnenberger, M., Henkel, D., Arentewicz, G. and Hasse, A. (1975) Studie zu einem Selbsthilfe-program fur zwangneurotische Patienten. *Zeitschrift fur Klinische Psychologie,* 4, 124-36.

Worsley, J. (1970) The causation and treatment of obsessionality. In *Behavior Therapy in the '70s,* edited by L. Burns and J. Worsley. Bristol: John Wright.

Yamagami, T. (1971) The treatment of an obsession by thought stopping. *J. of Behavior Ther. and Exp. Psychiat.,* 2, 133-35.

Yarywa-Tobias, J. A. (1975) The action of clomipramine in obsessive-compulsive neurosis: A pilot study. *Current Therapeutic Research,* 17, 111-16.

Yates, A. (1970) *Behavior Therapy.* New York: Wiley.

Young, J., Fenton, G. and Lader, M. (1971) The inheritance of neurotic traits. *Brit. J. Psychiatry,* 119, 393-98.

Author Index

Subject Index